TRADE PROTECTION IN THE UNITED STATES

Trade Protection in

Gary Clyde Hufbauer was a Senior Fellow at the Institute for International Economics while working on this book. He is now the Marcus Wallenberg Professor of International Financial Diplomacy at Georgetown University. Hufbauer was formerly Deputy Assistant Secretary for International Trade and Investment Policy of the US Treasury; Director of the International Tax Staff at the Treasury; and Professor of Economics at the University of New Mexico.

Diane T. Berliner was a Research Assistant at the Institute while working on this volume. She is currently completing the requirements for a Masters degree in American foreign policy and international economics at the Johns Hopkins School of Advanced International Studies.

Kimberly Ann Elliott is a Research Assistant at the Institute and has a Masters from the Johns Hopkins School of Advanced International Studies.

The authors thank Virginia Rizzo for her research assistance on several of the case studies, Deborah A. McGuire for her diligent typing of the manuscript, and Michelle K. Smith for editorial assistance.

G.C.H.   D.T.B.   K.A.E.

INSTITUTE FOR INTERNATIONAL ECONOMICS
11 Dupont Circle, NW
Washington, DC 20036
(202) 328-0583 Telex:248329 CEIP
C. Fred Bergsten, *Director*
Kathleen A. Lynch, *Director of Publications*
Stephen Kraft, *Designer*

The Institute for International Economics was created, and is principally funded, by the German Marshall Fund of the United States.

The views expressed in this publication are those of the authors. This publication is part of the overall program of the Institute, as endorsed by its Board of Directors, but does not necessarily reflect the views of individual members of the Board or the Advisory Committee.

Copyright © 1986 Institute for International Economics. All rights reserved. No part of this book may be reproduced or utilized in any form or by any means, electronic or mechanical, including photocopying, recording, or by information storage or retrieval system, without written permission from the Institute.

Library of Congress Cataloging-in-Publication Data
Hufbauer, Gary Clyde.
Trade Protection in the United States.
Bibliography: p. 41
1. United States—Commercial policy—Case studies. 2. Free trade and protection—Protection—Case studies. I. Berliner, Diane T. II. Elliott, Kimberly Ann, 1960- . III. Title.

HF1455.H788 1985 382.7'3'0973 85-18067
ISBN 0-88132-040-4

GARY CLYDE HUFBAUER
DIANE T. BERLINER
KIMBERLY ANN ELLIOTT

the United States: 31 Case Studies

INSTITUTE FOR INTERNATIONAL ECONOMICS
Washington, DC 1986

Contents

1 Introduction   1
   Routes to Special Protection   2
     Exceptionally High Tariffs   6
     Escape Clause Relief   7
     Presidential Use of Inherent Constitutional Powers   8
     Statutory Frameworks for Discretionary Protection   8
     Statutory Quotas   9
   Characteristics of Special Protection   9
     The Rise of Quantitative Restraints   10
     Duration and Review   11
     Price, Import, and Employment Effects   12
     Costs of Special Protection   13
     Adjustment during Special Protection   16
   Assessment of Special Protection   20
   A New Approach to Troubled Industries   23
     A Refurbished Escape Clause   23
     Unraveling Existing Special Protection   24
     Illustrative Examples   28

2 Methodology   31
   Import Restraints   31
     Definitions for Import Restraint Parameters   35
     Relations between Import Restraint Parameters   36
   Industry Adjustment   37
     Definitions for Adjustment Parameters   38
     Relations between Adjustment Parameters   38

Bibliography   41

Appendix: Case Studies — 43

Prefatory Note — 45

Manufacturing Cases

  Case M–1 Book Manufacturing — 47

  Case M–2 Benzenoid Chemicals — 55

  Case M–3 Household Glassware — 63

  Case M–4 Rubber Footwear — 72

  Case M–5 Ceramic Articles — 80

  Case M–6 Ceramic Tiles — 90

  Case M–7 Frozen Concentrated Orange Juice — 100

  Case M–8 Canned Tuna — 108

  Case M–9 Textiles and Apparel: Phase I — 117

  Case M–10 Textiles and Apparel: Phase II — 128

  Case M–11 Textiles and Apparel: Phase III — 139

  Case M–12 Carbon Steel: Phase I — 154

  Case M–13 Carbon Steel: Phase II — 162

  Case M–14 Carbon Steel: Phase III — 170

  Case M–15 Ball Bearings — 185

  Case M–16 Specialty Steel — 193

  Case M–17 Nonrubber Footwear — 206

  Case M–18 Color Television Receivers — 218

  Case M–19 CB Radios — 226

  Case M–20 Bolts, Nuts, and Large Screws of Iron or Steel — 234

  Case M–21 Prepared Mushrooms — 241

  Case M–22 Automobiles — 249

  Case M–23 Heavyweight Motorcycles — 263

Services Cases

  Case S–1 Maritime Industries — 270

Agriculture and Fisheries Cases

  Case A–1 Sugar — 286

  Case A–2 Dairy Products — 302

  Case A–3 Peanuts — 314

  Case A–4 Meat — 323

  Case A–5 Fish in the Conservation Zone — 334

Mining Cases

  Case E–1 Petroleum — 343

  Case E–2 Lead and Zinc — 355

Text Tables

1.1	Characteristics of special protection	3
1.2	Distribution of costs and benefits from special protection	14
1.3	Adjustment during special protection	17
1.4	Special protection related to total trade	21
1.5	Characteristics of hypothetical adjustment programs	26

Text Figures

2.1	The effect of trade restraints on demand and price for imported good	32
2.2	The effect of trade restraints on demand and price for domestic good	32

INSTITUTE FOR INTERNATIONAL ECONOMICS
11 Dupont Circle, NW
Washington, DC 20036
(202) 328–0583 Telex:248329 CEIP

C. Fred Bergsten, *Director*

BOARD OF DIRECTORS

Peter G. Peterson, *Chairman*
Raymond Barre
W. Michael Blumenthal
Douglas A. Fraser
Alan Greenspan
Abdlatif Y. al-Hamad
Reginald H. Jones
Frank E. Loy
Donald F. McHenry
Saburo Okita
I. G. Patel
Karl Otto Pöhl
David Rockefeller
Donna E. Shalala
Mario Henrique Simonsen
Anthony M. Solomon
Dennis Weatherstone
Andrew Young

Ex officio
C. Fred Bergsten
Richard N. Cooper

Honorary Directors
George P. Shultz
John N. Turner

ADVISORY COMMITTEE

Richard N. Cooper, *Chairman*
Robert Baldwin
Lester R. Brown
Rimmer de Vries
Juergen B. Donges
Rudiger Dornbusch
Robert J. Flanagan
Isaiah Frank
Jacob A. Frenkel
Gottfried Haberler
Mahbub ul Haq
Arnold C. Harberger
Dale E. Hathaway
Nurul Islam
Peter B. Kenen
Lawrence R. Klein
Ryutaro Komiya
Lawrence B. Krause
Paul R. Krugman
Roger M. Kubarych
Robert Z. Lawrence
Assar Lindbeck
Harald B. Malmgren
Richard R. Nelson
Joseph S. Nye, Jr.
Rudolph A. Oswald
Jacques J. Polak
Jeffrey D. Sachs
Ernest Stern
Philip K. Verleger, Jr.
Henry C. Wallich
Marina v.N Whitman
Alan Wm. Wolff

Preface

In a major research project over the past two years, the Institute has studied the postwar adjustment to trade competition of troubled industries in the United States and in five other countries. Common themes have been sought that may warn of the onset of competitive problems, permitting both industries and public policy to address them more rapidly. Lessons have been drawn from the adjustment efforts of the past to help devise effective remedies for the future.

The project, directed by Gary Clyde Hufbauer and Howard F. Rosen, will produce three publications. One, released concurrently with this volume, is *Trade Policy for Troubled Industries*—the fifteenth in our POLICY ANALYSES IN INTERNATIONAL ECONOMICS series—which summarizes the analytical conclusions and presents the policy recommendations resulting from the entire study. (Some of the central conclusions were cited in *Trading for Growth: The Next Round of Trade Negotiations*, by Dr. Hufbauer and Jeffrey J. Schott, released by the Institute in September 1985.) *Domestic Adjustment and International Trade*, scheduled for release later in 1986, will contain the papers commissioned on specific aspects of the problem (including adjustment experiences abroad).

The present volume provides detailed analyses of thirty-one cases in which trade volumes exceed $100 million and the United States has applied "special" trade protection—exceptional restraints on imports implemented through high tariffs, quotas, or other unusual limitations. It is thus a companion source book to *Trade Policy for Troubled Industries*, and can be used independently to look at the details of US "special protection" in these sectors. A common methodology was developed and applied to a series of disparate remedies for very different economic sectors, thus permitting meaningful comparisons of measures adopted and results achieved. Diane T. Berliner and Kimberly Ann Elliott worked with Dr. Hufbauer on the preparation of the case studies and this volume.

The Ford Foundation provided substantial support for the entire adjustment project, and I would like to convey a special word of thanks for its help. In particular, all of the researchers engaged in this effort at the Institute wish to express their gratitude to Thomas O. Bayard, a Foundation Program Officer, for his important intellectual inputs to the project—on a topic to which he has made a number of pioneering contributions in the past.

The Institute for International Economics is a private nonprofit research institution for the study and discussion of international economic policy. Its purpose is to analyze important issues in that area and to develop and communicate practical new approaches for dealing with them. The Institute is completely nonpartisan.

The Institute was created in November 1981 through a generous commitment of funds from the German Marshall Fund of the United States. Support is being received from other private foundations and corporations, and the Institute is now broadening and diversifying its financial base. As noted, the Ford Foundation provided substantial support for this study.

The Board of Directors bears overall responsibility for the Institute and gives general guidance and approval to its research program—including identification of topics that are likely to become important to international economic policymakers over the medium run (generally, one to three years) and which thus should be addressed by the Institute. The Director, working closely with the staff and outside Advisory Committee, is responsible for the development of particular projects and makes the final decision to publish an individual study.

The Institute hopes that its studies and other activities will contribute to building a stronger foundation for international economic policy around the world. Comments as to how it can best do so are invited from readers of these publications.

C. FRED BERGSTEN
Director
March 1986

1

Introduction

With bipartisan regularity, American presidents since Franklin Delano Roosevelt have proclaimed the virtues of free trade. They have inaugurated bold international programs to reduce tariff and nontariff barriers. But almost in the same breath, most presidents have advocated or accepted special measures to protect problem industries. Together, these two strands of policy have produced a contradictory profile. On the one hand, the United States has dramatically liberalized its tariff barriers since the Smoot–Hawley Tariff of 1930.[1] On the other hand, the United States has imposed numerous regimes of "special protection" to insulate important manufacturing and agricultural sectors from foreign competition.

In recent years, dollar overvaluation and high unemployment in certain hard-hit sectors have dramatically heightened the cry for special protection; but the underlying quest transcends year-to-year fluctuations in the exchange rate and the business cycle. Early in the twentieth century, important instances of special protection included book manufacturing, the maritime industry, and sugar. In the post–World War II period, Presidents Dwight D. Eisenhower and John F. Kennedy launched America on a new trajectory of special protection, first with "voluntary" restraints on Japanese exports of cotton textiles that ripened into the Short-Term and Long-Term Cotton Textile Arrangements, and then with voluntary and mandatory controls on oil imports. President Lyndon B. Johnson ushered in the legal apparatus for restricting meat imports. In the wake of oil scarcity, President Richard M. Nixon allowed oil import controls to lapse, but he also restrained imports of steel (implementing a voluntary restraint agreement negotiated under Johnson) and tightened textile restrictions with the first Multi-Fiber Arrangement. President Gerald R. Ford contributed specialty steel to the

---

1. The ratio of duties collected to dutiable imports dropped from 53.5 percent in 1933 to 5.2 percent in 1982 (USTR, *Annual Report, 1983*, p. 187).

agenda of special protection, but little else, mainly because his short tenure in office coincided with the inauguration of the Tokyo Round of Multilateral Trade Negotiations (MTN). As part of the price for implementing the Tokyo Round agreements, however, President Jimmy Carter restricted imports of steel, textiles, and footwear. During his first term, President Ronald Reagan answered the prayers of the sugar, textile, automobile, and steel industries.

In short, the US response to the trade and structural problems of important industries has often been special protection. The purpose of special protection is to slow the pace of adjustment to changing realities in the international trading system, especially for industries that are already experiencing the aging pains of maturity.[2]

By "special protection" we mean exceptional restraints on imports, implemented through high tariffs, quota restraints, or other limitations that go well beyond normal tariff or border restrictions. Table 1.1 summarizes the 31 significant cases of special protection in the United States that are the substance of this reference volume. We have arbitrarily defined "significant" cases as those that affect trade volumes in excess of $100 million. From these cases, certain general themes can be drawn about the roads to special protection and the characteristics of special protection in the United States.

Routes to Special Protection

The US Constitution explicitly entrusts the regulation of foreign commerce to the Congress and implicitly entrusts the conduct of foreign affairs to the President.[3] Thus, the constitutional schema assigns roles to both the President and Congress in formulating international trade policy. This division of power often creates tension when a constituent-minded Congress pushes a globally-minded President to impose import restraints. The cases summarized in table 1.1 illustrate five distinct legal paths to special protection, each reflecting the pull and haul between Congress and the President. These paths are outlined in the next several sections.

---

2. A large literature has developed that seeks to explain the "political market" for protection. Among the variables emphasized are numbers of employees, value added per employee, degree of concentration, extent of financial adversity, and import share. See, for example, Magee, 1980; Messerlin, 1981; Anderson and Baldwin, October 1981; Baldwin, October 1984a and October 1984b; Cline, 1984; Cassing, McKeown and Ochs, 1984; and Pugel and Walter, 1984.

3. Tribe, 1978, pp. 165–67.

Table 1.1 Characteristics of special protection

Case	Route and termination[a] (symbols)	Relief period[b] (dates)	Import value (million dollars)	Tariff or equivalent (percentage)	Induced increase in domestic price (percentage)	Induced decrease in imports (million dollars)	Induced increase in employment[c]
Manufacturing							
M–1 Book Manufacturing	(E), (1)	1891–present	481 (1984)	40.0	12.0	421	5,000
M–2 Benzenoid Chemicals	(A), (1)	1922–86	2,698 (1984)	15.0	4.5	750	300
M–3 Glassware	(A), (1)	1922–present	312 (1983)	19.0	12.0	118	1,000
M–4 Rubber Footwear	(A), (1)	1930–present	331 (1983)	42.0	21.0	125	7,800
M–5 Ceramic Articles	(A, B), (1)	1930–present	498 (1984)	14.0	7.0	126	2,000
M–6 Ceramic Tiles	(A), (1)	1930–present	249 (1984)	21.6	17.3	66	850
M–7 Orange Juice	(A), (1)	1930–present	304 (1983)	44.0	35.0	363	2,200
M–8 Canned Tuna	(A), (1)	1951–present	137 (1983)	12.5	10.0	52	1,200
M–9 Textiles and Apparel: Phase I	(A, D), (1)	1957–73	3,497 (1973)	20.0	16.0	8,600	420,000
M–10 Textiles and Apparel: Phase II	(A, D), (1)	1974–81	9,500 (1981)	27.0	22.0	15,000	540,000
M–11 Textiles and Apparel: Phase III	(A, D), (1)	1982–present	16,498 (1984)	30.0	24.0	27,900	640,000
M–12 Carbon Steel: Phase I	(C), (2)	1969–74	4,830 (1974)	13.3	5.3	1,420	8,100
M–13 Carbon Steel: Phase II	(C, D), (1)	1978–82	8,958 (1982)	15.9	6.4	2,146	7,000

Table 1.1 Characteristics of special protection (continued)

Case	Route and termination[a] (symbols)	Relief period[b] (dates)	Import value (million dollars)	Tariff or equivalent (percentage)	Induced increase in domestic price (percentage)	Induced decrease in imports (million dollars)	Induced increase in employment[c]
M–14 Carbon Steel: Phase III	(B, C, D), (1)	1982–present	10,206 (1984)	30.0	12.0	3,038	9,000
M–15 Ball Bearings	(B), (2)	1974–78	199 (1978)	12.0	2.4	6	500
M–16 Specialty Steel	(B), (3)	1976–80	404 (1984)	25.0	15.0	77	500
	(B), (1)	1983–86					
M–17 Nonrubber Footwear	(B), (3)	1977–81	2,480 (1981)	18.5	5.5	248	12,700
M–18 Color Televisions	(B), (3)	1977–82	1,543 (1982)	15.0	6.0	125	1,000
M–19 CB Radios	(B), (3)	1978–81	54 (1981)	21.0	21.0	132	600
M–20 Bolts, Nuts, Large Screws	(B), (3)	1979–82	311 (1982)	15.0	6.0	10	200
M–21 Prepared Mushrooms[d]	(B), (3)	1980–83	110 (1983)	20.0	10.0	16	300
M–22 Automobiles	(C), (1)	1981–present[e]	29,260 (1984)	11.0	4.4	5,800	55,000
M–23 Motorcycles	(B), (1)	1983–88	124 (1984)	30.0	15.0	163	700
Services							
S–1 Maritime Industries	(E), (1)	1789–present	15,000 (1983)	0.0	60.0	7,000	11,000
Agriculture and Fisheries							
A–1 Sugar	(D), (1)	1934–present	1,258 (1984)	30.0	30.0	1,288	15,300 1,350,000 (acres)

A-2 Dairy Products	(D), (1)	1953–present	588 (1983)	80.0	40.0	2,300	25,000 (cows) 3,000,000 (acres)
A-3 Peanuts	(D), (1)	1953–present	2 (1983)	28.0	28.0	200	170,000 (acres)
A-4 Meat	(D), (1)	1965–present	1,363 (1983)	14.0	7.0	1,500	11,000 8,000,000 (head)
A-5 Fish	(E), (1)	1977–present	3,627 (1983)	10.0	10.0	280	27,000
Mining							
E-1 Petroleum	(D), (2)	1959–73	7,858 (1973)	96.0	96.0	6,550	43,000
E-2 Lead and Zinc	(B), (2)	1958–65	141 (1964)	9.5	9.5	45	2,200

a. The symbols used to identify the route of initiation of special protection are as follows: A—high tariffs; B—escape clause action; C—executive use of inherent constitutional powers (e.g., voluntary export restraints); D—statutory framework for discretionary protection (e.g., Section 22 of the Agricultural Adjustment Act of 1933); E—statutes explicitly limiting imports (e.g., the Magnuson Act restricting foreign fishing in the US Fishery Conservation Zone). The symbols used to identify the means of termination of special protection are as follows: 1—not applicable as protection is either ongoing or has been replaced by another phase or means of relief; 2—protection terminated because of a revival of demand and/or an increase in prices; 3—protection terminated or phased out following industry adjustment through downsizing, product shifts, and/or reinvestment and modernization.

b. Termination dates in currently ongoing cases assume that tariffs are lowered and other types of protection are phased out as scheduled.

c. Unless otherwise specified, figures refer to the number of production jobs.

d. Prepared mushrooms have been treated only as an escape clause case even though the relatively high ad valorem equivalent (13.3 percent in 1984) makes it a borderline high tariff case as well.

e. The automobile case is defined as ongoing and in need of adjustment because of continuing Japanese export restraint.

f. Import values are for the shipping services sector only. There was no increase in import prices since protection was implemented through subsidization and cargo reservation.

Exceptionally High Tariffs

In the 1920s and 1930s, high tariffs were the main answer to troublesome competition from foreign quarters. The high tariffs remaining today are largely a legacy from the Fordney–McCumber Tariff of 1922 and the Smoot–Hawley Tariff of 1930, retained by industries with sufficient political strength to guard their ancestral ramparts against the erosion of seven tariff-cutting rounds conducted under the General Agreement on Tariffs and Trade (GATT). Prior to each round, certain industries have managed to persuade Congress that they cannot survive without their accustomed tariffs. This prejudgment may be given legal sanction by specific exclusion from the President's tariff-cutting authority;[4] or it may be conveyed by a special investigation that identifies "import-sensitive" industries;[5] or it may be urged informally but persuasively to the President by key senators and congressmen.

The average US tariff on dutiable imports has now dwindled to about 5 percent. By contrast, the tariff-based instances of special protection singled out in table 1.1 involve tariffs of about 15 percent and higher. These self-selected survivors of the Fordney-McCumber and Smoot-Hawley tariffs include the cases, Benzenoid Chemicals, Rubber Footwear, Ceramic Articles and Tiles, Glassware, Canned Tuna, Textiles and Apparel (Phases I, II, and III), and Orange Juice.[6] The Textiles and Apparel cases and the Ceramic Articles case involve additional forms of protection besides high tariffs. In terms of trade coverage, the big case is Textiles and Apparel: Phase III, involving $16.5 billion of imports in 1984. Among the ongoing cases, Benzenoid Chemicals is next at $2.7 billion of trade coverage in 1984. After that, the high tariff cases represent trade coverage in the hundreds of millions.

---

4. For example, Section 127 of the Trade Act of 1974 exempted goods subject to escape clause relief, and certain other goods, from tariff cuts. A similar exemption was first used in Section 225 of the Trade Expansion Act of 1962 (Metzger, 1964, p. 41).

5. The Trade Agreements Extension Act of 1951 required the US Tariff Commission (established in 1916 and transformed in 1975 into the US International Trade Commission) to designate "peril points" beyond which tariffs could not be safely cut. The Trade Expansion Act of 1962 eliminated the "peril point" concept, but required the Commission to designate "import-sensitive" industries. In both cases, while the designation was not binding on the President, it carried weight (Metzger, 1971a, pp. 320–21).

6. The case names used here and later in this chapter are the names used in the appendix. The high tariff cases listed in table 1.1 do not give a representative sample of the history of high tariffs as an instrument of special protection, since troubled industries that have already had their high tariffs cut are not listed.

Escape Clause Relief

Now granted under Section 201 of the Trade Act of 1974,[7] the escape clause in theory was meant to provide the major route to special protection. In practice, escape clause relief has become a secondary road. The award of escape clause relief is highly discretionary and relief has been granted far less often than it has been sought. Moreover, the escape clause contains features that are disagreeable to industry: it contemplates the decline of protection from year to year and the corresponding adjustment of the petitioning industry to the realities of international competition.

An industry seeking escape clause relief must clear two hurdles. First, the industry must persuade the US International Trade Commission (USITC) to find that the industry has been "seriously injured" or "threatened" with serious injury, and that rising imports are the most important cause of the actual injury or the threat of injury. Second, once half or more of the commissioners sitting on the case recommend trade relief, the industry must persuade the President that trade relief serves the national interest more than adjustment assistance or, indeed, no relief at all.

From 1975 to 1984, some 53 import relief petitions were brought to the USITC under Sections 201 and 203 (Section 203 enables an extension of prior relief).[8] A majority of the Commission recommended trade relief in 28 instances and the Commission was evenly split on 3 cases. Of these 31 cases (28 plus 3), the President granted trade relief in only 13 cases. Some of these 13 cases involved too little trade coverage to qualify as significant instances of special protection.[9] Significant instances of escape clause relief and end-year trade coverage include Ball Bearings ($199 million); Specialty Steel ($404 million); Nonrubber Footwear ($2,480 million); Color Tele-

---

7. Section 201 of the Trade Act of 1974 was preceded by several earlier versions of an escape clause: an industry consultation provision in the Reciprocal Trade Agreements Act of 1934; a formal "escape clause" in the 1942 bilateral trade agreement with Mexico; Executive Order 9832 of 1945 in which President Truman required that an escape clause be included in all future trade agreements; a legislative escape clause in Section 7 of the Trade Agreements Extension Act of 1951; and a revised escape clause in Section 301 of the Trade Expansion Act of 1962. The 1962 act required that trade concessions be the major cause of increased imports and that rising imports be a "major factor" in causing or threatening injury; the 1974 act dropped the linkage to trade concessions and relaxed the causation test to "substantial cause" (USITC, March 1982, pp. 1–4; Metzger, 1971b, pp. 319–21; Baldwin, October 1984a, chap. 3).

8. Baldwin, October 1984b, p. 19.

9. Recent escape clause relief cases that resulted in trade restrictions but did not involve significant amounts of trade include: Ferrochromium (TA-201-35); Clothespins (TA-201-36); and Non-Electric Cookware (TA-201-39).

visions ($1,543 million); Prepared Mushrooms ($110 million); Motorcycles ($124 million); CB Radios ($54 million);[10] Bolts, Nuts, and Large Screws ($311 million); and Ceramic Articles ($498 million).

Presidential Use of Inherent Constitutional Powers

The President may use his inherent responsibility for the conduct of foreign policy to persuade a foreign government both to limit its exports to the United States and to administer the necessary restraints. This low-visibility, high-flexibility form of protection has become a favored means of helping large troubled industries. The President can claim credit both for defending the principles of free trade (against more protective congressional or USITC solutions) and for defending the industry (against the dangers of unregulated commerce); moreover, the President can usually conceal the cost of protection from the public. In addition, the President can relax or remove the restraints rather easily once political attitudes or economic fortunes change.

An early example of the use of inherent constitutional powers was President Johnson's steel restraints (Carbon Steel: Phase I). The latest example was President Reagan's use of voluntary restraint agreements (VRAs) to limit steel shipments by Brazil, Korea, Spain, Japan, and other suppliers (Carbon Steel: Phase III). Another example was President Reagan's auto restraints.

As these examples indicate, the extent of trade coverage can be huge. In fact, minimizing diplomatic fallout is a major reason that presidents use their inherent constitutional powers to deal with cases involving large amounts of trade.

Statutory Frameworks for Discretionary Protection

Statutory frameworks often seem to give the President considerable latitude in deciding how to answer the trade problems of affected industries. In practice, that latitude may be narrowed by congressional surveillance. Examples are Section 204 of the Agricultural Act of 1956, used as the statutory vehicle for restraining textile and apparel imports, and Section 22

---

10. CB radio imports totaled $194 million in 1978, the first year of restraints. The large decline in subsequent years was principally due to declining demand for a "fad" item, rather than to trade restraints.

of the Agricultural Adjustment Act of 1933 (1935 amendment), currently used to limit dairy, peanut, cotton, and sugar imports.[11] In deploying both these statutes, presidents pay close attention to congressional sentiment.

Another statute, Section 232 of the Trade Expansion Act of 1962, permits trade restrictions for national security purposes. Section 232 was used to restrain petroleum imports between 1962 and 1973. More recently, the bolts, nuts, and large screws industry and the machine tool industry have tried— so far without success—to harness Section 232 to their protective desires.

Unusual quantitative relief in countervailing duty and antidumping duty cases is the latest variety of extraordinary restraint applied within a statutory framework. This approach was inaugurated in 1978 by the trigger price mechanism (Carbon Steel: Phase II). The same approach was followed in the settlement of subsidy complaints against Chinese textiles in 1983 (Textiles and Apparel: Phase III).

Statutory Quotas

These statutes represent the most decisive exercise of congressional power. They often set a rigid limit on imports, expressed as a percentage of consumption or as a residual between domestic consumption and domestic production, or they altogether bar foreign suppliers from the US market. Examples include the manufacturing clause of the copyright law, the Jones Act, the Meat Act, and the Magnuson Fisheries Act. Each of these laws strictly limits foreign entry, allowing presidential discretion only as to details of implementation.

Characteristics of Special Protection

Special protection has several characteristics that merit comment: the widespread use of quantitative restraints; the duration and review of protection; the costs to consumers and the efficiency loss to the nation; and the extent of adjustment during the life of trade restraints.

---

11. Since its enactment in 1935, Section 22 has been used from time to time to restrict imports of cotton, wheat, almonds, dairy, peanuts, flaxseed, filberts, oats, rye, barley, tungnuts, and sugar (CRS, 1984, 9).

The Rise of Quantitative Restraints

In the postwar period, high tariffs have infrequently been used to inaugurate new cases of special protection.[12] Instead, special protection—especially in big cases—has usually entailed quantitative restraints (QRs), ranging from VRAs in which the restraints are imposed by the foreign country, to orderly marketing agreements (OMAs) in which restraints are monitored by the United States, to global and bilateral quotas in which the US Customs Service allows only fixed quantities to enter the United States.[13]

The use of QRs rather than high tariffs to restrain imports answers a strong preference of both domestic producers and foreign exporters. Domestic producers prefer QRs for three reasons: first, their share of the domestic market is more certain; second, domestic prices are less variable since fluctuations in foreign supply conditions do not so greatly affect quantities offered for sale in the US market; third, for a given degree of political "clout," the domestic industry can secure more protection through quantitative restraints than through tariffs, since the American public seems to understand the impact of tariffs but is easily persuaded that QRs barely affect prices (this may be less true now than in the past because of the publicity given the auto and other recent cases).

Foreign exporters prefer quantitative restraints for somewhat different reasons, and their reasons vary depending on whether they are traditional suppliers or new entrants to the US market. In the postwar period, most QRs have been selective: "well-behaved" exporting countries that are not seen to be disrupting the domestic market are usually exempt from control. For this reason, traditional suppliers prefer QRs. They need not cut back their own exports; moreover, restrictions on third-country competitors may improve price levels in the US market and limit those countries' increases in market share.

By contrast, the foreign exporters that are affected—normally the "aggressive" new entrants—prefer QRs to tariffs because QRs are customarily implemented in a way that confers valuable scarcity rents on the restrained exporters. Rents are created by artificial scarcity in the US market. They devolve on restrained exporters because quotas are allocated to foreign

---

12. New instances of special protection implemented with duties have largely been confined to escape clause cases. See table 1.1.

13. Unilateral quantitative restrictions made a "modern" appearance as early as 1463 when the British Parliament imposed a zero quota on a range of manufactured articles. By contrast, "voluntary" restraints on exports, negotiated between governments and implemented by the supplying country, date from US policy initiatives in the 1930s, first spawned by the National Industrial Recovery Act (Metzger, 1971b, pp. 167–70).

governments which in turn distribute the rights to established firms.[14] As C. Fred Bergsten first pointed out,[15] both the United States and foreign exporters view this means of allocating quota rights as a method of payment to compensate restrained suppliers for their reduced export volumes. This trade-off between volume and price makes QRs far more palatable than tariffs.

Duration and Review

Cases of special protection vary widely in terms of the duration of protection and the frequency of review. At one extreme are instances of short-term relief lasting five years or less, exemplifed by Carbon Steel: Phase I, Nonrubber Footwear, Color Televisions, possibly Automobiles,[16] and Motorcycles. In these instances, relief was only designed to provide "breathing room." Restrictive measures were subject to periodic review, either by the explicit terms of the escape clause (Nonrubber Footwear, Televisions, Motorcycles, and numerous other cases) or by presidential design (Carbon Steel: Phase I and Automobiles).

At the other extreme are protective measures designed to insulate the domestic industry from foreign competition for an extended period. "Indefinite protection" describes most of the high tariffs still standing from the Tariff Acts of 1922 and 1930. Other instances include the maritime laws (dating from 1789), the manufacturing clause in the US copyright law (dating from 1891), and the Magnuson Fisheries Act (dating from 1977).

Between these two extremes are cases in which presidential review is permitted by statute but constrained by custom. Section 22 of the Agricultural Adjustment Act of 1933 gives the Secretary of Agriculture authority to review sugar, dairy, peanut and other agricultural quotas—subject always to the watchful eye of the domestic industries and their powerful congressional allies. Not surprisingly, sugar imports have been controlled since 1934 (with brief interludes during periods of soaring prices, in World War

---

14. The United States almost never auctions quota rights and seldom allocates them to US importers or producers—two methods of distribution that would deprive foreign suppliers of the scarcity rents. However, Australia, New Zealand, Brazil, the United Kingdom, and other countries have experimented with these alternative approaches.

15. Bergsten, 1975, chap. 15.

16. The US-Japanese "voluntary" restraint agreement on automobile imports was replaced, in April 1985, by a voluntary export restraint system designed solely by the Japanese government, but implemented largely in response to congressional resolutions. Thus, trade restraints on automobiles remain in place.

II and the mid-1970s), while dairy and peanuts imports have been limited since 1953. Similarly, Section 204 of the Agricultural Act of 1956 nominally allows the President great flexibility in setting textile and apparel quotas—but in fact every decision is carefully monitored by Congress and the industry.

In terms of end-games, the 31 cases can be divided into three broad categories. The first and largest category, covering 22 cases, includes cases that were either ongoing in 1985, or, at an earlier date, had been rolled over into another phase of protection (the textiles and apparel, and carbon steel cases).

The second category, covering four cases, includes situations where special protection was terminated because of a cyclical revival in demand and an upsurge in product prices. This description applies to Carbon Steel: Phase I (the 1974 revival); Ball Bearings (the 1978 revival); Petroleum (tighter markets in the early 1970s, even before OPEC burst on the scene), and Lead and Zinc (Vietnam War demand in the mid-1960s).

The third category, covering six instances of special protection,[17] includes cases where protection was terminated following adjustment—involving some combination of downsizing, product shifts, and modernization.

This categorization of cases suggests that, while adjustment occasionally points to the end of special protection, in far more cases protection endures indefinitely, or is brought to an end only by the happenstance of cyclical revival.

Price, Import, and Employment Effects

The last four columns of table 1.1 give rough estimates of the tariff or tariff-equivalent of trade restraints, the induced increase in the price of domestically produced competing goods, the induced decrease in imports, and the induced increase in production jobs (or agricultural acreage or livestock). Much could be said about these estimates, but we shall confine our comments to a few highlights.

Tariff-equivalent rates of protection range from about 10 percent for automobiles and fisheries to nearly 100 percent for dairy and petroleum. Most cases fall in the 15 percent to 40 percent bracket. The impact on prices charged by the domestic industry is a matter of controversy. In our judgment, the "coefficient of price response" (the ratio of induced increase in the domestic price to the tariff-equivalent rate of protection) usually lies in the

---

17. Speciality Steel is counted both as a case where protection was terminated in 1980 and, after being revived in 1983, as an ongoing case of protection.

range of 0.3 to 0.5. Only for standardized commodities, such as orange juice and textiles, do we assign coefficients as high as 0.7 to 0.9. The coefficients of price response are almost always less than 1.0 because imported and domestic commodities are imperfect substitutes (both in product characteristics and in channels of distribution) and because the domestic industry often exhibits "sticky" price behavior, characteristic of oligopolies.

Estimates for the induced decreases in imports are dominated by a few large cases: Textiles and Apparel; Carbon Steel; Automobiles; Maritime; Sugar; Dairy Products; Meat; and Petroleum. In big cases, imports are often reduced by $1 billion, $5 billion, or more.

Estimates for induced increases in production jobs are dominated by the same cases, with the addition of four others: Book Manufacturing; Rubber Footwear; Nonrubber Footwear; and Fish. Apart from Textiles and Apparel, estimates of production jobs "saved" are decidedly small. Seldom do the figures exceed 10,000 workers. The estimates of jobs saved do not, however, include white collar employees, workers in ancillary industries (for example, workers making tires for automobiles), or retail and service employees in the immediate locality. On the other hand, the estimates make no allowance for the fact that higher costs in the protected industry undermine competitiveness in industries that use protected goods as inputs, or for the fact that real consumer purchasing power is cut. All in all, the estimates in table 1.1 of jobs saved probably exaggerate the employment induced by special protection.

Costs of Special Protection

Table 1.2 presents estimates of the cost of special protection expressed both in terms of the total annual cost to consumers and in terms of the annual cost to consumers per production job "saved" (or per acre or head of livestock saved). Table 1.2 also gives estimates of the gains enjoyed by producers, both total and per job in the industry (or per acre or head of livestock). In addition, table 1.2 records estimates of the gains to foreigners, tariff revenues, and the efficiency losses to the economy.

Costs to consumers of special protection are huge. These costs represent a giant off-budget transfer from consumers on the one hand to producers and foreign suppliers on the other. In Phase III of Textiles and Apparel, the costs are running about $27.0 billion per year; in Phase III of Carbon Steel, about $6.8 billion; in Automobiles, about $5.8 billion; in Dairy Products, about $5.5 billion; and in most other ongoing cases, the amounts exceed $100 million annually.

Against these total costs, the production jobs "saved" in the affected

Table 1.2 Distribution of costs and benefits from special protection

	Cost of restraints to consumers		Gain from restraints to producers			Welfare costs of restraints		
Case	Totals (million dollars)	Per job saved[a] (dollars)	Totals (million dollars)	Per job[a] (dollars)	Gain to foreigners (million dollars)	Tariff revenue (million dollars)	Efficiency loss (million dollars)
Manufacturing							
M–1 Book Manufacturing	500	100,000	305	9,000	neg.	0	29
M–2 Benzenoid Chemicals	2,650	over 1 million	2,250	37,000	neg.	252	14
M–3 Glassware	200	200,000	130	11,000	neg.	54	13
M–4 Rubber Footwear	230	30,000	90	6,400	neg.	139	33
M–5 Ceramic Articles	95	47,500	25	3,100	neg.	69	6
M–6 Ceramic Tiles	116	135,000	62	10,000	neg.	55	11
M–7 Orange Juice	525	240,000	390	90,000	neg.	128	130
M–8 Canned Tuna	91	76,000	74	5,500	7	10	4
M–9 Textiles and Apparel: Phase I	9,400	22,000	8,700	4,000	neg.	1,158	1,100
M–10 Textiles and Apparel: Phase II	20,000	37,000	18,000	8,700	350	2,143	3,100
M–11 Textiles and Apparel: Phase III	27,000	42,000	22,000	11,100	1,800	2,535	4,850
M–12 Carbon Steel: Phase I	1,970	240,000	1,330	3,400	330	290	50
M–13 Carbon Steel: Phase II	4,350	620,000	2,770	9,700	930	556	120
M–14 Carbon Steel: Phase III	6,800	750,000	3,800	22,000	2,000	560	330

M–15 Ball Bearings	45	90,000	21	500	neg.	18	neg.
M–16 Specialty Steel	520	1,000,000	420	60,000	50	32	30
M–17 Nonrubber Footwear	700	55,000	250	2,000	220	262	16
M–18 Color Televisions	420	420,000	190	9,000	140	77	7
M–19 CB Radios	55	93,000	14	6,400	neg.	32	5
M–20 Bolts, Nuts, Large Screws	110	550,000	60	5,500	neg.	16	1
M–21 Prepared Mushrooms	35	117,000	13	4,300	neg.	25	0.8
M–22 Automobiles	5,800	105,000	2,600	4,300	2,200	790	200
M–23 Motorcycles	104	150,000	67	20,000	neg.	21	17
Services							
S–1 Maritime Industries	3,000	270,000	2,000	130,000	neg.	10[b]	1,000
Agriculture and Fisheries							
A–1 Sugar	930	60,000	550	27,000	410	5	130
		690/acre		180/acre			
A–2 Dairy Products	5,500	220,000	5,000	53,000	250	34	1,370
		1,800/cow		450/cow			
A–3 Peanuts	170	1,000/acre	170	120/acre	neg.	9	14
A–4 Meat	1,800	160,000	1,600	9,500	135	44	145
		225/head		20/head			
A–5 Fish	560	21,000	200	900	170	177	15
Mining							
E–1 Petroleum	6,900	160,000	4,800	61,500	2,000[c]	70	3,000
E–2 Lead and Zinc	67	30,000	46	2,300	4	11	5

Neg. Negligible.

a. Unless otherwise specified, figures are per worker.
b. Estimated duties collected on ship repairs performed abroad.
c. In this case, because of the way the quotas were allocated, the gains to importers accrued to domestic refiners rather than foreign exporters.

industries are, on the whole, rather modest. By far the largest jobs saved number is in Textiles and Apparel (640,000); followed by Automobiles (55,000), Fish (27,000), and Dairy (25,000). As a consequence, costs per production job saved are quite large, usually in the range of $20,000 to $100,000 per year, and often exceeding $150,000. The fact that costs to consumers per production job saved are so high underpins the strategy for an alternative approach that would liberally compensate departing workers for moving to new industries or early retirement.

Gains to producers *averaged over all jobs* are usually in the $4,000 to $20,000 per year range—a significant fraction of earnings per worker. In exceptional cases, such as Orange Juice and Petroleum, the calculated gains per worker substantially exceeded the annual wage bill per worker.

When trade restraints are imposed either through tariffs or through outright exclusion from the US market (as in Book Manufacturing and Maritime), foreign exporters gain nothing from the apparatus of protection. On the other hand, when quotas are assigned to foreign suppliers, the gains to foreign exporters from higher prices, although they may not fully offset losses in export volumes, can be handsome. For example, restraints imposed in Phase III of Carbon Steel probably enrich foreign suppliers to the extent of about $2.0 billion annually.

The last column of table 1.2 cites efficiency losses to the economy. Efficiency losses to the economy are, of course, much smaller than costs to the consumer, since most of the consumer costs are reflected in higher producer income. Only in large cases do efficiency losses exceed $1.0 billion dollars annually.

Adjustment During Special Protection

Table 1.3 summarizes the adjustment experience during episodes of special protection. The outstanding feature of this summary is that a great deal of adjustment does in fact take place, both in concluded cases and in ongoing cases.

In terms of labor force adjustment, the number of production jobs almost always dropped during the episodes. Carbon steel employment has declined by over 10 percent per year since 1980; the rubber footwear, glassware, industrial fastener, maritime, orange juice, and automobile industries have shed labor at rates in excess of 4 percent annually. Textile and apparel employment has dropped by about 1.6 percent annually since 1980. Likewise, the acreage or livestock in protected industries generally falls. Even sugar acreage has dropped by more than 2 percent annually since 1973. These rates of labor and cropland adjustment represent a signal accomplishment.

At the same time, the import share of the domestic market has usually been allowed to rise, if at constrained rates. Typically, the market share rise

Table 1.3 Adjustment during special protection[a]

	Employment[b]			Import share		
Case	Pre-restraint (thousands)	Post-restraint (thousands)	Annual change (percentage)	Pre-restraint (percentage)	Post-restraint (percentage)	Annual change (percentage points)
Manufacturing						
M–1 Book Manufacturing	37 (1979)	33 (1984)	–2.2	10.0 (1979)	19.5 (1984)	1.9
M–2 Benzenoid Chemicals	70 (1978)	61 (1984)	–2.1	1.0 (1978)	1.6 (1984)	0.1
M–3 Glassware	15 (1978)	12 (1983)	–4.0	10.5 (1978)	21.6 (1983)	2.2
M–4 Rubber Footwear	22 (1975)	14 (1983)	–4.5	39.8 (1975)	62.4 (1983)	2.8
M–5 Ceramic Articles	10 (1978)	8 (1984)	–3.3	50.7 (1976)	66.0 (1984)	1.9
M–6 Ceramic Tiles	7 (1972)	6 (1984)	–1.2	33.2 (1976)	57.9 (1984)	3.1
M–7 Orange Juice	5 (1978)	4 (1984)	–4.0	16.2 (1979)	29.5 (1983)	2.7
M–8 Canned Tuna	15 (1979)	13 (1983)	–2.2	6.8 (1978)	17.9 (1983)	2.2
M–9 Textiles and Apparel: Phase I	2,137 (1955)	2,140 (1974)	0.0	6.3 (1960)	8.4 (1974)	0.2
M–10 Textiles and Apparel: Phase II	2,194 (1972)	2,067 (1981)	–0.6	9.6 (1972)	14.0 (1981)	0.5
M–11 Textiles and Apparel: Phase III	2,112 (1980)	1,980 (1984)	–1.6	12.1 (1980)	20.4 (1984)	2.1

Table 1.3 Adjustment during special protection[a] *(continued)*

Case	Employment[b]			Import share		
	Pre-restraint (thousands)	Post-restraint (thousands)	Annual change (percentage)	Pre-restraint (percentage)	Post-restraint (percentage)	Annual change (percentage points)
M–12 Carbon Steel: Phase I	421 (1968)	339 (1975)	−2.8	16.7 (1968)	13.5 (1975)	−0.5
M–13 Carbon Steel: Phase II	337 (1977)	286 (1981)	−3.8	17.8 (1977)	21.8 (1982)	0.8
M–14 Carbon Steel: Phase III	292 (1980)	171 (1984)	−10.4	16.4 (1980)	26.7 (1984)	2.6
M–15 Ball Bearings	44 (1973)	43 (1979)	−0.4	23.7 (1973)	30.1 (1979)	1.1
M–16 Specialty Steel	16 (1975)	14 (1984)	−1.3	18.1 (1975)	16.8 (1984)	−0.1
M–17 Nonrubber Footwear	136 (1975)	122 (1982)	−1.5	41.3 (1975)	59.0 (1982)	2.5
M–18 Color Televisions	27 (1976)	21 (1982)	−3.7	38.5 (1979)	34.2 (1983)	−1.1
M–19 CB Radios	3 (1976)	neg. (1982)	−15.2	94.0 (1976)	97.0 (1983)	0.5
M–20 Bolts, Nuts, Large Screws	13 (1978)	10 (1982)	−5.3	40.9 (1978)	49.9 (1982)	2.3
M–21 Prepared Mushrooms	3 (1979)	3 (1982)	0.0	51.8 (1979)	62.4 (1984)	2.1
M–22 Automobiles	779 (1979)	605 (1984)	−4.5	28.3 (1979)	34.2 (1984)	1.2
M–23 Motorcycles	2 (1982)	3 (1984)	25.0	69.0 (1982)	31.0 (1984)	−19.0

Services						
S–1 Maritime Industries	37 (1970)	14 (1984)	–4.4	65.2 (1970)	62.3 (1983)	–0.2
Agriculture and Fisheries						
A–1 Sugar	29	20	–4.4	50.3 (1974)	34.5 (1984)	–1.6
	2,300 (acres) (1976)	1,800 (acres) (1983)	–3.1			
A–2 Dairy Products	97	94	–0.6	4.5 (1978)	4.2 (1983)	–0.1
	10,900 (cows) (1978)	11,100 (cows) (1983)	0.4			
A–3 Peanuts	6	6	–1.2	neg.	neg.	neg.
	1,520 (acres) (1974)	1,410 (acres) (1983)	–0.8			
A–4 Meat	189	168	–0.6	3.6 (1964)	5.9 (1983)	0.1
	108,000 (head) (1963)	114,000 (head) (1983)	0.3			
A–5 Fish	173 (1976)	216 (1982)	4.1	62.5 (1976)	61.5 (1983)	–0.1
Mining						
E–1 Petroleum	140 (1954)	75 (1975)	–2.7	9.9 (1954)	25.8 (1975)	0.8
E–2 Lead and Zinc	28 (1957)	20 (1966)	–3.4	58.2 (1957)	37.6 (1966)	–2.3

Neg. Negligible.

a. In lengthy and ongoing cases, the pre- and post-restraint figures are actually the first and the last years of data that we included in the case.

b. Unless otherwise specified, figures refer to the number of production jobs in the industry.

is 0.5 percent to as much as 3 percent annually. Again, these are significant figures.

Special protection as practiced in the United States cannot, for the most part, be faulted for freezing the status quo. Instead, it should be criticized for providing rather little assistance to workers and firms that depart the troubled industry; for imposing huge costs on consumers; for not promoting a smooth transition to the realities of international competition; and for engendering widespread opposition to trade liberalization.

Assessment of Special Protection

The US system of special protection is far from the worst system imaginable. Indeed, the system has several virtues. In the first place, a presidential policy of making slow and grudging concessions to troubled industries, coupled with less-than-watertight regimes of protection, allows a great deal of adjustment to take place. Before trade restraints are put in place, the industry usually sheds a substantial number of workers and concedes market share to imports. Even after restraints are in place, the import share of the market typically rises and employment continues to shrink. Moreover, relief often turns out to be temporary. Despite the fears of skeptics and the hopes of industry, many instances of special protection do not ripen into a maritime story, a book printing story, or an apparel story. Although highly inefficient from an economic standpoint, the use of VRAs, OMAs, and other QRs minimizes international abrasion so long as quota rents are conferred on foreigners. Finally, special protection for problem industries has not so far precluded liberalization in other sectors of the economy, notably through seven rounds of GATT negotiations.

In short, the US system of special protection has its strong points. Scholars of the Bert Lance school might say, "If it ain't broke, don't fix it." Yet, while not completely broke, the system has six conspicuous defects by comparison with a policy framework that would place greater stress on the original purposes of the GATT Article XIX escape clause—namely, time-limited, degressive protection, applied on a most-favored-nation (MFN) basis.

First, the trade coverage of special protection is growing. Table 1.4 gives summary statistics. The trade coverage in 1955 was $0.6 billion; in 1960, $3.4 billion; in 1970, $9.7 billion; in 1980, $28.9 billion; and in 1984, $67.6 billion. As a percentage of US imports, special protection tapered off after the end of petroleum restraints, but grew from 8 percent of imports in 1975 to 21 percent in 1984. The reduction of US imports on account of special protection rose from $12.4 billion in 1975 to some $44.4 billion in 1984. The rise in special protection since 1980 is closely related to the appreciation

Table 1.4 Special protection related to total trade[a]

Year	Total US imports (billion dollars)	US imports covered by special protection		Consumer cost of special protection[b]		Induced decrease in imports		Tariff equivalent of special protection		Division of tariff equivalent		Relative wholesale prices[e] (1975=100)
		Annual average (million dollars)	Share of total imports (percentage)	Annual average (million dollars)	Share of total imports (percentage)	Annual average (million dollars)	Share of total imports (percentage)	(million dollars)	(percentage)	Tariff revenue[c] (million dollars)	Implied quota rents[d] (million dollars)	
1955	11.6	577	5	703	6	629	5	180	31	21	159	118.6
1960[f]	15.1	3,380	22	6,352	42	5,917	39	1,931	57	302	1,629	126.2
1965[f]	21.5	4,759	22	9,627	45	8,720	41	2,665	56	440	2,225	116.5
1970[f]	40.2	9,655	24	16,439	41	14,631	36	4,499	47	847	3,652	118.2
1975	99.3	7,894	8	13,117	13	12,424	12	2,202	28	1,375	827	100.0
1980	245.3	28,928	12	32,749	13	22,619	9	6,147	21	3,445	2,702	93.9
1984[g]	328.7	67,597	21	53,474	16	44,431	13	13,713	20	6,123	7,590	135.5

a. These figures do not include the maritime case (S–1) since the import statistics are not comparable with those in other cases.
b. The consumer cost for those years not included in the cases themselves and in which protection was ongoing, was derived by relating the current year cost to current year trade and adjusting the cost with the trade level of other years.
c. The tariff equivalent and tariff revenue were estimated by applying the rates in the case to all years in which the case was ongoing, even though some variation in tariff and quota levels undoubtedly occurred.
d. The quota rents were derived simply by subtracting the estimated tariff revenue from the dollar value of the tariff equivalent.
e. The figures for 1955 and 1960 are based on Helen B. Junz and Rudolf R. Rhomberg, "Prices and Export Performance of Industrial Countries, 1953–63," *IMF Staff Papers* 12, no. 2 (July 1965): table 9, p. 269. The figures for 1965 to 1984 are based on the table, "Cost and Price Comparisons for Mfg." in IMF, *International Financial Statistics*.
f. The unusually high levels of protection and relative consumer costs in the years 1960, 1965, and 1970 are due to restricted petroleum imports which accounted for an average 42 percent of covered trade in those years.
g. Some of the figures are for 1983.

of the dollar against major foreign currencies.[18] Between 1980 and 1984, US wholesale prices rose, relative to the wholesale prices expressed in US dollars of major trading partners, from an index level of 93.9 to an index level of 135.5 (table 1.4). Once the dollar corrects against foreign currencies, much of the special protection witnessed in the mid-1980s should begin to erode; nevertheless, it seems likely that a good part of the edifice will remain.

Second, special protection is costly to consumers, both in total consumer costs and in consumer costs per production job "saved." Figures of $20,000 to $85,000 consumer costs per job-year saved are common, and figures above $150,000 occur all too often. These figures represent a high price for the goal usually announced—namely, to preserve blue collar employment in the afflicted industry.

Third, special protection diverts scarce resources to America's least promising industries. Almost by definition, industries that need special protection are industries that have lost their competitive edge in the world economy. These industries do not draw on the comparative strength of the US labor force. They are industries in which foreign technology is as good, or better, than US technology.

Fourth, special protection is associated with huge quota rents, largely accruing to foreign producers. In 1984, the figure was running at $7.6 billion annually. The creation and allocation of quota rents serves to entrench established patterns of production, on a worldwide scale, rather than encourage adjustment to changing comparative advantage. For example, Europe rather than Korea continues as a major supplier of carbon steel to the US market.

Fifth, in recent years, special protection has come to impede new initiatives for trade liberalization. In the days when special protection was limited to sugar, dairy, cotton textiles, oil, and selected other products, it did not seriously interfere with the Kennedy Round of trade negotiations. Now that special protection has spread to autos, steel, nearly all textiles, meat, and many other goods, it stands as a major obstacle to multilateral trade liberalization.

Sixth and finally, special protection is highly inequitable as between industries. Large industries with political clout—dairy, apparel, automobiles—are able to shake the US political system for massive benefits. Small industries with only regional influence—footwear, copper, CB radios—at best get escape clause relief and often get nothing. Unfairness may be a fact of political life, but it is not an attractive fact.

---

18. The connection between dollar overvaluation and trade protection is often stressed by Bergsten. See, for example, Bergsten and Williamson, 1983.

A New Approach to Troubled Industries

Our companion monograph suggests a new trade policy for troubled industries.[19] Only the basic elements will be summarized here. The cases give very rough illustrative calculations as to how the new approach might affect industries that are beneficiaries of ongoing special protection.

The problems of declining industries often reflect domestic events—stagnant demand and high productivity—to a greater extent than foreign competition. Trade relief is not a proper solution for problems of domestic origin. However, it would be difficult or impossible to distinguish a particular worker displaced by imports from a fellow worker displaced by weak demand. Thus, our approach proposes that all workers present in the industry on a defined date should be equally eligible for assistance, but that funding for adjustment optimally would be divided between domestic and trade relief sources according to the relative role of each in contributing to the industry's decline.

A general premise of the plan is that continued contraction will be necessary, however unpleasant, for most industries forced to adjust to a changing competitive environment. Therefore, neither public nor coerced private investment should be a prerequisite for other types of government assistance. To be sure, even in a contracting industry, new investment may be highly productive, but private risk takers are the best judge of what type and how much new investment should be undertaken.

A Refurbished Escape Clause

The plan calls for centralizing relief under a refurbished escape clause.[20] Why the escape clause? This provision has been a durable, if underutilized, component of US trade policy for more than 40 years. It makes practical political sense to build on familiar foundations. Escape clause relief requires that injury be demonstrated in an adversarial setting. The purpose of relief under the new plan, as under the existing escape clause, is to provide temporary "breathing room" for orderly adjustment, not to provide a facade for indefinite protection. Of all forms of special protection, escape clause relief has most reliably functioned in a time-limited fashion.

The USITC is called upon to design a menu of relief alternatives, while

---

19. Hufbauer and Rosen, 1986.

20. Hufbauer and Rosen (1986) explain how the escape clause should be restructured so as to make it a more attractive relief option relative to unfair trade procedures or other special statutory provisions.

the US Trade Representative (USTR) is charged with selecting the actual course to be followed. The relief provided should address both "domestic" causes of decline—unemployment from slow demand growth and fast productivity growth—and "international" causes of decline—unemployment from greater import penetration. The remedy package should be based on the relative contribution of these two sources of injury, if practicable.

Assured funding for adjustment purposes is built into the plan. This is an important point: since general revenues are always scarce, self-financed options are a key ingredient of the relief menu. Self-financing is generated by tariffs, auctioned quotas, or taxes on the industry's products. However, under certain circumstances, use of general budget revenues may be most appropriate.

The four basic components that the USITC would draw on in designing alternative adjustment programs would include:

- a tariff on imports of the product; or quantitative restrictions on imports with quota rights auctioned by the US Treasury; in both cases with the proceeds earmarked to assist the industry[21]
- quantitative restraints on imports, either allocated to the domestic import-competing industry or assigned to individual exporting countries; with worker and firm adjustment programs funded either by the industry or by general budget receipts
- a special tax on the product, levied *both* on domestic production and on imports (and rebated on exports), with the proceeds used to assist the industry[22]
- the use of general budget revenues to finance adjustment, with no import restraints.

Unraveling Existing Special Protection

The procedures outlined under the new plan would strictly apply to future cases in which industries seek relief from fair trade. Existing cases of special protection may, however, require custom tailoring, because entire industries and regions have come to depend on federal barriers to foreign competition.

---

21. The idea of converting quotas to tariffs or auctioned quotas and dedicating the revenues to adjustment purposes has been advocated by Bhagwati, 1982, and Schultz and Schumacher, May/June 1984.

22. Taxes of this sort have been widely used in US agricultural programs, for example in the Jones-Costigan Act of 1934 that regulated sugar production and imports.

In some cases, adjustment has been postponed so long that a huge chasm separates the US industry from its foreign competitors.

The adjustment process in existing cases should be initiated by a request from the USTR directing the USITC to design degressive relief measures. The USTR request would be made only after consultation with other executive branch agencies and key congressional committees. The menu of degressive remedies would be much the same as for new escape clause cases. Among other options, the menu would include programs designed to convert existing quantitative restrictions into tariffs or auctioned quotas. However, the phase-out horizon might be longer than for new cases, because the starting level of protection is higher. As a working assumption, we would project a 1 percent to 3 percent decrease in tariff or tariff-equivalent protection per year. In an industry like apparel, where the tariff equivalent of protection probably exceeds 39 percent, the phase-out might require 15 years or more.

The US decision to implement adjustment programs in existing cases of specific protection would very likely be conditioned on similar pledges from Japan, Europe, Canada, and advanced developing countries such as Brazil and Mexico. Japan, for example, might inaugurate an adjustment program for its rice, beef, and citrus farmers in exchange for an American automobile program. International commitments would be phrased in terms of several goals: a specified reduction of protective barriers; a specified growth in the market share held by imports; minimum and optional maximum rates of exit of workers, plant capacity, and farmland. Within these commitments, each country should be free to develop its own adjustment programs.[23]

In the case of existing programs of special protection that spring from statutory relief schemes, the USTR choice of an alternative adjustment program would require "fast-track" approval by Congress.[24] This would apply, for example, to relief under Section 204 of the Agricultural Act of 1956, Section 22 of the Agricultural Adjustment Act of 1933, the Meat Act, the Jones Act, and so forth. "Fast-track" review would give Congress an opportunity to consider the views of affected constituents, to examine reciprocal international concessions, and to exercise its constitutional role in regulating foreign commerce.

---

23. Hufbauer and Schott explain how this could be part of a new round of trade negotiations.

24. The "fast-track" approval process was devised in the Trade Act of 1974. Under this process, the President gives Congress 90 days notification prior to submitting legislation; Congress then votes on the legislation, without amendment, within 60 days of submission.

Table 1.5 Characteristics of hypothetical adjustment programs

	Employment[a]				Import market share			Program cost	
Case	1984[b] (thousand)	1990[b] (thousand)	Annual change due to domestic factors[c] (percentage)	Annual change due to rising import share (percentage)	1984 (percentage)	1990 (percentage)	Annual change (percentage points)	Assumed adjustment cost per worker[b] (dollars)	Net budgetary surplus (cost) of adjustment program[a] (million dollars)
Manufacturing									
M–1 Book Manufacturing	33	22	−3.0	−2.5	20.0	32.0	2.0	24,000	(199)
M–3 Glassware	12	10	−1.9	−1.2	23.0	30.0	1.2	20,000	185
M–4 Rubber Footwear	15	10	−1.0	−5.2	64.0	76.0	2.0	17,000	744
M–5 Ceramic Articles	8	6	−1.9	−2.3	66.0	71.4	0.9	17,000	306
M–6 Ceramic Tiles	6	5	−1.9	−0.9	48.7	52.1	0.6	17,000	191
M–7 Orange Juice	4	4	2.1	−2.8	30.0	41.0	1.8	17,000	944
M–8 Canned Tuna	13	11	−1.9	−0.6	15.7	19.9	0.7	16,000	(35)
M–11 Textiles and Apparel: Phase III	1,980	1,696	−1.0	−1.4	20.4	27.7	1.2	17,500	15,210
M–14 Carbon Steel: Phase III	170	128	−3.3	−0.8	26.7	25.5	−0.2	35,000	15,223
M–16 Specialty Steel	14	10	−4.2	−1.1	16.4	23.6	1.2	35,000	35
M–22 Automobiles	605	460	−2.7	−1.3	33.7	41.9	1.4	35,000	6,100

Services								
S–1 Maritime Industries	14	8	–2.6	65.0	77.0	2.0	36,000	11,131
Agriculture and Fisheries								
A–1 Sugar	20	12	–0.2	37.4	57.1	3.3	15,000	158
	1,800	1,100	–0.2				1,000/acre	
	(acres)	(acres)						
A–2 Dairy Products	94	69	–3.5	4.3	10.2	1.0	15,000	557
	11,100	8,700	–2.7				600/cow	
	(cows)	(cows)						
A–3 Peanuts	1,400	1,310	0.0	neg.	6.2	1.0	1,500/acre	(110)
	(acres)	(acres)						
A–4 Meat	168	140	–1.9	6.0	12.0	1.0	20,000	(259)
	114,000	114,000	0.9				500/head	
	(head)	(head)						
A–5 Fish	200	216	1.3	60.0	62.5	0.4	15,000	770

Neg. Negligible.

a. The annual changes due to productivity and consumption growth and rising import share are based on figures to be found in the cases. The net effect on employment as derived from the percentage figures may not agree with the percentage change derived from employment figures in this table since these have been rounded to the nearest thousand.

b. All figures, unless otherwise specified, refer to workers in the industry.

c. These are changes due to increases in productivity and consumption growth.

d. These figures represent the net budgetary surplus (outlay) of the hypothetical adjustment programs over the period 1985–90.

Illustrative Examples

The United States could certainly do worse than its present approach to special protection. But the United States could also do much better. As a way of illustrating the better alternative, we have prepared numerical examples of possible adjustment programs that might replace existing cases of special protection. These examples, summarized in table 1.5, appear in individual cases in the appendix.

In the examples, rough assumptions were made about various parameters—consumption growth, productivity growth, elasticities of demand, and so forth. The programs are designed to adjust resources unemployed *both* from "international" and from "domestic" causes. Protection is scheduled to decline at one to three percentage points per year, expressed in tariff-equivalent terms. All in all, the adjustment programs do not entail a marked increase in the rate of labor or acreage exit, or the pace of import penetration, when compared to recent trends.

Employment in the troubled industries is projected to decline, generally by 2 percent to 5 percent annually. This is about the same as past experience in these industries. Less than half the decline is associated with imports. The rest stems from domestic causes. The adjustment programs would, of course, cover workers, farmland, and livestock, no matter why they are dislocated.

The share of the domestic market supplied by importers rises about 1 percent per year under the hypothetical programs. Again, this is about the same as past experience with troubled industries.

The programs envisage large on-budget, self-financed payments to the workers and firms that face the burden of adjustment. We assume that costs of the program would work out to twice the average annual wage of each separated worker. This figure includes allowances for early retirement, retraining, relocation, and industry adjustment. Wage costs are estimated in the range of $15,000 to $36,000 per separated worker per year. Thus, adjustment costs are calculated in the $30,000 to $72,000 per worker range. This is very much larger than the past history of trade adjustment assistance programs, amounting to under $3,000 per worker.[25] The cost for retiring farmland was set at $1,000 to $1,500 per acre, and the cost for retiring livestock at $500 to $600 per head. We have deliberately set high cost figures, both to make the new program attractive by comparison with special protection and to allow for a margin of error in the number of workers (or acres) receiving assistance.

---

25. USTR 1984, p. 150.

We assumed that quantitative restraints would either be converted to tariffs or sold as auctioned quotas. On this assumption, it appears possible to fund the envisaged levels of assistance—without using product taxes or general budget receipts. This result reflects the recapture of very high quota rents that are now garnered by private foreign suppliers and US importers. Nevertheless, in the spirit of dividing the funding burden between domestic and international causes of decline, and as a matter of international comity, in many instances the program should be partly funded with general revenues and product taxes.

2
Methodology

This chapter outlines a simple comparative statics framework for estimating the quantitative impact of import restraints. It then presents a simple framework for calculating industry adjustment under a policy of degressive tariffs or quotas. These frameworks were used as rough guideposts in preparing the case studies.

Import Restraints

The framework rests on three assumptions:

- The imported good and the domestic good are imperfect substitutes.
- The supply schedule for imports is perfectly elastic.
- The supply schedule for domestically produced goods is upwardly sloped.

Figures 2.1 and 2.2 illustrate the effect of trade restraints—either tariffs or quantitative limitations—on the US demand and price for the imported good and the domestic good. Physical units of each good are conveniently defined so that the price of each unit, in the absence of trade restraints, is 1.0.

In the absence of restraints, the quantity Q_m would be imported. Immediately after a tariff is imposed, the quantity $(Q_m - q_m)$ would be imported. Higher import prices will shift some demand to domestic production and thereby raise domestic prices and output. In turn, this will cause an outward shift in the demand schedule for imports.[1] Once equilibrium is reestablished,

---

1. If binding quota restraints are imposed, any outward shift in the demand for imports would simply be reflected in higher prices. For expositional convenience, we may consider that the point e in figure 2.1 is reached either by tariff restraints or by quota restraints.

Figure 2.1   The effect of trade restraints on demand and price for imported good

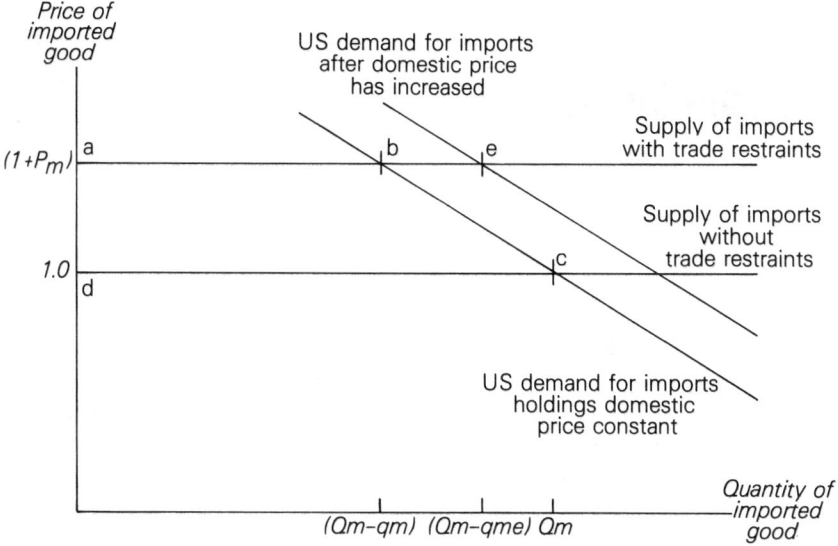

Figure 2.2   The effect of trade restraints on demand and price for domestic good

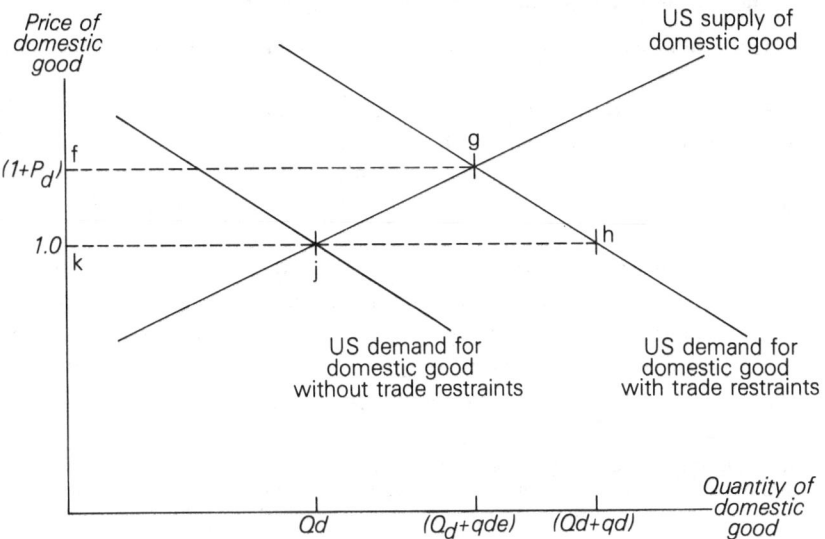

imports have declined by the quantity q_{me}, while the price per unit has increased by P_m. Meanwhile, the demand schedule for domestic goods has shifted to the right, and the equilibrium quantity of domestic output has shifted from Q_d to $(Q_d + q_{de})$.

Foreign exporters may gain or lose from the restraints depending in part on how restraints are imposed. At one extreme, if the quantity q_{me} is excluded from the US market by a quota, and the quotas are allocated to importers (either foreign or domestic firms), then the importers will receive a quota rent, measured as the increase in price, P_m, times the new quantity ($Q_m - q_{me}$). At the other extreme, if a tariff is imposed equal to the entire price increase, then importers will receive no scarcity rents. A mixture of quantitative and tariff restraints, such as a tariff-rate quota, will divide the scarcity rents between importers and the US Treasury.

In real life, foreign supply schedules may not be perfectly elastic. This helps explain why foreign suppliers usually resist quotas, even if the quota mechanism assigns all the scarcity rents to them. It also helps explain why domestic firms are more eager for quota restraints than seemingly equivalent tariffs. Since the measurement of gains or losses to foreign suppliers is not our main focus, we will adhere to the assumption of perfectly elastic foreign supply schedules.

Import restraints are often imposed on only one or two suppliers. The decrease in imports from all foreign suppliers taken together may be less than the decrease from the one or two suppliers subject to restrictions, because other foreign suppliers may replace the restricted foreign suppliers. Moreover, quantitative restraints may be offset by quality upgrading. The quantity q_{me} in figure 2.1 is drawn to reflect both offsetting supplies from unrestricted suppliers (q_{me} may be smaller than the quantity nominally excluded by restraints) and any quality upgrading (physical units are defined in quality-equivalent terms).

Figure 2.2 depicts the impact of import restraints on domestic producers. Physical units are again conveniently defined so that the price of each unit, in the absence of trade restraints, is 1.0. The diminished supply and higher price of imports shifts the demand schedule for domestic goods to the right. The increased quantity of domestic goods demanded at equilibrium prices is represented by q_{de}.

The ratio, (q_{de}/q_{me}), may be denoted as the coefficient of quantity response, Ø. The coefficient Ø reflects both imperfect substitution between domestic goods and imported goods, and the likelihood that a rise in the relative price of imported goods will shift some demand to domestic goods. The coefficient Ø will normally exhibit a value between one and zero: the additional quantity of domestic product demanded will be positive but less than the quantity of imports excluded from the US market. The coefficient

Ø may be expressed in terms of the elasticity of supply of domestically produced goods, E_s; the cross-elasticity of the physical quantity of imports relative to the price of domestic goods, E_{md}; and the ratio between imports and domestic production, MR:

(1) $\quad \emptyset = q_{de}/q_{me} = (E_s)/(E_{md} \cdot MR)$.

Equation (1) says that, if any three of the four variables are known (Ø, E_s, E_{md}, MR), then the fourth is also known.

The supply schedule for domestically produced goods is assumed to have an upward slope. Hence, the higher demand causes the price of domestically produced goods to rise by P_d. The ratio, (P_d/P_m), may be denoted as the coefficient of price response, θ. Presumably θ is less than one and greater than zero. The coefficient θ may be expressed in terms of the domestic supply elasticity, E_s, and the cross-elasticity of physical output of the domestic good relative to the price of the imported good, E_{dm}:

(2) $\quad \theta = E_{dm}/E_s$.

Equation (2) says that, if any two of the three variables are known (θ, E_{dm}, E_s), then the third is also known. Given the relationship between the cross-elasticity of output, E_{dm}, and the cross-elasticity of demand for the domestic good relative to the price of the imported good, E_{ddm}, equation (2) may also be written:

(3) $\quad \theta = (E_{ddm})/(E_s + E_d)$.

Equation (3) says that, if any three of the four variables are known (E_{ddm}, E_s, E_d, and θ), then the fourth is also known.

The rise in domestic prices imposes a cost to consumers in their purchase of domestic goods, represented by the area [fghk] in figure 2.2. The total cost experienced by consumers is the sum of the additional cost for their purchases of imports at higher prices (area [aecd] in figure 2.1) and the additional cost for their purchases of domestically produced goods at higher prices (area [fghk] in figure 2.2). This total cost is approximately represented by the change in the price of imports times the quantity of imports, plus the change in the price of domestic output times the quantity of domestic output.

Offsetting the additional cost to consumers is the gain to domestic producers, GD, represented in figure 2.2 by the area [fgjk]. This is approximately equal to the change in the price of domestic output times the quantity of domestic output. Also offsetting the cost to consumers is the revenue (if any) collected by the US Treasury through the imposition of a tariff or the auction of quotas.

The efficiency loss, EL, to the United States from increasing domestic production is given by the triangular area [ghj] in figure 2.2. This represents the difference between the loss of consumers' surplus (area [fghk]) and the gain of producers' surplus (area [fgjk]). This formulation assumes that the area [mhk] represents consumers' surplus (both from domestic and foreign purchases) prior to the trade restraint. In fact, consumers' surplus was probably greater than [mhk] because consumers were forced to an inferior demand curve by trade restraints. Note that this formulation of the efficiency loss takes no account of transitional unemployment, which can be very substantial.

The gain to foreign exporters, GF, is represented by the quota premium, if any, on quotas assigned to foreign suppliers times the quantity of imports. In most cases, this quota premium is the same as the change in import price less the tariff. However, in some cases quota rights may be assigned to domestic importers. The overall welfare cost to the US economy, WD, may be defined as the efficiency loss, EL, plus the gain to foreign importers, GF.

These and other relationships are summarized in the following summary of definitions and relations.

Definitions for Import Restraint Parameters

P_m = percentage increase in the price of imported goods owing to import restraint.

P_d = percentage increase in the price of domestically produced goods as a consequence of the higher import price.

θ = coefficient relating the response of the price of domestic goods to the price of imported goods. By definition: $\theta = P_d/P_m$. By hypothesis: $0<\theta<1$.

Q_m = quantity of imported goods without the import restriction. Quantity units are defined so that the pre-restraint price is 1.0 per unit.

q_m = initial decrease in quantity of imports as a result of the import restraint.

q_{me} = equilibrium decrease in quantity of imports as a result of the import restraint and the induced impact on domestic prices.

Q_d = quantity of domestically produced goods without the import restriction. Quantity units are defined so that the pre-restraint price is 1.0 per unit.

q_d = initial increase in quantity of domestically produced goods demanded at constant prices as a result of the import restraint.

q_{de} = equilibrium increase in the quantity of domestically produced goods as a result of the import restriction.

$\emptyset$ = coefficient relating the equilibrium change in the quantity of

E_s = domestic goods purchased to the change in the quantity of imported goods purchased. By definition: $\emptyset = q_{de}/q_{me}$. By hypothesis: $0<\emptyset<1$.

E_s = elasticity of supply of domestically produced goods. By definition: $E_s = (q_{de}/Q_d)/(P_d)$.

E_d = elasticity of demand for domestically produced goods. By definition: $E_d = [(q_d - q_{de})/(Q_d + q_{de})]/(P_d) = [(q_d - q_{de})/Q_d]/(P_d)$.
Note: the use of Q_d in the second version of this definition gives an analytically convenient approximation.

E_m = elasticity of demand for imported goods. By definition: $E_m = (q_m/Q_m)$.

E_{ddm} = cross-elasticity of demand for domestically produced goods relative to the price of imported goods, holding the price of domestic goods constant. By definition: $E_{ddm} = (q_d/Q_d)/(P_m)$.

E_{dm} = cross-elasticity of physical output of domestically produced goods relative to the price of imported goods, taking into account the impact of higher import prices on both domestic supply and domestic demand. By definition: $E_{dm} = (q_{de}/Q_d)/(P_m)$.

E_{md} = cross-elasticity of physical quantity of imported goods relative to the price of domestically produced goods. By definition: $E_{md} = (q_{me}/Q_m)/(P_d)$.

MR   = import ratio in the absence of restrictions. By definition: $MR = (Q_m/Q_d)$.

CD   = cost of import restraints to domestic consumers.
GD   = gain from import restraints to domestic producers.
GF   = gain from import restraints to foreign exporters.
EL   = efficiency loss to the United States from larger domestic production. By definition, this is the triangular area [ghj] in figure 2.2.
WD   = welfare cost of import restraints to the United States. By definition: $WD = GF + EL$.
t = ad valorem tariff rate imposed by the United States, or tariff-rate equivalent of quotas sold at auction.
T = tariff revenue collected by the United States.

Note: Price elasticities are defined as positive numbers.

Relations Between Import Restraint Parameters

(1) $P_d = \theta(P_m)$
(2) $\theta = P_d/P_m = E_{dm}/E_s = (E_{ddm})/(E_s + E_d)$
(3) $q_{de} = \emptyset(q_{me})$
(4) $\emptyset = q_{de}/q_{me} = (E_s)/(E_{md} \cdot MR)$
(5) $q_{de} = E_s \cdot P_d \cdot Q_d$

(6) $q_m = E_m \cdot P_m \cdot Q_m$
(7) $E_{dm} = (E_{ddm})/(1 + E_d/E_s)$
(8) $E_{md} = (E_{dm})(\emptyset \cdot \theta \cdot MR)$
(9) $CD \approx P_m(Q_m - q_{me}) + P_d(Q_d + q_{de})$
(10) $GD \approx P_d(Q_d + q_{de})$
(11) $GF = P_m(Q_m - q_{me}) - T$
(12) $EL = 0.5P_d(q_{de}) + 0.5P_d(q_d - q_{de}) =$
    $0.5P_d(q_{de}) + 0.5[P_d \cdot P_d \cdot E_d \cdot (Q_d + q_{de})]$
(13) $WD = GF + EL$
(14) $T = t(Q_m - q_{me})$

The relations listed above were used as rough guideposts in estimating the parameters that appear in the case studies. Exact conformity between the relations and the parameters was not sought.

Industry Adjustment

The industry adjustment profiles in the case studies in the appendix are calculated under a number of severe simplifying assumptions. Our purpose is to illustrate orders of magnitude, not to give definitive quantitative analyses. The key assumptions are:

- US consumption in real terms grows by a fixed percentage each year.
- Imports in real terms grow by a predetermined increase in the quota. See equation (4) below. In some cases, the tariff is scheduled to decrease by a predetermined amount each year. In those cases, the change in the quantity of imports is a derived number, based on the elasticity of import demand.
- US production is the difference between consumption and imports. See equation (5).
- US employment is determined by the level of production and a predetermined rate of productivity growth. See equation (6).
- The annual budget cost of the adjustment program is twice the wage and benefit payments to workers laid off in the previous year. See equation (1) below.
- The revenue available to fund adjustment equals the quota auction revenue plus the tariff revenue.
- The total protective barrier—the quota auction rate plus the tariff rate—declines to reflect the percentage increase in import quantity and the elasticity of import demand.

Definitions for Adjustment Parameters

- n = subscript denoting the year.
- t = quota auction rate plus tariff rate.
- dt = change in the quota auction rate plus tariff rate.
- T = annual revenue collected by the United States, defined as imports times the quota auction rate plus tariff rate.
- R = annual cost of the adjustment program, defined as two times the wage and benefit payments to workers laid off in the previous year.
- Q_m^* = actual imports (quantity, or value at constant prices).
- ΔQ_m^* = predetermined increase in imports (quantity, or value at constant prices).
- Q_d^* = domestic production (quantity, or value at constant prices).
- E_m = elasticity of demand for imports with respect to a change in the quota auction plus tariff rate of protection.
- C = domestic consumption, defined as the sum of imports and production (inventories held constant).
- g = annual rate of growth in consumption.
- A = domestic employment in the affected industry.
- k = coefficient that relates domestic employment to domestic production, taking into account productivity growth.
- W = wage rate in constant dollars.

Relations Between Adjustment Parameters

(1) $R_n = 2.0(W_n)(A_{n-1} - A_n)$
(2) $T_n = t_n(Q_m^*)_n$
(3) $dt = [(\Delta Q_m^*)/(Q_m^*)]/(E_m)$
(4) $(Q_m^*)_n = (Q_m^*)_{n-1} + \Delta Q_m^*$
(5) $(Q_d^*)_n = C_n - (Q_m^*)_n$
(6) $A_n = k_n(Q_d^*)_n$

The relations between adjustment parameters were used as rough guideposts in designing the hypothetical adjustment programs that appear in the case studies of those industries where special protection was ongoing in 1985 (and was not in prospect of an early phase-out by Tokyo Round tariff cuts or other measures). Exact conformity between the adjustment programs and the relations was not imposed.

The 31 cases appear in the appendix. Each case includes a brief history of protective measures; a summary of key statistics; a quantitative profile of important parameters, showing, among other data, the costs to consumers and the benefits to producers; and, for ongoing cases, a hypothetical adjustment plan.

Bibliography

This bibliography lists only general reference works, including but not limited to items referenced in the text. A detailed bibliography accompanies each case study.

Anderson, Kym, and Robert E. Baldwin. 1981. "The Political Market for Protection in Industrial Countries: Empirical Evidence." World Bank Staff Working Paper, no. 492. Washington, October.
Bailey, Pat (Federal Trade Commission). 1984. "The Perils of Protectionism." Charles Francis Adams Lecture, Fletcher School of Law and Diplomacy, Medford, Mass., October.
Balassa, Bela, and Carol Balassa. 1984. "Industrial Protection in the Developed Countries." *The World Economy,* vol. 7, no. 2 (June).
Baldwin, Robert E. 1984a. "The Political Economy of US Import Policy." University of Wisconsin, Madison, October.
―――. 1984b. "Rent-seeking and Trade Policy: An Industry Approach." University of Wisconsin, Madison, October.
Baldwin, Robert E., and Anne O. Krueger, eds. 1984. *The Structure and Evolution of Recent US Trade Policy.* National Bureau of Economic Research Conference Report. Chicago: University of Chicago Press.
Bergsten, C. Fred, ed. 1975. *Toward a New World Trade Policy: The Maidenhead Papers.* Lexington, Mass.: Lexington Books, D.C. Heath and Co.
Bergsten, C. Fred and John Williamson. 1983. "Exchange Rates and Trade Policy." In *Trade Policy in the 1980s.* Edited by William R. Cline. Washington: Institute for International Economics.
Bhagwati, Jagdish N. 1982. "Shifting Comparative Advantage, Protectionist Demands, and Policy Response." In *Import Competition and Response,* edited by Jagdish N. Bhagwati. National Bureau of Economic Research Conference Report. Chicago: University of Chicago Press.
Cable, Vincent. 1983. *Protectionism and Industrial Decline.* London: Hodder and Stoughton for the Overseas Development Institute.
Cassing, James, Timothy J. McKeown, and Jack Ochs. 1984. "Firms, Regions, Business Cycles, and the Demand for Tariffs." Paper read at the Annual Meeting of the American Political Science Association. University of Pittsburgh, Pa., September.
Cline, William R. 1984. "US Trade and Industrial Policy: The Experience of Textiles, Steel, and Automobiles." Paper read at Trade 1984, Conference Marking the 50th Anniversary of the US Export–Import Bank. Washington, October.
Collyns, Charles. 1982. *Can Protection Cure Unemployment?* Thames Essay No. 31. London: Trade Policy Research Centre.
Hufbauer, Gary Clyde, and Howard F. Rosen. 1986. *Trade Policy for Troubled Industries.* POLICY ANALYSES IN INTERNATIONAL ECONOMICS 15. Washington: Institute for International Economics, March.

———, eds. 1986. *Domestic Adjustment and International Trade*. Washington: Institute for International Economics, forthcoming.

Lawrence, Robert Z. 1984. *Can America Compete?* Washington: Brookings Institution.

Magee, Stephen P. 1980. "Three Simple Tests of the Stoper–Samuelson Theorem." In *Issues in International Economics*. Edited by P. Oppenheimer. London: Oriel Press.

Messerlin, Patrick A. 1981. "The Political Economy of Protectionism: The Bureaucratic Case." *Weltwirtschaftliches Archiv*, vol. 117, no. 3.

Metzger, Stanley D. 1964. *Trade Agreements and the Kennedy Round*. Fairfax, Va.: Coiner Publications.

———. 1971a. "Adjustment Assistance." In President's Commission on International Trade and Investment Policy (Williams Commission). *United States International Economic Policy in an Interdependent World: Compendium of Papers*. Vol. 1. Washington.

———. 1971b. "Injury and Market Disruption from Imports." In President's Commission on International Trade and Investment Policy (Williams Commission). *United States International Economic Policy in an Interdependent World: Compendium of Papers*. Vol. 1. Washington.

Pugel, Thomas A., and Ingo Walter. 1983. "US Corporate Interests and the Political Economy of Trade Policy." New York University, Graduate School of Business Administration, December.

Schultz, Siegfried, and Dieter Schumacher. 1984. "The Reliberalization of World Trade." *Journal of World Trade Law*, vol. 18, no. 3, (May/June).

Tribe, Lawrence. 1978. *American Constitutional Law*. Mineola, NY: Foundation Press.

US Congressional Research Service. 1984. "Agriculture in the GATT: Toward the Next Round of Multilateral Trade Negotiations." Report 84–169. Washington, September.

US International Trade Commission. 1982. *The Effectiveness of Escape Clause Relief in Promoting Adjustment to Import Competition*. USITC Publication no. 1229. Washington, March.

US Trade Representative. 1984. *Annual Report of the President on the Trade Agreements Program, 1983*. Washington, April.

Appendix: Case Studies

Prefatory Note

Acronyms have been used in the citations to the cases when referring to agencies of the US government, and to three frequently cited international entities, the GATT, the IMF, and the OECD. Other sources are cited by abbreviated title or author's name.

The full bibliographic reference for each case citation may be found in the reference list at the end of the case. With the exception of USITC, USTC, and USTR, government agency acronyms do not carry the prefix "US." However, the sources for these citations may be found under "US" in the reference lists. For example, AID is the acronym for United States Agency for International Development. Sources for citations that refer to bureaus or offices that are part of larger departments will be found under the higher division as shown below.

KEY TO ACRONYMS USED

AID	Agency for International Development
BC	Bureau of the Census, Department of Commerce
BEA	Bureau of Economic Analysis, Department of Commerce
BIE	Bureau of Industrial Economics, Department of Commerce
BLS	Bureau of Labor Statistics, Department of Labor
BM	Bureau of Mines, Department of Interior
CBO	Congressional Budget Office
CRS	Congressional Research Service
DIBA	Domestic and International Business Administration (later the International Trade Administration), Department of Commerce
DMSD	Data Management and Statistics Division, National Marine Fisheries Service, Department of Commerce
DOA	Department of Agriculture
FTC	Federal Trade Commission
GAO	General Accounting Office

IRA	Industrial Resource Administration, Department of Commerce
ITA	International Trade Administration, Department of Commerce
MARAD	Maritime Administration
NMFS	National Marine Fisheries Services, Department of Commerce
OTA	Office of Technology Assessment, Congress
USITC	United States International Trade Commission
USTC	United States Tariff Commission (predecessor to USITC)
USTR	United States Trade Representative (prior to 1979 called STR, Special Trade Representative, or Special Representative for Trade Negotiations)

Non-US Entities

GATT	General Agreement on Tariffs and Trade
IMF	International Monetary Fund
OECD	Organization for Economic Cooperation and Development

CASE M-1

Book Manufacturing

PERIOD OF RELIEF

1891 to present

SUPPLIERS AFFECTED

Global (primarily East Asia)

RELIEF ACTION

Since passage of the International Copyright Act on 3 March 1891, the US book printing industry has been more or less insulated from foreign competition. The 1891 act included the so-called "manufacturing clause," which required that books and periodicals published in the United States also be printed and bound in the United States in order to qualify for US copyright protection. (BIE 1982, 87)

"The manufacturing clause was amended by the 1909 copyright act to generally require that English-language books and periodicals be manufactured in the United States in order to be registered for copyright purposes and that foreign-language works of domestic origin be domestically manufactured as well." By 1955 the scope of the clause had been narrowed to English-language works by US authors or domiciliaries. (USITC 1402, 1-2)

In the Copyright Act of 1976 (17 USC 601), Congress narrowed effective coverage of the manufacturing clause to only those works "consisting preponderantly of nondramatic literary material by US authors or domiciliaries that are in the English language and are protected by US copyright law." Thus, the current law does not extend to dramatic, musical, pictoral, or graphic works; foreign language, bilingual, or multilingual works; public domain materials; or works consisting mostly of material not subject to the manufacturing requirement. However, the act extended the scope of the clause to cover the "literary portion" of other printed matter in directories, catalogs, and even greeting cards. (USITC 841, 5)

The European Community (EC) asked that the manufacturing clause be put on the negotiating table during the Tokyo Round of multilateral trade negotiations (MTN), but dropped the issue following assurances that the clause would expire in 1982.

In July 1982, however, Congress overrode a presidential veto and extended the clause until 1 July 1986. The EC considered the extension a violation of commitments made in the MTN and argued that it upset the balance of concessions negotiated. Following two rounds of discussion in the winter of 1982–83 under General Agreement on Tariffs and Trade (GATT) Articles XXII and XXIII, the EC demanded $250 million in compensation. The United States offered only $7 million, thus stalemating the discussions. On 20 April 1983, the EC requested formation of a GATT panel to settle the compensation issue, but to date no final decision has been reached. Further, industry experts expect that the clause will be extended again in 1986, for at least another four years, if not indefinitely. (USITC 1402, xi; BIE 1983, 7–9; Lofquist)

CHANGES IN THE INDUSTRY

HR 6198 (1982), which extended the manufacturing clause, also included a provision directing the US International Trade Commission (USITC) to investigate the economic effects of terminating the clause. The Commission concluded that termination would have a relatively small impact on the US printing and publishing industry as a whole, and that the long-term effect on the US competitive position would be generally insignificant. (USITC 1402)

The printing and publishing industry is one of the 10 largest industries in the US manufacturing sector. It is divided into three major segments: commercial publishing and printing, book publishing, and book manufacturing. Of these three segments, according to the Commission's findings, book manufacturing would be the most affected by termination of the manufacturing clause. The Commission estimated that 2 percent to 10 percent of the books published in the United States, with an approximate value of $50 million to $250 million, would be printed and bound abroad if not for the requirements of the copyright law. Industry representatives claim that termination of protection would result in the printing of 30 percent to 45 percent of US-published books overseas. (USITC 1402, xiv, 93)

The Commission found that the US industry is generally competitive with other world producers in terms of production costs, but not labor costs. Thus, the books that would be more profitable to manufacture abroad would be those that are relatively labor intensive, primarily short-run books with color or sewn bindings. Even for these books, much of the labor cost advantage of East Asian producers would be obviated by communication and transportation costs. (USITC 1402, xii–xiv)

The effect on newspapers and periodicals of terminating the manufacturing clause would be negligible because of the time factor. Catalogs and directories would also be minimally affected. These can already be printed overseas, because more space is devoted to pictures than words, but for cost reasons they are not. (USITC 1402, xv–xvi)

Key Statistics

The following data are for the book manufacturing industry only, as this segment of the publishing and printing industry would be most affected by suspension of the manufacturing clause. About half of all imported printed matter is books.

Imports from all sources

Year (during restraints)	Volume (million units)	Value (million dollars)	Source
1979	204	264	BC, FT 246
1980	217	297	BC, FT 246
1981	237	286	BC, FT 246
1982	284	306	BC, FT 246
1983	353	357	BC, FT 246
1984	480	481	BC, FT 246

Apparent consumption[a]

Year (during restraints)	Volume (million units)	Value (million dollars)	Source
1979	2,034	1,850	authors' estimate
1980	2,038	2,033	authors' estimate
1981	2,073	2,245	authors' estimate
1982	2,148	2,060	authors' estimate
1983	2,393	2,348	authors' estimate
1984	2,466	2,656	authors' estimate

a. Estimates based on domestic output plus imports, minus exports.

Market share of imports (percentage of apparent consumption, by volume)

Year (during restraints)	Share	Source
1979	10.0	authors' estimate
1980	10.6	authors' estimate
1981	11.4	authors' estimate
1982	13.2	authors' estimate
1983	14.8	authors' estimate
1984	19.5	authors' estimate

Output of domestic industry

Year (during restraints)	Volume[a] (million units)	Value (million dollars, producers' shipments)	Source
1979	2,268	2,024	Dessauer, 136; BIE 1983, 7–9
1980	2,330	2,245	Dessauer, 136; BIE 1983, 7–9
1981	2,433	2,556	Dessauer, 136; BIE 1984, 7–10
1982	2,502	2,392	Dessauer, 136; BIE 1985, 27–9
1983	2,645	2,600[b]	Dessauer, 137; BIE 1985, 27–9
1984	2,827	2,845[b]	Dessauer, 137; BIE 1985, 27–9

a. These figures reflect the number of books delivered by manufacturers to publishers, including books exported. They include a small number of books manufactured abroad for US publishers. Given the constraints of the manufacturing clause, such books are likely to be art books or others that consist primarily of illustrations.

b. Preliminary estimate.

Employment in the domestic industry

Year (during restraints)	Production jobs (average number)	Source
1979	37,100	BIE 1983, 7–9
1980	37,700	BIE 1983, 7–9
1981	39,600	BIE 1984, 7–10
1982	34,500	BIE 1985, 27–9
1983	31,100	BIE 1985, 27–9
1984	33,000[a]	BIE 1985, 27–9

a. Preliminary estimate.

Wages

Year (during restraints)	Dollars per hour	Source
1979	6.30	BIE 1983, 7–9
1980	6.94	BIE 1983, 7–9
1981	7.60	BIE 1984, 7–10
1982	8.38	BIE 1985, 27–9
1983	8.95	BIE 1985, 27–9
1984	9.14[a]	BIE 1985, 27–9

a. Preliminary estimate.

Industry profits

Figures on profits are not available.

Industry capacity utilization

Figures on capacity utilization are not available.

Quantitative Profile

Item	Amount	Source
Number of years restraints in force (1891 to present)	94 years	
Induced increase in price of imported goods	31.2 to 42.4 percent 40 percent	Morici, 28[a] authors' estimate[a]
Induced increase in price of domestic goods	12 percent	authors' estimate
Coefficient of price response	0.3	authors' estimate
Quantity and value of imports (1984)	480 million units $481 million	BC, FT 246 BC, FT 246
Induced decrease in imports due to restraints	420 million units $421 million	authors' estimate authors' estimate
Quantity and value of domestic production (1984)	2,827 million units $2,845 million	Dessauer, 137 BIE 1985, 27–9
Induced increase in domestic production due to restraints	2 to 10 percent (by value) 30 to 45 percent (by volume) 10 to 19 percent (by value) 15 percent (by volume) 420 million units	USITC 1402, 93[b] CRS, 142[c] CRS, 159 authors' estimate authors' estimate
Coefficient of quantity response	1.0	authors' estimate
Elasticity of demand for imports	1.46 to 3.00 1.4	Stern, 9[d] Morici, 15
Elasticity of supply of domestic goods	2.0	authors' estimate
Elasticity of demand for domestic goods	0.3	authors' estimate
Cross-elasticity of demand for domestic goods relative to price of imported goods	2.72 to 3.01 0.7	Stern, 9[d] authors' estimate
Cross-elasticity of output of domestic goods relative to price of imported goods	0.6	authors' estimate
Cross-elasticity of quantity of imported goods relative to price of domestic goods	5.0	authors' estimate
Cost of restraints to US consumers (1984)	$500 million	authors' estimate
Gain from restraints to US producers (1984)	$305 million	authors' estimate
Tariff revenue and implied average tariff rate	none	Morici, 28

Quantitative Profile (continued)

Item	Amount	Source
Gain from restraints to foreigners	negligible	authors' estimate[e]
Efficiency loss from larger domestic production to the United States (1984)	$29 million	authors' estimate
Welfare cost of restraints to the United States (1984)	$29 million	authors' estimate
Employment in protected US industry	37,100 (1979)	BIE 1983, 7–9
	33,000 (1984)	BIE 1985, 27–9
Induced increase in employment	730 to 3,530	USITC 1402, 99
	14,000 to 21,000	CRS, 170[f]
	5,000 (1984)	authors' estimate
Cost of restraints to US consumers per job saved (1984)	$100,000	authors' estimate
Gain from restraints to US producers per job (1984)	$9,000	authors' estimate

a. Morici's and Megna's estimate reflects the tariff equivalent of the manufacturing clause, and is based on the Congressional Research Service's (CRS) estimate that imports would rise in the long run, by 10 percent to 19 percent of the value of US producers' shipments. Our estimate, likewise, is based not on current imports but on the estimated increase in imports after termination of the clause.

b. This estimate reflects the number of books currently manufactured domestically that would be printed overseas if the clause were terminated.

c. The Book Manufacturing Institute provided this estimate to the CRS.

d. This elasticity is for the printing and publishing industry as a whole.

e. We estimate negligible gains to importers, since one category of books is banned entirely, while all others are permitted to enter freely.

f. This figure reflects the Book Manufacturing Institute's estimate of employment loss in the book printing and publishing industries should the clause be terminated.

Hypothetical Adjustment Program

	1984	1985	1986	1987	1988	1989	1990
US purchases of books (million units)							
Assumed annual consumption growth of 4 percent	2,466	2,565	2,667	2,774	2,885	3,000	3,120
Imports from all sources							
Assumed annual consumption growth of 4 percent and no change in import restraints (million units)	480	513	533	554	577	600	624

Hypothetical Adjustment Program (continued)

	1984	1985	1986	1987	1988	1989	1990
Assumed annual consumption growth of 4 percent and liberalized protection (million units)	480	564	640	721	808	900	998
Import share of consumption with degressive protection (percentage)	20	22	24	26	28	30	32
Hypothetical quota auction rate							
Quota auction rate liberalized by 3 percentage points per year[a] (percent)	40	37	34	31	28	25	22
Quota auction revenue (million 1984 dollars)[a]	—	19	36	52	65	75	82
US production for the domestic market (million units)							
Assumed annual consumption growth of 4 percent and constant import share	1,986	2,052	2,134	2,220	2,308	2,400	2,496
Assumed annual consumption growth of 4 percent and rising import share	1,986	2,001	2,027	2,053	2,077	2,100	2,122
US employment in domestic book manufacturing (thousand workers)							
Assumed 8 percent annual productivity growth and constant import share	33	32	31	30	29	28	27
Assumed 8 percent annual productivity growth and rising import share	33	31	29	27	25	24	22
Year-to-year employment changes (thousand workers)							
Changes induced by consumption and productivity growth with constant import share	—	−1	−1	−1	−1	−1	−1

Hypothetical Adjustment Program (continued)

	1984	1985	1986	1987	1988	1989	1990
Changes induced by rising import share	—	−1	−1	−1	−1	—	−1
Total employment changes	—	−2	−2	−2	−2	−1	−2
Benefit and budget calculations (1984 prices)							
Annual wage cost per worker assuming constant $10 per hour and 2,400 hours (dollars)	24,000	24,000	24,000	24,000	24,000	24,000	24,000
Benefits calculated at two times annual wage cost per worker (million dollars)	—	96	96	96	96	48	96
Projected program surplus or deficit: tariff revenue less benefits (million dollars)	—	−77	−60	−44	−31	27	−14

— Not applicable.

a. These estimates assume a domestic supply elasticity of 2.0 and a domestic demand elasticity of 0.3. The quota auction would apply only to new exports of books previously excluded by the clause. Thus, the quota auction revenue is based on the difference between imports with no change in restraints and imports under liberalization.

BIBLIOGRAPHY

Dessauer, John P. 1984. *Book Industry Trends: The 8th Annual Compilation of Book Industry Statistics, 1979–88.* New York: Book Industry Study Group.

Lofquist, William (Department of Commerce). 1985. By communication, 24–28 June.

Morici, Peter, and Laura L. Megna. 1983. *US Economic Policies Affecting Industrial Trade: A Quantitative Assessment.* Report no. 200. Washington: National Planning Association.

Stern, Robert M. 1984. "Comments on Data, Elasticities, and Other Key Parameters." Seminar Discussion Paper no. 134. Paper read at conference, General Equilibrium Trade Policy Modelling, Columbia University, 5–6 April.

US Congressional Research Service. 1981. *Economic Concerns Relating to the Elimination of the Manufacturing Clause of the US Copyright Law.* Report no. 81–178E. Washington.

US Department of Commerce. Bureau of the Census. Various years. *US Imports for Consumption and General Imports.* FT 246. Washington.

———. Bureau of Industrial Economics. 1982–85. *US Industrial Outlook.* Washington.

US International Trade Commission. 1983. *Study of the Economic Effects of Terminating the Manufacturing Clause of the Copyright Law.* USITC Publication no. 1402. Washington, July.

———. 1983. *Summary of Trade and Tariff Information: Books, Magazines, Newspapers, and Other Cultural Printed Material.* USITC Publication no. 841, control no. 2–5–19. Washington, December.

CASE M-2

Benzenoid Chemicals

PERIOD OF RELIEF

1922 to 1986

SUPPLIERS AFFECTED

Global

RELIEF ACTION

Before World War I, little synthetic organic chemical production existed in the United States; instead, the United States depended almost entirely on Germany. Severe supply disruptions accompanying the war led to the creation of a domestic industry with encouragement and protection from the US government. (USITC 1427, 1)

Benzenoid chemicals, a subgroup of synthetic organic chemicals, are derived from coal tar or crude petroleum. In the protection scheme devised by Congress in the Tariff Act of 1922, imports of these chemicals and their products (primarily dyes and pigments, drugs, pesticides, and their intermediates) were divided into two categories. "Competitive" benzenoid chemicals and products were subject both to high ad valorem tariffs and the American Selling Price (ASP) system of customs valuation. "Noncompetitive" imports of these goods were subject to somewhat lower ad valorem tariffs and the normal US value system of customs valuation. (USITC 1427, 1–2)

Under the ASP system, tariffs were calculated by applying the ad valorem rate to the wholesale price of a like or competitive domestic product. By contrast, under the normal US value system, tariffs are based on the export price in the country of origin. The ASP system allowed duty rates to be set that appeared lower than their US value equivalents. "Indeed, the Congress apparently introduced the system on benzenoid chemical products . . . to provide the industry a very high degree of protection without placing tariffs of over 100 percent in the U.S. Tariff Schedule." Even as late as 1964, real duties on particular categories often exceeded 100 percent on a US value basis. In that year, the average duty on these products on an ASP basis was 40 percent; on a US value basis, the average duty exceeded 65 percent. (Baldwin, 134–35)

During the Kennedy Round of multilateral trade negotiations (MTN), the European Community (EC) and United Kingdom urged the United States to abolish the ASP system. Since US negotiators did not have the requisite legislative authority to abolish the system, they concluded a separate agreement on chemicals under which the EC and the United Kingdom would implement a second tier of tariff reductions following congressional termination of the ASP system. Congress refused to act, however, and in December 1972, the EC decided not to implement its part of the separate agreement. Thus, the final duty reductions on benzenoid chemicals were 50 percent for the United States and only 36 percent to 39 percent for the EC. (USITC 1427, 2–3)

Following the Tokyo Round, the ASP system was finally terminated, effective 1 July 1980, by the Trade Agreements Act of 1979, which served as implementing legislation for the General Agreement on Tariffs and Trade (GATT) Customs Valuation Code. Tokyo Round concessions also included a series of staged tariff reductions on benzenoid chemicals and products, scheduled for completion by 1 January 1987. In 1983, the average ad valorem tariff on all benzenoid chemicals and products, including duty-free cyclic crudes, was 13.6 percent. By 1987, the average ad valorem duty on a range of chemicals is estimated to decline to about 10.5 percent.[1] (USITC 1427, 3–4)

CHANGES IN THE INDUSTRY

Initial data suggest that termination of the ASP system and tariff reductions in the Tokyo Round have had little effect on US chemical imports. During 1984–85, however, the US economic recovery and overvalued dollar caused imports to balloon, growing by 67 percent in just one year. Dollar overvaluation and sluggish foreign demand also caused US exports to stagnate. Nonetheless, imports remained well below 2 percent of US consumption in 1984 as revived demand in the auto, construction, and other industrial sectors increased demand for intermediate chemicals and their end products. (USITC 1427, 38; BIE, 12–7)

---

1. This very rough estimate is based on 153 of the benzenoid chemicals included in part 1, schedule 4, of the Tariff Schedules of the United States (TSUS). It underestimates the reduction in tariff rates because it excludes specific duties, which in many cases are being eliminated. Further, it overestimates the overall ad valorem equivalent for benzenoid chemicals and products since it does not take into account cyclic crudes. Thus, a figure comparable to the 1983 rate of 13.6 percent would be lower than 10.5 percent.

Key Statistics

Imports affected[a]

Year	Volume (million pounds)	Value (million dollars)	Source
During ASP			
1978	515.7	629.4	USITC 1427, 95
1979	519.4	696.6	USITC 1427, 95
1980	597.6	992.3	USITC 1427, 95
After ASP			
1981	660.9	938.7	USITC 1427, 95
1982	689.4	874.4	USITC 1427, 95
1983	711.0	902.0	authors' estimate
1984	1,182.0	1,500.0	authors' estimate

a. These figures include imports of "competitive" benzenoid chemicals and products, the only ones subject to the ASP system.

Total imports: intermediate chemicals and finished products[a]

Year	Volume (million pounds)	Value (million dollars)	Source
During ASP			
1978	693.7	1,177	USITC 1427, 89
1979	747.2	1,376	USITC 1427, 89
1980	697.2	1,444	USITC 1427, 89
After ASP			
1981	856.7	1,604	USITC 1427, 89
1982	842.4	1,569	USITC 1427, 89
1983	868.3[b]	1,622	authors' estimate; BC, IM 146
1984	1,444.3[b]	2,698	authors' estimate; BC, IM 146

a. Benzenoid crudes are not included since they enter the United States duty free.

b. This figure was derived using the average unit value for the years 1978–82 ($1.868 per pound).

Apparent consumption: intermediate chemicals and finished products

Year	Volume (million pounds)	Value (million dollars)	Source
During ASP			
1978	70,019	30,721	USITC 1427, 89
1979	74,407	37,877	USITC 1427, 89
1980	65,076	41,190	USITC 1427, 89

Apparent consumption: intermediate chemicals and finished products
(continued)

Year	Volume (million pounds)	Value (million dollars)	Source
After ASP			
1981	68,424	44,502	USITC 1427, 89
1982	61,006	35,078[a]	USITC 1427, 89; authors' estimate
1983[a]	75,286	41,244	authors' estimate
1984[a]	89,788	50,606	authors' estimate

a. These estimates assume that the volume of exports remained steady at 5 percent of output while the value of exports remained at 3 percent of the value of production.

Market share of imports (percentage of apparent consumption, by volume)

Year	Affected imports	Total imports	Source
During ASP			
1978	0.7	1.0	USITC 1427, 89
1979	0.7	1.0	USITC 1427, 89
1980	0.9	1.1	USITC 1427, 89
After ASP			
1981	1.0	1.3	USITC 1427, 89
1982	1.1	1.4	USITC 1427, 89
1983	0.9	1.2	authors' estimate
1984	1.3	1.6	authors' estimate

Output of domestic industry: intermediate chemicals and finished products

Year	Volume (million pounds)	Value (million dollars)	Source
During ASP			
1978	73,750	31,713	USITC 1427, 89
1979	78,362	39,181	USITC 1427, 89
1980	68,488	42,622	USITC 1427, 89
After ASP			
1981	71,880	46,003	USITC 1427, 89
1982	64,692	36,163[c]	USITC 1427, 89; authors' estimate
1983	79,248[b]	42,520[c]	authors' estimate
1984[a]	94,514[b]	52,171[c]	authors' estimate

a. Preliminary estimates.

b. These estimates assume that output of intermediate benzenoid chemicals and products expanded at the same rate as that of primary organic chemicals. (BIE, 12–8)

c. These estimates assume that the value of production of intermediate benzenoid chemicals and products increased (decreased) at the same rate as that of industrial organic chemicals. (BIE, 12–7)

Employment[a]

Year	Production workers (average number)	Source
During ASP		
1978	70,300	BIE, 12–9
1979	71,800	BIE, 12–9
1980	70,800	BIE, 12–9
After ASP		
1981	67,200	BIE, 12–9
1982	63,900	BIE, 12–9
1983	62,800	BIE, 12–9
1984[b]	61,400	BIE, 12–9

a. These figures are for workers in the industrial organic chemical industry, including some workers producing chemicals other than benzenoids, but not workers producing finished products.

b. Preliminary estimate.

Wages[a]

Year	Dollars per hour	Source
During ASP		
1978	9.03	BIE, 12–9
1979	9.90	BIE, 12–9
1980	10.76	BIE, 12–9
After ASP		
1981	11.71	BIE, 12–9
1982	13.11	BIE, 12–9
1983	14.09	BIE, 12–9
1984[b]	14.90	BIE, 12–9

a. These figures reflect wages of workers in the industrial organic chemical industry, including some workers producing chemicals other than benzenoids, but not workers producing finished products.

b. Preliminary estimate.

Industry profits: chemicals and allied products (million dollars)

Year	Profits	Source
During ASP		
1980	13,271	FTC
After ASP		
1981	18,937	FTC
1982	13,859	FTC
1983	16,814	FTC
1984[a]	16,487	FTC

a. This figure reflects profits for the first three quarters of 1984.

Industry capacity utilization: entire chemical industry (average in December)

Year	Percentage	Source
During ASP		
1978	83	BEA
1979	83	BEA
1980	78	BEA
After ASP		
1981	70	BEA
1982	66	BEA
1983	78	BEA
1984	n.a.	

n.a. Not available.

Quantitative Profile

Item	Amount	Source
Number of years restraints in force (ASP and high tariffs, 1922–86)	64 years	
Induced increase in price of imported benzenoid chemicals	2.7 percent (1976)	Morici, 35[a]
	15 percent (1984)	authors' estimate
Induced increase in price of domestic benzenoid chemicals (1984)	4.5 percent	authors' estimate
Coefficient of price response	0.3	authors' estimate
Quantity and value of imports (1984)	1,444 million pounds	authors' estimate
	$2,698 million	authors' estimate
Induced decrease in imports due to restraints (1984)	400 million pounds	authors' estimate
	$750 million	authors' estimate
Quantity and value of domestic production (1984)	94,514 million pounds	authors' estimate
	$52,171 million	authors' estimate
Induced increase in domestic production due to restraints (1984)	300 million pounds	authors' estimate
Coefficient of quantity response	0.75	authors' estimate
Elasticity of demand for imported benzenoid chemicals	1.65	Morici, 108[b]
	2.53 to 6.82	Stern, 9[c]
	3.0	authors' estimate
Elasticity of supply of domestic benzenoid chemicals	1.0	authors' estimate
Elasticity of demand for domestic benzenoid chemicals	0.2	authors' estimate
Cross-elasticity of demand for domestic benzenoid chemicals relative to price of imported benzenoid chemicals	2.61 to 9.85	Stern, 9[c]
	0.4	authors' estimate

Quantitative Profile (continued)

Item	Amount	Source
Cross-elasticity of output of domestic benzenoid chemicals relative to price of imported benzenoid chemicals	0.3	authors' estimate
Cross-elasticity of quantity of imported benzenoid chemicals relative to price of domestic benzenoid chemicals	large	authors' estimate
Cost of restraints to US consumers	$829 million (1980) $2,650 million (1984)	Munger, 9 authors' estimate
Gain from restraints to US producers (1984)	$2,250 million	authors' estimate
Tariff revenue and implied average tariff rate (1983)	$252 million 15.5 percent	BC, IM 146 BC, IM 146[d]
Gain from restraints to foreigners	negligible	authors' estimate
Efficiency loss from larger domestic production to the United States (1984)	$14 million	authors' estimate
Welfare cost of restraints to the United States (1984)	$14 million	authors' estimate
Employment in protected US industry	70,300 (1978) 61,400 (1984)	BIE, 12–9[e] BIE, 12–9[e]
Induced increase in employment (1984)	300	authors' estimate
Cost of restraints to US consumers per job saved (1984)	over $1 million	authors' estimate
Gain from restraints to US producers per job (1984)	$37,000	authors' estimate

a. This estimate reflects only the effect of the ASP system on import prices.

b. This coefficient applies to the chemical and allied products industry as a whole.

c. These estimates are for the industrial chemicals segment of the industry.

d. This figure is based on the dutiable value of intermediate benzenoid chemicals and their products and does not include the duty-free cyclic crudes.

e. This figure reflects the number of production workers in the industrial organic chemicals industry as a whole and do not include workers producing final products derived from benzenoid chemicals.

BIBLIOGRAPHY

Baldwin, Robert E. 1970. *Nontariff Distortions of International Trade.* Washington: Brookings Institution.

Metzger, Stanley D. 1974. *Lowering Nontariff Barriers.* Washington: Brookings Institution.

Morici, Peter, and Laura L. Megna. 1983. *US Economic Policies Affecting Industrial Trade: A Quantitative Assessment.* Report no. 200. Washington: National Planning Association.

Munger, Michael C. 1983. *The Costs of Protectionism: Estimates of the Hidden Tax of Trade Restraint.* Working Paper no. 80. Washington University, Center for the Study of American Business, July.

Stern, Robert M. 1984. "Comments on Data, Elasticities, and Other Key Parameters." Seminar Discussion Paper no. 134. Paper read at conference, General Equilibrium Trade Policy Modelling, Columbia University, 5–6 April.

US Congress. House. Committee on Ways and Means. 1979. *Trade Agreements Act of 1979.* Committee Report. 96 Cong., 1 sess., July.

US Department of Commerce. Bureau of the Census. Various years. *US Imports for Consumption.* IM 146. Washington, December.

———. Bureau of Economic Analysis. Various years. *Survey of Current Business.* Washington, March.

———. Bureau of Industrial Economics. 1985. *US Industrial Outlook.* Washington.

US Federal Trade Commission. Various years. *Quarterly Financial Review.* Washington, December.

US International Trade Commission. 1982a. *Summary of Trade and Tariff Information: Benzenoid Cyclic Intermediates—Commodity Chemicals.* USITC Publication no. 841, control no. 4–1–12. Washington, May.

———. 1982b. *Summary of Trade and Tariff Information: Benzenoid Cyclic Intermediates—Specialty Chemicals.* USITC Publication no. 841, control no. 4–1–16. Washington, November.

———. 1983. *An Assessment of the Multilateral Trade Negotiations on Benzenoid Chemicals.* USITC Publication no. 1427. Washington, September.

———. 1984a. *Summary of Trade and Tariff Information: Benzenoid Cyclic Intermediates—Commodity Chemicals.* USITC Publication no. 841, control no. 4–1–12 (Supp.). Washington, September.

———. 1984b. *Summary of Trade and Tariff Information: Benzenoid Cyclic Intermediates—Specialty Chemicals.* USITC Publication no. 841, control no. 4–1–16 (Supp.). Washington, October.

CASE M-3

Household Glassware

PERIOD OF RELIEF

1922 to present

SUPPLIERS AFFECTED

Global (primarily Western Europe)

RELIEF ACTION

The Tariff Act of 1922 set duty rates of 55 percent ad valorem on articles of household glassware.[1] The Tariff Act of 1930 (Smoot-Hawley) increased rates to 60 percent ad valorem. General Agreement on Tariffs and Trade (GATT) negotiations reduced by half the US tariff rates on most glassware items. (USTC 1948, 39)

In 1952, duty rates on many household glassware articles were further reduced, with cuts ranging from 15 percent to as much as 67 percent of the Smoot-Hawley rates. In 1963, the classification system was changed under Section 201 of the Tariff Classification Act of 1962, which subdivided categories of glassware, reduced duty rates for some categories, and left others unchanged. (USTC 257, 89)

The Kennedy Round of trade negotiations resulted in sequential rate reductions from 1968 to 1972. By 1972, most-favored-nation (MFN) duty rates for many categories were 50 percent to 83 percent below the Smoot-Hawley rates, although the rates for many other categories remained high. The Tokyo Round reduced rates on about half the categories of household glassware. By the last staged reduction (1 January 1987),

---

1. With its products protected by an average ad valorem tariff equivalent of 12 percent in 1983, the entire glass and glass products industry represents a borderline case within our framework. However, because of the problems in aggregating and analyzing data across such a broad variety of products, only the subcategory of household glassware, with an ad valorem equivalent of 19 percent in 1983, has been included. Further, the average tariff on the broader category should fall to below 10 percent by 1987 while the ad valorem equivalent for household glassware will still be around 13 percent at that time.

these duty rates will be about 25 percent to 60 percent below the Kennedy Round levels. Based on current import values and shares, these reductions should end in an average ad valorem equivalent of about 13 percent on household glassware items. (USTC 257, 85–88; USITC 1192)

CHANGES IN THE INDUSTRY

Household glassware is made either by machines that automatically blow or press molten glass into molds, or by hand. Although more than 80 percent of household glassware is machine-made, the industry is nevertheless highly labor-intensive, as even the mechanical process requires much supervision and inspection. Another major cost is energy, specifically natural gas. Although natural gas prices and supplies have stabilized over the past several years, inexpensive fuel resource availability is a constant industry concern. (USITC 841, 1983, 7–8)

During 1981–83, the industry took a downturn because of producers' inability to meet high energy and labor costs, especially in the handmade glassware sector, and a 40 percent increase in glassware imports, prompted in large part by the strong dollar. The number of firms in 1983 was about 10 percent less than in 1978, profits fell drastically between 1978 and 1983, output declined approximately 20 percent, and imports doubled. (USITC 841, 1984, 1)

To lower production costs and remain competitive with foreign suppliers, the US industry has begun to use computer and microprocessing manufacturing technology, especially in the highly automated machine-made glassware sector. Firms are also redesigning furnaces to use less fuel in the melting process, and to use other fuel sources such as oil and electricity. Marketing efforts have been stepped up, with an emphasis on direct sales and wholesale distribution. (USITC 841, 1983, 8)

Key Statistics

Imports from all sources

Year (during restraints)	Volume (million pieces)	Value (million dollars)	Source
1978	164	154	USITC 841, 1983, 26
1979	199	192	USITC 841, 1984, 12
1980	207	220	USITC 841, 1984, 12
1981	227	252	USITC 841, 1984, 12
1982	243	260	USITC 841, 1984, 12
1983	322	312	USITC 841, 1984, 12

Apparent consumption

Year (during restraints)	Volume[a] (million pieces)	Value (million dollars)	Source
1978	1,563	922	authors' estimate; USITC 841, 1983, 26
1979	1,501	991	authors' estimate; USITC 841, 1984, 12
1980	1,277	1,107	authors' estimate; USITC 841, 1984, 12
1981	1,295	1,179	authors' estimate; USITC 841, 1984, 12
1982	1,187	1,215	authors' estimate; USITC 841, 1984, 12
1983	1,493	1,463	authors' estimate; USITC 841, 1984, 12

a. These figures reflect the volume of US producers' shipments plus imports, minus exports. Export figures are estimated, as official sources do not provide volume data for two categories of household glassware. Because these categories together account for approximately 3 percent of total production, their exclusion only slightly affects the volume of apparent consumption, and, therefore, the import penetration ratio.

Market share of imports (percentage of apparent consumption, by volume)

Year (during restraints)	Share	Source
1978	10.5	authors' estimate
1979	13.3	authors' estimate
1980	16.2	authors' estimate
1981	17.5	authors' estimate
1982	20.5	authors' estimate
1983	21.6	authors' estimate

Output of domestic industry[a]

Year (during restraints)	Volume (million pieces)	Value (million dollars)	Source
1978	1,591	858	BC, MA–32E; USITC 841, 1983, 26
1979	1,458	887	BC, MA–32E; USITC 841, 1984, 12
1980	1,214	989	BC, MA–32E; USITC 841, 1984, 12
1981	1,224	1,041	BC, MA–32E; USITC 841, 1984, 12
1982	1,040	1,038	BC, MA–32E; USITC 841, 1984, 12
1983	1,243	1,214	BC, MA–32E

a. Producers' shipments.

Employment in domestic industry[a]

Year (during restraints)	Production workers (average number)	Source
1978	15,100	authors' estimate
1979	14,900	authors' estimate
1980	14,600	authors' estimate
1981	14,500	authors' estimate
1982	12,000	authors' estimate
1983	12,500	authors' estimate

a. Employment figures are based on information provided for industries 3229 and 3231, which represent, respectively, glassware produced from glass made in the same establishment and glassware produced from glass purchased or transferred from other establishments. From 1977 to 1982, the value of shipments of household glassware (3229) accounted for 30 percent to 37 percent of shipments of all products in 3229. The value of shipments of household glassware (3231) accounted for 3 percent to 9 percent of shipments of all products in 3231. (BC, Census of Manufactures, 3)

Wages (dollars per hour)

Year (during restraints)	SIC 3229[a]	SIC 3231	Source
1978	6.56	5.48	BC, MC 82, 3
1979	7.14	6.19	BC, MC 82, 3
1980	7.64	6.78	BC, MC 82, 3
1981	8.57	7.63	BC, MC 82, 3
1982	9.37	7.68	BC, MC 82, 3
1983	n.a.	n.a.	BC, MC 82, 3

n.a. Not available.

a. Figures for SIC 3229 cover the segment of the industry producing glassware made from glass manufactured in the same establishment. SIC 3231 covers that segment of the industry producing glassware made from glass purchased or transferred from another establishment.

Industry profits[a] (million dollars)

Year (during restraints)	Profits[b]	Source
1978	26.0	Morris, 160
1979	16.4	Morris, 160
1980	14.2	Morris, 160
1981	12.4	Morris, 160
1982	13.4	Morris, 160
1983	8.1	Morris, 163

a. Industry profits are based on data provided by 29 to 33 establishments whose products are classified in industry 3229.

b. Net income before taxes.

Industry capacity utilization (percentage)

Year (during restraints)	SIC 3229[a]	SIC 3231	Source
1978	79	83	BC, MQ–C1
1979	82	66	BC, MQ–C1
1980	74	68	BC, MQ–C1
1981	70	65	BC, MQ–C1
1982	64	54	BC, MQ–C1
1983	n.a.	n.a.	BC, MQ–C1

n.a. Not available.

a. Figures for SIC 3229 cover the segment of the industry producing glassware made from glass manufactured in the same establishment. SIC 3231 covers that segment of the industry producing glassware made from glass purchased or transferred from another establishment.

Quantitative Profile

Item	Amount	Source
Number of years restraints in force (since 1922)	63 years	
Induced increase in price of imported glassware (1983)	19 percent	authors' estimate[a]
Induced increase in price of domestic glassware (1983)	12 percent	authors' estimate
Coefficient of price response	0.65	authors' estimate
Quantity and value of imports (1983)	322 million pieces $312 million	USITC 841, 1984, 12 USITC 841, 1984, 12
Induced decrease in imports due to restraints (1983)	122 million pieces $118 million	authors' estimate authors' estimate
Quantity and value of domestic production (1983)	1,243 million pieces $1,214 million	BC, MA–32E BC, MA–32E
Induced increase in domestic production due to restraints (1983)	100 million pieces $98 million	authors' estimate authors' estimate
Coefficient of quantity response	0.8	authors' estimate
Elasticity of demand for imported glassware	2.9 2.0	Stern, 9[b] authors' estimate
Elasticity of supply of domestic glassware	2.0	authors' estimate
Elasticity of demand for domestic glassware	1.0	authors' estimate
Cross-elasticity of demand for domestic glassware relative to price of imported glassware	4.3 2.0	Stern, 9[b] authors' estimate
Cross-elasticity of output of domestic glassware relative to price of imported glassware	1.3	authors' estimate

Quantitative Profile (continued)

Item	Amount	Source
Cross-elasticity of quantity of imported glassware relative to price of domestic glassware	10.0	authors' estimate
Cost of restraints to US consumers	$906 million (1980) $200 million (1983)	Munger, 9[c] authors' estimate
Gain from restraints to US producers (1983)	$130 million	authors' estimate
Tariff revenue and implied average tariff rate (1983)	$54 million 18.9 percent	BC, IM 146 authors' estimate
Gain from restraints to foreigners (1983)	negligible	authors' estimate
Efficiency loss from larger domestic production to the United States (1983)	$13 million	authors' estimate
Welfare cost of restraints to the United States (1983)	$13 million	authors' estimate
Employment in protected US industry	15,100 (1978) 12,500 (1983)	authors' estimate
Induced increase in employment (1983)	1,000	authors' estimate
Cost of restraints to US consumers per job saved (1983)	$200,000	authors' estimate
Gain from restraints to US producers per job (1983)	$11,000	authors' estimate

a. This figure is based on the 1983 average ad valorem tariff.

b. This coefficient is for all glass and glass products.

c. Munger's estimate represents the cost to consumers of high tariffs on all glass and glass products.

Hypothetical Adjustment Program

	1984	1985	1986	1987	1988	1989	1990
US purchases of glassware (million pieces)							
Assumed annual consumption growth of 0 percent	1,500	1,500	1,500	1,500	1,500	1,500	1,500
Imports from all sources							
Assumed annual consumption growth of 0 percent and no change in import restraints (million pieces)	350	350	350	350	350	350	350

Hypothetical Adjustment Program (continued)

	1984	1985	1986	1987	1988	1989	1990
Assumed annual consumption growth of 0 percent and degressive tariff (import price elasticity of 2.0) (million pieces)	350	364	379	394	409	426	443
Import share of consumption with degressive tariff (percentage)	23	24	25	26	27	28	30
Hypothetical tariff rate							
Tariff degressive at 2 percentage points per year (percent)	19	17	15	13	11	9	7
Tariff revenue (million 1984 dollars)	65	60	56	50	44	37	30
US production for the domestic market (million pieces)							
Assumed annual consumption growth of 0 percent and constant import share	1,150	1,150	1,150	1,150	1,150	1,150	1,150
Assumed annual consumption growth of 0 percent and rising import share	1,150	1,136	1,121	1,106	1,091	1,074	1,057
US employment in the domestic glassware industry (thousand workers)							
Assumed 2 percent annual productivity growth and constant import share	12.5	12.3	12.0	11.8	11.5	11.3	11.1
Assumed 2 percent annual productivity growth and rising import share	12.5	12.1	11.7	11.3	10.9	10.6	10.2
Year-to-year employment changes (thousand workers)							
Changes induced by consumption and productivity growth with constant import share	—	−0.2	−0.3	−0.2	−0.3	−0.2	−0.2

Hypothetical Adjustment Program (continued)

	1984	1985	1986	1987	1988	1989	1990
Changes induced by rising import share	—	−0.2	−0.1	−0.2	−0.1	−0.1	−0.2
Total employment changes	—	−0.4	−0.4	−0.4	−0.4	−0.3	−0.4
Benefit and budget calculations (1984 prices)							
Annual wage cost per worker assuming constant $10 per hour and 2,000 hours (dollars)	20,000	20,000	20,000	20,000	20,000	20,000	20,000
Benefits calculated at two times annual wage cost per worker (million dollars)	—	16	16	16	16	12	16
Projected program surplus or deficit: tariff revenue less benefits (million dollars)	65	44	40	34	28	25	14

— Not applicable.

BIBLIOGRAPHY

Morris, Robert, and Associates. 1982, 1983. *Annual Statement Studies.* Philadelphia.

Munger, Michael C. 1983. *The Costs of Protectionism: Estimates of the Hidden Tax of Trade Restraint.* Working Paper no. 80. Washington University, Center for the Study of American Business, July.

Stern, Robert M. 1984. "Comments on Data, Elasticities, and Other Key Parameters." Seminar Discussion Paper no. 134. Paper read at conference, General Equilibrium Trade Policy Modelling, Columbia University, 5–6 April.

US Department of Commerce. Bureau of the Census. 1983. *US Imports for Consumption.* IM 146. Washington, December.

———. Various years. *Current Industrial Reports: Consumer, Scientific, Technical and Industrial Glassware.* Publication no. MA–32E. Washington.

———. Various years. *Current Industrial Reports: Survey of Plant Capacity.* Publication no. MQ–C1. Washington.

———. Various years. *US Exports.* FT 446. Washington.

———. 1984a. *Census of Manufactures: Pressed and Blown Glass.* Publication no. MC82–I–32A–3(P). Washington, August.

———. 1984b. *Census of Manufactures: Products of Purchased Glass.* Publication no. MC82–I–32A–4(P). Washington, August.

———. Bureau of Industrial Economics. 1985. *US Industrial Outlook.* Washington.

US International Trade Commission. 1981. *History of the Tariff Schedules of the United States Annotated.* USITC Publication no. 1192. Washington.

———. 1983. *Summary of Trade and Tariff Information: Household Glassware.* USITC Publication no. 841, control no. 5–3–10. Washington, February.

———. 1984. *Summary of Trade and Tariff Information: Household Glassware.* USITC Publication no. 841, control no. 5–3–10 (Supp.). Washington, October.

US Tariff Commission. 1948. *Summaries of Tariff Information: Earths, Earthenware and Glassware.* Vol. 2. Washington.

———. 1952. *United States Import Duties.* USTC Publication no. TC 1.10: IM 7/4/52. Washington.

———. 1963. *United States Import Duties Annotated.* Washington.

———. 1968. *Summaries of Trade and Tariff Information: Pressed and Blown Glassware.* USTC Publication No. 257. Washington.

CASE M-4

Rubber Footwear

PERIOD OF RELIEF

June 1930 to present

SUPPLIERS AFFECTED

Global (primarily China, Hong Kong, Korea, Mexico, Taiwan, and Thailand)

RELIEF ACTION

Imports have penetrated the domestic market for rubber footwear more deeply than the market for nonrubber footwear. Despite this, the rubber footwear industry has not generally sought special protection, as has the nonrubber footwear sector, because it continues to be protected by high tariffs nearly unchanged since the Tariff Act of 1930 (the Smoot-Hawley tariff). In addition, the domestic industry benefited from the American Selling Price (ASP) system of customs valuation from 1933 until its termination in 1981. Under the ASP system, the dutiable import value is the wholesale price of the like product in the United States, rather than the wholesale price or export value in the country of origin. The ASP system sometimes resulted in ad valorem tariff rates double or more the nominal rate. (USITC 841, 1981, 1; Baldwin, 134)

The rubber footwear industry has two major segments: protective footwear (e.g., hunting boots, galoshes, and overshoes); and casual footwear with rubber soles and fabric uppers (e.g., some athletic footwear, sport oxfords, sneakers, and specialty shoes designed for leisure use, primarily espadrilles). Imports of such products, including zoris (inexpensive rubber-thonged sandals) for which there is no domestically produced equivalent, increased from 19 percent of consumption in 1965 to 65 percent in 1981. (BIE 1982, 145)

In 1979, 75 percent (by quantity) of rubber footwear imports entered the United States under Tariff Schedules of the United States (TSUS) item 700.60, dutiable at 20 percent ad valorem and valued on an ASP basis. This category included casual footwear (except zoris). US acceptance of the Customs Valuation Code in the Tokyo Round of multilateral trade negotiations (MTN) signaled the end of the ASP system, which was terminated for rubber footwear on 30 June 1981. New nomenclature and tariff rates were established to replace the old category TSUS 700.60. (USITC 841, 1981, v, 1–7)

Ad valorem tariffs on protective rubber footwear (TSUS items 700.51–700.53) ranged from 12.5 percent to 25 percent to 37.5 percent prior to 1980. The lower rate will eventually decrease to 6.6 percent as a result of concessions in the Tokyo Round. The two higher rates, which are the Smoot-Hawley rates, will not change. Ad valorem duties on casual footwear (TSUS items 700.57–700.71) now range from 20 percent to 48 percent, and, with specific duties added on, the highest level has an ad valorem equivalent of approximately 67 percent. Tariffs on zoris (TSUS item 700.54), at 6 percent, are already low and will further decrease to 2.4 percent by 1988. Zoris are also the only category of rubber footwear eligible for reduced tariff treatment under the Generalized System of Preferences (GSP), and major suppliers such as Hong Kong, Taiwan, Thailand, and China are eligible for GSP benefits. (USITC 841, 1981, v, 1–7)

CHANGES IN THE INDUSTRY

Since the 1960s, the number of US manufacturers of rubber footwear has declined, dropping from 107 in 1972 to approximately 50 ten years later. About 40 of these manufacturers produce fabric-upper footwear, primarily jogging shoes and other athletic footwear, which accounted for 88 percent of total domestic output in 1983. (USITC 841, 1984b, 1)

Most athletic footwear is made with a combination of rubber and nonrubber materials, and, depending on the proportion of each, can be classified under either tariff category. Producers of such footwear suffered from the orderly marketing agreements (OMAs) with Korea and Taiwan restricting nonrubber footwear[1] because foreign suppliers simply shifted the ratio between the two types of materials and shipped similar products classified as rubber footwear during the period covered by the OMAs and as nonrubber footwear thereafter. Imports of rubber footwear increased nearly 50 percent from 1975 to 1977, then dropped by 30 percent in 1982, after the OMAs expired, to their lowest level since 1975. Even with the decline in imports, however, domestic output has continued downward, dropping 25 percent from 1982 to 1983.

---

1. See Case M–17, Nonrubber Footwear.

Key Statistics

Imports from all sources

Year (during restraints)	Volume (million pairs)	Value (million dollars)	Source
1975	98.3	392.2	USITC 841, 1981, 36; BIE 1985, 18–9
1977	145.3	642.3	USITC 841, 1981, 36; BIE 1985, 18–9
1979	147.7	470.7	USITC 841, 1981, 36; USITC 841, 1984, 20
1980	149.1	648.6	USITC 841, 1984, 20
1981	166.4	647.4	USITC 841, 1984, 20
1982	127.7	334.7	USITC 841, 1984, 20
1983	132.3	331.1	USITC 841, 1984, 20

Apparent consumption

Year (during restraints)	Volume (million pairs)	Value (million dollars)	Source
1975	247.1	618.1	USITC 841, 1981, 36
1977	252.2	684.5	USITC 841, 1981, 36
1979	253.6	938.3	USITC 841, 1981, 36
1980	258.8	1,175.2	USITC 841, 1984, 20
1981	270.3	1,261.2	USITC 841, 1984, 20
1982	229.0	955.4	USITC 841, 1984, 20
1983[a]	212.0	823.6	USITC 841, 1984, 20

a. Preliminary estimates.

Market share of imports (percentage of apparent consumption, by volume)

Year (during restraints)	Share	Source
1975	39.8	USITC 841, 1981, 36
1977	57.6	USITC 841, 1981, 36
1979	58.2	USITC 841, 1981, 36
1980	57.6	authors' estimate
1981	61.2	authors' estimate
1982	55.8	authors' estimate
1983	62.4	authors' estimate

Output of domestic industry[a]

Year (during restraints)	Volume (million pairs)	Value (million dollars)	Source
1975	149.7	459.6	USITC 841, 1981, 36
1977	108.1	404.8	USITC 841, 1981, 36
1979	107.8	480.2	USITC 841, 1981, 36
1980	112.0	546.2	USITC 841, 1984, 20
1981	106.0	634.1	USITC 841, 1984, 20
1982	103.3	638.7	USITC 841, 1984, 20
1983[b]	82.3	504.7	USITC 841, 1984, 20

a. Producers' shipments.
b. Preliminary estimates.

Employment in domestic industry

Year (during restraints)	Production workers (average number)	Source
1975	22,300	BLS 1983, 208
1977	20,900	BLS 1983, 208
1979	19,900	BLS 1983, 208
1980	19,800	BLS 1983, 208
1981	19,000	BLS 1983, 208
1982	16,200	BLS 1984
1983	14,100	BLS 1984

Wages

Year (during restraints)	Dollars per hour	Source
1975	2.76	BIE 1984, 15–8
1977	3.86	BIE 1984, 15–8
1979	4.20	BIE 1984, 15–8
1980	4.45[a]	authors' estimate
1981	4.73	BIE 1984, 15–8
1982	5.36	BIE 1985, 18–9
1983	5.73	USITC 841, 1984, 20

a. Based on trends.

Industry profits

Figures on profits are not available.

Industry capacity utilization

Figures on capacity utilization are not available.

Quantitative Profile

Item	Amount	Source
Number of years restraints in force (1930 to present)	55 years	
Induced increase in price of imported rubber footwear	4.3 percent (1976) 42 percent (1983)	Morici, 34–5[a] authors' estimate
Induced increase in price of domestic rubber footwear	21 percent (1983)	authors' estimate
Coefficient of price response	0.5	authors' estimate
Quantity and value of imports (1983)	132 million pairs $331 million	USITC 841, 1984, 20 USITC 841, 1984, 20
Induced decrease in imports due to restraints	50 million pairs $125 million	authors' estimate authors' estimate
Quantity and value of domestic production (1983)	82.3 million pairs $505 million	USITC 841, 1984, 20 USITC 841, 1984, 20
Induced increase in domestic production due to restraints	45 million pairs $276 million	authors' estimate authors' estimate
Coefficient of quantity response	0.9	authors' estimate
Elasticity of demand for imported rubber footwear	under 1.0 1.0	USITC 1545, A110 authors' estimate
Elasticity of supply of domestic rubber footwear	2.0	authors' estimate
Elasticity of demand for domestic rubber footwear	1.0	authors' estimate
Cross-elasticity of demand for domestic rubber footwear relative to price of imported rubber footwear	1.33 to 4.07 1.5	USITC 1545, A110 authors' estimate
Cross-elasticity of output of domestic rubber footwear relative to price of imported rubber footwear	1.0	authors' estimate
Cross-elasticity of quantity of imported rubber footwear relative to price of domestic rubber footwear	0.5	authors' estimate
Cost of restraints to US consumers (1983)	$230 million	authors' estimate
Gain from restraints to US producers (1983)	$90 million	authors' estimate
Tariff revenue and implied average tariff rate (1983)	$139 million 41.9 percent	BC, IM 146 authors' estimate
Gain from restraints to foreigners (1983)	negligible	authors' estimate

Quantitative Profile (continued)

Item	Amount	Source
Efficiency loss from larger domestic production to the United States (1983)	$33 million	authors' estimate
Welfare cost of restraints to the United States (1983)	$33 million	authors' estimate
Employment in protected US industry	22,300 (1975) 14,000 (1983)	USITC 841, 1981, 36 BLS 1984
Induced increase in employment (1983)	7,800	authors' estimate
Cost of restraints to US consumers per job saved (1983)	$30,000	authors' estimate
Gain from restraints to US producers per job (1983)	$6,400	authors' estimate

a. This figure reflects an increase due to the American Selling Price (ASP) system of valuation only.

Hypothetical Adjustment Program

	1984	1985	1986	1987	1988	1989	1990
US purchases of rubber footwear (million pairs)							
Assumed annual consumption growth of 0 percent	250	250	250	250	250	250	250
Imports from all sources							
Assumed annual consumption growth of 0 percent and no change in import restraints (million pairs)	160	160	160	160	160	160	160
Assumed annual consumption growth of 0 percent and degressive tariff (import price elasticity of 1.0) (million pairs)	160	165	170	175	180	185	190
Import share of consumption with degressive tariff (percentage)	64	66	68	70	72	74	76

APPENDIX 77

Hypothetical Adjustment Program (continued)

	1984	1985	1986	1987	1988	1989	1990
Hypothetical tariff rate							
Tariff degressive at 2 percentage points per year (percent)	42	40	38	36	34	32	30
Tariff revenue (million 1984 dollars)	—	167	163	159	155	150	144
US production for the domestic market (million pairs)							
Assumed annual consumption growth of 0 percent and constant import share	90	90	90	90	90	90	90
Assumed annual consumption growth of 0 percent and rising import share	90	85	80	75	70	65	60
US employment in the domestic industry (thousand workers)							
Assumed 1 percent annual productivity growth and constant import share	15.30	15.15	15.00	14.85	14.70	14.56	14.41
Assumed 1 percent annual productivity growth and rising import share	15.30	14.31	13.33	12.37	11.43	10.52	9.61
Year-to-year employment changes (workers)							
Changes induced by consumption and productivity growth with constant import share	—	−150	−150	−150	−150	−140	−150
Changes induced by rising import share	—	−840	−830	−810	−790	−770	−760
Total employment changes	—	−990	−980	−960	−940	−910	−910
Benefit and budget calculations (1984 prices)							
Annual wage cost per worker assuming constant $7 per hour and 2,400 hours (dollars)	17,000	17,000	17,000	17,000	17,000	17,000	17,000

Hypothetical Adjustment Program (continued)

	1984	1985	1986	1987	1988	1989	1990
Benefits calculated at two times annual wage cost per worker (million dollars)	—	34	33	33	32	31	31
Projected program surplus or deficit: tariff revenue less benefits (million dollars)	—	133	130	126	123	119	113

— Not applicable.

BIBLIOGRAPHY

Baldwin, Robert E. 1970. *Nontariff Distortions of International Trade.* Washington: Brookings Institution.

Morici, Peter, and Laura L. Megna. 1983. *US Economic Policies Affecting Industrial Trade: A Quantitative Assessment.* Report no. 200. Washington: National Planning Association.

US Department of Commerce. Bureau of the Census. 1983. *US Imports for Consumption.* IM 146. Washington, December.

———. Bureau of Industrial Economics. Various years. *US Industrial Outlook.* Washington.

US Department of Labor. Bureau of Labor Statistics. 1983, 1984. *Supplement to Employment and Earnings.* Washington, July.

US International Trade Commission. 1981. *Summary of Trade and Tariff Information: Rubber and Plastic Footwear.* USITC Publication no. 841, control no. 7–1–11. Washington, March.

———. 1984a. *Nonrubber Footwear.* USITC Publication no. 1545. Washington, July.

———. 1984b. *Summary of Trade and Tariff Information.* USITC Publication no. 841, control no. 7–1–11 (2d Supp.). Washington, October.

CASE M-5

Ceramic Table and Kitchen Articles

PERIOD OF RELIEF

June 1930 to present

SUPPLIERS AFFECTED

Global (primarily Japan, Korea, Taiwan, United Kingdom, and West Germany)

RELIEF ACTION

High tariffs on certain ceramic articles[1] originated in the Tariff Act of 1930 (Smoot-Hawley bill), which increased duties on a wide variety of goods. Prior to the Kennedy Round (1963–67), statutory tariffs on ceramic kitchen and tableware ranged from 50 percent to 70 percent with additional specific duties of 10 cents per dozen pieces on most items. (Pastor, 77–78; USITC 893, 37–38)

In the Kennedy Round of multilateral trade negotiations (MTN), tariff concessions were granted on all earthen table and kitchen articles except dinnerware valued at over $7 but not over $12 per "norm," and on household china table and kitchen articles except dinnerware valued at not over $56 per norm.[2] The trade agreement

---

1. The articles examined here include certain fine-grained earthenware, stoneware, and chinaware table and kitchen articles that are chiefly used for preparing, serving, or storing food or beverages, or food or beverage ingredients. The average ad valorem equivalent for all ceramic articles, covered in the Tariff Schedules of the United States (TSUS), schedule 5, part 2, in 1984 was 13.1 percent. The high tariffs, however, are concentrated in subparts B and C, which include floor and wall tiles, and table and kitchen articles, respectively. Subparts A and D have average ad valorem tariffs of less than 8 percent. Subpart E, ceramic articles not specifically provided for, has an ad valorem equivalent of 12.7 percent, but the 1984 import value was only $15 million. See Case M–6, Ceramic Floor and Wall Tiles. (USITC 893, 4; USTC 574, 5–7; BC, IM 146)

2. "Norm" refers to the 77 pieces listed in appendix B of the Tariff Schedules of the United States (TSUS) as follows: 12 each of the specified size of plates, cups, saucers, soups, and fruits, and one each of the specified size of platter or chop dish, open vegetable, sugar, and creamer. (USTC 668, 8)

duty rates took effect on 1 January 1972. The average ad valorem equivalent was 25 percent (based on 1972 import values), substantially above the average for all manufactured goods. (USTC 574, 29–30; USITC 893, 37–38; Morici and Megna, 31)

On 22 February 1972, following its investigation (TEA–I–22) under Section 301(b) of the Trade Expansion Act of 1962 (TEA), the US Tariff Commission (later the US International Trade Commission) reported to President Richard M. Nixon that, primarily as a result of Kennedy Round trade agreement concessions, certain ceramic articles were being imported into the United States in such increased quantities as to seriously injure the domestic industry. The Commission recommended import relief in the form of increased tariffs. (USITC 893, 2–3)

Following the Commission's findings, on 22 April 1972, President Nixon issued presidential proclamation 4125 providing tariff increases ranging from 7 percent to 111 percent over the trade agreement rates. These escape action rates, reflecting an average ad valorem equivalent increase of 18.5 percent, took effect on 1 May 1972, and were to remain in effect for a period of not more than four years, unless extended by subsequent presidential action. President Nixon also permitted firms and workers in the domestic earthen tableware industry to apply to the Departments of Commerce and Labor, respectively, for adjustment assistance under the provisions of the TEA.[3] (USITC 893, 2–3; USTC 574, 2, 11; Morici and Megna, 48)

On 31 March 1976, the Commission completed a review investigation (TA–203–1) conducted under Sections 203(i)(2) and 203(i)(3) of the Trade Act of 1974. The Commission found that termination of the 1972 escape clause duties would have an adverse impact on the competitive segment of the domestic industry. Acting on the Commission's advice, President Gerald R. Ford extended and modified portions of the relief granted in presidential proclamation 4125 and terminated other portions of the relief package. Effective 1 May 1976, tariff increases granted in 1972 were continued for four TSUS categories at the then prevailing rates (36 percent average ad valorem) for one year, to decline approximately 4 percent to 9 percent on 1 May 1977 and 1 May 1978. These rates were set to expire on 30 April 1979, at which time the trade agreement rates would again take effect. Ford terminated escape clause rates for other categories as originally scheduled. (USITC 893, 3; Morici and Megna, 31)

On 30 March 1978, responding to a petition of 13 March 1978 filed by the Special Representative for Trade Negotiations, the US International Trade Commission (USITC) began an investigation under Section 203(i)(2) of the Trade Act of 1974. The investigation (TA–203–4) examined the probable economic effect on the domestic industry of the immediate termination of import relief in effect from 1 May 1976. (USITC 893, 1)

On 1 June 1978, the USITC advised President Jimmy Carter that the probable economic effect on the domestic industry of immediately terminating increased duty

---

3. As of 30 November 1975, 143 workers in one firm had received $367,000 in trade readjustment allowances. The Department of Labor later certified workers in two other firms and denied certification to workers in another. The Department of Commerce denied adjustment assistance to the one firm that applied for it. (USITC 893, 11)

rates applicable to earthen dinnerware and nondinnerware, and nonbone china nondinnerware, would be minimal. The increased duty rates had been effective in restraining imports from 1 May 1972 through 31 December 1975. However, in 1976 and 1977, imports of earthen and china table and kitchen articles increased substantially, largely because an increasing percentage of the imports originally subject to the higher rates of duty were entering under unprotected higher value tariff categories as a result of inflation and foreign currency revaluations. On 6 October 1978, following the USITC determination, President Carter terminated all escape clause rates and reinstated the trade agreement rates. (USITC 893, 1–2, 7; Morici and Megna, 31)

President Carter's action left the domestic industry with statutory tariff protection of about 20 percent ad valorem. In the Tokyo Round, the United States agreed to eight annual staged tariff rate reductions on ceramic articles beginning 1 January 1980. The reductions will lower the average ad valorem tariff rates from about 19 percent in 1980 to about 13 percent by 1 January 1987. The average ad valorem equivalent (based on import values and calculated duties) was already 14 percent in 1984. (USITC 841, 1981, 4–7; USITC 841, 1984, 2–5; BC, IM 146)

On 24 May 1982, responding to a petition filed on 14 May 1982 by the American Dinnerware Emergency Committee, the USITC instituted an investigation under Section 406 of the Trade Act of 1974. On 3 August 1982, the USITC (with one dissenting vote) determined that imports from the People's Republic of China of ceramic household articles chiefly used for preparing, storing, or serving food or beverages, or food or beverage ingredients, had not resulted in domestic market disruption. (USITC 841, 1984, 6)

CHANGES IN THE INDUSTRY

Since 1972, domestic producers have improved productivity and product quality and design. Management has increased capital expenditures and introduced labor-saving machinery. Research and development, plant, and capital equipment expenditures increased from $1.5 million in 1973 to $6.3 million in 1977. The industry has implemented production process innovations such as automatic and semiautomatic clay-forming machines, semiautomatic color-dipping machines, and underglaze stamping machines. These innovations have contributed to the industry's declining employment and increasing productivity. (USITC 893, 14)

Further work force reduction was achieved in a collective bargaining agreement negotiated between US producers and the International Brotherhood of Pottery and Allied Workers. A new job combination clause authorized the elimination and combination of certain job descriptions. (USITC 893, 13–14)

But since the granting of escape clause relief in 1972, several factors have worked against the earthenware industry's international competitiveness. The 1974–75 recession reduced domestic demand for earthen tableware; the natural gas shortage and substantial price increases disrupted production and added to production costs; and increased emphasis on environmental protection and job health and safety requirements led to unplanned capital expenditures. Many foreign producers do not bear comparable environmental and safety costs. (USITC 893, 14–15)

Key Statistics

Imports from all sources

Year (during restraints)	Volume (million dozen pieces)	Value (million dollars)	Source
1976	29.6	179.8	USITC 841, 1981, 34
1978	35.9	289.1	USITC 841, 1984, 16
1980	38.1	326.7	USITC 841, 1984, 16
1981	44.4	370.6	USITC 841, 1984, 16
1982	45.6	362.4	USITC 841, 1984, 16
1983	60.2	439.3	BC, FT 210; BC, FT 246
1984	63.4	497.5	BC, FT 210; BC, FT 246

Apparent consumption

Year (during restraints)	Volume[a] (million dozen pieces)	Value (million dollars)	Source
1976	58.4	387.2	authors' estimate; USITC 841, 1981, 34
1978	65.2	517.7	authors' estimate; USITC 841, 1984, 16
1980	60.9	622.7	authors' estimate; USITC 841, 1984, 16
1981	67.7	696.7	authors' estimate; USITC 841, 1984, 16
1982	78.3	680.2	authors' estimate; USITC 841, 1984, 16
1983	91.0	808.3	authors' estimate
1984	96.1	889.5	authors' estimate

a. These figures reflect producers' shipments plus imports, minus exports. The estimates for 1983–84 are based on the volume of imports plus producers' shipments for those years; exports were small. (USITC 841, 1984, 16)

Market share of imports (percentage of apparent consumption, by volume)

Year (during restraints)	Share	Source
1976	50.7	authors' estimate
1978	55.1	authors' estimate
1980	62.6	authors' estimate
1981	65.6	authors' estimate
1982	58.2	authors' estimate
1983	66.2	authors' estimate
1984	66.0	authors' estimate

Output of domestic industry[a]

Year (during restraints)	Volume[b] (million dozen pieces)	Value (million dollars)	Source
1976	30.1	217.0	authors' estimate; USITC 841, 1981, 34
1978	30.8	240.0	authors' estimate; USITC 841, 1984, 16
1980	24.1	313.0	authors' estimate; USITC 841, 1984, 16
1981	24.6	344.0	authors' estimate; USITC 841, 1984, 16
1982	34.8	338.0	authors' estimate; USITC 841, 1984, 16
1983	30.8	369.0[c]	authors' estimate; BIE, 48–5
1984	32.7	392.0[c]	authors' estimate; BIE, 48–5

a. Producers' shipments.
b. Since USITC estimates for the volume of producers' shipments are not available, the figures for 1980–82 are based on the value of US producers' shipments divided by the unit value per dozen of US exports. The 1983–84 figures were derived using the average 1979–82 export unit value of $12 per dozen pieces. (USITC 841, 1981, 34; USITC 841, 1984, 16)
c. Preliminary estimate.

Employment in domestic industry

Year (during restraints)	Production workers (average number)	Source
1976	8,000	BIE, 48–8
1978	10,000	BIE, 48–8
1980	10,000	BIE, 48–8
1981	9,000	BIE, 48–8
1982	8,100	BIE, 48–5
1983	8,500[a]	BIE, 48–5
1984	8,000[a]	BIE, 48–5

a. Preliminary estimate.

Wages (dollars per hour)

Year (during restraints)	Chinaware	Earthenware	Source
1976	4.79	3.82	BIE, 48–8
1978	5.32	4.23	BIE, 48–8
1980	6.14	5.27	BIE, 48–8
1981	6.88	5.50	BIE, 48–8
1982	8.23	6.53	BIE, 48–5
1983	8.71	6.91[a]	BIE, 48–5
1984	9.13	7.24[a]	BIE, 48–5

a. Preliminary estimate.

Industry profits[a] (million dollars)

Year (during restraints)	Profits[b]	Source
1973	2.74	USITC 893, 15
1974	2.37	USITC 893, 15
1976	4.24	USITC 893, 15
1977	4.52	USITC 893, 15
1979	n.a.	
1980	n.a.	
1981	n.a.	
1982	n.a.	
1983	n.a.	
1984	n.a.	

n.a. Not available.

a. The figures for 1973–77 reflect profit experience on earthen tableware operations of nine US producers, accounting for approximately 90 percent of US production of earthenware.

b. Net operating profits before taxes.

Industry capacity utilization

Figures on capacity utilization are not available.

Quantitative Profile

Item	Amount	Source
Number of years restraints in force (1930 to present)	55 years	
Induced increase in price of imported ceramics	14 percent	BC, IM 146[a]
Induced increase in price of domestic ceramics	7 percent	authors' estimate
Coefficient of price response	0.5	authors' estimate
Quantity and value of imports (1984)	63 million dozen pieces $498 million	BC, FT 210 BC, FT 246
Induced decrease in imports due to restraints (1984)	16 million dozen pieces $126 million	authors' estimate[b] authors' estimate
Quantity and value of domestic production (1984)	33 million dozen pieces $392 million	authors' estimate BIE, 48–5
Induced increase in domestic production due to restraints (1984)	8 million dozen pieces	authors' estimate

Quantitative Profile (continued)

Item	Amount	Source
Coefficient of quantity response	0.5	authors' estimate
Elasticity of demand for imported ceramics	1.4	Stern, 9[c]
Elasticity of supply of domestic ceramics	1.2	authors' estimate
Elasticity of demand for domestic ceramics	3.0	authors' estimate
Cross-elasticity of demand for domestic ceramics relative to price of imported ceramics	2.1 1.7	Stern, 9[c] authors' estimate
Cross-elasticity of output of domestic ceramics relative to price of imported ceramics	0.5	authors' estimate
Cross-elasticity of quantity of imported ceramics relative to price of domestic ceramics	0.5	authors' estimate
Cost of restraints to US consumers (1984)	$95 million	authors' estimate
Gain from restraints to US producers (1984)	$25 million	authors' estimate
Tariff revenue and implied average tariff rate (1984)	$69 million 14 percent	authors' estimate authors' estimate
Gain from restraints to foreigners	negligible	authors' estimate[d]
Efficiency loss from larger domestic production to the United States (1984)	$6 million	authors' estimate
Welfare cost of restraints to the United States (1984)	$6 million	authors' estimate
Employment in protected US industry	10,000 (1978) 8,000 (1984)	BIE, 48–8 BIE, 48–5
Induced increase in employment (1984)	2,000	authors' estimate
Cost of restraints to US consumers per job saved (1984)	$47,500	authors' estimate
Gain from restraints to US producers per job	$3,100	authors' estimate

a. This estimate is based on the average ad valorem tariff on earthen and chinaware kitchen and table articles as derived from the proportion of calculated duty to dutiable value of imports. Because the value of imports covered in the escape clause case was so small, the costs of that program have not been considered here.

b. This figure is extrapolated from an observed 40 percent decline in imports of certain ceramic articles covered by escape clause rates from 1972–77 and was adjusted for the import demand elasticity of 1.4.

c. This coefficient is for pottery, china, and earthenware.

d. Imports have been restrained by tariffs, which do not confer rents on importers.

Hypothetical Adjustment Program

	1984	1985	1986	1987	1988	1989	1990
US purchases of ceramics (million dozen pieces)							
Assumed annual consumption growth of 4 percent	96.0	99.8	103.8	108.0	112.3	116.8	121.5
Imports from all sources							
Assumed annual consumption growth of 4 percent and no change in import restraints (million dozen pieces)	63.4	65.9	68.6	71.3	74.2	77.1	80.2
Assumed annual consumption growth of 4 percent and degressive tariff (import price elasticity of 1.4) (million dozen pieces)	63.4	66.8	70.4	74.2	78.2	82.3	86.7
Import share of consumption with degressive tariff (percentage)	66.0	66.9	67.8	68.7	69.6	70.5	71.4
Hypothetical tariff rate							
Tariff degressive at 1 percentage point per year (percent)	14	13	12	11	10	9	8
Tariff revenue (million 1984 dollars)	69	69	67	64	62	58	55
US production for the domestic market (million dozen pieces)							
Assumed annual consumption growth of 4 percent and constant import share	32.6	33.9	35.2	36.7	38.1	39.7	41.3
Assumed annual consumption growth of 4 percent and rising import share	32.6	33.0	33.4	33.8	34.1	34.5	34.8
US employment in the earthenware industry (workers)							
Assumed 6 percent annual productivity growth and constant import share	8,000	7,840	7,690	7,540	7,390	7,250	7,100

Hypothetical Adjustment Program (continued)

	1984	1985	1986	1987	1988	1989	1990
Assumed 6 percent annual productivity growth and rising import share	8,000	7,630	7,300	6,940	6,610	6,300	5,980
Year-to-year employment changes (workers)							
Changes induced by consumption and productivity growth with constant import share	—	−160	−150	−150	−150	−140	−150
Changes induced by rising import share	—	−210	−180	−210	−180	−170	−170
Total employment changes	—	−370	−330	−360	−330	−310	−320
Benefit and budget calculations (1984 prices)							
Annual wage cost per worker assuming constant $8.50 per hour and 2,000 hours (dollars)	17,000	17,000	17,000	17,000	17,000	17,000	17,000
Benefits calculated at two times annual wage cost per worker (million dollars)	—	12.6	11.2	12.2	11.2	10.5	10.9
Projected program surplus or deficit: tariff revenue less benefits (million dollars)	69.0	56.4	55.8	51.8	50.8	47.5	44.1

— Not applicable.

BIBLIOGRAPHY

Morici, Peter, and Laura L. Megna. 1983. *US Economic Policies Affecting Industrial Trade: A Quantitative Assessment.* Report no. 200. Washington: National Planning Association.

Pastor, Robert A. 1980. *Congress and the Politics of US Foreign Economic Policy 1929–1976.* Los Angeles: University of California Press.

Stern, Robert M. 1984. "Comments on Data, Elasticities, and Other Key Parameters." Seminar Discussion Paper no. 134. Paper read at conference, General Equilibrium Trade Policy Modelling, Columbia University, 5–6 April.

US Department of Commerce. Bureau of the Census. 1984. *Census of Manufactures.* Publication No. MC82–I–32C–3(P). Washington, April.

US International Trade Commission. 1976. *Certain Ceramic Tableware: Report to the President on Investigation No. TA–203–1 Under Sections 203(i)(2) and 203(i)(3) of the Trade Act of 1974*. USITC Publication no. 766. Washington.

———. 1978. *Certain Ceramic Articles: Report to the President on Investigation No. TA–203–4 Under Section 203 of the Trade Act of 1974*. USITC Publication no. 893. Washington, June.

———. 1981. *Summary of Trade and Tariff Information*. USITC Publication no. 841, control no. 5–2–6. Washington, November.

———. 1982a. *Certain Ceramic Kitchenware and Tableware from the People's Republic of China: Report to the President on Investigation No. TA–406–8 Under Section 406 of the Trade Act of 1974*. USITC Publication no. 1279. Washington, August.

———. 1982b. *Summary of Trade and Tariff Information*. USITC Publication no. 841, control no. 5–2–8. Washington, December.

———. 1984. *Summary of Trade and Tariff Information*. USITC Publication no. 841, control no. 5–2–6 (Supp.). Washington, February.

US Tariff Commission. 1972. *Ceramic Table and Kitchen Articles, Including Dinnerware: Report to the President on Investigation No. TEA–I–22 Under Section 301(b) of the Trade Expansion Act of 1962*. USTC Publication no. 466. Washington, February.

———. 1973. *Certain Ceramic Tableware: Report to the President on Investigation No. TEA–IR–10–73 Under Section 351(d)(1) of the Trade Expansion Act of 1962*. USTC Publication no. 574. Washington, May.

———. 1974. *Certain Ceramic Tableware: Report to the President on Investigation No. TEA–IR–10–74 Under Section 351(d)(1) of the Trade Expansion Act of 1962*. USTC Publication no. 668. Washington, May.

CASE M–6

Ceramic Floor and Wall Tiles

PERIOD OF RELIEF

June 1930 to present

SUPPLIERS AFFECTED

Global (primarily Brazil, Canada, Italy, Japan, Mexico, Spain, and West Germany)

RELIEF ACTION

High tariffs on ceramic floor and wall tiles[1] originated in the Smoot-Hawley bill, enacted by Congress as the Tariff Act of 1930, which established ad valorem tariffs on tiles averaging 53.8 percent. In the early 1960s, tariffs on all ceramic floor and wall tiles were reduced by more than 50 percent. Effective 31 August 1963, the average ad valorem most-favored-nation (MFN) tariff rate dropped to 23.9 percent; the tariff on imported mosaic and glazed tiles fell from 55 percent ad valorem to 24.5 percent, and the rate on all other imported tiles declined from 50 percent to 24 percent. These rates remained effective through 31 December 1979 for mosaic tiles and through 31 December 1981 for glazed and other imported tiles. (USITC 841, 1981, 4)

On 1 January 1980, most of the initial tariff rates negotiated under the Tokyo Round of multilateral trade negotiations (MTN) became effective. These rates take effect through eight annual staged reductions, ending 1 January 1987. The average ad valorem tariff rate was 23.5 percent on 1 January 1980 and is scheduled to be reduced to 19.8 percent by 1 January 1987. Despite the Kennedy and Tokyo Round tariff reductions, the tariff on tiles will remain substantially above the average for all manufactured goods. (USITC 841, 1981, 4; USITC 841, 1983, 3)

---

1. Ceramic floor and wall tiles are thin surfacing units (less than 1.25 inches thick) composed primarily of shaped and fired mixtures of nonmetallic minerals (Standard Industrial Classification 3253; Tariff Schedules of the United States [TSUS] items 532.20 to 532.27). Both industry practice and US tariff treatment distinguish three major types of tiles: glazed or unglazed mosaic, glazed nonmosaic, and unglazed nonmosaic. (USITC 841, 1981, v, 2)

On 30 March 1980, certain tiles were designated as eligible articles under the Generalized System of Preferences (GSP) in response to petitions from the governments of Colombia and Malaysia; the Guatemala Export Promotion Center; and Stylex, SA, Honduras. They had requested duty-free treatment for all mosaic tiles; however, such treatment was granted only to certain small or irregularly shaped mosaic tiles (virtually none of which are produced in the United States) covered under TSUS item 532.22. (USITC 841, 1981, 3)

In other actions, the Tile Council of America, Inc. (a trade association of US ceramic tile manufacturers), filed a petition on 5 October 1981, with the Department of Commerce alleging that the government of Mexico subsidized producers and exporters of glazed and unglazed nonmosaic tiles. The Department initiated a countervailing duty investigation on 30 October 1981, and announced a final affirmative determination and a countervailing duty order on 10 May 1982. Countervailing duties of 15.84 percent ad valorem were imposed, with one exception. The rate was set at zero percent for imports from one Mexican firm that verified it did not benefit from any of the cited subsidies. (USITC 1442, 4)

On 20 October 1981, the Oil, Chemical and Atomic Workers International Union filed a petition for trade adjustment assistance with the Department of Labor on behalf of workers at H&R Johnson, Inc., Keyport, New Jersey, alleging injury to workers from increased imports. The department initiated an investigation on 26 October 1981, and published an affirmative recommendation on 30 August 1982, certifying workers as being eligible to apply for worker adjustment assistance as of 31 August 1982. Also, on 26 March 1982, the Department of Commerce revoked a 1971 Department of Treasury ruling that certain ceramic tiles from the United Kingdom were being dumped.[2] (USITC 1442, 4)

CHANGES IN THE INDUSTRY

The US ceramic floor and wall tile industry is both highly specialized and concentrated, dominated by multiplant firms and larger plants. The industry comprised 61 companies and 79 manufacturing establishments in 1977, the most recent year for which official statistics are available. (USITC 841, 1983, 1)

The industry is believed to have become more concentrated during the period 1978 to 1982. Seven US firms that operated a total of 24 plants in 1982 increased their share of US production during 1978–82 from 66 percent to 70 percent. Foreign interests are known to control five companies and eight establishments and accounted for at least 20 percent of US producers' shipments in 1982. (USITC 1442, 6; USITC 841, 1983, 1)

The industry's new plant construction and facility upgrading peaked (along with US consumption) in 1979. Capital expenditures, which increased to $20 million in 1979, decreased to $19 million in 1980, and $14 million in 1981. (USITC 841, 1983, 1)

---

2. On 2 January 1980, authority for administering the antidumping law was transferred from the Department of Treasury to the Department of Commerce.

Industry analysts anticipate that the 1980s will bring long-term growth in the volume of US tile consumption. Tile qualities such as aesthetic appeal, durability, ease of maintenance, and fire resistance have been attracting new customers. For the short term, however, analysts expect periodic downward fluctuations in consumption growth resulting from the cyclical nature of the residential construction market. (USITC 841, 1981, v–vi; USITC 1442, 6)

Key Statistics

Imports from all sources

Year	Volume (million square feet)	Value (million dollars)	Source
Before MTN rates			
1976	136.1	55.6	USITC 841, 1981, 22
1977	217.9	86.6	USITC 841, 1981, 22
1978	253.9	116.4	USITC 1442, 23
1979	291.6	149.9	USITC 1442, 23
During MTN rates			
1980	255.4	170.4	USITC 1442, 23
1981	254.7	187.8	USITC 1442, 23
1982	225.8	144.9	USITC 1442, 23
1983	297.5	174.0	BC, FT 246
1984	452.8	248.8	Lukes

Apparent consumption

Year	Volume (million square feet)	Value (million dollars)	Source
Before MTN rates			
1976	410.0	254.7	USITC 841, 1981, 22
1977	477.4	297.7	USITC 841, 1981, 22
1978	549.8	372.3	USITC 1442, 23
1979	597.7	440.5	USITC 1442, 23
During MTN rates			
1980	545.1	472.3	USITC 1442, 23
1981	531.0	531.3	Tile Council 1985b, 23; authors' estimate
1982	509.6	484.0	Tile Council 1985b, 23; authors' estimate
1983	621.8	565.6	Tile Council 1985b, 23; authors' estimate
1984	781.5	656.9	Tile Council 1985b, 23; authors' estimate

Market share of imports (percentage of apparent consumption, by volume)

Year	Share	Source
Before MTN rates		
1976	33.2	USITC 841, 1981, 22
1977	45.6	USITC 841, 1981, 22
1978	46.2	USITC 1442, 26
1979	48.8	USITC 1442, 26
During MTN rates		
1980	46.9	USITC 1442, 26
1981	48.0	Tile Council 1985b, 23
1982	44.3	Tile Council 1985b, 23
1983	47.8	Tile Council 1985b, 23
1984	57.9	Tile Council 1985b, 23

Output of domestic industry[a]

Year	Volume (million square feet)	Value (million dollars)	Source
Before MTN rates			
1976	277.2	200.4	USITC 841, 1981, 22
1977	265.0	214.2	USITC 841, 1981, 22
1978	301.7	260.7	USITC 1442, 23
1979	312.8	297.0	USITC 1442, 23
During MTN rates			
1980	297.6	309.3	USITC 1442, 23
1981	287.5	356.9	Tile Council 1985b, 23; USITC 1442, 23
1982	295.7	366.8	Tile Council 1985b, 23; Lukes
1983	334.3	405.4	Tile Council 1985b, 23; Lukes
1984	337.0	420.0	Tile Council 1985b, 23; Lukes

a. Producers' shipments.

Employment in domestic industry[a]

Year	Production workers (average number)	Source
Before MTN rates		
1972	6,800	USITC 841, 1981, 6
1977	6,400	USITC 841, 1981, 6
1978	6,300	USITC 841, 1983, 1
1979	6,322	authors' estimate

Employment in domestic industry[a] (continued)

Year	Production workers (average number)	Source
During MTN rates		
1980	6,637	authors' estimate
1981	6,294	authors' estimate
1982	5,901	authors' estimate
1983	5,983	authors' estimate
1984	5,970	authors' estimate

a. The estimates for 1979–82 are derived from data provided by seven US firms representing 67 percent of US shipments in 1982. The 1983–84 figures assume that employment increased with production in those years, but only by a fraction.

Wages

Year	Dollars per hour	Source
Before MTN rates		
1972	3.10	USITC 841, 1981, 20
1977	4.41	USITC 841, 1981, 20
1978	4.94	USITC 1442, 11
1979	5.34	USITC 1442, 11
During MTN rates		
1980	5.85	USITC 1442, 11
1981	6.42	USITC 1442, 11
1982	6.83	USITC 1442, 11
1983	7.23	BLS, 38
1984	7.50	authors' estimate

Industry profits[a] (million dollars)

Year	Profits[b]	Source
Before MTN rates		
1976	n.a.	
1977	n.a.	
1978	22.6	USITC 1442, 12
1979	25.6	USITC 1442, 12
During MTN rates		
1980	25.5	USITC 1442, 12
1981	25.0	USITC 1442, 12
1982	23.6	USITC 1442, 12
1983	n.a.	
1984	n.a.	

n.a. Not available.

a. The figures reflect profit experience of seven US firms that accounted for 67 percent, by volume, of US production in 1982.

b. Net profits before taxes.

Industry capacity utilization[a]

Year	Percentage	Source
Before MTN rates		
1976	78.8	authors' estimate
1977	75.6	authors' estimate
1978	76.8	USITC 1442, 8
1979	81.4	USITC 1442, 8
During MTN rates		
1980	80.6	USITC 1442, 8
1981	75.8	USITC 1442, 8
1982	66.7	USITC 1442, 8
1983	75.5	authors' estimate
1984	71.5	authors' estimate

a. The figures reflect capacity utilization of seven US firms that accounted for 70 percent of US production in 1982. The estimates for 1976–77 and 1983–84 are based on data trends for US production and capacity. (USITC 1442, 8)

Quantitative Profile

Item	Amount	Source
Number of years restraints in force (1930 to present)	55 years	
Induced increase in price of imported tiles (1984)	21.6 percent	USITC 841, 1983, 3[a]
Induced increase in price of domestic tiles (1984)	17.3 percent	authors' estimate
Coefficient of price response	0.8	authors' estimate
Quantity and value of imports (1984)	453 million square feet $249 million	Lukes Lukes
Induced decrease in imports due to restraints (1984)	120 million square feet $66 million	authors' estimate authors' estimate
Quantity and value of domestic production (1984)	337 million square feet $420 million	Tile Council 1985b, 23 Lukes
Induced increase in domestic production due to restraints (1984)	48 million square feet	authors' estimate
Coefficient of quantity response	0.4	Tile Council 1985a
Elasticity of demand for imported tiles	0.5	Tile Council 1985a

Quantitative Profile (continued)

Item	Amount	Source
Elasticity of supply of domestic tiles	1.5	authors' estimate
Elasticity of demand for domestic tiles	1.2	authors' estimate
Cross-elasticity of demand for domestic tiles relative to price of imported tiles	2.0	Stern, 9[b]
Cross-elasticity of output of domestic tiles relative to price of imported tiles	1.2	authors' estimate
Cross-elasticity of quantity of imported tiles relative to price of domestic tiles	3.0	authors' estimate
Cost of restraints to US consumers (1984)	$116 million	authors' estimate
Gain from restraints to US producers (1984)	$62 million	authors' estimate
Tariff revenue and implied average tariff rate (1984)	$55 million 22 percent	authors' estimate BC, IM 146
Gain from restraints to foreigners (1984)	negligible	authors' estimate
Efficiency loss from larger domestic production to the United States (1984)	$11 million	authors' estimate
Welfare cost of restraints to the United States (1984)	$11 million	authors' estimate
Employment in protected US industry	6,400 (1977) 5,970 (1984)	USITC 841, 1981, 6 authors' estimate
Induced increase in employment (1984)	850	authors' estimate
Cost of restraints to US consumers per job saved (1984)	$135,000	authors' estimate
Gain from restraints to US producers per job (1984)	$10,000	authors' estimate

a. Prior to the MTN negotiations, the average ad valorem equivalent decreased from 53.8 percent (effective June 1930 to August 1963) to 23.9 percent (effective August 1963 to December 1979), reflecting an average pre-MTN ad valorem equivalent of 38.9 percent.

b. This is the elasticity for the classification "other nonmetallic mineral products," which excludes rubber, plastic, pottery, china, earthenware, or glass products.

Hypothetical Adjustment Program

	1984	1985	1986	1987	1988	1989	1990
US purchases of tiles (million square feet)							
Assumed annual consumption growth of 4 percent	596.0	619.8	644.6	670.4	697.2	725.1	754.1
Imports from all sources							
Assumed annual consumption growth of 4 percent and no change in import restraints (million square feet)	290.0	301.6	313.7	326.2	339.2	352.8	366.9
Assumed annual consumption growth of 4 percent and degressive tariff (import price elasticity of 1.2) (million square feet)	290.0	305.1	321.0	337.7	355.3	373.8	393.2
Import share of consumption with degressive tariff (percentage)	48.7	49.2	49.8	50.4	51.0	51.6	52.1
Hypothetical tariff rate							
Tariff degressive at 1 percentage point per year (percent)	22	21	20	19	18	17	16
Tariff revenue (million 1984 dollars)	37	38	38	38	37	37	37
US production for the domestic market (million square feet)							
Assumed annual consumption growth of 4 percent and constant import share	306.0	318.2	330.9	344.2	358.0	372.3	387.2
Assumed annual consumption growth of 4 percent and rising import share	306.0	314.7	323.6	332.7	341.9	351.3	360.9
US employment in the domestic tile industry (workers)							
Assumed 6 percent annual productivity growth and constant import share	6,000	5,880	5,762	5,647	5,534	5,423	5,315

Hypothetical Adjustment Program (continued)

	1984	1985	1986	1987	1988	1989	1990
Assumed 6 percent annual productivity growth and rising import share	6,000	5,820	5,645	5,476	5,312	5,153	4,998
Year-to-year employment changes (workers)							
Changes induced by consumption and productivity growth with constant import share	—	−120	−118	−115	−113	−111	−108
Changes induced by rising import share	—	−60	−57	−54	−51	−48	−47
Total employment changes	—	−180	−175	−169	−164	−159	−155
Benefit and budget calculations (1984 prices)							
Annual wage cost per worker assuming constant $8.50 per hour and 2,000 hours (dollars)	17,000	17,000	17,000	17,000	17,000	17,000	17,000
Benefits calculated at two times annual wage cost per worker (million dollars)	—	6.1	6.0	5.7	5.6	5.4	5.3
Projected program surplus or deficit: tariff revenue less benefits (million dollars)	—	31.9	32.0	32.3	31.4	31.6	31.7

— Not applicable.

BIBLIOGRAPHY

Lukes, James (US International Trade Commission). 1985. By communication, 13 May.

Pastor, Robert A. 1980. *Congress and the Politics of US Foreign Economic Policy 1929–1976*. Los Angeles: University of California Press.

Stern, Robert M. 1984. "Comments on Data, Elasticities, and Other Key Parameters." Seminar Discussion Paper no. 134. Paper read at conference, General Equilibrium Trade Policy Modelling, Columbia University, 5–6 April.

US Department of Commerce. Bureau of the Census. 1983. *US Imports for Consumption*. IM 146. Washington, December.

———. 1983. *US Imports for Consumption and General Imports.* FT 246. Washington.

———. Bureau of Economic Analysis. 1985. *Survey of Current Business.* Washington, March.

US Department of Labor. Bureau of Labor Statistics. 1983. *Supplement to Employment and Earnings.* Washington, July.

US International Trade Commission. 1981. *Summary of Trade and Tariff Information: Ceramic Floor and Wall Tiles.* USITC Publication no. 841, control no. 5–2–2. Washington, May.

———. 1983. *Summary of Trade and Tariff Information: Ceramic Floor and Wall Tiles.* USITC Publication no. 841, control no. 5–2–2 (Supp.). Washington, August.

———. 1983. *Competitive Assessment of the US Ceramic Floor and Wall Tile Industry.* USITC Publication no. 1442. Washington, October.

Washington Economic Research Consultants. 1985a. "Estimated Impact of Trade Remedies or Exchange Rate Revaluation on the US Ceramic Tile Industry." Prepared for Tile Council of America, Inc. Washington, September.

———. 1985b. "Ceramic Floor and Wall Tiles, Statistical Report, Fourth Quarter 1984." Prepared for Tile Council of America, Inc. Washington.

CASE M–7

Frozen Concentrated Orange Juice

PERIOD OF RELIEF

June 1930 to present

SUPPLIERS AFFECTED

Global (primarily Brazil)

RELIEF ACTION

The Tariff Act of 1930 (the Smoot-Hawley tariff) established a duty of 70 cents per gallon for frozen concentrated orange juice (FCOJ).[1] In October 1948, negotiations with Brazil under the General Agreement on Tariffs and Trade (GATT) reduced the rate 50 percent, and the lower rate was extended to other countries under GATT's most-favored-nation (MFN) clause. The 35-cents-per-gallon rate has been in effect since 1948 and is not scheduled for reduction. Imports from Caribbean Basin Initiative (CBI) countries, but not other developing countries, are eligible for duty-free entry under the Generalized System of Preferences (GSP). (USITC 1623, A4–5)

The Trade and Tariff Act of 1984 reclassified orange juice products in order to close a loophole under which foreign exporters were avoiding the high tariff on FCOJ by adding water offshore and shipping it as nonconcentrated orange juice, which is assessed a duty of only 20 cents per gallon. The revised tariff schedules retain the lower duty for reconstituted juice of a concentration lower than 1.5 but raise the duty for all other reconstituted juice to the higher 35 cents per gallon. (Alexander)

CHANGES IN THE INDUSTRY

Frozen concentrated orange juice is made by extracting the juice from fresh oranges, evaporating the moisture until a desired degree of concentration is achieved, and

---

1. Other juices—namely other concentrated citrus fruit juices, concentrated grape juice, and frozen concentrated grape juice—are also protected by high tariffs. Because their import values are rather low ($29 million, $1 million, and $0.2 million, respectively), they were not included in this case study. (BC, IM 146)

then freezing the concentrate. The oranges used in the production process are "round" oranges, as distinct from "eating" oranges.

Extensive co-ownership characterizes the industry, as is evidenced by the many grower-owned cooperatives and processor-owned groves in production. For this reason the US International Trade Commission defines the industry to include both FCOJ processors and growers of round oranges. (USITC 1623, 27–29, A3)

The domestic industry's decline from 1978 to 1983 was primarily caused by the effects of two back-to-back freezes in Florida during the 1981 and 1982 seasons.[2] Since Florida growers account for 85 percent to 90 percent of the oranges used in processing, the freezes severely affected FCOJ production. The 1980–81 freeze reduced the output of round oranges by 17 percent and lowered FCOJ production by 28 percent. The 1981–82 freeze reduced round orange and FCOJ output by another 27 percent. Due to the lower price of Brazilian FCOJ (partly a result of government subsidization, but largely the result of the Florida freezes), imports as a percentage of total available FCOJ increased irregularly from 8 percent in 1979–80, when Florida growers registered a record crop, to 30 percent in 1982–83. (USITC 1623, 12)

Based on information provided by 11 corporations, investment in FCOJ production facilities increased at varying rates between 1979 and 1983. The book value increased 32 percent in 1979–80, 28 percent in 1980–81, 16 percent in 1981–82, and 34 percent in 1982–83. Research and development (R&D) is performed by private firms, state agencies, and grower associations. R&D expenditures reported by 17 producers reached a high of $3.1 million in 1982. (USITC 1623, A18–19; USITC 1406, A23)

---

2. The crop year for round oranges runs from 1 December to 30 November. Thus, the 1981 season is actually 1 December 1980 to 30 November 1981.

Key Statistics

All volume figures refer to the single-strength equivalent of FCOJ, which requires a 3-to-1 dilution with water.

Imports from all sources

Year (during restraints)	Volume (million gallons, crop year[a])	Value (million dollars)	Source
1979	173	118	USITC 1406, A24
1980	103	69	USITC 1623, A21
1981	208	171	USITC 1623, A21
1982	374	302	USITC 1623, A21
1983	377	304	USITC 1623, A21

a. A crop year runs from 1 December to 30 November (e.g., crop year 1979 is actually 1 December 1978 to 30 November 1979).

Apparent consumption[a]

Year (during restraints)	Volume (million gallons)	Value (million dollars)	Source
1979	967	945	authors' estimate
1980	980	906	authors' estimate
1981	1,001	1,372	authors' estimate
1982	1,136	1,567	authors' estimate
1983	1,238	1,682	authors' estimate

a. These figures reflect the volume and value of US producers' shipments plus imports, minus exports. Net sales figures are used to represent the value of US producers' shipments. (USITC 1623, A12–13, A15, A21; USITC 1406, A15–16, A18, A24)

Market share of imports[a] (percentage of total available FCOJ, by volume)

Year (during restraints)	Share	Source
1979	16.2	authors' estimate
1980	8.1	authors' estimate
1981	17.6	authors' estimate
1982	31.4	authors' estimate
1983	29.5	authors' estimate

a. Most imported FCOJ is used at the processor level for blending with domestic FCOJ, and is either consumed domestically or re-exported. Since it is impossible to determine the proportion of FCOJ that is re-exported, the usual measure of import penetration (the ratio of imports to apparent consumption) is not as useful as the comparison of imports with total available FCOJ.

Output of domestic industry

Year (during restraints)	Volume[a] (million gallons)	Value[b] (million dollars)	Source
1979	758	908	USITC 1406, A14; A18
1980	1,013	934	USITC 1406, A14; A18
1981	733	1,340	USITC 1623, A11; A15
1982	538	1,392	USITC 1623, A11; A15
1983	685	1,506	USITC 1623, A11; A15

a. These figures represent US production of FCOJ from Florida's orange crop. During the years 1978–83, Florida's orange crop accounted for about 85 percent to 90 percent of oranges used in processing FCOJ.

b. Net sales figures are used to represent the value of domestic output.

Employment in domestic industry[a]

Year (during restraints)	Production workers (average number)	Source
1979	4,848	authors' estimate
1980	4,518	authors' estimate
1981	4,440	authors' estimate
1982	4,446	authors' estimate
1983	4,400	authors' estimate

a. These estimates are based on the assumption that job-year employment in FCOJ processing is about 6 percent of employment in the frozen foods industry, the same as its proportion of shipments value in 1978–79.

Wages[a]

Year (during restraints)	Dollars per hour	Source
1979	5.12	Brown
1980	5.59	Brown
1981	6.16	Brown
1982	6.53	Brown
1983	6.95	Brown

a. These figures are based on SIC industry 2037, "frozen fruits and vegetables," which includes frozen concentrated fruit juices, dried citrus pulp, and frozen fruits and vegetables.

Acreage in round orange growing

Year (during restraints)	Thousand acres	Source
1979	799	USITC 1406, A9
1980	806	USITC 1623, A6
1981	795	USITC 1623, A6
1982	777	USITC 1623, A6
1983	749	USITC 1623, A6

Industry profits[a] (million dollars)

Year (during restraints)	Profits[b]	Source
1979	26.6	USITC 1406, A18
1980	30.6	USITC 1406, A18
1981	159.6	USITC 1623, A15
1982	140.8	USITC 1623, A15
1983	138.9	USITC 1623, A15

a. Figures for crop years 1979–80 are based on information provided to the USITC by 12 corporations on FCOJ operations. Figures for the remaining years are based on information provided by 14 US producers, 10 of which are corporations and 4 of which are cooperatives. In 1983, the 10 corporations accounted for about 44 percent of total domestic shipments, while the 4 cooperatives accounted for 19 percent.

b. Net profits before taxes.

Industry capacity utilization

During the processing season, orange processors continuously operate at full capacity until all fresh fruit is processed. After the season, they close fresh-fruit operations and the equipment sits idle until the next season. (USITC 1623, A11)

Quantitative Profile

Item	Amount	Source
Number of years restraints in force (1930 to present)	55 years	
Induced increase in price of imported FCOJ (1983)	44 percent	authors' estimate
Induced increase in price of domestic FCOJ (1983)	35 percent	authors' estimate
Coefficient of price response	0.9	authors' estimate
Quantity and value of imports (1983)	377 million gallons $304 million	USITC 1623, A21 USITC 1623, A21
Induced decrease in imports due to restraints (1983)	450 million gallons $363 million	authors' estimate authors' estimate
Quantity and value of domestic production (1983)	685 million gallons $1,506 million	USITC 1623, A11 USITC 1623, A15
Induced increase in domestic production (1983)	340 million gallons	authors' estimate
Coefficient of quantity response	0.75	authors' estimate
Elasticity of demand for imported FCOJ	2.4	USITC 1623, A64[a]
Elasticity of supply of domestic FCOJ	3.0	USITC 1623, A65
Elasticity of demand for domestic FCOJ	0.5	USITC 1623, A65[b]

Quantitative Profile (continued)

Item	Amount	Source
Cross-elasticity of demand for domestic FCOJ relative to price of imported FCOJ	3.2	authors' estimate
Cross-elasticity of output of domestic FCOJ relative to price of imported FCOJ	2.7	authors' estimate
Cross-elasticity of quantity of imported FCOJ relative to price of domestic FCOJ	7.3	authors' estimate
Cost of restraints to US consumers (1983)	$525 million	authors' estimate
Gain from restraints to US producers (1983)	$390 million	authors' estimate
Tariff revenue and implied average tariff rate (1983)	$128 million 43.5 percent	BC, IM 146 authors' estimate
Gain from restraints to foreigners	negligible	authors' estimate
Efficiency loss of larger domestic production to the United States (1983)	$130 million	authors' estimate
Welfare costs of restraints to the United States (1983)	$130 million	authors' estimate
Employment in protected US industry	4,848 (1979) 4,400 (1983)	authors' estimate authors' estimate
Induced increase in employment (1983)	2,200	authors' estimate
Cost of restraints to US consumers per job saved (1983)	$240,000	authors' estimate
Gain from restraints to US producers per job (1983)	$90,000	authors' estimate

a. Elasticities obtained from USITC 1623 were derived from estimated equations based on crop-year data from 1965–82. The elasticity of demand for imported FCOJ is the percentage decrease in imports that result from a 1 percent increase in the ratio of the import price to the cost of round oranges.

b. Demand at the consumer level is much more price elastic (1.0) than demand of intermediate buyers. (USITC 1623, A65)

Hypothetical Adjustment Program

	1984	1985	1986	1987	1988	1989	1990
US purchases of FCOJ (million gallons)							
Assumed annual consumption growth of 4 percent	1,300	1,352	1,406	1,462	1,521	1,582	1,645

Hypothetical Adjustment Program (continued)

	1984	1985	1986	1987	1988	1989	1990
Imports from all sources							
Assumed annual consumption growth of 4 percent and no change in import restraints (million gallons)	390	406	422	439	456	474	493
Assumed annual consumption growth of 4 percent and degressive tariff (import price elasticity of 2.4) (million gallons)	390	425	463	506	553	607	668
Import share of consumption with degressive tariff (percentage)	30	31	33	35	36	38	41
Hypothetical tariff rate							
Tariff degressive at 2 percentage points per year (percent)	44	42	40	38	36	34	32
Tariff revenue (million 1984 dollars)	140	144	150	156	161	167	173
US production for the domestic market (million gallons)							
Assumed annual consumption growth of 4 percent and constant import share	910	946	984	1,023	1,065	1,108	1,152
Assumed annual consumption growth of 4 percent and rising import share	910	927	943	956	968	975	977
US employment in the domestic FCOJ industry (workers)[a]							
Assumed 2 percent annual productivity growth and constant import share	4,400	4,488	4,578	4,669	4,763	4,858	4,955
Assumed 2 percent annual productivity growth and rising import share	4,400	4,398	4,387	4,363	4,329	4,275	4,202

Hypothetical Adjustment Program (continued)

	1984	1985	1986	1987	1988	1989	1990
Year-to-year employment changes (workers)							
Changes induced by consumption and productivity growth with constant import share	—	88	90	91	94	95	97
Changes induced by rising import share	—	−90	−101	−115	−128	−149	−170
Total employment changes	—	−2	−11	−24	−34	−54	−73
Benefit and budget calculations (1984 prices)							
Annual wage cost per worker assuming constant $8.50 per hour and 2,000 hours (dollars)	17,000	17,000	17,000	17,000	17,000	17,000	17,000
Benefits calculated at two times annual wage cost per worker (million dollars)	—	neg.	0.4	0.8	1.2	1.8	2.5
Projected program surplus or deficit: tariff revenue less benefits (million dollars)	140	144	150	155	160	165	170

— Not applicable.

a. The processing of orange juice is highly seasonal, and these figures are estimates expressed on a job-year equivalent basis.

BIBLIOGRAPHY

Alexander, Wayne (House Ways and Means Subcommittee on International Trade). 1985. By communication, June.

Brown, Harold (Bureau of Labor Statistics). 1985. By communication, April.

US Bureau of the Census. 1983. *US Imports for Consumption.* IM 146. Washington, December.

US International Trade Commission. 1983. *Frozen Concentrated Orange Juice from Brazil.* USITC Publication no. 1406. Washington, July.

———. 1984a. *Summary of Trade and Tariff Information: Fruit Juices.* USITC Publication no. 841, control no. 1–12–50. Washington, September.

———. 1984b. *Frozen Concentrated Orange Juice from Brazil.* USITC Publication no. 1623. Washington, December.

Ward, R., and D. Tilley. 1980. "Time Varying Parameters with Random Components: The Orange Juice Industry." *Southern Journal of Agricultural Economics* (December).

CASE M-8

Canned Tuna

PERIOD OF RELIEF

1951 to present

SUPPLIERS AFFECTED

Global (primarily affecting Japan, the Philippines, Taiwan, and Thailand)

RELIEF ACTION

In 1951, following the termination of a trade agreement with Mexico, the ad valorem tariff on imports of canned tuna in oil was doubled from 22.5 percent to 45 percent. Effective September 1955, that tariff was lowered to 35 percent as a concession to Japan in negotiations under the General Agreement on Tariffs and Trade (GATT). The 35 percent duty remains in effect today. (USITC 1558, A6)

Prior to the doubling of the tariff rate in 1951, almost all imports of canned tuna were packed in oil. Shortly thereafter, tuna packed in brine (now spring water) became commercially important for the first time. Today, 98 percent of imported canned tuna is packed in water. (USITC 1558, A6)

The tariff on canned tuna not in oil had been set at 25 percent by the Tariff Act of 1930 (Smoot-Hawley), but was lowered to 15.5 percent in 1943 pursuant to a trade agreement with Iceland. In 1956, the agreement with Iceland was withdrawn, and a tariff-rate quota (TRQ) negotiated with Japan went into effect on 14 April 1956. The TRQ permitted imports under 20 percent of the previous year's domestic pack to enter at 12.5 percent ad valorem, while imports over that level were dutiable at 25 percent. Concessions in the Kennedy Round of multilateral trade negotiations (MTN) subsequently lowered the two rates to 6 percent and 12.5 percent, respectively, effective 1 January 1972. No tariff concessions were made in the Tokyo Round. (USITC 1558, A16)

On 15 February 1984, the US International Trade Commission initiated an investigation under Section 201 of the Trade Act of 1974, in response to a petition from the United States Tuna Foundation and allied groups (including representatives of the tuna fishing fleet)[1] claiming injury from imports and requesting escape clause relief. The petitioners sought an increase in the tariff on imports of tuna canned in water to 35 percent (equivalent to that for tuna canned in oil). On 25 July 1984, the USITC found, by a 4 to 1 vote, that while imports were rising and the industry had been injured, overexpansion and a shift in the fishing grounds from the eastern to the western Pacific were more important causes of domestic injury. (FTC, 1; USITC 1558, 1, 16)

CHANGES IN THE INDUSTRY

The US tuna industry has responded to changing consumer tastes and increasing imports of canned tuna in water by shifting domestic production to the preferred product. From 1979 to 1983, US firms increased production of tuna canned in water by 54 percent and decreased production of tuna canned in oil by 34 percent. (USITC 1558, A30)

---

1. The USITC decided, and the petitioners concurred, that the industry definition included boats, fishermen, and processors. (USITC 1558, 7)

Key Statistics

Volume of imports from all sources (million pounds)

Year (during restraints)	Canned tuna (not in oil)				Canned tuna (in oil)	Source
	Under-quota	Over-quota	Total per Customs[a]	Total per Census[a]		
1956	27.8	—	27.8	n.a.	n.a.	NMFS 1970, 46
1961	56.2	—	56.2	58.2	0.4	NMFS 1970, 46
1965	49.2	—	49.2	50.8	0.2	NMFS 1970, 46
1970	70.1	0.8	70.9	72.1	0.2	NMFS 1970, 46
1972	54.5	—	54.5	56.1	0.4	NMFS 1975, 58
1974	52.2	—	52.2	52.5	0.2	NMFS 1983, 65
1976	56.4	—	56.4	58.6	0.3	NMFS 1983, 65
1978	50.0	—	50.0	51.6	0.2	NMFS 1983, 65
1980	109.1	5.1	114.2	63.1	0.4	NMFS 1983, 65
1982	92.8	—	92.8	87.4	0.2	NMFS 1983, 65
1983	91.9	28.3	120.2	122.1	0.2	NMFS 1983, 65

— Not applicable.
n.a. Not available.
a. The Bureau of the Census figures do not agree with US Customs figures because some imported tuna is stored in bonded warehouses before being entered for consumption and counted against the quota.

Value of imports from all sources (million dollars)

Year (during restraints)	Canned tuna (not in oil)	Source
1974	51.4	DOA 1979, 583
1976	67.6	DOA 1979, 583
1978	64.2	DOA 1982, 547
1980	96.7	USITC 1558, A23
1982	112.9	USITC 1558, A23
1983	136.9	USITC 1558, A23

Apparent consumption

Year (during restraints)	Volume (million pounds)		Value[a] (million dollars)	Source
	Canned tuna (in oil and in water)	Canned tuna (in water only)		
1961	369.3	n.a.	n.a.	NMFS 1970, 46
1965	409.4	n.a.	n.a.	NMFS 1970, 46
1970	510.3	n.a.	n.a.	NMFS 1970, 46
1972	676.3	n.a.	n.a.	NMFS 1975, 58
1974	713.1	n.a.	881.0	NMFS 1983, 65; authors' estimate
1976	658.1	n.a.	924.0	NMFS 1983, 65; authors' estimate
1978	756.6	n.a.	1,337.5	NMFS 1983, 65; authors' estimate
1980	665.6	350.8	1,235.7	NMFS 1983, 65; USITC 1558, A67; authors' estimate
1982	626.1	434.5	1,031.4	NMFS 1983, 65; USITC 1558, A67; authors' estimate
1983	683.4	509.2	958.3	NMFS 1983, 65; USITC 1558, A67; authors' estimate

n.a. Not available.

a. These estimates are derived from the value of imports plus domestic output.

Market share of imports (percentage of apparent consumption, by volume[a])

Year (during restraints)	Share	Source
1961	15.9	NMFS 1970, 46
1965	12.4	NMFS 1970, 46
1970	14.2	NMFS 1970, 46
1972	8.4	NMFS 1975, 58
1974	7.4	NMFS 1983, 65
1976	9.0	NMFS 1983, 65
1978	6.8	NMFS 1983, 65
1980	9.6	NMFS 1983, 65
1982	14.0	NMFS 1983, 65
1983	17.9	NMFS 1983, 65

a. Volume based on Census figures.

Output of domestic industry[a]

Year (during restraints)	Volume (million pounds, canned weight)	Value (million dollars)	Source
1961	310.6	n.a.	NMFS 1970, 46
1965	358.4	n.a.	NMFS 1970, 46
1970	438.1	n.a.	NMFS 1970, 46
1972	619.8	n.a.	NMFS 1975, 58
1974	660.3	829.6	NMFS 1983, 65; DOA 1982, 546
1976	599.2	856.4	NMFS 1983, 65; DOA 1982, 546
1978	704.8	1,273.3	NMFS 1983, 65; DOA 1982, 546
1980	602.1	1,149.0	NMFS 1983, 65; DOA 1982, 546
1982	538.5	918.5	NMFS 1983, 65; DOA 1982, 546
1983	561.1	821.4	NMFS 1983, 65; NMFS 1983, xiii

n.a. Not available.
a. From domestic landings and imports of fresh and frozen tuna.

Employment in domestic industry

Year (during restraints)	Employees[a]	Hours worked (million)	Vessels[b]	Source
1979	14,668	25.7	79	USITC 1558, A48, A64
1980	14,906	23.6	83	USITC 1558, A48, A64
1981	14,581	23.9	86	USITC 1558, A48, A64
1982	13,436	21.7	102	USITC 1558, A48, A64
1983	13,397	24.0	93	USITC 1558, A48, A64

a. Average number of production workers in canneries.
b. Because crews of US tuna boats usually are foreign nationals and only the officers are American nationals, the number of vessels rather than individual fishermen has been used here. These figures are based on responses to the USITC and represent 65 percent to 81 percent of the domestic tuna fleet. The fleet as a whole declined from 129 vessels in 1979 to 125 in 1983, but overall capacity increased because larger boats were added to the fleet. (USITC 1558, 12–14; A63; A64)

Wages and benefits

Year (during restraints)	Total[a] (million dollars)	Hourly (dollars per hour)	Source
1979	134.9	5.26	USITC 1558, A48
1980	146.0	6.17	USITC 1558, A48
1981	153.3	6.41	USITC 1558, A48
1982	146.8	6.76	USITC 1558, A48
1983	160.9	6.71	USITC 1558, A48

a. Packers only.

Industry profits[a] (million dollars)

Year (during restraints)	Processors	Boat owners	Source
1979	54.7	(3.7)	USITC 1558, A55, A64
1980	61.9	13.0	USITC 1558, A55, A64
1981	28.2	(7.1)	USITC 1558, A55, A64
1982	(172.3)	(40.9)	USITC 1558, A55, A64
1983	(6.8)	(14.3)	USITC 1558, A55, A64

a. Net profits (loss) before taxes.

Industry capacity utilization

Year (during restraints)	Capacity[a] (million pounds)	Utilization rate (percent)	Source
1979	888.5	69.5	USITC 1558, A29
1980	976.4	65.5	USITC 1558, A29
1981	990.3	65.5	USITC 1558, A29
1982	984.0	57.8	USITC 1558, A29
1983	863.7	72.4	USITC 1558, A29

a. Processors only.

Quantitative Profile

Item	Amount	Source
Number of years restraints in force (since 1951)	34 years	
Induced increase in price of imported tuna (1983)	12.5 percent	authors' estimate[a]
Induced increase in price of domestic tuna (1983)	10 percent	authors' estimate
Coefficient of price response	0.8	authors' estimate
Quantity and value of imports (1983)	122.1 million pounds $136.9 million	NMFS 1983, 65 USITC 1558, A23
Induced decrease in imports due to restraints (1983)	50 million pounds $52 million	authors' estimate
Quantity and value of domestic production (1983)	561.1 million pounds $821.4 million	NMFS 1983, 65 NMFS 1983, xiii
Induced increase in domestic production due to restraints (1983)	50 million pounds $73 million	authors' estimate authors' estimate
Coefficient of quantity response	1.0	authors' estimate
Elasticity of demand for imported canned tuna	3.3	authors' estimate

Quantitative Profile (continued)

Item	Amount	Source
Elasticity of supply of domestic canned tuna	0.32 1.0	FTC, app. A, 15[b] authors' estimate[b]
Elasticity of demand for domestic canned tuna	0.30	FTC, app. A, 15[b]
Cross-elasticity of demand for domestic tuna relative to price of imported tuna	1.0	authors' estimate
Cross-elasticity of output of domestic tuna relative to price of imported tuna	0.8	authors' estimate
Cross-elasticity of quantity of imported tuna relative to price of domestic tuna	4.6	authors' estimate
Cost of restraints to US consumers (1983)	$91 million	authors' estimate
Gain from restraints to US producers (1983)	$74 million	authors' estimate
Tariff revenue and implied average tariff rate (1983)	$10 million 7.5 percent	authors' estimate authors' estimate[c]
Gain from restraints to foreigners (1983)	$7 million	authors' estimate
Efficiency loss from larger domestic production to the United States (1983)	$4 million	authors' estimate
Welfare cost of restraints to the United States (1983)	$11 million	authors' estimate
Employment in protected US industry	14,668 (1979) 13,397 (1983)	USITC 1558, A48 USITC 1558, A48
Induced increase in employment (1983)	1,200	authors' estimate
Cost of restraints to US consumers per job saved (1983)	$76,000	authors' estimate
Gain from restraints to US producers per job (1983)	$5,500	authors' estimate

a. This figure is attributable to the 35 percent tariff on tuna canned in oil and a 12.5 percent above-quota tariff on tuna canned in water, and is based on the assumption that above-quota tuna canned in water sets the import price for both types.

b. The staff of the Federal Trade Commission (FTC) regards these elasticity estimates as the "best available" coefficients. The supply elasticity is for all fish and forestry products (see Richardson and Mutti). We believe the true coefficient for supply of canned tuna is higher, owing to the relatively low levels of capacity utilization in recent years.

c. This figure is based on the difference between the above-quota tariff of 12.5 percent and the below-quota tariff of 6 percent.

Hypothetical Adjustment Program

	1984	1985	1986	1987	1988	1989	1990
US purchases of canned tuna (million pounds)							
Assumed annual consumption growth of 0 percent	700	700	700	700	700	700	700
Imports from all sources							
Assumed annual consumption growth of 0 percent and no change in import restraints (million pounds)	110	110	110	110	110	110	110
Assumed annual consumption growth of 0 percent and degressive tariff (import price elasticity of 2.0) (million pounds)	110	114	119	123	128	133	139
Import share of consumption with degressive tariff (percentage)	15.7	16.3	17.0	17.6	18.3	19.0	19.9
Hypothetical tariff rate							
Tariff degressive at 2 percentage points per year[a] (percent)	12.5	10.5	8.5	6.5	4.5	2.5	0.5
Tariff revenue (million 1984 dollars)	14.5	12.7	10.7	8.5	6.1	3.5	0.7
US production for domestic market (million pounds)[b]							
Assumed annual consumption growth of 0 percent and constant import share	590	590	590	590	590	590	590
Assumed annual consumption growth of 0 percent and rising import share	590	586	581	577	572	567	561
US employment in domestic tuna processing industry (thousand workers)							
Assumed 2 percent annual productivity growth and constant import share	13.4	13.1	12.9	12.6	12.4	12.1	11.9

Hypothetical Adjustment Program (continued)

	1984	1985	1986	1987	1988	1989	1990
Assumed 2 percent annual productivity growth and rising import share	13.4	13.0	12.7	12.4	12.1	11.7	11.4
Year-to-year employment changes (thousand workers)							
Changes induced by consumption and productivity growth with constant import share	—	−0.3	−0.3	−0.3	−0.3	−0.3	−0.3
Changes induced by rising import share	—	−0.1	−0.1	−0.1	−0.1	−0.1	−0.1
Total employment changes	—	−0.4	−0.4	−0.4	−0.4	−0.4	−0.4
Benefit and budget calculations (1984 prices)							
Annual wage cost per worker assuming constant $8 per hour and 2,000 hours (dollars)	16,000	16,000	16,000	16,000	16,000	16,000	16,000
Benefits calculated at two times annual wage cost per worker (million dollars)	—	12.8	12.8	12.8	12.8	12.8	12.8
Projected program surplus or deficit: tariff revenue less benefits (million dollars)	14.5	−0.1	−2.1	−4.3	−6.7	−9.3	−12.1

— Not applicable.

a. Assuming that the tariff on tuna canned in oil is harmonized with the over-quota tariff on tuna canned in water, which then would apply to all imports of canned tuna following elimination of the quota.

b. Calculated as US purchases minus imports.

BIBLIOGRAPHY

Richardson, J. David, and John H. Mutti. 1976. "Industrial Displacement through Environment Controls: The International Competitive Aspect." In *Studies in International Environmental Economics*. Edited by Ingo Walter. New York: John Wiley & Sons.

US Department of Agriculture. 1979, 1982. *Agricultural Statistics*. Washington.

US Department of Commerce. National Marine Fisheries Service. Various years. *Fisheries of the United States*. Washington.

US Federal Trade Commission. 1984. *Proceedings before the US International Trade Commission: Certain Canned Tuna Fish*. Prehearing brief. Washington, May.

US International Trade Commission. 1984. *Certain Canned Tuna Fish*. USITC Publication no. 1558. Washington, August.

CASE M–9

Textiles and Apparel: Phase I

Voluntary Restraint Agreement with Japan (VRA)

Short-Term Arrangement Regarding International Trade in Cotton Textiles (STA)

Long-Term Arrangement Regarding International Trade in Cotton Textiles (LTA)

PERIOD OF RELIEF

VRA: January 1957 to January 1962
STA: 1 October 1961 to 30 September 1962
LTA: 1 October 1962 to 31 December 1973

SUPPLIERS AFFECTED

VRA: Japan

STA: 16 importing and exporting countries accounting for 90 percent of free world trade in cotton textiles. (Loewinger, 4)

LTA: 19 countries signed the LTA by 1972; the United States imposed quota restrictions against 37 suppliers. (USITC 850, 10; Keesing and Wolf, 39)

RELIEF ACTION

Prewar Restraints on Japanese Exports

From 1935 to 1940, the United States sought to limit textile imports from Japan through voluntary restraints, selective tariff increases, and industry-to-industry agreements. Similar restraints were imposed by the United Kingdom, France, and many other countries. (GATT, 62–63)

Postwar "Voluntary" Restraints

In 1956, prodded by Section 204 of the Agricultural Act of 1956, President Dwight D. Eisenhower opened negotiations with Japan aimed at restraining US textile imports. In January 1957, Japan agreed to a five-year voluntary restraint program on cotton textile exports. Throughout the 1950s, the United Kingdom and Western Europe maintained quantitative restrictions against Japanese exports of cotton textiles. In 1959, through industry-to-industry consultations, the United Kingdom restricted cotton fabric imports from Hong Kong, India, and Pakistan. These bilateral arrangements paved the way for the Short-Term Arrangement. (GATT, 64; Keesing and Wolf, 15)

117

In 1959, at US urging, discussions on cotton textile trade were conducted under the General Agreement on Tariffs and Trade (GATT) in order to define "market disruption." In November 1960, a GATT paper, "Avoidance of Market Disruption," laid the groundwork for a new injury test involving a less restrictive definition of trade impact than the serious injury test for escape clause relief under GATT Article XIX. The new test looked to potential increases in imports, price differentials between domestic and import prices, and selective application of restraints against foreign countries. (GATT, 65)

The Short-Term Arrangement

At the insistence of President John F. Kennedy, a series of meetings was held that culminated in the July 1961 Geneva talks, which gave birth to the Short-Term Arrangement Regarding International Trade in Cotton Textiles (STA). The key feature of the STA was the "market disruption" provision borrowed from the November 1960 GATT paper. The existence or threat of market disruption would enable the importing country to request the exporting country to restrain its exports, unilaterally or by agreement, to a level not lower than imports during the 12-month period ending two to three months before initiation of the restraint. The STA covered 64 categories of cotton textiles. (Keesing and Wolf, 16)

The Long-Term Arrangement

The STA included machinery to create the Long-Term Arrangement Regarding International Trade in Cotton Textiles (LTA). The LTA was concluded on 9 February 1962, and became effective 1 October 1962. As an additional concession to the US industry, textiles were largely exempted from tariff cuts in the Trade Expansion Act of 1962, which ushered in the Kennedy Round of multilateral trade negotiations (MTN) (1964–67). (Keesing and Wolf, 16–17)

The LTA covered textiles containing more than 50 percent cotton by weight or by value. It permitted bilateral quotas on terms "not inconsistent" with LTA objectives. Quotas could be imposed unilaterally by the importing country, but at levels not less than actual imports during the previous period. Under normal circumstances, quotas were to allow import growth of 5 percent annually. (GATT, 72)

The LTA was renewed in 1967, at the insistence of President Lyndon B. Johnson, and again in 1970 at the insistence of President Richard M. Nixon. In response to the growing role of synthetic fibers, in 1971, the United States negotiated bilateral agreements with Japan, Hong Kong, Taiwan, and Korea that covered wool and man-made fiber textiles as well as cotton. European nations did likewise. These agreements led to the first Multi-Fiber Arrangement. (See Case M–10, Textiles and Apparel: Phase II; GATT, 72; USITC 850, 12; Loewinger, 5–8; Pelzman 1982, 3–4)

CHANGES IN THE INDUSTRY

"An important factor in the difficulties of the textile industry during the 1950s was the protection benefiting United States cotton growers. This permitted foreign cotton textile manufacturers to obtain their raw material at much lower prices than their United States competitors. Such negative 'effective protection' had contributed to demands for non-tariff protection in the late 1950s." (OECD, 151)

"Since the LTA applied only to cotton textiles, foreign exporters shifted their production to textiles made of synthetic fibers. Declining production costs, the technical virtues of synthetic fibers, and the economic boom of the 1960s greatly enlarged the market for man-made fibers. Between 1960 and 1979, the share of world fiber production accounted for by man-made fibers rose from 5 percent to 36 percent. United States imports of man-made fiber goods increased ten-fold between 1960 and 1970, from 31 million pounds to 329 million pounds.

"Between 1962 and 1967, the U.S. textile industry accommodated itself to the regime of protection found in the LTA. New capital investment was devoted to man-made fibers. Firms moved into the south and west from the northeast. The market share of a very few large companies increased dramatically: the share of the eight largest textiles firms in the shipment of cotton fabric rose from 29 percent in 1954 to 48 percent in 1972 and their share in the shipment of synthetic fabrics rose from 39 percent to 54 percent in the same period.

"The 1963–73 decade witnessed an explosion in exports of clothing based on man-made fibers from developing countries. The explosion was ignited by quotas on cotton textiles, and the favorable economics of man-made fibers. Thus, U.S. imports of apparel made of cotton grew by only a third from 1964 to 1972, from 415 to 545 million square yards equivalent, while imports of apparel made of man-made fibers jumped more than seventeen times, from 92 to 1,606 million square yards equivalent. By 1973, Hong Kong, South Korea, and Taiwan accounted for more than three-quarters of the total apparel exports of developing countries.

"The domestic apparel industry adjusted poorly to its increased exposure to the imports of man-made fibers. American firms became less competitive due to a rise in nominal labor costs at the same time the dollar exchange rate increased. Cyclical stagnation in 1970–71 added to the industry's woes." (Loewinger, 6–7)

Key Statistics

Imports affected: cotton textiles and apparel

Year	Volume (million pounds)	Source
During VRA		
1960	252	USITC 850, C3
During LTA		
1965	361	USITC 850, C3
1970	463	USITC 850, C3
1971	493	USITC 850, C3
1972	611	USITC 850, C3
1973	564	USITC 850, C3
During MFA		
1974	503	USITC 850, C3

Imports from all sources: cotton, wool, and man-made textiles and apparel

Year	Volume (million pounds)	Value (million dollars)	Source
During VRA			
1960[a]	416	873	USITC 850, C3; BIE 1966
During LTA			
1965	596	1,426	USITC 850, C3; BIE 1970
1970	909	2,275	USITC 850, C3; Morkre, 141
1971	1,034	2,761	USITC 850, C3; Morkre, 141
1972	1,187	3,215	USITC 850, C3; Morkre, 141
1973	1,119	3,497	USITC 850, C3; Morkre, 141
During MFA			
1974	948	3,693	USITC 850, C3; Morkre, 141

a. Data for 1960 are unavailable; this figure reflects the value of imports for 1961. (BIE 1966)

Apparent consumption affected: cotton textiles and apparel

Year	Volume (million pounds)	Source
During VRA		
1960	4,210	USITC 850, C3
During LTA		
1965	4,709	USITC 850, C3
1970	4,118	USITC 850, C3
1971	4,253	USITC 850, C3
1972	4,185	USITC 850, C3
1973	3,897	USITC 850, C3
During MFA		
1974	3,420	USITC 850, C3

Apparent consumption: cotton, wool, and man-made textiles and apparel

Year	Volume (million pounds)	Value[a] (billion dollars)	Source
During VRA			
1960	6,563	28.5	USITC 850, C3; authors' estimate
During LTA			
1965	8,804	38.7	USITC 850, C3; authors' estimate
1970	10,151	46.7	USITC 850, C3; authors' estimate
1971	11,356	50.0	USITC 850, C3; authors' estimate

Apparent consumption: cotton, wool, and man-made textiles and apparel
(continued)

Year	Volume (million pounds)	Value[a] (billion dollars)	Source
1972	12,335	55.3	USITC 850, C3; authors' estimate
1973	12,947	61.4	USITC 850, C3; authors' estimate
During MFA			
1974	11,241	62.5	USITC 850, C3; authors' estimate

a. These figures are derived from the value of imports from all sources plus domestic output, with minor adjustment for exports.

Market share of imports (percentage of apparent consumption, by volume)

Year	Affected imports	Total imports	Source
During VRA			
1960	6.0	6.3	authors' estimate
During LTA			
1965	7.7	6.8	authors' estimate
1970	11.2	9.0	authors' estimate
1971	11.6	9.1	authors' estimate
1972	14.6	9.6	authors' estimate
1973	14.5	8.6	authors' estimate
During MFA			
1974	14.7	8.4	authors' estimate

Output of domestic industry

Year	Volume[a] (combined, million pounds)	Value (billion dollars) Textiles	Value (billion dollars) Apparel	Source
During VRA				
1960	6,477	13.8	13.8	USITC 850, C3; BIE 1966
During LTA				
1965	8,523	18.3	19.0	USITC 850, C3; BIE 1970
1970	9,595	22.6	23.5	USITC 850, C3; BIE 1975
1971	10,708	24.0	25.0	USITC 850, C3; BIE 1975
1972	11,649	27.4	27.0	USITC 850, C3; BIE 1975
1973	12,474	31.1	30.0	USITC 850, C3; BIE 1976
During MFA				
1974	11,102	32.8	30.6	USITC 850, C3; BIE 1977

a. These figures reflect mill consumption of cotton, wool, and man-made fibers.

Employment in domestic industry (thousand production workers)

Year	Textiles	Apparel	Source
Prior to VRA			
1955	1,050	1,087	BLS, 504, 547
During VRA			
1960	924	1,098	BLS, 504, 547
During LTA			
1965	926	1,206	BLS, 504, 547
1970	975	1,196	BLS, 504, 547
1971	955	1,178	BLS, 504, 547
1972	986	1,208	BLS, 504, 547
1973	1,010	1,250	BLS, 504, 547
During MFA			
1974	965	1,175	BLS, 504, 547

Wages (dollars per hour)

Year	Textiles	Apparel	Source
Prior to VRA			
1955	1.38	1.37	BLS, 504, 548
During VRA			
1960	1.61	1.59	BLS, 504, 548
During LTA			
1965	1.87	1.83	BLS, 504, 548
1970	2.45	2.39	BLS, 504, 548
1971	2.57	2.49	BLS, 504, 548
1972	2.75	2.60	BLS, 504, 548
1973	2.95	2.76	BLS, 504, 548
During MFA			
1974	3.20	2.97	BLS, 504, 548

Industry profits[a] (million dollars)

Year	Textiles	Apparel	Source
During VRA			
1960	659	320	Predicasts 1974, 89, 105
During LTA			
1965	1,112	619	Predicasts 1982, 205, 229
1970	884	754	Predicasts 1982, 205, 229

Industry profits[a] (million dollars) (continued)

Year	Textiles	Apparel	Source
1971	968	876	Predicasts 1982, 205, 229
1972	1,024	1,077	Predicasts 1982, 205, 229
1973	1,317	1,231	Predicasts 1982, 205, 229
During MFA			
1974	995	915	Predicasts 1982, 205, 229

a. Net profits before taxes.

Industry capacity utilization (textiles only, average in December)

Year	Percentage	Source
During VRA		
1960	n.a.	
During LTA		
1965	93	BEA 1974, 51
1970	81	BEA 1974, 51
1971	86	BEA 1974, 51
1972	91	BEA 1974, 51
1973	89	BEA 1974, 51
During MFA		
1974	69	BEA 1975, 18

n.a. Not available.

Tariff rates (weighted averages, ad valorem equivalent)

Year	Thread and yarn	Fabrics	Made-up articles	Clothing	Source
During VRA					
1962	11.5	24.0	19.0	25.0	GATT, 67–69
During LTA, MFA I, and MFA II					
1973	14.5	16.0	13.5	27.0	GATT, 67–69
Post-Tokyo Round					
1987	9.0	11.5	7.5	22.5	GATT, 67–69

Quantitative Profile

Item	Amount	Source
Number of years restraints in force (VRA, STA, and LTA, 1957–73)	16 years	
Induced increase in price of imports (average 1962–73)		
Textiles	14.5 percent	authors' estimate[a]
Apparel	27.0 percent	authors' estimate[a]
Combined	20.0 percent	authors' estimate
Induced increase in price of domestic goods (average 1962–73)		
Textiles	11.6 percent	authors' estimate
Apparel	21.6 percent	authors' estimate
Combined	16.0 percent	authors' estimate
Coefficient of price response (textiles and apparel combined)	0.8	authors' estimate
Quantity and value of imports (1974)	948 million pounds $3.7 billion	USITC 850, C3 Morkre, 141
Induced decrease in imports due to restraints (1974)	2,200 million pounds $8.6 billion	authors' estimate[b] authors' estimate
Quantity and value of domestic production (1974)	11,102 million pounds $63.4 billion	USITC 850, C3 BIE 1977
Induced increase in domestic production due to restraints (1974)	2,200 million pounds	authors' estimate[b]
Coefficient of quantity response	1.0	authors' estimate
Elasticity of demand for imports		
Textiles	1.14 to 1.41	Stern, 9
	1.10 to 1.30	Morkre, 152
	1.2	authors' estimate
Apparel	0.52 to 3.92	Stern, 9
	3.77	Morkre, 152
	2.0	authors' estimate
Combined	1.6	authors' estimate
Elasticity of supply of domestic goods		
Textiles	1.0	authors' estimate
Apparel	1.0 (Canada)	Jenkins, 27
Combined	1.0	authors' estimate
Elasticity of demand for domestic goods		
Textiles	0.34	Bell, 181
Apparel	0.50 (Canada)	Jenkins, 27
Combined	0.4	authors' estimate

Quantitative Profile (continued)

Item	Amount	Source
Cross-elasticity of demand for domestic goods relative to price of imported goods		
Textiles	1.15 to 2.58	Stern, 9
	1.9	authors' estimate
Apparel	1.62 to 4.27	Stern, 9
	2.9	authors' estimate
Combined	1.4	authors' estimate
Cross-elasticity of output of domestic textiles and apparel combined relative to price of imported goods	1.0	authors' estimate
Cross-elasticity of quantity of imported textiles and apparel combined relative to price of domestic goods	10.0	authors' estimate
Cost of restraints to US consumers	$1.3 billion (1973)	Bergsten, 3[c]
	$9.4 billion (1974)	authors' estimate[d]
Gain from restraints to US producers (1974)	$8.7 billion	authors' estimate
Tariff revenue and implied average tariff rate (1976)		
Textiles	$243 million	BC, IM 146
	16.1 percent	BC, IM 146
Apparel	$915 million	BC, IM 146
	28.6 percent	BC, IM 146
Gain from restraints to foreigners (1974)	negligible	authors' estimate
Efficiency loss from larger domestic production to the United States (1974)	$1,100 million	authors' estimate
Welfare cost of restraints to the United States (1974)	$1,100 million	authors' estimate
Employment in protected US industry		
Textiles	1,050,000 (1955)	BLS, 504, 547
	965,000 (1974)	BLS, 504, 547
Apparel	1,087,000 (1955)	BLS, 504, 547
	1,175,000 (1974)	BLS, 504, 547
Induced increase in employment (1974)		
Textiles	120,000	authors' estimate
Apparel	300,000	authors' estimate
Combined	420,000	authors' estimate

Quantitative Profile (continued)

Item	Amount	Source
Cost of restraints to US consumers per job saved (1974)	$22,000	authors' estimate
Gain from restraints to US producers per job (1974)	$4,000	authors' estimate

a. These estimates are based on tariff rates, and assume that quota restrictions on cotton textiles exerted no additional upward pressure on prices because imports of man-made textiles and apparel put a ceiling on domestic prices.

b. These estimates assume that tariff restraints increased the average price of textiles and apparel imports by 20 percent.

c. This figure is based on the cost to consumers of restrictions on apparel imports on woolen and synthetic textiles imposed in 1971. It does not reflect the cost of restrictions on imports of other textiles. (Bergsten, 3)

d. This figure assumes a 20 percent average tariff on consumption of $63.4 billion of affected textiles.

BIBLIOGRAPHY

Bell, Thomas M., Kathryn Kobe, and Sam Evans. 1979. "The Supply and Demand for Textile Fibers with Emphasis on Cotton." *Proceedings: Beltwide Cotton Production Research Conference*. Memphis, Tenn.: National Cotton Council of America, December.

Bergsten, C. Fred. 1973. *The Costs of Import Restrictions to American Consumers*. New York: American Importers Association.

GATT Secretariat. 1984. *Textiles and Clothing in the World Economy*. Text and appendices I–IV. Geneva, July.

Jenkins, Glenn P. 1982. "Cost and Consequences of the New Protectionism: The Case of Canada's Clothing Sector" (revised). Ottawa: North-South Institute, December.

Keesing, Donald B., and Martin Wolf. 1980. *Textile Quotas against Developing Countries*. Thames Essay no. 23. London: Trade Policy Research Centre.

Loewinger, Andrew. 1982. "Textile and Apparel Trade." In *US International Economic Policy 1981: A Draft Report*. Edited by Gary Clyde Hufbauer. Washington: International Law Institute, April.

Morkre, Morris E., and David G. Tarr. 1980. *Effects of Restrictions on United States Imports: Five Case Studies and Theory*. US Federal Trade Commission, Bureau of Economics. Washington, June.

OECD (Organization for Economic Cooperation and Development). 1981. *Structural Problems and Policies Related to the OECD Textile and Clothing Industries*. DSTI/IND/80.36 (3rd draft). Paris, July.

Pelzman, Joseph. 1980. "The Competitiveness of the US Textile Industry." College of Business Administration, University of South Carolina.

———. 1984. "The Multifiber Arrangement and Its Effect on the Profit Performance of the US Textile Industry." In *The Structure and Evolution of Recent US Trade Policy*. Edited by Robert E. Baldwin and Anne O. Krueger. National Bureau of Economic Research Conference Report. Chicago: University of Chicago Press.

Predicasts, Inc. 1974, 1982. *Predicasts' Basebook*. Cleveland, Ohio.

Stern, Robert M. 1984. "Comments on Data, Elasticities, and Other Key Parameters." Seminar Discussion Paper no. 134. Paper read at conference, General Equilibrium Trade Policy Modelling, Columbia University, 5–6 April.

US Department of Commerce. Bureau of the Census. Various years. *US Imports for Consumption*. IM 146. Washington, December.

———. Bureau of Economic Analysis. 1974. *Survey of Current Business*. Washington, July.

———. 1975. *Survey of Current Business*. Washington, March.

———. Bureau of Industrial Economics. Various years. *US Industrial Outlook*. Washington.

US Department of Labor. Bureau of Labor Statistics. 1979. *Employment and Earnings, United States, 1909–78*. Washington, July.

US International Trade Commission. 1978. *The History and Current Status of the MFA*. USITC Publication no. 850. Washington, January.

———. 1981a. *The Multifiber Arrangement, 1973 to 1980*. 2 vols. USITC Publication no. 1131. Washington, March.

———. 1981b. *The Multifiber Arrangement, 1973 to 1980*. USITC Publication no. 1146 (Supp.). Washington, May.

Wolf, Martin. 1983. "Managed Trade in Practice: Implications of the Textile Arrangements." In *Trade Policy in the 1980s*. Edited by William R. Cline. Washington: Institute for International Economics.

CASE M-10

Textiles and Apparel: Phase II

First Arrangement Regarding International Trade in Textiles (also known as the first Multi-Fiber Arrangement or MFA I)

Second Arrangement Regarding International Trade in Textiles (also known as the second Multi-Fiber Arrangement or MFA II)

PERIOD OF RELIEF

MFA I: 1 January 1974 to 31 December 1977
MFA II: 1 January 1978 to 31 December 1981

SUPPLIERS AFFECTED

By November 1980, the United States had negotiated bilateral restraint agreements with some 21 countries, covering all important suppliers of textiles and apparel outside Europe and Canada. (USITC 1131, 11; OECD, 188)

RELIEF ACTION

MFA I was preceded by "voluntary" restraints on Japanese textiles (beginning in 1957), the Short-Term Arrangement Regarding International Trade in Cotton Textiles (STA), and the Long-Term Arrangement Regarding International Trade in Cotton Textiles (LTA). (See Case M-9, Textiles and Apparel: Phase I)

MFA I covered imports of man-made fiber and wool products, in addition to cotton textiles. It carried over the "market disruption" concept, the bilateral agreement powers, and the unilateral quota powers of the LTA. As preconditions of the Trade Act of 1974, Congress insisted on the negotiation of MFA I, and the partial exemption of textiles from tariff cuts. (Keesing and Wolf, 16–17, 71–72)

As a concession to exporters, MFA I provided that bilateral restraint agreements should enable an annual growth of physical imports generally not less than 6 percent, and it provided three types of "flexibility provisions": transferability of quotas (to the extent of 5 percent to 7 percent) among product categories during a particular year, known as "swing"; limited adjustment between years for a particular product, known as "carry forward" (borrowing from next year's quota up to 10 percent); and "carry over" (carrying over a quota to a future year up to 10 percent, less any carry forward). (Das, 98)

On 14 December 1977, the Protocol of 1977 extended MFA I for an additional four years. Together, the protocol and MFA I are known as MFA II. The protocol included a provision that allowed for "reasonable departures" from the framework of MFA I with the mutual agreement of the importing and exporting members. (Das, 96, 98)

In February 1979, under pressure from the US textile industry, which made its support of the multilateral trade negotiations (MTN) contingent on further trade relief, the Carter administration issued a White Paper that ushered in a new wave of restrictions on the negotiation of bilateral textile agreements. The White Paper:

- introduced the concept that import growth should be related to domestic market growth
- introduced the concept that "import surges" could trigger tighter controls
- introduced the practice of renegotiating existing agreements with more restrictive "flexibility provisions"
- promised a "snapback" clause that would restore textile and apparel tariffs to pre-MTN levels if the MFA did not continue in effect.

The Carter White Paper set the tone for MFA III. (See Case M–11, Textiles and Apparel: Phase III; DOC 1979; Loewinger, 8–9; Keesing and Wolf, 71–72)

CHANGES IN THE INDUSTRY

As a result of changes in the structure of protection incorporated in MFA I and MFA II, the composition of imports changed. "From 1971 to 1979, the percentage share of apparel to total textile imports grew from 35 to 58 percent and imports from LDCs [less developed countries] grew from 41 to 70 percent. Moreover, the share of the big three [South Korea, Taiwan, and Hong Kong] grew from 30 percent in 1971 to 42 percent in 1979." (Loewinger, 11)

The textile mill industry retained some degree of international competitiveness in this period. This competitiveness was due, in part, to government cotton dust regulations that forced firms to replace old equipment. Many firms invested in state-of-the-art technology while, at the same time, consolidating into larger firms. The US apparel industry, however, has become steadily less competitive internationally. Import penetration ratios, particularly for products supplied by countries not subject to bilateral agreements, have continued to grow. (Loewinger, 15, 18–19)

Key Statistics

Imports affected[a]

Year	Volume[b] (million pounds)	Source
During LTA		
1972	950	authors' estimate
During MFA I		
1974	758	authors' estimate
1975	776	authors' estimate
1976	1,034	USITC 1471, A5
1977	1,005	USITC 1471, A5
During MFA II		
1978	1,268	USITC 1471, A5
1979	1,128	USITC 1471, A5
1980	1,190	USITC 1471, A5
1981	1,458	USITC 1471, A5

a. These figures reflect imports from up to 23 countries that are subject to bilateral restraints. They have been converted from million equivalent square yards, using the following conversion factors: (1976) 3.87, (1977) 3.78, (1978) 3.55, (1979) 3.37, (1980) 3.36, (1981) 3.36.

b. The figures for 1972–75 are estimated as 80 percent of total imports from all sources.

Imports from all sources

Year	Volume (million pounds)	Value (billion dollars)	Source
During LTA			
1972	1,187	3.2	USITC 1131, v.2, E3; Morkre, 141
During MFA I			
1974	948	3.7	USITC 1131, v.2, E3; Morkre, 141
1975	970	3.7	USITC 1131, v.2, E3; Morkre, 141
1976	1,287	4.9	USITC 1131, v.2, E3; Morkre, 141
1977	1,317	5.4	USITC 1131, v.2, E3; Morici, 15
During MFA II			
1978	1,617	7.1	USITC 1131, v.2, E3; Morici, 15
1979	1,381	7.2	USITC 1131, v.2, E3; Morici, 15
1980	1,455	8.2	USITC 1471, A6; Morici, 15
1981	1,715	9.5	USITC 1471, A6; Morici, 15

Apparent consumption

Year	Volume (million pounds)	Value[a] (billion dollars)	Source
During LTA			
1972	12,335	56.5	USITC 1471, A6; authors' estimate
During MFA I			
1974	11,240	62.5	USITC 1471, A6; authors' estimate
1975	10,826	62.1	USITC 1471, A6; authors' estimate
1976	12,095	71.1	USITC 1471, A6; authors' estimate
1977	12,734	86.8	USITC 1471, A6; authors' estimate
During MFA II			
1978	13,197	93.0	USITC 1471, A6; authors' estimate
1979	13,064	94.7	USITC 1471, A6; authors' estimate
1980	12,026	98.3	USITC 1471, A6; authors' estimate
1981	12,246	107.4	USITC 1471, A6; authors' estimate

a. These figures are derived from the value of imports and domestic output, with an adjustment for exports.

Market share of imports (percentage of apparent consumption, by volume)

Year	Affected imports	Total imports	Source
During LTA			
1972	7.7	9.6	USITC 1471, A6; authors' estimate
During MFA I			
1974	6.7	8.4	USITC 1471, A6; authors' estimate
1975	7.2	9.0	USITC 1471, A6; authors' estimate
1976	8.5	10.6	USITC 1471, A6; authors' estimate
1977	7.9	10.3	USITC 1471, A6; authors' estimate
During MFA II			
1978	9.6	12.3	USITC 1471, A6; authors' estimate
1979	8.6	10.6	USITC 1471, A6; authors' estimate
1980	10.0	12.1	USITC 1471, A6; authors' estimate
1981	11.9	14.0	USITC 1471, A6; authors' estimate

Output of domestic industry

Year	Volume[a] (combined, million pounds)	Value (billion dollars)		Source
		Textiles	Apparel	
During LTA				
1972	11,649	28.0	27.8	USITC 1471, A6; BIE, 44–8, 45–7
During MFA I				
1974	11,102	32.8	30.6	USITC 1471, A6; BIE, 44–8, 45–7
1975	10,553	31.1	31.4	USITC 1471, A6; BIE, 44–8, 45–7
1976	11,617	36.4	34.8	USITC 1471, A6; BIE, 44–8, 45–7
1977	12,167	40.6	40.2	USITC 1471, A6; BIE, 44–8, 45–7
During MFA II				
1978	12,391	42.3	42.7	USITC 1471, A6; BIE, 44–8, 45–7
1979	12,773	45.1	43.0	USITC 1471, A6; BIE, 44–8, 45–7
1980	11,890	47.2	45.8	USITC 1471, A6; BIE, 44–8, 45–7
1981	11,548	50.1	49.8	USITC 1471, A6; BIE, 44–8, 45–7

a. These figures reflect mill consumption of cotton, wool, and man-made fibers.

Employment in domestic industry (thousand production workers)

Year	Textiles	Apparel	Source
During LTA			
1972	985.7	1,208.0	BLS 1979, 504, 546
During MFA I			
1974	965.0	1,174.9	BLS 1979, 504, 546
1975	867.9	1,066.0	BLS 1979, 504, 546
1976	918.8	1,134.3	BLS 1979, 504, 546
1977	910.2	1,316.3	BLS 1983, 153, 165
During MFA II			
1978	899.1	1,332.3	BLS 1983, 153, 165
1979	885.1	1,304.3	BLS 1983, 153, 165
1980	847.7	1,263.5	BLS 1983, 153, 165
1981	823.0	1,244.4	BLS 1983, 153, 165

Wages (dollars per hour)

Year	Textiles	Apparel	Source
During LTA			
1972	2.75	2.53	BIE, 44–8, 45–7
During MFA I			
1974	3.20	2.97	BLS 1979, 506, 548
1975	3.42	3.17	BLS 1979, 506, 548
1976	3.69	3.40	BLS 1979, 506, 548
1977	4.07	3.56	BIE, 44–8, 45–7
During MFA II			
1978	4.41	3.80	BIE, 44–8, 45–7
1979	4.75	3.97	BIE, 44–8, 45–7
1980	5.28	4.25	BIE, 44–8, 45–7
1981	5.58	4.53	BIE, 44–8, 45–7

Industry profits[a] (million dollars)

Year	Textiles	Apparel	Source
During LTA			
1972	1,024	1,077	Predicasts, 205, 229
During MFA I			
1974	995	915	Predicasts, 205, 229
1975	720	1,244	Predicasts, 205, 229
1976	1,440	1,422	Predicasts, 205, 229
1977	1,924	1,818	Predicasts, 205, 229
During MFA II			
1978	1,918	1,634	Predicasts, 205, 229
1979	1,998	1,617	Predicasts, 205, 229
1980	1,408	1,825	BEA 1984
1981	1,300	2,020	BEA 1984

a. Net profits before taxes.

Industry capacity utilization (textiles only, average in December)

Year	Percentage	Source
During LTA		
1972	91	BEA, March
During MFA I		
1974	69	BEA, March
1975	85	BEA, March
1976	84	BEA, March
1977	87	BEA, March

Industry capacity utilization (textiles only, average in December) (continued)

Year	Percentage	Source
During MFA II		
1978	85	BEA, March
1979	82	BEA, March
1980	80	BEA, March
1981	75	BEA, March

Tariff rates (weighted averages, ad valorem equivalent)

Year	Thread and yarn	Fabrics	Made-up articles	Clothing	Source
During VRA					
1962	11.5	24.0	19.0	25.0	GATT, 67–69
During LTA, MFA I, and MFA II					
1973	14.5	16.0	13.5	27.0	GATT, 67–69
Post-Tokyo Round					
1987	9.0	11.5	7.5	22.5	GATT, 67–69

Quantitative Profile

Item	Amount	Source
Number of years restraints in force (MFA I and MFA II only, 1974–81)	7 years	
Induced increase in price of imported goods		
Textiles	19 percent (1979)	authors' estimate[a]
Apparel	35 percent (1979) (Canada)	Jenkins, 47[b]
	46 percent (1981)	Hamilton, 8
	35 percent (1979)	authors' estimate[a]
Combined	27 percent (1979)	authors' estimate[a]
Induced increase in price of domestic goods (1979)		
Textiles	15 percent	authors' estimate
Apparel	28 percent	authors' estimate
Combined	22 percent	authors' estimate
Coefficient of price response (textiles and apparel combined)	0.8	authors' estimate
Quantity and value of imports (1981)	1.72 billion pounds	USITC 1471, A5
	$9.5 billion	authors' estimate

Quantitative Profile (continued)

Item	Amount	Source
Induced decrease in imports due to restraints	0.71 billion pounds (1977)	Morkre, 154[c]
	3.0 billion pounds (1981)	authors' estimate
	$15.0 billion (1981)	authors' estimate
Quantity and value of domestic production (1981)	11.55 billion pounds	USITC 1471, A6
	$99.9 billion	BIE, 44–8, 45–7
Induced increase in domestic production due to restraints	0.71 billion pounds (1977)	Morkre, 154[c]
	3.0 billion pounds (1981)	authors' estimate
Coefficient of quantity response (textiles and apparel combined)	1.0	authors' estimate
Elasticity of demand for imports		
Textiles	1.14 to 1.41	Stern, 9
	1.10 to 1.30	Morkre, 152
	1.2	authors' estimate
Apparel	0.52 to 3.92	Stern, 9
	3.77	Morkre, 152
	2.0	authors' estimate
Combined	1.6	authors' estimate
Elasticity of supply of domestic goods		
Textiles	1.0	authors' estimate
Apparel	1.0 (Canada)	Jenkins, 27
Combined	1.0	authors' estimate
Elasticity of demand for domestic goods		
Textiles	0.34	Bell, 181
Apparel	0.50 (Canada)	Jenkins, 27
Combined	0.4	authors' estimate
Cross-elasticity of demand for domestic goods relative to price of imported goods		
Textiles	1.15 to 2.59	Stern, 9
	1.9	authors' estimate
Apparel	1.62 to 4.27	Stern, 9
	2.9	authors' estimate
Combined	1.4	authors' estimate
Cross-elasticity of output of domestic textiles and apparel combined relative to price of imported goods	1.0	authors' estimate
Cross-elasticity of quantity of imported textiles and apparel combined relative to price of domestic goods	7.0	authors' estimate

Quantitative Profile (continued)

Item	Amount	Source
Cost of restraints to US consumers		
Textiles	$6 billion (1981)	authors' estimate
Apparel	$14 billion (1981)	authors' estimate
Combined	$18.4 billion (1980)	Consumers
	$20 billion (1981)	authors' estimate
Gain from restraints to US producers (1981)		
Textiles	$5.4 billion	authors' estimate
Apparel	$12.6 billion	authors' estimate
Combined	$18 billion	authors' estimate
Tariff revenue and implied average tariff rate (1981)		
Textiles	$388 million	BC, IM 146
	14.8 percent	authors' estimate
Apparel	$1,755 million	BC, IM 146
	26.3 percent	authors' estimate
Combined	23.0 percent	authors' estimate
Gain from restraints to foreigners (1981)	$350 million	authors' estimate
Efficiency loss from larger domestic production to the United Sates (1981)	$3,100 million	authors' estimate
Welfare cost of restraints to the United States (1981)	$3,450 million	authors' estimate
Employment in protected US industry		
Textiles	985,700 (1972)	BLS 1979, 504
	823,000 (1981)	BLS 1983, 153
Apparel	1,208,000 (1972)	BLS 1979, 546
	1,244,400 (1981)	BLS 1983, 165
Induced increase in employment (1981)		
Textiles	150,000	authors' estimate
Apparel	390,000	authors' estimate
Combined	540,000	authors' estimate
Cost of restraints to US consumers per job saved		
Textiles	$40,000 (1981)	authors' estimate
Apparel	$36,000 (1981)	authors' estimate
Combined	$81,000 (1978)	Council, 70
	$37,000 (1981)	authors' estimate

Quantitative Profile (continued)

Item	Amount	Source
Gain from restraints to producers per job (1981)		
Textiles	$6,600	authors' estimate
Apparel	$10,100	authors' estimate
Combined	$8,700	authors' estimate

a. These figures include the effect of existing tariffs (14.8 percent for textiles, 26.3 percent for apparel, 21 percent combined) and the additional scarcity premium created by quotas (4.2 percent for textiles, 8.7 percent for apparel, 6 percent combined).

b. This figure reflects the average effect of total protection to net landed cost for 16 apparel items, assuming that quota protection added 4 to 5 percent to tariff protection.

c. This figure is based on an estimate of $5.4 billion imports.

BIBLIOGRAPHY

Bell, Thomas M., Kathryn Kobe, and Sam Evans. 1979. "The Supply and Demand for Textile Fibers with Emphasis on Cotton." *Proceedings: Beltwide Cotton Production Research Conference.* Memphis, Tenn.: National Cotton Council of America, December.

Cabinet Committee on Price Stability. 1968. "International Trade." Washington.

Consumers for World Trade. 1984. "How Much Do Consumers Pay for US Trade Barriers?" CWT Information Paper. Washington, Winter.

Council on Wage and Price Stability. Executive Office of the President. 1978. "Textiles/Apparel: A Study of the Textile and Apparel Industries." Washington.

Das, Bhagirath L. 1983. "The GATT Multi-Fibre Arrangement." *Journal of World Trade Law* 17, no. 2 (March–April): 5.

GATT Secretariat. 1984. "Textiles and Clothing in the World Economy." Text and appendices I–IV. Geneva, July.

Hamilton, Carl. 1984. "Voluntary Export Restraints on Asia: Tariff Equivalents, Rents and Trade Barrier Formation." Seminar Paper 276. Institute for International Economic Studies, University of Stockholm, April.

Jenkins, Glenn P. 1982. "Cost and Consequences of the New Protectionism: The Case of Canada's Clothing Sector" (revised). Ottawa. North–South Institute, December.

Keesing, Donald B., and Martin Wolf. 1980. *Textile Quotas against Developing Countries.* Thames Essay no. 23. London: Trade Policy Research Centre.

Loewinger, Andrew. 1982. "Textile and Apparel Trade." In *US International Economic Policy 1981: A Draft Report.* Edited by Gary Clyde Hufbauer. Washington: International Law Institute, April.

Morici, Peter, and Laura L. Megna. 1983. *US Economic Policies Affecting Industrial Trade: A Quantitative Assessment.* Report no. 200. Washington: National Planning Association.

Morkre, Morris E., and David G. Tarr. 1980. *Effects of Restrictions on United States Imports: Five Case Studies and Theory.* US Federal Trade Commission, Bureau of Economics. Washington, June.

OECD (Organization for Economic Cooperation and Development). 1981. *Structural Problems and Policies Related to the OECD Textile and Clothing Industries.* DSTI/IND/80.36 (3rd draft). Paris, July.

Pelzman, Joseph. 1980. "The Competitiveness of the US Textile Industry." College of Business Administration, University of South Carolina.

———. 1984. "The Multifiber Arrangement and Its Effect on the Profit Performance of the US Textile Industry." In *The Structure and Evolution of Recent US Trade Policy*. Edited by Robert E. Baldwin and Anne O. Krueger. National Bureau of Economic Research Conference Report. Chicago: University of Chicago Press.

Predicasts, Inc. 1982. *Predicasts' Basebook*. Cleveland, Ohio.

Stern, Robert M. 1984. "Comments on Data, Elasticities, and Other Key Parameters." Seminar Discussion Paper no. 134. Paper read at conference, General Equilibrium Trade Policy Modelling, Columbia University, 5–6 April.

US Department of Commerce. 1979. "Administration Textile Program" (Carter White Paper). News release. Washington, 15 February.

———. Bureau of the Census. Various years. *US Imports for Consumption*. IM 146. Washington, December.

———. Bureau of Economic Analysis. Various years. *Survey of Current Business*. Washington, March.

———. 1984. *Survey of Current Business*. Washington, July.

———. Bureau of Industrial Economics. 1985. *US Industrial Outlook*. Washington.

US Department of Labor. Bureau of Labor Statistics. 1979. *Employment and Earnings, United States, 1909–1978*. Washington, July.

———. 1983. *Supplement to Employment and Earnings*. Washington, July.

US International Trade Commission. 1978. *The History and Current Status of the Multifiber Arrangement*. USITC Publication no. 850. Washington, January.

———. 1981. *The Multifiber Arrangement 1973 to 1980*. USITC Publication no. 1131. 2 vols. Washington, March.

———. 1983. *US Imports of Textile and Apparel Products under the Multifiber Arrangement, 1976–1982, and January–June 1983*. USITC Publication no. 1471. Washington, December.

Wolf, Martin, Hans Hinrich Glismann, Joseph Pelzman, and Dean Spinanger. 1984. *Costs of Protecting Jobs in Textiles and Clothing*. Thames Essay no. 37. London: Trade Policy Research Centre.

CASE M-11

Textiles and Apparel: Phase III

Third Arrangement Regarding International Trade in Textiles
(also known as the third Multi-Fiber Arrangement or MFA III)

PERIOD OF RELIEF

1 January 1982 to 31 July 1986

SUPPLIERS AFFECTED

By 1985, the United States had negotiated bilateral restraint agreements with 31 countries, entailing some 650 separate quotas, covering all important suppliers of textiles and apparel outside of Europe and Canada. (USITC 1539, foreword; Lenahan, 8)

RELIEF ACTION

MFA III was preceded by "voluntary" restraints on Japanese textiles (beginning in 1957), the Short-Term Arrangement (STA), the Long-Term Arrangement (LTA), the first Multi-Fiber Arrangement (MFA I), and the second Multi-Fiber Arrangement (MFA II). (See Cases M-9 and M-10, Textiles and Apparel: Phase I and Phase II)

On 22 December 1981, at the urging of the European Community (EC), and with the acquiescence of President Ronald Reagan, the Protocol of 1981 was negotiated. This protocol, together with MFA I, is known as MFA III. MFA III incorporated several restrictive approaches built into the earlier Carter White Paper on textile trade:

☐ The normal minimum import growth rate of 6 percent (in volume terms) may be abandoned for: "dominant suppliers" (e.g., Hong Kong, Taiwan, Korea, Macao) of all three fibers and cases of "market disruption" (e.g., when importing countries face a threat to their "minimum viable production").

☐ "Anti-surge" clauses can be used to preclude full utilization of previously unused quotas, with compensation to be paid on other products.

☐ "Market disruption" is redefined to refer to the overall growth of the market for the product in the importing country, and thus takes into account any decline in growth resulting from shifting patterns of demand.

The net result of these three changes is that the import growth rate both from the major suppliers and in sensitive categories will often be limited to the market growth rate. The US-Hong Kong bilateral agreement, for example, limits export growth from 1982 to 1987 to 0.5 percent to 1.5 percent per year, for 26 restricted categories covering 60 percent of Hong Kong textile exports to the United States. (Das, 96)

Imports of textiles and apparel continued to increase rapidly in 1983 and 1984. The failure of the quotas to slow import growth has three major explanations: the soaring value of the dollar in exchange markets; increases in shipments (due to the dollar overvaluation) from countries outside the MFA, Italy being one of the most prominent; and transshipments of semifinished apparel from countries with filled quotas to countries with unfilled quotas where the pieces were then assembled and exported to the United States under the unfilled quota. (*Journal of Commerce*, 14 February 1985, 1A)

To address these problems, the Reagan administration tightened the regulations governing textile imports. In December 1983, the United States set specific percentages of import growth that would indicate "market disruption" and hence trigger a "call," namely the extension of quotas to a previously unrestricted category of textile or apparel products. The soaring value of the dollar, however, caused imports to continue to increase at an unprecedented rate, prompting President Reagan to issue a proclamation on 9 May 1984 calling for more stringent regulations. (*Wall Street Journal*, 8 August 1984, 1)

On 1 August 1984, US Customs Commissioner William von Raab announced that the regulations governing the determination of the country of origin would be tightened beginning 9 September 1984. The new rules defined the country of origin as the country where the cloth was cut rather than where it was sewn, the previous definition. Importers and retailers vigorously criticized the new rules, claiming they would disrupt the "vital Christmas buying season." To avoid such disruption, US Treasury Secretary Donald Regan announced on 23 August 1984 a delay in the effective date of interim regulations until 31 October 1984 for goods ordered before 3 August 1984 and shipped before the end of October. Following analysis of public comments received while the interim regulations were in effect, the final regulations were published in the Federal Register in March and became effective 4 April 1985. (*Journal of Commerce*, 27 August 1984, 1A; USITC 1693, 16)

In early February 1985, 10 developing countries formed the International Textile and Clothing Bureau in Geneva. The bureau seeks to keep the MFA from being renewed beyond its expiration date in July 1986. (*Journal of Commerce*, 15 February 1985, 1A)

On 8 March 1985, William A. Andres, chairman of the Retail Industry Trade Action Coalition (RITAC), called for a "consumer impact test" to be applied "before erecting new trade barriers." He estimated that quotas cost consumers $4.4 billion annually, and that every worker in the textile and apparel industries could be provided with $15,000 in adjustment assistance in place of quota protection. (Retail)

On 19 March 1985, Congressman Ed Jenkins (D-Ga.) and Senator Strom Thurmond (R-SC) introduced the Textile and Apparel Trade Enforcement Act of 1985 in the House and Senate, respectively. If it had been adopted unchanged, the bill would have rolled back sharply imports from major suppliers, including Taiwan, South Korea, Hong Kong, China, and Japan, and would have restricted future growth to 1 percent a year. Smaller exporters (those providing less than 1.5 percent of US imports annually) would be allowed 6 percent annual growth in their quotas. Under the bill, Europe and Canada would continue to be exempt from the restrictions. In addition to setting new quotas on wool, cotton, and man-made fiber products, the bill would extend quotas to silk, linen, and ramie, fibers not previously covered by the MFA. (*Journal of Commerce*, 20 March 1985, 1A; 11 July 1985, 1A)

Hong Kong's congressional lobbyist, Victor French, predicted that implementation of the House bill would raise retail apparel prices by 25 percent to 30 percent within a year. RITAC predicted price increases of 16 percent and 33 percent on apparel and textiles respectively. Donald V. Siebert, co-chair of RITAC, further predicted that more jobs would be lost in the retail sector than would be saved in apparel manufacturing. Industry and labor representatives disagreed, claiming that up to 1 million jobs could be lost if the current annual growth rate of imports continues. Testifying against the original version of the bill before the Senate Subcommittee on International Trade, Secretary of Commerce Malcolm Baldridge noted that the Council of Economic Advisers, based on estimates by the Commerce Department that the Jenkins bill would reduce imports from some countries by 30 percent to 40 percent, had predicted that the Jenkins bill could raise prices by an average 10 percent and cost consumers $14 billion annually, nearly $140,000 per job saved. (*Journal of Commerce*, 30 May 1985, 15A; 3 June 1985, 5A; 11 July 1985, 1A; Baldridge)

As of early July, the so-called Jenkins bill had 285 cosponsors in the House and 53 in the Senate. It passed in the House on 9 October by a vote of 262 to 159, not enough to override a presidential veto, and several votes less than the bill had cosponsors. (*Journal of Commerce*, 11 July 1985, 1A; *Washington Post*, 20 September 1985, E1; 27 September 1985, E1; 10 October 1985, E1)

On 25 September, Thurmond introduced into the Senate a revised version of the bill that he hoped would avoid a presidential veto. The less restrictive bill redefines major exporters as those that provide more than 10 percent of US imports and thus reduces the number of "major exporting nations" from 12 to 3—Taiwan, Hong Kong, and Korea. "This saves two key countries from the worst effects of the bill: China, which has threatened to retaliate[1] and with whom the Reagan administration is trying to build better relations, and Brazil, the world's largest debtor nation." (*Washington Post*, 27 September 1985, E1)

Under the Thurmond version, quotas for the top three exporters would be rolled back to a level that would have existed if imports from those countries had increased at just the 6 percent per year provided by the MFA, from 1980 through 1984. The 1984 level would then become the base and subsequent growth would be limited to 1 percent a year. Intermediate suppliers, those providing between 1.5 percent and 10 percent of US annual imports, would not be rolled back but would have their 1985 quotas frozen at the 1984 level and would be permitted only 1 percent growth thereafter. Smaller exporters would be allowed 6 percent annual growth as under the

---

1. China did, in fact, retaliate in 1983 when the United States restricted the import of Chinese textiles and apparel during the negotiation of their bilateral agreement under the MFA. China responded at that time by suspending the purchase of American agricultural products valued at $550 million.

Jenkins version. The bill also would use quotas to restrict shoe imports to 60 percent of the US market for the next eight years. (*Congressional Quarterly Weekly Report,* 7 September 1985, 1755; 5 October 1985, 2017; *Washington Post,* 14 November 1985, E1)

In order to avoid a threatened filibuster, Thurmond and co-sponsor Senator Ernest F. Hollings (D-SC) attached the measure to the budget reconciliation bill on 24 October 1985. The bill survived a procedural vote 54 to 42, but was withdrawn from the floor by Majority Leader Robert J. Dole (R-Kan.) when passage of the budget reconciliation was threatened by a flood of other amendments, sparked by the addition of the textile bill. The textile provision was later separated from the budget reconciliation and was passed by the Senate, after copper had been added to attract additional votes, 60 to 39 on 13 November. The House passed the bill on 3 December but, as expected, the President vetoed it on 17 December 1985. Congressman Jenkins announced that he would call for an override vote in August 1986 if the President's negotiators did not achieve sufficient tightening of restraints in discussions to renew the MFA. (*Washington Post,* 25 October 1985, A7; 14 November 1985, E1; 18 December 1985, A1; 19 December 1985, G1; *New York Times,* 4 December 1985, D5)

CHANGES IN THE INDUSTRY

The apparel industry—with financial assistance from the Department of Commerce, the textile industry, and the Amalgamated Clothing and Textile Workers' Union—is attempting to match international competition with automation. These four entities have contributed $2 million over the past three years to research and development in robotics. The result has been a "complex computerized service system that can fold and sew pieces of limp fabric to make sleeves, the back of suit coats and vests, with a speed and precision that few human clothing workers can manage...." Organized labor has supported the new system in hopes that more efficient domestic production will stem the tide of imports, and thereby make up for jobs lost through automation. If continued financing is available, the invention will go into production in 1986. (*Washington Post,* 13 May 1984, G1)

In addition to developing and making better use of advanced technology, "experts say that textile and apparel producers must begin planning now to: diversify their companies to achieve growth in areas where foreign competitors aren't strong; develop more specialized product lines and market segments; consolidate through mergers; and develop stronger markets for exports.... There are few indications, however, that the industry is ready to implement comprehensive long-range planning and marketing strategies that would make it more competitive. It is a very scattered industry, dominated by small, family-owned companies, making it difficult to amass the capital for major technology research or to obtain the clout to enlist the retail industry in its cause." (*Washington Post,* 15 October 1985, D2)

Key Statistics

Imports affected

Year	Volume[a] (million pounds)		Value[b] (million dollars)		Source
	Textiles	Apparel	Textiles	Apparel	
During MFA II					
1980	432	811	1,684	4,586	ITA; authors' estimate
1981	590	891	2,069	5,425	ITA; authors' estimate
During MFA III					
1982	548	849	1,894	6,058	ITA
1983	755	957	2,165	6,879	ITA
1984	1,075	1,150	3,075	8,396	ITA

a. These figures have been converted from million equivalent square yards by using the following conversion factors: (1980) 3.36, (1981) 3.36, (1982) 3.48, (1983) 3.51, (1984) 3.27.
b. The 1980–81 estimates assume that the proportion of affected imports to total imports of textiles and apparel, respectively, were the same in 1980–81 as in 1982–83.

Imports from all sources

Year	Volume[a] (million pounds)		Value (million dollars)		Source
	Textiles	Apparel	Textiles	Apparel	
During MFA II					
1980	595	858	2,440	5,732	ITA; BC, IM 146
1981	785	933	2,999	6,781	ITA; BC, IM 146
During MFA III					
1982	734	972	2,738	7,448	ITA; BC, IM 146
1983	1,008	1,109	3,186	8,720	ITA; BC, IM 146
1984	1,548	1,444	4,400	12,098	ITA; BC, IM 146

a. These figures have been converted from million equivalent square yards by using the following conversion factors: (1980) 3.36; (1981) 3.36; (1982) 3.48; (1983) 3.51; (1984) 3.27.

Apparent consumption

Year	Volume (combined, million pounds)	Value[a] (billion dollars)		Source
		Textiles	Apparel	
During MFA II				
1980	12,026	49.8	51.5	USITC 1539, A6; authors' estimate
1981	12,246	53.3	56.6	USITC 1539, A6; authors' estimate

Apparent consumption (continued)

Year	Volume (combined, million pounds)	Value[a] (billion dollars) Textiles	Apparel	Source
During MFA III				
1982	11,103	50.5	60.8	USITC 1539, A6; authors' estimate
1983	13,555	57.1	64.1	USITC 1539, A6; authors' estimate
1984	14,636[b]	62.2	69.4	USITC 1635, A6; authors' estimate

a. These figures are derived from the value of imports from all sources plus the value of domestic output.
b. This figure is extrapolated from data for the first six months of 1984.

Market share of imports (percentage of apparent consumption, by volume)

Year	Affected imports	Total imports	Source
During MFA II			
1980	10.3	12.1	authors' estimate
1981	12.1	14.0	authors' estimate
During MFA III			
1982	12.6	15.4	authors' estimate
1983	12.6	15.6	authors' estimate
1984	15.2	20.4	authors' estimate

Output of domestic industry

Year	Volume (combined, million pounds)	Value (billion dollars) Textiles	Apparel	Source
During MFA II				
1980	11,890	47.4	45.8	USITC 1539, A6; BIE 1983, 39–2, 40–6
1981	11,548	50.3	49.8	USITC 1539, A6; BIE 1984, 40–1, 41–10
During MFA III				
1982	10,100	47.8	53.4	USITC 1539, A6; BIE 1985, 44–1, 45–1
1983	12,000	53.9	55.4	USITC 1539, A6; BIE 1985, 44–1, 45–1
1984[a]	12,328	57.8	57.3	USITC 1635, A6; BIE 1985, 44–1, 45–1

a. Preliminary estimates.

Employment in domestic industry (thousand production workers)

Year	Textiles	Apparel	Source
During MFA II			
1980	848	1,264	BLS 1983, 153, 165
1981	823	1,244	BLS 1983, 153, 165
During MFA III			
1982	750	1,161	BLS 1983, 153, 165
1983	743	1,164	BLS 1984, 174, 188
1984[a]	765	1,215	authors' estimate

a. Derived from preliminary data. (BEA)

Wages (dollars per hour)

Year	Textiles	Apparel	Source
During MFA II			
1980	5.07	4.56	BLS 1984, 174, 188
1981	5.52	4.97	BLS 1984, 174, 188
During MFA III			
1982	5.83	5.20	BLS 1984, 174, 188
1983	6.18	5.37	BLS 1984, 174, 188
1984	6.41	5.48	authors' estimate

Industry profits[a] (million dollars)

Year	Profits[b]	Source
During MFA II		
1980	1,866	FTC
1981	1,988	FTC
During MFA III		
1982	1,447	FTC
1983	2,697	FTC
1984	2,113[c]	FTC

a. Textiles only.

b. Net profits before taxes.

c. This figure reflects industry profits for the first three quarters of 1984.

Industry capacity utilization (textiles only, average in December)

Year	Percentage	Source
During MFA II		
1980	80	BEA
1981	75	BEA
During MFA III		
1982	74	BEA
1983	86	BEA
1984	n.a.	

n.a. Not available.

Tariff rates (percent, weighted averages)

Year	Thread and yarn	Fabrics	Made-up articles	Clothing	Source
During VRA					
1962	11.5	24.0	19.0	25.0	GATT, 67–69
During LTA, MFA I, and MFA II					
1973	14.5	16.0	13.5	27.0	GATT, 67–69
Post-Tokyo Round					
1987	9.0	11.5	7.5	22.5	GATT, 67–69

Quantitative Profile

Item	Amount	Source
Number of years restraints in force (MFA III, 1982–86)	4 years	
Induced increase in price of imported goods (1983)		
Textiles	21 percent	authors' estimate[a]
Apparel	39 percent	authors' estimate[a]
	50 percent	Hamilton 1985a, 21[a]
	46 to 76 percent	Hickok, 6[a]
Combined	30 percent	authors' estimate
Induced increase in price of domestic goods		
Textiles	17 percent (1983)	authors' estimate
Apparel	46 percent (1981)	Hamilton 1984, 8
	31 percent (1983)	authors' estimate
Combined	24 percent (1983)	authors' estimate
Coefficient of price response	0.8	authors' estimate

Quantitative Profile (continued)

Item	Amount	Source
Quantity and value of imports (1984)		
Textiles	1,548 million pounds	ITA
	$4,400 million	BC, IM 146
Apparel	1,444 million pounds	ITA
	$12,098 million	BC, IM 146
Combined	$16,498 million	BC, IM 146
Induced decrease in imports due to restraints (1984)		
Textiles	500 million pounds	authors' estimate
	$1.3 billion	authors' estimate
Apparel	3,500 million pounds	authors' estimate
	$26.6 billion	authors' estimate
Combined	$27.9 billion	authors' estimate
Quantity and value of domestic production (1984)	12.3 billion pounds	USITC 1635, A6
	$115.1 billion	BIE 1985, 44–1, 45–1
Induced increase in domestic production due to restraints (1984)		
Textiles	500 million pounds	authors' estimate
Apparel	3,500 million pounds	authors' estimate
Combined	4,000 million pounds	authors' estimate
Coefficient of quantity response		
Textiles	1.0	authors' estimate
Apparel	1.0	authors' estimate
Combined	1.0	authors' estimate
Elasticity of demand for imports		
Textiles	1.14 to 1.41	Stern, 9
	1.10 to 1.30	Morkre, 152
	1.2	authors' estimate
Apparel	0.52 to 3.92	Stern, 9
	3.77	Morkre, 152
	2.0	authors' estimate
Combined	1.8	authors' estimate
Elasticity of supply of domestic goods		
Textiles	1.0	authors' estimate
Apparel	1.0 (Canada)	Jenkins, 27
Combined	1.0	authors' estimate
Elasticity of demand for domestic goods		
Textiles	0.34	Bell, 181
Apparel	0.50 (Canada)	Jenkins, 27
Combined	0.4	authors' estimate

Quantitative Profile (continued)

Item	Amount	Source
Cross-elasticity of demand for domestic goods relative to price of imported goods		
Textiles	1.15 to 2.58	Stern, 9
	1.9	authors' estimate
Apparel	1.62 to 4.27	Stern, 9
	2.9	authors' estimate
Combined	1.4	authors' estimate
Cross-elasticity of output of domestic textiles and apparel combined relative to price of imported goods	1.4	authors' estimate
Cross-elasticity of quantity of imported textiles and apparel combined relative to price of domestic goods	1.0	authors' estimate
Cost of restraints to US consumers (1984)		
Textiles	$9 billion	authors' estimate
Apparel	$8.5 to $12.0 billion	Hickok, 18–19
	$18 billion	authors' estimate
Combined	$23 billion	Retail[b]
	$27 billion	authors' estimate
Gain from restraints to US producers (1984)		
Textiles	$8.4 billion	authors' estimate
Apparel	$13.6 billion	authors' estimate
Combined	$22.0 billion	authors' estimate
Tariff revenue and implied average tariff rate (1983)		
Textiles	$400 million	BC, IM 146
	13.9 percent	authors' estimate
Apparel	$2,135 million	BC, IM 146
	24.7 percent	authors' estimate
Combined	22 percent	authors' estimate
Gain from restraints to foreigners		
Textiles	$300 million (1984)	authors' estimate
Apparel	$219 million (1981)	Hamilton 1984, 8
	$1,500 million (1984)	authors' estimate
Combined	$1,800 million (1984)	authors' estimate
Efficiency loss of larger domestic production to the United States (1984)		
Textiles	$350 million	authors' estimate
Apparel	$4,500 million	authors' estimate
Combined	$4,850 million	authors' estimate

Quantitative Profile (continued)

Item	Amount	Source
Welfare cost of restraints to the United States (1984)		
Textiles	$650 million	authors' estimate
Apparel	$6,000 million	authors' estimate
Combined	$6,650 million	authors' estimate
Employment in protected US industry		
Textiles	848,000 (1980)	BLS 1983, 153
	765,000 (1984)	authors' estimate
Apparel	1,264,000 (1980)	BLS 1983, 165
	1,215,000 (1984)	authors' estimate
Induced increase in employment (1984)		
Textiles	180,000	authors' estimate
Apparel	460,000	authors' estimate
Combined	640,000	authors' estimate
Cost of restraints to US consumers per job saved (1984)		
Textiles	$50,000	authors' estimate
Apparel	$39,000	authors' estimate
Combined	$42,000	authors' estimate
Gain from restraints to US producers per job (1984)		
Textiles	$11,000	authors' estimate
Apparel	$11,200	authors' estimate
Combined	$11,100	authors' estimate

a. Authors' figures assume that MFA III added 2 percent to total protection of textiles by comparison with MFA II, and that MFA III added 4 percent to total protection of apparel. For textiles, tariff protection is estimated to be 13.9 percent and quota protection 7.1 percent; for apparel, tariff protection is estimated to be 24.7 percent and quota protection 14.3 percent. Carl Hamilton has estimated that apparel imports from Hong Kong are 23 percent more expensive due to tariffs and 27 percent more expensive due to quotas. Susan Hickok uses a USITC estimate of 26 percent for the tariff on clothing and adds an estimate of 20 percent to 50 percent for the tariff equivalent of the quotas. Taking quality upgrading into account, Hickok concludes that imported clothing prices are 108 percent higher because of import restraints. She assumes no effect on domestic producer prices and, thus, comes up with an estimated 17 percent to 25 percent overall price increase.

b. The Retail Industry Trade Action Coalition estimates the cost of quotas to US consumers to be $4.4 billion and the cost of tariffs, $19 billion.

Hypothetical Adjustment Program

	1984	1985	1986	1987	1988	1989	1990
US purchases of textiles and apparel combined (billion pounds)							
Assumed annual consumption growth of 2 percent	14.64	14.93	15.23	15.54	15.85	16.16	16.49
Imports from all sources							
Assumed annual consumption growth of 2 percent and no change in import restraints (billion pounds)	2.99	3.05	3.11	3.17	3.24	3.30	3.37
Assumed annual consumption growth of 2 percent and quotas rising at 0.20 billion pounds per year (billion pounds)	2.99	3.25	3.51	3.77	4.04	4.30	4.57
Import share of consumption with rising quotas (percentage)	20.4	21.8	23.0	24.3	25.5	26.6	27.7
Hypothetical quota auction and existing tariffs							
Quota auction							
Rate (percent)	—	6.4	3.4	0.4	—	—	—
Revenue (million 1984 dollars)	—	1,150	660	80	—	—	—
Tariff							
Rate (percent)	21.7	21.7	21.7	21.7	18.1	15.1	12.1
Revenue (million 1984 dollars)	3,580	3,890	4,200	4,510	4,030	3,580	3,050
Total							
Rate (percent)	21.7	28.1	25.1	22.1	18.1	15.1	12.1
Revenue (million 1984 dollars)	3,580	5,040	4,860	4,590	4,030	3,580	3,050
US production for the domestic market[a] (billion pounds)							
Assumed annual consumption growth of 2 percent and constant import share	11.65	11.88	12.12	12.37	12.61	12.86	13.12
Assumed annual consumption growth of 2 percent and rising import share	11.65	11.68	11.72	11.77	11.81	11.86	11.92

Hypothetical Adjustment Program (continued)

	1984	1985	1986	1987	1988	1989	1990
US employment in textile and apparel industry combined (thousand workers)							
Assumed 3 percent annual productivity growth and constant import share	1,980	1,960	1,942	1,924	1,904	1,885	1,867
Assumed 3 percent annual productivity growth and rising import share	1,980	1,927	1,878	1,831	1,783	1,738	1,696
Year-to-year employment changes (thousand workers)							
Changes induced by consumption and productivity growth with constant import share	—	−20	−18	−18	−20	−19	−18
Changes induced by rising import share	—	−33	−31	−29	−28	−26	−24
Total employment changes	—	−53	−49	−47	−48	−45	−42
Benefit and budget calculations for textiles and apparel combined (1984 prices)							
Annual wage cost per worker assuming constant $7 per hour and 2,500 hours (dollars)	17,500	17,500	17,500	17,500	17,500	17,500	17,500
Benefits calculated at two times annual wage cost per worker (million dollars)	—	1,855	1,715	1,645	1,680	1,575	1,470
Projected program surplus or deficit: tariff revenue less benefits (million dollars)	—	3,185	3,145	2,945	2,350	2,005	1,580

— Not applicable.

a. These figures reflect calculated US purchases less imports.

BIBLIOGRAPHY

Balassa, Carol. 1984. "Levels of Protection on Manufactured Goods: The US, EC, Canada, Japan." Office of the US Trade Representative. Washington.

Baldridge, Malcolm (Secretary of Commerce). 1985. Statement before the Senate Committee on Finance, Subcommittee on International Trade. Washington, 15 July.

Bell, Thomas M., Kathryn Kobe, and Sam Evans. 1979. "The Supply and Demand for Textile Fibers with Emphasis on Cotton." *Proceedings: Beltwide Cotton Production Research Conference.* Memphis, Tenn.: National Cotton Council of America, December.

Choi, Ying-Pik, Hwa Soo Chung, and Nicolas Marian. 1985. *The Multi-Fibre Arrangement in Theory and Practice.* London: Frances Pinter.

Das, Bhagirath. 1983. "The Gatt Multi-Fibre Arrangement." *Journal of World Trade Law* 17, no. 2 (March–April): 5.

GATT Secretariat. 1984. "Textiles and Clothing in the World Economy." Text and appendices I–IV. Geneva, July.

Hamilton, Carl. 1984. "Voluntary Export Restraints on Asia: Tariff Equivalents, Rents and Trade Barrier Formation." Seminar Paper 276. Institute for International Economic Studies, University of Stockholm, April.

———. 1985a. "An Assessment of Voluntary Restraints on Hong Kong Exports to Europe and the USA." Institute for International Economic Studies, University of Stockholm.

———. 1985b. "Temporarily Higher Tariffs or a New Multifibre Arrangement." Institute for International Economic Studies, University of Stockholm.

Hickok, Susan. 1985. "The Consumer Cost of US Trade Restraints." *Federal Reserve Bank of New York: Quarterly Review* 10, no. 2 (Summer): 1–12.

Jenkins, Glenn P. 1982. "Cost and Consequences of the New Protectionism: The Case of Canada's Clothing Sector" (revised). Ottawa: North-South Institute, December.

Keesing, Donald B., and Martin Wolf. 1980. *Textile Quotas against Developing Countries.* Thames Essay no. 23. London: Trade Policy Research Centre.

Lenahan, Walter C. (Deputy Assistant Secretary of Commerce for Textiles and Apparel). 1985. Statement before the House Ways and Means Committee, Subcommittee on Trade. Washington, 3 April.

Loewinger, Andrew. 1982. "Textile and Apparel Trade." In *US International Economic Policy 1981: A Draft Report.* Edited by Gary Clyde Hufbauer. Washington: International Law Institute, April.

Morkre, Morris E., and David G. Tarr. 1980. *Effects of Restrictions on United States Imports: Five Case Studies and Theory.* US Federal Trade Commission, Bureau of Economics. Washington, June.

Mutti, Jack (Council of Economic Advisers). 1985. By communication, October.

OECD (Organization for Economic Cooperation and Development). 1981. *Structural Problems and Policies Relating to the OECD Textile and Clothing Industries.* DSTI/IND/80.36 (3rd draft). Paris, July.

Retail Industry Trade Action Coalition. 1985. "Retail Group Calls for Consumer Impact Test on Trade Barriers." Press release. Washington, 8 March.

Stern, Robert M. 1984. "Comments on Data, Elasticities, and Other Key Parameters." Seminar Discussion Paper no. 134. Paper read at conference, General Equilibrium Trade Policy Modelling, Columbia University, 5–6 April.

US Department of Commerce. Bureau of the Census. Various years. *US Imports for Consumption.* IM 146. Washington, December.

———. Bureau of Economic Analysis. Various years. *Survey of Current Business*. Washington, March.

———. Bureau of Industrial Economics. Various years. *US Industrial Outlook*. Washington.

———. International Trade Administration, Office of Textiles and Apparel. Various years. *Major Shippers of Cotton, Wool, and Man-Made Fiber Textiles and Apparel*. Washington.

US Department of Labor. Bureau of Labor Statistics. 1983, 1984. *Supplement to Employment and Earnings*. Washington, July.

US Federal Trade Commission. Various years. *Quarterly Financial Report*. Washington, December.

US General Accounting Office. 1983. *Implementation of Trade Restrictions for Textiles and Apparel*. Washington, November.

US International Trade Commission. 1984. *US Imports of Textiles and Apparel under the Multifiber Arrangement, 1976–1983*. USITC Publication no. 1539. Washington, June.

———. 1985a. *US Imports of Textiles and Apparel under the Multifiber Arrangement, January–June 1984*. USITC Publication no. 1635. Washington, January.

———. 1985b. *The Multifiber Arrangement, 1980–84*. USITC Publication no. 1693. Washington, May.

———. 1985c. *Emerging Textile-Exporting Countries, 1984*. USITC Publication no. 1716. Washington, July.

Wolf, Martin. 1983. "Managed Trade in Practice: Implications of the Textile Arrangements." In *Trade Policy in the 1980s*. Edited by William R. Cline. Washington: Institute for International Economics.

CASE M-12

Carbon and Alloy Steel Products: Phase I

PERIOD OF RELIEF

1 January 1969 to 31 December 1974

SUPPLIERS AFFECTED

European Community (EC), Japan, and United Kingdom

RELIEF ACTION

In the fall of 1968, Senator Vance Hartke (D-Ind.) introduced a bill to limit steel imports[1] to 9.6 percent of the US market (the 1964–66 import share). To forestall this initiative, both Japan and the European Community (EC) agreed in December 1968 to restrict voluntarily their steel exports to the United States (accounting for 82 percent of total US steel imports) for three years. (USITC 1256, 4–5; Mintz, 79–81)

Under these voluntary restraint agreements (VRAs), the Japanese and Europeans were to limit steel exports to the United States to 5.75 million tons each in 1969 (as compared with shipments of 7.3 million tons, Japan, and 7.1 million tons, EC, in 1968), 6.04 million tons in 1970, and 6.35 million tons in 1971. The VRAs affected the level of total imports; they did not restrict specific steel products from individual countries. As a result of the VRAs, suppliers shifted their export product mix toward more expensive stainless and alloy steel products, notwithstanding Japan's promise to "try not to change greatly the product mix and pattern of distribution of trade as compared with the present." (USITC 1256, 4–5; Mintz, 79–81)

On 1 January 1972, the VRAs were extended for three years, whereupon the United Kingdom joined the restraining group. The extended agreements contained precise

---

1. The carbon and alloy steel products discussed in this case include alloy and other than alloy steel (except stainless steel, heat resisting steel, and certain tool steel), including ingots, blooms, billets, slabs, and sheet bars provided for in items 606.6705, 606.6710, 606.6715, 606.6720, 606.6725, 606.6730, 606.6735, 606.6740, 606.6926, 606.6929, 606.6932, 606.6935, 606.6938, 606.6941, 606.6944, and 606.6947 of the Tariff Schedules of the United States (TSUS).

import tonnage limitations on specific steel mill products, and lowered the annual increase in tonnage of allowable imports from 5 percent to 2.5 percent. (USITC 1256, 4–5)

The VRAs expired on 31 December 1974, in the context of strong US demand for steel mill products. An informal understanding with Japan apparently continued to the effect that Japan's annual steel shipments would not exceed 6 million tons. The economic downturn of 1977, however, brought a renewed call for relief from steel imports. (See Case M–13, Carbon and Alloy Steel Products: Phase II; Walter, 495; Morici and Megna, 20; USITC 1256, 4–5)

CHANGES IN THE INDUSTRY

The growth of imports slowed through 1970, but resumed again in 1971 and 1972. During the next two years the VRAs were not generally binding, as exporters turned away from US markets that were subject to US price controls. Between 1971 and 1973, the US dollar depreciated against foreign currencies, providing US steel producers with breathing room, and rising profit margins, after years of steadily rising imports. (Crandall 1981, 35–38; Crandall 1982, 18)

The years 1972 and 1973 were characterized by rising production, increasing exports, and declining imports. During 1973–74, the US steel industry operated at almost full capacity, increased exports, and generally shared in the worldwide commodity boom. In 1973, the United Steelworkers secured generous wage and benefit increases (annual increases estimated at 9.3 percent for three years) in a contract signed 18 months before the expiration of the old contract. The VRAs expired in 1974, at a time of general excess demand for steel and expiring US price controls. (Crandall 1981, 35–38)

Key Statistics

Imports affected from Japan, EC, UK[a]

Year	Volume (million tons)	Value (million dollars)	Source
Before restraints			
1968	14.39	1,662	USITC 1256, 61; Crandall 1981, 126
During restraints			
1969	11.45	1,404	USITC 1256, 61; Crandall 1981, 126
1970	10.69	1,558	USITC 1256, 61; Crandall 1981, 126
1972	14.22	2,292	USITC 1256, 61; Crandall 1981, 126
1974	12.58	3,805	USITC 1256, 61; Crandall 1981, 126
After restraints			
1975	9.97	2,960	Walter, 489; Crandall 1981, 126

a. The figures for 1968–70 exclude the United Kingdom, which did not join the restraining group until 1972. (USITC 1256, 61)

Imports from all sources

Year	Volume (million tons)	Value (million dollars)	Source
Before restraints			
1968	17.96	2,074	USITC 1256, 61; Crandall 1981, 126
During restraints			
1969	14.03	1,720	USITC 1256, 61; Crandall 1981, 126
1970	13.36	1,948	USITC 1256, 61; Crandall 1981, 126
1972	17.68	2,849	USITC 1256, 61; Crandall 1981, 126
1974	15.97	4,830	USITC 1256, 61; Crandall 1981, 126
After restraints			
1975	12.01	3,566	Walter, 489; Crandall 1981, 126

Apparent consumption

Year	Volume (million tons)	Value (million dollars)	Source
Before restraints			
1968	107.6	18,661	Walter, 488; USITC 1256, 59
During restraints			
1969	102.7	18,663	Walter, 488; USITC 1256, 59
1970	97.1	18,779	Walter, 488; USITC 1256, 59
1972	106.6	23,520	Walter, 488; USITC 1256, 59
1974	119.6	34,402	Walter, 488; USITC 1256, 59
After restraints			
1975	89.0	29,696	Walter, 488; USITC 1256, 59; American Iron, 17

Market share of imports (percentage of apparent consumption, by volume)

Year	Affected imports	Total imports	Source
Before restraints			
1968	13.4	16.7	authors' estimate; Walter, 489
During restraints			
1969	11.1	13.7	authors' estimate; Walter, 489
1970	11.0	13.8	authors' estimate; Walter, 489
1972	13.3	16.6	authors' estimate; Walter, 489
1974	10.5	13.4	authors' estimate; Walter, 489
After restraints			
1975	11.2	13.5	authors' estimate; Walter, 489

Output of domestic industry[a]

Year	Volume (million tons)	Value (million dollars)	Source
Before restraints			
1968	91.9	12,615	Walter, 488; Crandall 1981, 126
During restraints			
1969	93.9	13,305	Walter, 488; Crandall 1981, 126
1970	90.8	13,762	Walter, 488; Crandall 1981, 126
1972	91.8	15,881	Walter, 488; Crandall 1981, 126
1974	109.5	26,402	Walter, 488; Crandall 1981, 126
After restraints			
1975	80.0	21,398	Walter, 488; Crandall 1981, 126

a. Producers' shipments.

Employment in domestic industry

Year	Production workers (average number)	Source
Before restraints		
1968	420,684	American Iron, 21
During restraints		
1969	415,301	American Iron, 21
1970	403,115	American Iron, 21
1972	364,074	American Iron, 21
1974	393,212	American Iron, 21
After restraints		
1975	339,945	American Iron, 21

Wages and benefits

Year	Dollars per hour	Source
Before restraints		
1968	5.03	American Iron, 22
During restraints		
1969	5.38	American Iron, 22
1970	5.68	American Iron, 22
1972	7.08	American Iron, 22
1974	9.08	American Iron, 22
After restraints		
1975	10.59	American Iron, 22

Industry profits (million dollars)

Year	Profits[a]	Source
Before restraints		
1968	992	OTA, 120
During restraints		
1969	879	OTA, 120
1970	532	OTA, 120
1972	775	OTA, 120
1974	2,475	OTA, 120
After restraints		
1975	1,595	OTA, 120

a. Net profits before taxes.

Industry capacity utilization

Year	Percentage	Source
Before restraints		
1968	86.4	Crandall 1981, 24
During restraints		
1969	92.5	Crandall 1981, 24
1970	85.5	Crandall 1981, 24
1972	85.3	Crandall 1981, 24
1974	92.8	Crandall 1981, 24
After restraints		
1975	74.1	Crandall 1981, 24

Quantitative Profile

Item	Amount	Source
Number of years restraints in force (1969–74)	5 years	
Induced increase in price of imported steel (1974)	6.3 to 8.3 percent 13.3 percent	Crandall 1981, 105–6 authors' estimate[a]
Induced increase in price of domestic steel (average 1969–74)	3.8 percent 5.3 percent	USITC 1256, vi, 8[b] authors' estimate[b]
Coefficient of price response	0.4	authors' estimate
Quantity and value of imports (1974)	15,97 million tons $4,830 million	USITC 1256, 61 Crandall 1981, 126

Quantitative Profile (continued)

Item	Amount	Source
Induced decrease in imports due to restraints (average 1969–74)	3.2 million tons	USITC 1256, 8, 27[c]
	$1.02 billion	USITC 1256, 8, 27[c]
	4.5 million tons	authors' estimate[c]
	$1.42 billion	authors' estimate[c]
Quantity and value of domestic production (1974)	109.5 million tons	Walter, 488
	$26,402 million	Crandall 1981, 126
Induced increase in domestic production due to restraints (average 1969–74)	1.62 million tons	USITC 1256, vi, 10[d]
	$465 million	USITC 1256, vi, 10[d]
	2.25 million tons	authors' estimate[d]
	$646 million	authors' estimate[d]
Coefficient of quantity response	0.5	authors' estimate
Elasticity of demand for imported steel	0.7	USITC 1256, 49
	2.1 to 5	Crandall 1981, 131[e]
	2.5	authors' estimate
Elasticity of supply of domestic steel	1.4	Jondrow 1978, 24–25
	3.5	Crandall 1981, 132
	2.0	authors' estimate
Elasticity of demand for domestic steel	0.5	USITC 1256, 48
	0.5 to 2.0	Crandall 1981, 131[e]
	1.0	authors' estimate
Cross-elasticity of demand for domestic steel relative to price of imported steel	0.6	USITC 1256, 48
	0.3 to 1.1	Crandall 1981, 131[e]
	1.2	authors' estimate
Cross-elasticity of output of domestic steel relative to price of imported steel	0.8	authors' estimate
Cross-elasticity of quantity of imported steel relative to price of domestic steel	3.5 to 14.4	Crandall 1981, 131[e]
	2.2	authors' estimate
Cost of restraints to US consumers	$1,254 million (1977)	Crandall 1978, 431
	$1,970 million (1974)	authors' estimate
Gain from restraints to US producers (1974)	$1,330 million	authors' estimate
Tariff revenue and implied average tariff rate (1974)	$290 million	authors' estimate[f]
	6 percent	BC, IM 146
Gain from restraints to foreigners	$175 million (1969)	Magee, 672
	$568 million (1969)	Jondrow 1980, 8
	$330 million (1974)	authors' estimate
Efficiency loss from larger domestic production to the United States (1974)	$50 million	authors' estimate
Welfare cost of restraints to the United States	$386 million (1969)	Magee, 672
	$380 million (1974)	authors' estimate
Employment in protected US industry	420,684 (1968)	American Iron, 21
	393,212 (1974)	American Iron, 21
Induced increase in employment (1974)	19,117	USITC 1256, 11[g]
	8,100	authors' estimate[g]

APPENDIX 159

Quantitative Profile (continued)

Item	Amount	Source
Cost of restraints to US consumers per job saved	$63,000 (1977) $240,000 (1974)	Crandall 1978, 431 authors' estimate
Gain from restraints to US producers per job (1974)	$3,400	authors' estimate

a. This estimate includes the effect of the average ad valorem tariff of 6 percent, plus the 7.3 percent increase in prices attributable to the VRAs.

b. The USITC estimates that VRA-induced increases in the annual average producer price of steel mill products ranged from 1.3 percent ($2.84 per ton) in 1973 to 5.7 percent ($11.83 per ton) in 1970, with a six-year average estimate of 3.8 percent ($8.28 per ton). Our estimate includes the effect of both the VRAs and the tariff. (USITC 1256, vi, 8)

c. The estimated annual reductions in the volume of steel imports due to the VRAs ranged from 6.5 percent of actual imports in 1973 to 32.8 percent in 1970, with an average annual reduction of 20.1 percent. Over the six-year period, the VRAs reduced imports by an estimated 19.04 million tons (valued at $6.1 billion in 1974 dollars), with an average annual reduction of 3.2 million tons ($1.02 billion). Our estimate includes the effect of both the VRAs and the tariff, and is calculated on the basis of the ratio between the total domestic price effect (5.3 percent) and the VRA-induced price effect (3.8 percent), times the VRA-induced increase in production, adjusted by the coefficient of quantity response. (USITC 1256, 8, 27)

d. The estimated annual effects of the VRAs on domestic production ranged from 0.14 million tons in 1969 to 4.79 million tons in 1971, with a total increase during the six-year period of 9.7 million tons (annual average of 1.62 million tons), valued at $2.79 billion in 1974 dollars (annual average of $465 million). The total cumulative increase in domestic production over the period was 33.3 million tons, about 29 percent of which was accounted for by the effect of the VRAs. Most of the increase in domestic production was attributable to fluctuations in world market conditions and increased demand for steel. Our estimate includes the effect of both the VRAs and the tariff; see note c for the methodology. (USITC 1256, vi, 10)

e. Crandall's demand elasticities represent a range of estimates for five categories of steel: hot-rolled sheet; cold-rolled sheet; bars; structurals; and plate.

f. In 1976, the average ad valorem tariff rate for steel mill products, including specialty steel products, was 6.1 percent. A 6 percent tariff rate has been assumed for 1974 and applied to total 1974 imports to estimate tariff revenue.

g. Over the six-year period, the VRAs increased domestic employment by 144,702 man-years in steel and related industries. The estimated annual effects of the VRAs on employment ranged from 1,657 man-years in 1969 to 55,223 man-years in 1971, or an annual average of 19,117 jobs. Our own estimate includes the effect of both the VRAs and the tariff but does not include the effect on related industries. (USITC 1256, 11, 27)

BIBLIOGRAPHY

American Iron and Steel Institute. 1981. *Annual Statistical Report*. Washington.

Crandall, Robert W. 1978. "Federal Government Initiatives to Reduce the Price Level." *Brookings Papers on Economic Activity* 2.

———. 1981. *The US Steel Industry in Recurrent Crisis: Policy Options in a Competitive World*. Washington: Brookings Institution.

———. 1982. *Steel Imports: Dumping or Competition?* Brookings General Series Reprint 381. Washington: Brookings Institution.

Jondrow, James M. 1978. "Effects of Trade Restrictions on Imports of Steel." In *The Impact of International Trade and Investment on Employment*. US Department of Labor, Bureau of International Labor Affairs. Washington.

———. 1980. *Effects of Trade Restrictions on Imports of Steel.* Professional Paper 165. Alexandria, Va.: Public Research Institute, November.

Jondrow, James M., E. Levine, L. Jacobsen, A. Katz, and D. O'Neill. 1975. *Removing Restrictions on Imports of Steel.* Arlington, Va.: Public Research Institute, May.

Magee, Stephen P. 1972. "The Welfare Effects of Restrictions on US Trade." *Brookings Papers on Economic Activity* 3.

Mintz, Ilse. 1973. *US Import Quotas: Costs and Consequences.* Domestic Affairs Study 10. Washington: American Enterprise Institute, February.

Morici, Peter, and Laura L. Megna. 1983. *US Economic Policies Affecting Industrial Trade: A Quantitative Assessment.* Report no. 200. Washington: National Planning Association.

Munger, Michael C. 1983. *The Costs of Protectionism: Estimates of the Hidden Tax of Trade Restraint.* Working Paper no. 80. Washington University, Center for the Study of American Business, July.

Takacs, Wendy E. 1975. *Quantitative Restrictions and the US Steel Industry.* Ph.D. diss. Johns Hopkins University, May.

US Congress. Office of Technology Assessment. 1980. *Technology and Steel Industry Competitiveness.* Washington, June.

US Department of Commerce. Bureau of the Census. Various years. *US Imports for Consumption.* IM 146. Washington, December.

US International Trade Commission. 1982. *Economic Effects of Export Restraints.* USITC Publication no. 1256. Washington, June.

Walter, Ingo. 1983. "Structural Adjustment and Trade Policy in the International Steel Industry." In *Trade Policy in the 1980s.* Edited by William R. Cline. Washington: Institute for International Economics.

CASE M–13

Carbon and Alloy Steel Products: Phase II (Trigger Price Mechanism)

PERIOD OF RELIEF

January 1978 to March 1980
October 1980 to February 1982

SUPPLIERS AFFECTED

Global (primarily European Community [EC] and Japan)

RELIEF ACTION

In September 1977, responding to an overwhelming number of antidumping petitions filed with the Treasury Department, President Jimmy Carter directed Under Secretary of the Treasury Anthony Solomon to devise a relief plan for the US steel industry. The centerpiece of the Solomon Report was a systematic import-relief scheme designed to protect the US industry from the possible sale of foreign steel products at "less than fair value," a legal benchmark used in the US antidumping statute. (Walter, 491–92; Crandall 1981, 42–43, 107; GAO, 1–2)

In January 1978, as recommended in the Solomon Report, the Carter administration introduced the trigger price mechanism (TPM).[1] The TPM established "fair value" import reference prices (trigger prices) for steel products constructed on the basis of Japanese unit costs of production, profit margins, and the cost of transportation to the US market. Under the TPM, steel imports entering the US market below the trigger prices were presumed to be dumped and therefore subject to "fast-track" antidumping investigations. (Walter, 491–92; GAO, 2–3)

Trigger prices were revised quarterly, within a 5 percent flexibility band, to allow for changes in production costs and the yen-dollar exchange rate. TPM coverage

---

1. The trigger price mechanism (TPM) was announced on 3 January 1978. Initially the Treasury Department stated that trigger prices would not apply to shipments embarking prior to that date. Since the lag between the date of departure from Japan or Europe and the clearing of customs in the United States is generally two months, and since many trigger prices were not announced for another one or two months, the system was not fully effective until May 1978. (Crandall 1981, 107)

expanded from about 65 percent of steel mill imports in the first half of 1978 to about 85 percent in the second quarter of 1979, and extended to approximately 70 different steel products. (Walter, 491–92; GAO, 2)

In return for the TPM, the US steel industry withdrew numerous antidumping complaints against European and Japanese exporters. The TPM did not succeed, however, in eliminating protectionist sentiment within the domestic steel industry and Congress. The gap between Japanese and European production costs allowed European producers to cut their export prices and still enter the US market above the trigger prices. In March 1980, the United States Steel Corporation filed a massive number of new antidumping suits against European suppliers. In response, the Carter administration immediately suspended the TPM. (Walter, 492)

In October 1980, in an accord between the Carter administration and the domestic steel industry, stimulated in part by European threats of retaliation against US antidumping actions, the TPM was reinstated. The renewed TPM established significantly higher trigger prices (an average increase of 12 percent), as well as special provisions for the imposition of quantitative import restrictions in the event of future import "surges." (Walter, 492)

The revitalized TPM notwithstanding, steel imports rose steadily during 1981. In early February 1982, domestic steel producers filed a new wave of petitions claiming unfair trading practices by European producers. Beginning in October 1982, in response to these petitions, the United States negotiated a series of voluntary restraint agreements with major foreign suppliers. (See Case M–14, Carbon and Alloy Steel Products: Phase III; Walter, 491–92; Morici and Megna, 21; GAO, 1–5)

CHANGES IN THE INDUSTRY

The TPM increased the risk of administrative action against imports, whether or not dumped, and whether or not a cause of material injury to the US industry. As a result, the TPM deterred imports of low-priced steel in general and caused the Japanese import share of the US market to drop dramatically from 1977 to 1978. The TPM also coincided with the beginning of a two-year decline in the exchange value of the dollar. This decline caused import prices to rise, but the rise was assisted somewhat by the TPM. (Walter, 493; Crandall 1984, 9; CBO, 9)

After 1979, the gap between US steel prices and world steel prices widened markedly. The rise in the value of the dollar, beginning in mid-1980, placed the US steel industry in a difficult situation. Rather than cut prices, US producers held prices relatively stable, causing US imports to rise. Increased imports led to lower operating rates and declining profit margins. In response, the US industry began to sharply criticize the TPM, to challenge the Japanese industry's cost data, and to question the program's enforcement. (Crandall 1984, 11).

In 1982, the industry operated at less than 50 percent capacity, with fewer shipments and lower production than at any time since the late 1940s. These conditions precipitated a substantial number of layoffs and industry-wide operating losses. Although the US industry obtained modest relief in 1982 from its wage agreement with the United Steelworkers, price-cost margins fell dramatically as demand plummeted during the year. (Crandall 1984, 11; CBO, xv)

Key Statistics

Imports from all sources

Year	Volume (million tons)	Value[a] (million dollars)	Source
Before restraints			
1977	19.31	5,040	CBO, 15; authors' estimate
During TPM			
1978	21.14	6,257	CBO, 15; authors' estimate
1979	17.52	6,780	CBO, 15; authors' estimate
1980	15.50	6,634	CBO, 15; authors' estimate
1981	19.90	9,930	CBO, 15; authors' estimate
Nascent MSA			
1982	16.66	8,958	CBO, 15; USITC 1578, 3

a. These estimates reflect the average unit value per ton of US imports of carbon and alloy steel products as follows: $261 (1977), $296 (1978), $387 (1979), $428 (1980), and $499 (1981). (USITC 1064, A51–52; USITC 1553, A54)

Apparent consumption

Year	Volume (million tons)	Value[a] (million dollars)	Source
Before restraints			
1977	108.45	33,208	USITC 1553, A39; authors' estimate
During TPM			
1978	116.65	39,962	USITC 1553, A39; authors' estimate
1979	114.96	48,484	USITC 1553, A39; authors' estimate
1980	95.25	43,239	USITC 1553, A39; authors' estimate
1981	105.44	54,496	USITC 1578, 2; authors' estimate
Nascent MSA			
1982	76.39	39,181	USITC 1578, 2; authors' estimate

a. These figures reflect the value of imports and domestic output, with minor adjustments for exports.

Market share of imports (percentage of apparent consumption, by volume)

Year	Share	Source
Before restraints		
1977	17.8	USITC 1553, A39
During TPM		
1978	18.1	USITC 1553, A39
1979	15.2	USITC 1553, A39
1980	16.3	USITC 1553, A39
1981	18.9	USITC 1553, A39
Nascent MSA		
1982	21.8	USITC 1553, A39

Output of domestic industry[a]

Year	Volume (million tons)	Value[b] (million dollars)	Source
Before restraints			
1977	91.15	28,803	USITC 1553, A39; authors' estimate
During TPM			
1978	97.94	34,573	USITC 1553, A39; authors' estimate
1979	100.26	42,911	USITC 1553, A39; authors' estimate
1980	83.85	38,487	USITC 1553, A39; authors' estimate
1981	88.45	46,082	USITC 1578, 2; authors' estimate
Nascent MSA			
1982	61.57	31,154	USITC 1578, 2; authors' estimate

a. Producers' shipments.
b. These figures reflect the average unit value per ton of US shipments of carbon and alloy steel products as follows: $316 (1977), $353 (1978), $428 (1979), $459 (1980), $521 (1981), and $506 (1982). (USITC 1064, A46; USITC 1553, A77)

Employment in domestic industry

Year	Production workers (average number)	Source
Before restraints		
1977	337,396	American Iron 1980, 21
During TPM		
1978	339,155	American Iron 1980, 21
1979	341,931	American Iron 1980, 21
1980	292,000	USITC 1553, A84
1981	286,000	USITC 1578, 1
Nascent MSA		
1982	198,000	USITC 1578, 1

Wages and benefits

Year	Dollars per hour	Source
Before restraints		
1977	13.04	USITC 1553, A85
During TPM		
1978	14.30	USITC 1553, A85
1979	15.92	USITC 1553, A85
1980	18.45	USITC 1553, A85
1981	20.16	USITC 1553, A85
Nascent MSA		
1982	23.78	USITC 1553, A85

Industry profits (million dollars)

Year	Profits (loss)[a]	Source
Before restraints		
1977	22	American Iron 1983, 9
During TPM		
1978	1,277	American Iron 1983, 9
1979	1,155	American Iron 1983, 9
1980	1,735	American Iron 1983, 9
1981	2,601	American Iron 1983, 9
Nascent MSA		
1982	(3,206)	American Iron 1983, 9

a. Net income (loss) before taxes.

Industry capacity utilization

Year	Percentage	Source
Before restraints		
1977	78.4	American Iron 1983, 9
During TPM		
1978	86.8	American Iron 1983, 9
1979	87.8	American Iron 1983, 9
1980	72.8	American Iron 1983, 9
1981	78.3	American Iron 1983, 9
Nascent MSA		
1982	48.4	American Iron 1983, 9

Quantitative Profile

Item	Amount	Source
Number of years restraints in force (TPM only; 1978–82 excluding 6-month hiatus)	3.5 years	
Induced increase in price of imported steel	10.3 percent (1978–79) 15.9 percent (1979–81)	Crandall 1981, 109–10 authors' estimate[a]
Induced increase in price of domestic steel	0.8 to 1.1 percent (1979) 6.4 percent (1979–81)	Crandall 1981, 111[b] authors' estimate
Coefficient of price response	0.4	authors' estimate
Quantity and value of imports (1981)	19.9 million tons $9,930 million	CBO, 15 authors' estimate
Induced decrease in imports due to restraints	6 to 6.7 million tons (1979) 4.3 million tons (1981) $2,146 million (1981)	Crandall 1981, 134 authors' estimate authors' estimate
Quantity and value of domestic production (1981)	88.5 million tons $46,082 million	USITC 1578, 2 authors' estimate
Induced increase in domestic production due to restraints	2.2 to 3.1 million tons (1979) 2.2 million tons (1979–81)	Crandall 1981, 134 authors' estimate
Coefficient of quantity response	0.5	authors' estimate
Elasticity of demand for imported steel	0.7 2.1 to 5 2.5	USITC 1256, 49 Crandall 1981, 131[c] authors' estimate
Elasticity of supply of domestic steel	1.4 3.5 2.0	Jondrow, 24–25 Crandall 1981, 132 authors' estimate
Elasticity of demand for domestic steel	0.5 0.5 to 2.0 1.0	USITC 1256, 48 Crandall 1981, 131[c] authors' estimate
Cross-elasticity of demand for domestic steel relative to price of imported steel	0.6 0.3 to 1.1 1.2	USITC 1256, 48 Crandall 1981, 131[c] authors' estimate
Cross-elasticity of output of domestic steel relative to price of imported steel	0.8	authors' estimate
Cross-elasticity of quantity of imported steel relative to price of domestic steel	1.4	authors' estimate
Cost of restraints to US consumers	$1,135 million (1980) $4,350 million (1981)	Munger, 18 authors' estimate

Quantitative Profile (continued)

Item	Amount	Source
Gain from restraints to US producers	$640 million (1979) $2,770 million (1981)	Crandall 1981, 134 authors' estimate
Tariff revenue and implied average tariff rate (1981)	$556 million 5.6 percent	authors' estimate BC, IM 146
Gain from restraints to foreigners	$519 million (1979) $930 million (1981)	Crandall 1981, 134 authors' estimate
Efficiency loss from larger domestic production to the United States (1981)	$120 million	authors' estimate
Welfare cost of restraints to the United States (1981)	$1,050 million	authors' estimate
Employment in protected US industry	337,396 (1977) 286,000 (1981)	American Iron 1980, 21 USITC 1578, 1
Induced increase in employment	12,400 (1979) 7,000 (1981)	Crandall 1981, 134 authors' estimate
Cost of restraints to US consumers per job saved	$110,000 (1980) $620,000 (1981)	Munger, 25 authors' estimate
Gain from restraints to US producers per job (1981)	$9,700	authors' estimate

a. This figure includes Crandall's estimate that the TPM raised steel import prices by 10.3 percent, plus the average ad valorem tariff of 5.6 percent in 1981.

b. Although US steel prices rose by 10.6 percent in 1978 and by another 10.5 percent in 1979, Crandall attributes most of the rise to domestic cost and demand pressures (e.g., stronger demand, accelerating general inflation, increased costs of material and labor). (Crandall 1981, 111–15)

c. Crandall's demand elasticities represent a range of estimates for five categories of steel: hot-rolled sheet; cold-rolled sheet; bars; structurals; and plate.

BIBLIOGRAPHY

American Iron and Steel Institute. 1980, 1983. *Annual Statistical Report.* Washington.

Crandall, Robert W. 1978. "Federal Government Initiatives to Reduce the Price Level." *Brookings Papers on Economic Activity* 2.

———. 1980. "Steel Imports: Dumping or Competition?" *Regulation,* July–August, pp. 17–24.

———. 1981. *The US Steel Industry in Recurrent Crisis.* Washington: Brookings Institution.

———. 1984. "The EEC-US Steel Trade Crisis." Paper presented at symposium, Euro-American Relations and Global Economic Interdependence. Bruges, Belgium, College of Europe, 13 September.

Finger, J. Michael. 1981. *The United States Trigger Price Mechanism for Steel Imports.* Washington: World Bank.

Jondrow, James M. 1978. "Effects of Trade Restrictions on Imports of Steel." In *The Impact of International Trade and Investment on Employment.* US Department of Labor, Bureau of International Labor Affairs. Washington.

Morici, Peter, and Laura L. Megna. 1983. *US Economic Policies Affecting Industrial Trade: A Quantitative Assessment.* Report no. 200. Washington: National Planning Association.

Munger, Michael C. 1983. *The Costs of Protectionism: Estimates of the Hidden Tax of Trade Restraint.* Working Paper no. 80. Washington University, Center for the Study of American Business, July.

Solomon, Anthony. 1977. "Report to the President: A Comprehensive Program for the Steel Industry." US Department of the Treasury. Washington.

US Congress. House. Committee on Ways and Means, Subcommittee on Trade. 1978. *Steel: Background Data on the American Steel Industry and International Steel Trade.* 95 Cong., 2 sess., 16 May.

US Congressional Budget Office. 1984. *The Effects of Import Quotas on the Steel Industry.* Washington, July.

US Department of Commerce. Bureau of the Census. Various years. *US Imports for Consumption.* IM 146. Washington, December.

US General Accounting Office. 1980. *Report to the Congress: Administration of the Steel Trigger Price Mechanism.* Report no. 1D–80–15. Washington, 23 July.

US International Trade Commission. 1980. *Certain Carbon Steel Products from Belgium, the Federal Republic of Germany, France, Italy, Luxembourg, the Netherlands, and the United Kingdom.* USITC Publication no. 1064. Washington, May.

———. 1982. *Economic Effects of Export Restraints.* USITC Publication no. 1256. Washington, June.

———. 1984a. *Carbon and Certain Alloy Steel Products.* 2 vols. USITC Publication no. 1553. Washington, July.

———. 1984b. *Monthly Report on Selected Steel Industry Data.* USITC Publication no. 1578. Washington, September.

Walter, Ingo. 1983. "Structural Adjustment and Trade Policy in the International Steel Industry." In *Trade Policy in the 1980s.* Edited by William R. Cline. Washington: Institute for International Economics.

CASE M–14

Carbon and Alloy Steel Products: Phase III (Nascent Multi-Steel Arrangement)

PERIOD OF RELIEF

November 1982 to present

SUPPLIERS AFFECTED

Argentina, Australia, Brazil, European Community (EC), Japan, Korea, Mexico, South Africa, Spain, and others

RELIEF ACTION

In January 1982, seven domestic steelmakers filed approximately 110 antidumping and countervailing duty petitions with the US International Trade Commission (USITC) and the International Trade Administration (ITA) of the Department of Commerce against 41 suppliers of 9 steel products in 11 countries.[1] These petitions covered about 20 percent of total US carbon steel imports in 1981. ITA calculated preliminary duties ranging from 1 percent to 26 percent.

On 21 October 1982, as a means of settling the suits against European producers, the US government negotiated a voluntary restraint agreement (VRA) with the European Community (EC). The VRA, with a stated lifetime of 1 November 1982 to 31 December 1985, contained the following terms:

☐ The EC agreed to limit exports of 11 carbon steel products to 5.5 percent of the projected US market, with subceilings for individual products. In 1981, EC shipments were 5.9 percent of the US market.

☐ The EC agreed to limit pipe and steel tube to 5.9 percent of the US market, subject to further negotiation (compared to 6.2 percent in 1981).

---

1. Under the Trade Agreements Act of 1979, the Department of Commerce is responsible for determining the existence and magnitude of dumping margins and subsidies, while the US International Trade Commission must rule on the extent and source of injury, if any. Imposition of antidumping or countervailing duties requires an affirmative finding by both.

☐ The US agreed to initiate talks with third-country suppliers with a view to limiting the growth in their share of the US market. (Morici and Megna, 21; Walter, 493)

The policy focus turned next to third-country suppliers. Since the late 1960s, Japan has limited its steel shipments to between 5 percent and 6.5 percent of the total US market, pursuant to understandings with successive US administrations. In April 1984, as a means of settling a countervailing duty complaint, Mexico agreed to limit exports to the United States to 395,000 tons annually for 1984, 1985, and 1986, with a possible extension to 1987 (down from 600,000 tons in 1983). Also in April 1984, the Brazilian government announced it would implement voluntary export restraints, reducing its steel shipments by 47.2 percent (430,000 metric tons) between 1 May 1984 and 30 April 1985, but these restraints did not succeed in persuading the US steel industry to drop its unfair trade cases. In early 1984, South Africa agreed to limit its steel exports to the United States. (*New York Times*, 27 August 1984, D1; *Journal of Commerce*, 20 April 1984, 3A; *Washington Post*, 27 April 1984, D12; *Inside US Trade*, 7 September 1984, 4; Cases M–12 and M–13, Carbon and Alloy Steel Products: Phase I and Phase II)

On 24 January 1984, following receipt of a petition filed on behalf of the United Steelworkers of America and the Bethlehem Steel Corporation, the USITC instituted an escape clause investigation under Section 201 of the Trade Act of 1974. On 12 June 1984, the USITC determined by a 3 to 2 vote that five industries[2] accounting for 74 percent of domestic shipments were injured by imports of carbon and alloy steel products. On 11 July 1984, the USITC recommended to President Ronald Reagan that a mixture of tariffs, quotas, and tariff-rate quotas be imposed on 70 percent of all US steel imports for five years. (USITC 1553, 1–5; CRS 1984c, 1; Tarr and Morkre, 127)

In April 1984, under the leadership of David M. Roderick, the American Iron and Steel Institute mounted a campaign for the Fair Trade in Steel Act of 1984 (S 2380, HR 5081). The bill would have limited imports of all grades of steel products, including specialty steel, to 15 percent of domestic consumption (approximately the 1979–81 average level of 15.8 million tons) for a five-year period.

On 17 September 1984, presidential candidate Walter F. Mondale urged imposition of a quota that would limit imports of carbon steel products to 17 percent of the US market for five years. On 18 September 1984, President Reagan determined that the USITC recommendation for relief was not in the national economic interest, and directed the US Trade Representative (USTR) to negotiate five-year "surge control" arrangements (basically VRAs) with all leading steel suppliers within 90 days, and to take "vigorous and comprehensive" action against foreign unfair trade practices. In addition, the USITC was directed to monitor steel industry modernization.

---

2. The USITC rejected the petitioners' argument that the domestic industry should be defined as including all those facilities producing raw steel and certain "first-tier" finished products. The Commission, instead, delineated nine separate industries competing with the targeted imports, five of which it found either to be injured or threatened with injury—semifinished products (ingots, blooms, billets, slabs, and sheet bars); plates; sheets and strips; wire and wire products; structural shapes and units.

(*Washington Post,* 18 September 1984, C1; USTR 1984, 1–4; *New York Times,* 20 September 1984, D1)

The USTR estimated that the resulting level of finished carbon steel imports would be 18.5 percent of the US market, and that the level of total imports (including not more than 1.7 million tons of semifinished steel) would be 20.5 percent of the US market. The USTR indicated that VRAs would be sought with steel-exporting countries that had more than 0.3 percent of the US market in 1983, for example, Brazil, Spain, Korea, and Japan. The Department of Commerce was ordered to self-initiate countervailing duty petitions against suspected unfair trade. (USTR 1984, 1–4; *Wall Street Journal,* 20 December 1984, 31, and 19 September 1984, 3; *New York Times,* 19 September 1984, 1; *International Trade Reporter,* 24 October 1984, 498)

In October 1984, the Trade and Tariff Act of 1984 passed the Congress, containing a "sense of Congress" resolution (Section 803) urging that steel imports be limited to between 17.0 percent and 20.2 percent of US apparent consumption and authorizing President Reagan to negotiate the necessary agreements. Section 803 also called upon the steel industry as a whole to commit substantially all of its net cash flow from steel operations to reinvestment and modernization of steel production facilities and to worker retraining programs. Also in October, the Cabinet Council on Commerce and Trade began formulating a plan of tax and regulatory concessions that would specifically benefit the steel industry. (CRS 1984c, 1; *Washington Post,* 27 April 1984, D11; 27 March 1984, C1; *Inside US Trade,* 5 October 1984, 4)

Citing the Trade and Tariff Act of 1984, which treats the 1982 agreement on steel imports as a formal US-EC "arrangement," the US Customs Service embargoed steel pipe and tube imports from the EC beginning 29 November 1984. Explaining this decision, the Reagan administration said that more imports than the 5.9 percent market share agreed to in 1982 had already entered the United States that year. (*Journal of Commerce,* 21 November 1984, 1A)

In an EC Council of Ministers meeting on 22 November 1984, after the embargo announcement, the EC Commission was instructed to negotiate an import limit on steel pipe and tube of 7.6 percent of the US market. The EC denied that the 1982 exchange of letters on steel export restraints constituted a formal US-EC arrangement. EC officials also said they would seek redress through the General Agreement on Tariffs and Trade (GATT) and if satisfactory compensation could not be agreed upon, they might retaliate. US importers also protested the action and took their case before the US Court of International Trade. (*Journal of Commerce,* 29 November 1984, 1A)

Negotiators finally resolved the dispute in January 1985 when the United States and EC agreed to limit EC exports to 7.6 percent of the US steel pipe and tube market in 1985 and 1986, down from about 14.5 percent in 1984. Under the compromise, US importers were able to bring in about 60,000 tons of pipe and tube in 1985 free of quota. The pipe and tube temporarily blocked by the November 1984 embargo (about 200,000 tons) were counted under the 1985 quota. The EC was allowed to ship about 785,000 tons of steel into the United States in 1985, counting the 60,000 tons entered without charge to the quota (compared to about 1.3 million tons in 1984). Under the plan, the EC established an export license system to control shipments to the United States. (*Journal of Commerce,* 7 January 1985, 3A; 26 November 1984, 5A)

Earlier, on 20 December 1984, the Reagan administration had announced that it had completed the first phase of negotiations with seven steel-producing countries—Japan, Korea, Spain, Brazil, Mexico, South Africa, and Australia—that had agreed to hold their 1985 exports to about 10.13 percent of the expected US market, a 29.70 percent reduction from 1984 levels. The administration did not include Canada in the negotiations, however, after it pledged itself to be "prudent and not take advantage of the situation." At the same time, David Roderick announced that US Steel had filed 28 new antidumping and countervailing duty petitions against eight foreign producers—Austria, Venezuela, Sweden, and five Eastern European countries (Poland, East Germany, Hungary, Romania, and Czechoslovakia)—apparently as a means of persuading the USTR to negotiate restraints with those nations. (*Wall Street Journal*, 20 December 1984, 31; *Washington Post*, 5 September 1985, E1)

By November 1985, the USTR had negotiated a total of 15 VRAs covering 80 percent of the US market. Delays in negotiating and implementing the various agreements, however, resulted in an import surge in the early part of 1985 with imported steel taking 31 percent of the domestic market in January. Import penetration gradually decreased to 22 percent in July, but still averaged 25.6 percent of US steel consumption for the first eight months of the year, barely below 1984's record 26 percent. (*Washington Post*, 5 September 1985, E1; 27 October 1985, D1)

EC steel shipments to the United States increased by 17 percent in the first eight months of 1985 and were responsible, along with unrestrained Canadian exports, for much of the import surge. US and EC negotiators finally agreed on 1 November to limit European Community shipments of finished steel products to 5.5 percent of the US market through September 1989. The pact allows a slight increase in the EC market share but extends restraints to 10 additional products, primarily stainless and other specialty steel products (many of which are already restrained under an earlier 201 action). No agreement was reached regarding semifinished steel products, however, and imports of pipe and tube will remain under a separate agreement. (*Journal of Commerce*, 4 November 1985, 3A; *Wall Street Journal*, 4 November 1985, 29; see also Case M–16, Specialty Steel)

CHANGES IN THE INDUSTRY

Shifts in the regional pattern of US imports suggest that increased shipments from nontraditional sources rapidly replaced (and more than replaced) the reductions resulting from the US-EC agreement and Japanese self-restraint. Also, despite assurances to the contrary, Canada increased its shipments to the United States to "record heights." Steel imports into the United States from sources other than the EC or Japan have soared since 1982, rising to 53 percent of all steel imports in the first half of 1984 from only 35 percent in 1978–82. The increased foreign exchange value of the dollar since 1980, and very low US operating rates in 1982 and 1983, have pushed US costs far above international norms. (Crandall 1984, 17–18; CBO, 12–13, 27)

One of the root problems of the world steel market is massive state intervention. Some state-owned and state-subsidized firms aggressively price export sales despite large and continuing losses. US firms have had difficulty meeting this kind of foreign competition. (Verner et al., 1984d, 3)

The combined impact of efficient competitors at home (the mini-mills) and abroad, falling demand, and the 1980 world recession devastated domestic integrated steelmakers. Since 1980, integrated mills have shut down roughly one-fifth of their steelmaking capacity. Analysts predict that the trend in the US steel industry toward less production, reduced capacity, and more layoffs will continue into the 1990s. (Wines, 604)

The industry claims that in 1979–83, long-term investment in plant and equipment exceeded net profits by over $1 billion. The thrust of modernization has been replacement of obsolete open-hearth capacity by the integrated mills and rapid expansion of electric furnace capacity by the mini-mills. Layoffs, and, to some extent, reduced compensation and benefit programs have lowered unit labor costs. Workers at nine Wheeling-Pittsburgh Steel Corporation mills went on strike 18 July after the company filed for bankruptcy and, with court approval, canceled its union contract and cut wages and benefits by 18 percent. The top five US steelmakers already have notified the United Steelworkers of America that they will break "a 30-year pattern of 'coordinated' bargaining and individually seek substantial concessions as contracts expire in 1986." (*Washington Post,* 7 September 1984, A14; 24 July 1985, A1)

Major steel firms have merged, notably Jones & Laughlin Steel and Republic Steel (the third and fifth largest US producers, respectively), which became LTV Steel Company in June 1984 (now the second largest US producer). These mergers facilitated the streamlining of antiquated plants and the attainment of operating economies and technological and marketing advantages. Diversification by US steel producers is also increasing. The industry leader, US Steel, bought Marathon Oil several years ago and recently added Texas Oil & Gas; Bethlehem Steel is exploring diversification; and National Intergroup has announced its plans to sell half of National Steel. (USITC 1553, A213–14; *Business Week,* 20 August 1984, 150)

Nevertheless, the integrated industry remains under severe pressure from efficient US mini-mills that recycle steel scrap (already about 20 percent of the US market), and from new suppliers overseas. Moreover, as the US economy matures, other materials are replacing steel (e.g., aluminum), and consumption of steel-intensive items is declining. US production capacity in the integrated mills will have to be further reduced in the mid-1980s, following a 13 percent reduction since 1979. Bankruptcy-law filings, foreign partnerships, and employee buyouts are likely to increase as the industry continues to restructure. As indicated by one expert, "the days of a dominant integrated steel industry may be numbered." (*Wall Street Journal,* 12 April 1985, 6; Wines, 607)

Key Statistics

Imports initially affected, from EC[a]

Year	Volume (million tons)	Value (million dollars)	Source
During TPM			
1980	3.89	1,665[b]	CBO, 13; authors' estimate
1981	6.48	3,234[b]	USITC 1651, 2; authors' estimate
Nascent MSA			
1982	5.60	2,921	USITC 1651, 2; USITC 1636, 3
1983	4.12	1,616	USITC 1651, 3
1984	6.34	2,526	USITC 1651, 3

a. Since 1981, total figures include Greece. Figures include carbon, stainless, and alloy steel, whether or not subject to the October 1982 arrangement. Carbon and alloy steel products subject to the VRA account for some 93 percent of imports from these countries. (CBO, 13; USITC 1578, 2)

b. This estimate is derived from the average unit value per ton of US imports of carbon and alloy steel products of $428 (1980) and $499 (1981). (USITC 1553, A54; USITC 1578, 3)

Imports from all sources

Year	Volume (million tons)	Value (million dollars)	Source
During TPM			
1980	15.50	6,634[a]	CBO, 15; authors' estimate
1981	19.90	9,930[a]	CBO, 15; authors' estimate
Nascent MSA			
1982	16.66	8,958	USITC 1636, 3
1983	17.07	6,393	USITC 1651, 3
1984	26.18	10,206	USITC 1651, 3

a. This estimate is derived from the average unit value per ton of US imports of carbon and alloy steel products. (USITC 1553, A54; USITC 1578, 3)

Apparent consumption

Year	Volume (million tons)	Value[a] (million dollars)	Source
During TPM			
1980	95.25	43,234	USITC 1553, A39; authors' estimate
1981	105.44	54,496	USITC 1651, 2; authors' estimate
Nascent MSA			
1982	76.39	39,181	USITC 1651, 2; authors' estimate
1983	83.46	36,136	USITC 1651, 2; authors' estimate
1984	98.21	44,925	USITC 1651, 2; authors' estimate

a. These figures are based on the value of imports from all sources plus domestic output, with minor adjustments. (USITC 1553, A39, A52; USITC 1578, 2; CRS 1984c, 9)

Market share of imports (percentage of apparent consumption, by volume)

Year	Affected imports	Total imports	Source
During TPM			
1980	4.1	16.4	authors' estimate
1981	6.1	18.9	USITC 1651, 2
Nascent MSA			
1982	7.3	21.8	USITC 1651, 2
1983	4.9	20.5	USITC 1651, 2
1984	6.5	26.7	USITC 1651, 2

Output of domestic industry[a]

Year	Volume (million tons)	Value[b] (million dollars)	Source
During TPM			
1980	83.85	38,487	USITC 1553, A39; authors' estimate
1981	88.45	46,082	USITC 1651, 2; authors' estimate
Nascent MSA			
1982	61.57	31,154	USITC 1651, 2; authors' estimate
1983	67.58	25,796	USITC 1651, 2; authors' estimate
1984	73.01	35,191	USITC 1651, 2; authors' estimate

a. Producers' shipments.

b. These estimates are based on average unit values (per ton) of US producers' shipments of carbon and alloy steel products of $459 (1980), $521 (1981), $506 (1982), $448 (1983), and $482 (1984). (USITC 1553, A77; *Washington Post*, 30 August 1984, D1)

Employment in domestic industry[a]

Year	Production workers (average number)	Source
During TPM		
1980	292,000	USITC 1553, A84
1981	286,000	USITC 1651, 1
Nascent MSA		
1982	198,000	USITC 1651, 1
1983	169,000	USITC 1651, 1
1984	171,000	USITC 1651, 1

a. From 1978 to 1983, total employment fell 56 percent or by over 200,000 workers. (*International Trade Reporter*, 14 November 1984, 594)

Wages and benefits[a]

Year	Dollars per hour	Source
During TPM		
1980	18.45	USITC 1553, A85
1981	20.16	USITC 1553, A85
Nascent MSA		
1982	23.78	USITC 1553, A85
1983	22.21	USITC 1553, A85
1984	22.21	authors' estimate

a. Steel wages were 130 percent of the national industrial average wage in 1970, and rose to 170 percent of that average in 1984. In March 1983, the United Steelworkers ratified a 41-month contract calling for a temporary 10 percent wage cut that reduced hourly compensation by $1.31. Under a court-approved bankruptcy plan, Wheeling-Pittsburgh Steel Corp., the nation's seventh largest, canceled its union contract and cut workers' wages and benefits from $21.40 per hour to $17.50 per hour. The workers went out on strike. (*New York Times*, 31 August 1984, A23; CBO, 21; *Washington Post*, 24 July 1985, A1)

Industry profits (million dollars)

Year	Profits (loss)[a]	Source
During TPM		
1980	2,823	American Iron, 12
1981	4,769	American Iron, 12
Nascent MSA		
1982	(2,119)	American Iron, 12
1983	(2,402)	American Iron, 12
1984	466[b]	O'Boyle

a. Net profits (loss) before taxes.

b. This figure reflects an American Iron and Steel Institute estimate of operating profit in the steel industry for the first three quarters of 1984. (*Wall Street Journal*, 24 January 1985, 4)

Industry capacity utilization

Year	Percentage	Source
During TPM		
1980	72.8	American Iron, 9
1981	78.3	American Iron, 9
Nascent MSA		
1982	48.4	American Iron, 9
1983	56.2	American Iron, 9
1984	67.6	USITC 1651, 1

Quantitative Profile

Item	Amount	Source
Number of years restraints in force (Phase III only, 1982 to present)	3 years	
Induced increase in price of imported steel (1984)	30 percent	authors' estimate[a]
Induced increase in price of domestic steel (1984)	12 percent	authors' estimate
Coefficient of price response	0.4	authors' estimate
Quantity and value of imports (1984)	26.2 million tons $10,206 million	USITC 1651, 3 USITC 1651, 3
Induced decrease in imports due to restraints (1984)	3.5 million tons (from EC and Japan) 7.8 million tons $3,038 million	authors' estimate[b] authors' estimate[c] authors' estimate
Quantity and value of domestic production (1984)	73.0 million tons $35,191 million	USITC 1651, 2 authors' estimate
Induced increase in domestic production due to restraints (1984)	3.9 million tons $1,880 million	authors' estimate[d] authors' estimate
Coefficient of quantity response	0.5	authors' estimate
Elasticity of demand for imported steel	0.7 2.1 to 5 2.5	USITC 1256, 49 Crandall 1981, 131[e] authors' estimate
Elasticity of supply of domestic steel	1.4 3.5 2.0	Jondrow, 24–25 Crandall 1981, 132 authors' estimate
Elasticity of demand for domestic steel	0.5 0.5 to 2.0 1.0	USITC 1256, 48 Crandall 1981, 131[e] authors' estimate
Cross-elasticity of demand for domestic steel relative to price of imported steel	0.64 0.3 to 1.1 1.2	USITC 1256, 48 Crandall 1981, 131[e] authors' estimate

Quantitative Profile (continued)

Item	Amount	Source
Cross-elasticity of output of domestic steel relative to price of imported steel	0.8	authors' estimate
Cross-elasticity of quantity of imported steel relative to price of domestic steel	3.5 to 14.4 10	Crandall 1981, 131[e] authors' estimate
Cost of restraints to US consumers	$1.1 billion (1983) $2.0 billion (1984) $4.3 billion to $5.9 billion (1983) $6.8 billion (1984)	Tarr, 25[f] Hickok, 8 CBO, 47[g] authors' estimate[h]
Gain from restraints to US producers	$428 million (1983) $1.5 billion to $3.4 billion (1983) $3.8 billion (1984)	Tarr, 25[f] CBO, 45[i] authors' estimate[h]
Tariff revenue and implied average tariff rate (1984)	$560 million 5.5 percent	authors' estimate BC, IM 146[j]
Gain from restraints to foreigners	$557 million (1983) $1.5 billion to $2.1 billion (1983) $2.0 billion (1984)	Tarr, 25[f] CBO, 46[k] authors' estimate
Efficiency loss from larger domestic production to the United States (1984)	$330 million	authors' estimate
Welfare cost of restraints to the United States	$0.9 billion (1983) $2.3 billion (1984)	CBO, 46[g] authors' estimate
Employment in protected US industry	292,000 (1980) 171,000 (1984)	USITC 1651, 1 USITC 1651, 1
Induced increase in employment	11,250 9,000	CRS, 24 Sept., 2[l] authors' estimate[m]
Cost of restraints to US consumers per job saved	$113,622 (1983) $750,000 (1984)	Tarr, 25[f] authors' estimate
Gain from restraints to US producers per job (1984)	$22,000	authors' estimate

a. In the first quarter of 1984, world carbon steel prices were about $100 per ton or 25 percent below US carbon steel prices. This estimate reflects average cost differences between, on the one hand, the United States ($482 per ton) and, on the other hand, Korea ($297 per ton), Japan ($387 per ton), and West Germany ($388 per ton). The 30 percent figure reflects a 5 percent tariff and a 25 percent scarcity premium resulting from the pre-1985 restraint agreement with the EC and the informal understanding with Japan. Robert Crandall estimates that the additional VRAs authorized by President Reagan in 1984, if they result in finished steel imports declining to 18.5 percent of the US market, will cause import prices to go up by an additional 20 percent. According to Peter Marcus, another analyst, domestic prices could rise an additional 7 percent to 10 percent. Hickok estimates that import prices would rise an additional 5 percent and domestic prices 4 percent, if finished steel imports are held to 18.5 percent of the US market. (*Washington Post*, 30 August 1984, D1, and 23 September 1984, G1; *Journal of Commerce*, 26 July 1984, 6A; Hickok, 8)

b. On 12 July 1984, the EC Commission issued a statement indicating that EC steel exports to the United States fell in 1983 by 27 percent as against their 1982 level. A figure of 1.5 million tons reflects 27 percent of a base value of 5.6 million tons. This estimate is based on the assumption that the pre-1985 Japanese self-restraint agreement exerted a somewhat larger impact on shipments than the pre-1985 VRA negotiated with the EC, and that imports from Japan decreased by 2.0 million tons. (BNA, 8 August, 14 November 1984)

c. The total decrease reflects the impact of these new restraints in addition to the decline induced by the trigger price mechanism. See Case M–13, Carbon and Alloy Steel Products: Phase II.

d. This figure reflects only restraints on the EC and Japan. Under President Reagan's September 1984 plan to limit finished steel imports to 18.5 percent of the US market, there would be an additional reduction in imports of about 25 percent and a corresponding increase in domestic output. (*Washington Post*, 23 September 1984, G1)

e. Crandall's demand elasticities are derived from a range of estimates for five categories of steel: hot-rolled sheet; cold-rolled sheet; bars; structurals; and plate.

f. This figure reflects the annual costs to US consumers of President Reagan's September 1984 plan to limit finished steel imports to 18.5 percent of the US market.

g. This figure reflects the projected additional cost of the 15-percent quota under the proposed Fair Trade in Steel Act. This quota would be significantly more restrictive than actions taken through 1984.

h. This figure reflects an additional $3.0 billion on the price of imported steel ($0.5 billion in tariffs and $2.5 billion in quota premiums), and $3.8 billion on the price of domestic steel.

i. This figure projects the income transferred to domestic steel companies as a result of the 15-percent quota under the proposed Fair Trade in Steel Act, an amount that would increase in current dollars from $1.7 billion in 1985 to $4.5 billion in 1989 (a range of $1.5 billion to $3.4 billion in 1983 dollars).

j. Due to Tokyo Round tariff cuts, tariff rates are expected to decline by roughly 0.3 percent per year over the next five years (1984–88). (Tarr and Morkre, 136–37)

k. The income transferred to foreign companies as a result of the proposed 15-percent quota under the Fair Trade in Steel Act would average roughly $2 billion in each year of the quota, reflecting a range of $1.5 billion to $2.1 billion in 1983 dollars. (CBO, 46)

l. This figure reflects the projected increase in employment in steel and related industries under President Reagan's September 1984 plan to limit finished steel imports to 18.5 percent of the US market. The 15-percent quota of the Fair Trade in Steel Act, if enacted, would increase employment by approximately 56,100 workers.

m. This figure reflects the increase in employment estimated to result from a 3.9 million ton induced increase in domestic output as a consequence of pre-1985 Japanese self-restraint and the VRA with the EC, as well as the effect of the trigger price mechanism.

Hypothetical Adjustment Program

	1984	1985	1986	1987	1988	1989	1990
US consumption of carbon steel (million tons)							
Assumed annual consumption growth of 0 percent	98.2	98.2	98.2	98.2	98.2	98.2	98.2
Imports from all sources							
Assumed annual consumption growth of 0 percent and no change in import restraints (million tons)	26.2	20.9	20.9	20.9	20.9	20.9	20.9

Hypothetical Adjustment Program (continued)

	1984	1985	1986	1987	1988	1989	1990
Assumed annual consumption growth of 0 percent and quotas rising at 1 percent per year, after dropping to 20.5 percent in 1985 (million tons)	26.2	20.9	21.9	23.0	24.0	25.0	26.0
Import share of consumption with increasing quotas (percentage)	26.7	20.5	21.5	22.5	23.5	24.5	25.5
Hypothetical quota auction rate and existing tariffs							
Quota increasing at 1 percentage point per year[a] (percent)	—	35.0	32.5	30.0	27.5	25.0	22.5
Quota auction revenue (million 1984 dollars)	—	2,770	2,700	2,610	2,500	2,380	2,230
Tariff revenue (million 1984 dollars)	570	440	460	490	510	530	550
Total revenue (million 1984 dollars)	570	3,210	3,160	3,100	3,010	2,910	2,780
US production for the domestic market (million tons)							
Assumed annual consumption growth of 0 percent and constant import share	73.0	81.1	81.1	81.1	81.1	81.1	81.1
Assumed annual consumption growth of 0 percent and rising import share	73.0	81.1	80.1	79.0	78.0	77.0	76.0
US employment in steel industry (thousand workers)							
Assumed 4 percent annual productivity growth and constant import share	170.0	166.0	159.6	153.5	147.6	141.9	136.5
Assumed 4 percent annual productivity growth and rising import share	170.0	166.0	157.6	149.5	142.0	134.7	127.9

Hypothetical Adjustment Program (continued)

	1984	1985	1986	1987	1988	1989	1990
Year-to-year employment changes (thousand workers)							
Changes induced by consumption and productivity growth with constant import share	—	−4.0	−6.4	−6.1	−5.9	−5.7	−5.4
Changes induced by rising import share	—	—	−2.0	−2.0	−1.6	−1.6	−1.4
Total employment changes	—	−4.0	−8.4	−8.1	−7.5	−7.3	−6.8
Benefit and budget calculations (1984 prices)							
Annual wage cost per worker assuming constant $22 per hour and 1,500 hours (dollars)	35,000	35,000	35,000	35,000	35,000	35,000	35,000
Benefits calculated at two times annual wage cost per worker (million dollars)	—	280	588	567	525	511	476
Projected program surplus or deficit: quota revenue less benefits (million dollars)	—	2,930	2,572	2,533	2,485	2,399	2,304

— Not applicable.
a. The figures assume that a quota increase equal to 1 percent of the domestic market depresses the quota auction rate by 2.5 percent.

BIBLIOGRAPHY

Adams, John M. 1982. "Voluntary Restraint Arrangements in United States Trade and Antitrust Law: The 1982 Steel Negotiations and Proposals for Procedural Reform." Seminar paper, Georgetown University Law Center. Summer.

American Iron and Steel Institute. 1983. *Annual Statistical Report*. Washington.

Balassa, Carol. 1984. "Levels of Protection on Manufactured Goods: the US, EC, Canada, Japan." Office of the US Trade Representative. Washington.

Bureau of National Affairs. 1984. "Current Reports." *International Trade Reporter*. Washington, 8 August.

———. 1984. "Steel." *International Trade Reporter*. Washington, 14 November.

Cline, William R. 1983. "Introduction and Summary." In *Trade Policy in the 1980s*. Edited by William R. Cline. Washington: Institute for International Economics.

Crandall, Robert W. 1981. *The US Steel Industry in Recurrent Crisis: Policy Options in a Competitive World.* Washington: Brookings Institution.

———. 1984. "The EEC-US Steel Trade Crisis." Paper presented at symposium, Euro-American Relations and Global Economic Interdependence. Bruges, Belgium, College of Europe, 13 September.

Farnsworth, Clyde H. 1984. "Voluntary Import Restraint, Effect Similar to Quotas." *New York Times,* 20 September, D1.

Hickok, Susan. 1985. "The Consumer Cost of US Trade Restraints." *Federal Reserve Bank of New York: Quarterly Review.* 10, no. 2 (Summer): 1–12.

Horlick, Gary N. 1983. "American Trade Law and the Steel Pact Between Brussels and Washington." *The World Economy* 6, no. 3 (September): 357–62.

Jondrow, James M. 1978. "Effects of Trade Restrictions on Imports of Steel." In *The Impact of International Trade and Investment on Employment.* US Department of Labor, Bureau of International Labor Affairs. Washington.

Lawrence, Richard. 1985. "US, EC Seal Steel Shipments Pact." *Journal of Commerce,* 7 January, 3A.

Morici, Peter, and Laura L. Megna. 1983. *US Economic Policies Affecting Industrial Trade: A Quantitative Assessment.* Report no. 200. Washington: National Planning Association.

O'Boyle, Thomas F. 1985. "Some Steel Firms Profit in Declining Industry by Narrowing Product Lines, Curbing Costs." *Wall Street Journal,* 24 January, 4.

Pressman, Steven. 1984. "Pressure Mounts on Protectionist Trade Bills." *Congressional Quarterly Weekly Report,* 4 August, 1896–99.

Tarr, David G., and Morris E. Morkre. 1984. *Aggregate Costs to the United States of Tariffs and Quotas on Imports: General Tariff Cuts and Removal of Quotas on Automobiles, Steel, Sugar, and Textiles.* US Federal Trade Commission, Bureau of Economics Staff Report. Washington, December.

US Congress. 1984. *Fair Trade in Steel Act of 1984* (S 2380, HR 5081). 98 Cong., 2 sess., March.

US Congressional Budget Office. 1984. *The Effects of Import Quotas on the Steel Industry.* Washington, July.

US Congressional Research Service. 1984a. "America's Steel Industry: Modernizing to Compete." Report [unnumbered] prepared by David J. Cantor. Washington, 23 April.

———. 1984b. "Output and Employment Effects of US Steel Imports." Report no. 84–658–E, prepared by David J. Cantor. Washington, 5 June.

———. 1984c. "Import Quotas for Steel: US International Trade Commission Remedy Recommendations vs. The Fair Trade in Steel Act of 1984." Report no. 84–703–E, prepared by David J. Cantor. Washington, 26 July.

———. 1984d. "Potential Effects of a 15-Percent Steel Import Quota on Costs of Production in Major Steel-Using Industries." Report [unnumbered] prepared by David J. Cantor. Washington, 18 September.

———. 1984e. "Steel Import Limits: Estimated Import Reduction Under Three Alternative Proposals." Report no. 84–750–E, prepared by David J. Cantor. Washington, 24 September.

US Department of Commerce. Bureau of the Census. 1984. *US Imports for Consumption.* IM 146. Washington, December.

US General Accounting Office. 1981. *New Strategy Required for Aiding Distressed Steel Industry.* EMD–81–29. Washington, 8 January.

US International Trade Commission. 1982. *Economic Effects of Export Restraints.* USITC Publication no. 1256. Washington, June.

———. 1984a. *Carbon and Certain Alloy Steel Products.* 2 vols. USITC Publication no. 1553. Washington, July.

———. 1984b. *Monthly Report on Selected Steel Industry Data.* USITC Publication no. 1578. Washington, September.

———. 1984c. *Monthly Report on Selected Steel Industry Data.* USITC Publication no. 1627. Washington, December.

———. 1985a. *Monthly Report on Selected Steel Industry Data.* USITC Publication no. 1636. Washington, January.

———. 1985b. *Monthly Report on Selected Steel Industry Data.* USITC Publication no. 1651. Washington, February.

US Trade Representative. 1982. *Twenty-sixth Annual Report of the President of the United States on the Trade Agreements Program 1981–82.* Washington, November.

———. 1984. "Brock Announces President's Steel Decision." Washington, 18 September.

Verner, Liipfert, Bernhard, McPherson, and Hand. 1984a. *Government Aid to the Steel Industry of the European Communities: Market Distortion in Europe and Its Impact on the US Steel Industry.* Washington: American Iron and Steel Institute.

———. 1984b. *Japanese Government Promotion of the Steel Industry: Three Decades of Industrial Policy.* Washington: American Iron and Steel Institute.

———. 1984c. *The Rise of Steelmaking in the Developing Countries: State Intervention in the Market and Its Effect on International Trade in Steel.* Washington: American Iron and Steel Institute.

———. 1984d. *Steel and the State: Government Intervention in the Market and Its Effect on International Trade in Steel.* Washington: American Iron and Steel Institute.

Walter, Ingo. 1983. "Structural Adjustment and Trade Policy in the International Steel Industry." In *Trade Policy in the 1980s.* Edited by William R. Cline. Washington: Institute for International Economics.

Wicker, Tom. 1984. "Damned Either Way." *New York Times,* 31 August, A23.

Wines, Michael. 1984. "Steel: Managing Decline." *National Journal,* 31 March, 603–7.

CASE M-15

Ball Bearings

PERIOD OF RELIEF

2 May 1974 to 1 May 1978

SUPPLIERS AFFECTED

Global (primarily Japan)

RELIEF ACTION

In response to a petition filed by the Antifriction Bearings Manufacturers Association requesting import relief on behalf of its member companies, the US Tariff Commission (renamed the US International Trade Commission by the Trade Act of 1974) instituted an investigation on 31 January 1973 under Section 301(b) of the Trade Expansion Act of 1962. On 30 July 1973, the Commission sent a report of its findings to President Richard M. Nixon. One commissioner dissented from the majority and two commissioners did not participate. (USTC 597, 1–2)

The Commission made an affirmative injury from imports determination for ball bearings with integral shafts and for radial ball bearings with an outside diameter of over nine millimeters, and rendered a negative decision for antifriction balls and for radial ball bearings with an outside diameter under nine millimeters. The Commission made no determination for parts of ball bearings, nor for antifriction balls, ball bearings with integral shafts, and radial ball bearings imported from Canada under the US-Canadian automotive agreement.[1] (USTC 597, 3–5)

On 28 September 1973, President Nixon requested supplemental information under Section 351(a)(4) of the Trade Expansion Act of 1962. This request was prompted by the receipt of preliminary evidence indicating an increase in costs abroad that would tend to make the domestic industry more competitive with foreign suppliers. On 4 October 1973, the Commission instituted an investigation and submitted a supplemental report to President Nixon in January 1974. (USTC 649, 1–2)

---

1. See Case M–22, Automobiles, for more details on the US-Canadian agreement.

The Commission recommended an increase in the duty rate for ball bearings with integral shafts to 12 percent ad valorem and an increase in the duty rate for radial ball bearings with an outside diameter of over nine millimeters to 3.4 cents a pound plus 15 percent ad valorem. Presidential proclamation 4279 of 29 March 1974 modified the duty rates for radial ball bearings with an outside diameter of nine to ten millimeters to 20 percent ad valorem. The President did not grant relief for ball bearings with integral shafts. On average, escape clause relief increased the ad valorem duty by about 4 percent. The relief period expired on 1 May 1978. (USTC 597, 3; BIE; BC, IM 146)

CHANGES IN THE INDUSTRY

Following a seven-year period of import expansion at an average annual rate of 25 percent, imports dropped 40 percent in volume terms in 1975 as a result of the application of increased duty rates, coupled with stagnation in domestic demand (particularly in the auto industry). During the remaining relief period, imports increased at an average annual rate of 22 percent, although most of the increase occurred in 1978 in response to the phasing out of escape clause duties. Between 1977 and 1978, imports increased 39 percent in volume terms. (BIE)

The bearings industry did not keep pace with the US recovery during the period of protection. The years 1975–77 were characterized by falling profits, reduced capacity utilization, lower domestic demand, and declines in output and export volumes. As a result of these conditions, and in an attempt to remain price competitive with foreign suppliers (especially the Japanese), manufacturers cancelled or cut back plans for expansion. (BIE)

In late 1977 and 1978, the industry finally participated in the recovery, experiencing increased profits and capacity utilization, an increase in employment to the 1973 level, and substantially higher output and demand. Manufacturers began to make plans to upgrade equipment and expand facilities. The bearings manufacturers did not petition for further protection, and escape clause duties were phased out on 1 May 1978. (BIE)

Key Statistics

Imports from all sources[a]

Year	Volume[b] (million units)	Value (million dollars)	Source
Before restraints			
1973	173	112	BC, FT 246
During restraints			
1974	178	122	BC, FT 246
1975	108	108	BC, FT 246
1976	124	108	BC, FT 246
1977	140	130	BC, FT 246
1978	195	199	BC, FT 246
After restraints			
1979	210	246	BC, FT 246

a. Import figures include data on miniature radial ball bearings, which were not subject to escape clause action. Imports of miniature ball bearings constitute an average of 2.3 percent of total imports.

b. Since volume data for ball bearings with integral shafts is available only in pounds, units data have been estimated. A factor of 11 percent was used, as the affected categories of ball bearings, on average, accounted for 11 percent of the total volume of imports.

Apparent consumption[a]

Year	Volume (million units)	Value (million dollars)	Source
Before restraints			
1973	724	603	authors' estimate
During restraints			
1974	707	690	authors' estimate
1975	602	690	authors' estimate
1976	587	700	authors' estimate
1977	562	824	authors' estimate
1978	689	1,049	authors' estimate
After restraints			
1979	694	1,255	authors' estimate

a. These estimates are derived from the volume of output and imports combined. The value estimates include an adjustment for exports but export volume data were unavailable. This should not significantly affect the estimates, as exports are quite small.

Market share of imports (percentage of apparent consumption, by volume)

Year	Share	Source
Before restraints		
1973	23.7	authors' estimate
During restraints		
1974	25.0	authors' estimate
1975	17.7	authors' estimate
1976	21.0	authors' estimate
1977	24.8	authors' estimate
1978	28.1	authors' estimate
After restraints		
1979	30.1	authors' estimate

Output of domestic industry[a]

Year	Volume[b] (million units)	Value (million dollars)	Source
Before restraints			
1973	551	533	DIBA; BC 1980
During restraints			
1974	529	624	DIBA; BC 1980
1975	495	646	authors' estimate; BC 1980
1976	462	655	authors' estimate; BC 1980
1977	421	750	BC, MA–35Q
1978	494	910	BC, MA–35Q
After restraints			
1979	484	1,076	BC, MA–35Q

a. Producers' shipments.
b. The 1975 and 1976 estimates are based on trend information.

Employment in the domestic industry[a]

Year	Production workers (average number)	Source
Before restraints		
1973	43,900	BC, MC82, 3
During restraints		
1974	45,000	BC, MC82, 3
1975	40,200	BC, MC82, 3
1976	39,900	BC, MC82, 3
1977	41,300	BC, MC82, 3
1978	43,200	BC, MC82, 3

Employment in the domestic industry[a] (continued)

Year	Production workers (average number)	Source
After restraints		
1979	43,100	BC, MC82, 3

a. This information is based on the ball and roller bearing industry (SIC 3562) as a whole. Data were not available specifically for the ball bearings industry.

Wages

Year	Dollars per hour	Source
Before restraints		
1973	5.16	BC, MC82, 3
During restraints		
1974	5.51	BC, MC82, 3
1975	6.04	BC, MC82, 3
1976	6.59	BC, MC82, 3
1977	7.04	BC, MC82, 3
1978	7.66	BC, MC82, 3
After restraints		
1979	8.46	BC, MC82, 3

Industry profits (million dollars)

Year	Profits[a]	Source
Before restraints		
1973	n.a.	
During restraints		
1974	n.a.	
1975	25.3	Morris
1976	37.5	Morris
1977	9.0	Morris
1978	29.8	Morris
After restraints		
1979	25.2	Morris

n.a. Not available.

a. Net profits before taxes.

Industry capacity utilization

Year	Percentage	Source
Before restraints		
1973	n.a.	
During restraints		
1974	86	BC, MQ–CI
1975	75	BC, MQ–CI
1976	80	BC, MQ–CI
1977	78	BC, MQ–CI
1978	87	BC, MQ–CI
After restraints		
1979	84	BC, MQ–CI

n.a. Not available.

Quantitative Profile

Item	Amount	Source
Number of years restraints in force (1974–78)	4 years	
Induced increase in price of imported ball bearings (1978)	12 percent	authors' estimate[a]
Induced increase in price of domestic ball bearings (1978)	2.4 percent	authors' estimate
Coefficient of price response	0.2	authors' estimate
Quantity and value of imports (1978)	195 million units	BC, FT 246
	$199 million	BC, FT 246
Induced decrease in imports due to restraints	6 million units	authors' estimate
	$6 million	authors' estimate
Quantity and value of domestic production (1978)	494 million units	BC, MA–35Q
	$910 million	BC, MA–35Q
Induced increase in domestic production due to restraints	6 million units	authors' estimate
Coefficient of quantity response	1.0	authors' estimate
Elasticity of demand for imported ball bearings	0.25	authors' estimate
Elasticity of supply of domestic ball bearings	2.0	authors' estimate
Elasticity of demand for domestic ball bearings	0.1	authors' estimate
Cross-elasticity of demand for domestic ball bearings relative to price of imported ball bearings	0.4	authors' estimate

Quantitative Profile (continued)

Item	Amount	Source
Cross-elasticity of output of domestic ball bearings relative to price of imported ball bearings	0.4	authors' estimate
Cross-elasticity of quantity of imported ball bearings relative to price of domestic ball bearings	5	authors' estimate
Cost of restraints to US consumers (1977)	$45 million	authors' estimate
Gain from restraints to US producers (1977)	$21 million	authors' estimate
Tariff revenue and implied average tariff rate (1979)	$18.0 million 7.8 percent	BC, IM 146 BC, IM 146
Gain from restraints to foreigners	negligible	authors' estimate
Efficiency loss from larger domestic production to the United States (1977)	under $1 million	authors' estimate
Welfare cost of restraints to the United States (1977)	under $1 million	authors' estimate
Employment in protected US industry	43,900 (1973) 43,200 (1978)	BC, MC82, 3 BC, MC82, 3
Induced increase in employment (1977)	500	authors' estimate
Cost of restraints to US consumers per job saved (1977)	$90,000	authors' estimate
Gain from restraints to US producers per job (1977)	$500	authors' estimate

a. This figure reflects an estimated existing tariff duty of 8 percent and an estimated escape clause duty of 4 percent.

BIBLIOGRAPHY

Morris, Robert, and Associates. Various years. *Annual Statement Studies*. Philadelphia.

US Department of Commerce. Bureau of the Census. Various years. *Current Industrial Reports*. Publication no. MA–35Q. Washington.

———. Various years. *Current Industrial Reports: Survey of Plant Capacity*. Publication no. MQ–CI. Washington.

———. Various years. *US Imports for Consumption and General Imports*. FT 246. Washington.

———. Various years. *US Exports*. FT 410. Washington.

———. 1978, 1979. *US Imports for Consumption*. IM 146. Washington, December.

———. 1980. *Annual Survey of Manufactures*. Washington.

———. 1984. *1982 Census of Manufactures: Ball and Roller Bearings*. Publication no. MC82–I–35E–2(P). Washington.

———. Bureau of Industrial Economics. 1978, 1979. *US Industrial Outlook*. Washington.

———. Domestic and International Business Administration. 1972–74. *Antifriction Bearings Shipments and Trade*. Washington.

US International Trade Commission. 1981. *Summary of Trade and Tariff Information: Ball and Roller Bearings and Parts*. USITC Publication no. 841, control no. 6–4–10. Washington, July.

US Tariff Commission. 1973. *Antifriction Balls and Ball Bearings, Including Ball Bearings with Integral Shafts, and Parts Thereof.* USTC Publication no. 597. Washington, July.
———. 1974. *Antifriction Balls and Ball Bearings, Including Ball Bearings with Integral Shafts, and Parts Thereof.* USTC Publication no. 649. Washington, January.

CASE M-16

Specialty Steel

PERIOD OF RELIEF

14 June 1976 to 13 February 1980
1 January 1983 to 1 January 1987

SUPPLIERS AFFECTED

Global (primarily Argentina, Brazil, Canada, European Community [EC], Japan, Korea, Mexico, Spain, and Sweden)

RELIEF ACTION

Following the expiration of voluntary restraints on Japanese and European steel imports in 1974 (see Case M-12, Carbon and Alloy Steel Products: Phase I), the specialty steel industry petitioned the US International Trade Commission (USITC) under Section 201 of the Trade Act of 1974 for escape clause relief from stainless steel and alloy tool steel imports. On 16 January 1976, the USITC reported an affirmative finding of injury to President Gerald R. Ford and recommended that quantitative restrictions be imposed on stainless steel sheet and strip, plate, bars, and wire rods, and alloy tool steel imports. The USITC made a negative determination with respect to imported ingots, blooms, billets, slabs, and sheet bars under investigation, and thus recommended no relief. (Morici and Megna, 21; USITC 968, A5–6)

President Ford accepted the USITC findings and recommendations but, before granting relief, attempted to negotiate orderly marketing agreements (OMAs) with leading US suppliers of stainless and alloy tool steel. Only Japan responded positively, and a three-year OMA was negotiated, effective 14 June 1976 through 13 June 1979, which set annual limits on the five categories of imported specialty steel causing injury to the domestic industry.[1] The sheet and strip allocation was slightly above the 1975 level of Japanese imports; the amounts provided in the other four categories

---

1. See Agreement on Specialty Steel Imports, June 1976, United States-Japan, TIAS No. 8442.

were 20 percent to 50 percent below the 1975 level. The agreement provided some flexibility in meeting current market conditions; the principal result was to increase sheet and strip levels at the expense of other categories. The Japanese agreement was extended eight months and terminated 13 February 1980. (Morici and Megna, 21–22; GATT, 44)

On 11 June 1976, President Ford issued presidential proclamation no. 4445 providing import relief in the form of quantitative restrictions against all other suppliers for three years. The relief was phased down during the three-year period by increasing quota levels 3 percent annually. Quotas were imposed on a trading area or country-by-country basis with respect to larger suppliers, while a basket quota was used for all other suppliers.[2] This enabled all small suppliers to obtain market shares on a competitive basis. The size of the basket could be expanded if the principal suppliers fell short of quota levels and such shortfalls were reallocated. (Morici and Megna, 21; USITC 968, A6; GATT, 45)

On 14 October 1976, the Special Representative for Trade Negotiations (known informally as the Special Trade Representative, STR) requested that the USITC conduct an investigation under Section 203(i)(2) of the Trade Act of 1974 on the probable economic effect of terminating the quantitative restrictions on bearing steel imposed by proclamation 4445. On 14 February 1977, the USITC advised President Jimmy Carter that the effect of terminating such relief would be negligible. On 15 June 1977, President Jimmy Carter issued proclamation 4509 terminating the restrictions. (USITC 1377, A4)

On 25 May 1977, the STR again requested advice from the USITC concerning the probable economic effect of terminating or reducing all relief for the specialty steel industry. As a result of the investigation, on 14 October 1977 two commissioners determined that termination or reduction of relief would have serious adverse economic effects; one commissioner advised that chipper knife steel and band saw steel could be removed from the quota without adverse effects; and one commissioner advised that termination or reduction of all relief would have no substantial adverse impact on the domestic industry. Following receipt of this advice, on 5 April 1978, President Carter issued proclamation 4559, excluding chipper knife steel and band saw steel from the quota on alloy tool steel. (USITC 1377, A4)

On 11 December 1978, industry representatives and the United Steelworkers of America petitioned the USITC to conduct a review investigation under Section 203 of the Trade Act of 1974. Petitioners also requested that the relief period be extended so that modernization plans could be completed. On 24 April 1979, the USITC rendered a split decision, with two commissioners favoring extended import relief and two opposed. The two commissioners favoring extended relief found that increases in foreign capacity and a projected economic downturn in the United States could lead to increased imports and injury to the domestic industry if quotas were terminated. The two other commissioners argued that the industry had adjusted successfully to

---

2. The six basic source categories were Japan, the European Community, Canada, Sweden, all other countries entitled to TSUS Column 1 rates of duty, and all other countries. (USITC 1377, A3)

foreign competition and that the economic health of the domestic industry was "exceptionally good and comparable to 1974, which was the industry's historic peak year." On 12 June 1979, President Carter issued proclamation 4665, extending the quotas for eight months. Import relief was terminated on 14 February 1980. (USITC 1377, A5)

On 26 February 1982 and 9 August 1982, in response to petitions filed by the Tool and Stainless Steel Industry Committee and the United Steelworkers of America, the US Trade Representative (USTR)[3] initiated investigations under Section 301(a)(2)(A) of the Trade Act of 1974. Based on findings that the European Community (EC), Austria, and Sweden subsidized stainless and alloy tool steel production, President Ronald Reagan directed the USTR to request an expedited USITC investigation on the effects of such imports under Section 201 of the 1974 trade act. In other words, an "unfair" trade investigation under Section 301 was converted, at White House direction, into a "fair-but-injurious" investigation under Section 201. The President also directed the USTR to initiate multilateral and/or bilateral discussions aimed at the elimination of all trade distortive practices in the specialty steel sector and to monitor imports of specialty steel subject to the Section 201 proceeding. (USITC 1377, 4–8, A2)

The USITC instituted its investigation on 9 December 1982, and on 24 March 1983 unanimously determined that imports were a substantial cause of serious injury to the domestic industry. On 27 April 1983, the USITC recommended that country-by-country quotas be imposed with retroactive effect beginning 1 January 1983. The USITC proposed that the quotas be based on the market share of imports during 1979–81, and recommended that the targeted amount for each calendar year equal the following market shares of forecast US consumption, but not be less than the following quantities: sheet and strip at 62,900 short tons (8 percent); plate at 10,700 short tons (10 percent); bars at 27,000 short tons (17 percent); rods at 19,100 short tons (42 percent); and alloy tool steel at 22,100 short tons (20 percent). These target market shares and minimum quantities were equal to import averages during 1972–82, exclusive of imports in the years 1975 and 1982. The quotas were to extend for three years terminating 31 December 1985. (USITC 1377, 4–8, 39–40)

On 5 July 1983, President Reagan granted four years of import relief, retroactive to 1 January 1983, in the form of degressive tariffs for stainless steel sheet and strip, and plate (about 55 percent of specialty steel imports), and quotas for stainless steel bars and rods, and alloy tool steel. For stainless steel sheet and strip, tariffs were increased by 10 percent ad valorem in the first year, declining by two percentage points per year over the next three years. For stainless steel plate, the tariff was increased by 8 percent ad valorem in the first year, declining to 6 percent in the second, and by one percentage point per year in the following two years. Global quotas on stainless steel bars and rods and alloy tool steel were based on the USITC-recommended minimum import tonnages, and were to expand at an annual rate of

---

3. Upon completion of the Tokyo Round of trade negotiations, Congress passed the Trade Act of 1979, which, among other things, renamed the Office of the Special Representative for Trade Negotiations (STR) as the Office of the US Trade Representative (USTR).

3 percent. Relief took effect within 15 days. (USITC, 1580, 3, 36–37; Reagan, 1; *Journal of Commerce*, 6 July 1983, 5A)

Following this action, the European Community (EC) asserted its rights under the General Agreement on Tariffs and Trade (GATT), and demanded up to $160 million a year in trade compensation in the form of lower US duties on EC steel and textile products. US-EC negotiations on the appropriate level of compensation broke down in November 1984. The EC later retaliated against US chemicals, plastics, and other products by increasing European duties about $160 million a year. (*Journal of Commerce*, 6 September 1983, 1A; 28 November 1983, 3A; *New York Times*, 1 September 1983, D1)

In 1984, US specialty steel producers argued that quotas were helping that segment of the industry protected by quantitative restrictions, but that increased tariffs on flat-rolled specialty steels were not preventing rising imports. On 3 July 1984, the industry asked President Reagan to remove the higher tariffs on stainless steel sheet, strip, and plate and replace them with quotas. On 20 August 1984, USTR William E. Brock responded that the administration would continue to monitor closely the trade in stainless steel sheet and strip, and would "pay particular close attention to any surges in imports that might occur." (*New York Times*, 22 August 1984, D1; *Journal of Commerce*, 19 July 1984, 5A; 6 September 1984, 1A)

CHANGES IN THE INDUSTRY

The US specialty steel sector produces high-value, technology-intensive products. These products increased from 8 percent of total US steel shipments in 1963 to 11 percent in 1983. US producers took advantage of import relief during 1976–80 to modernize and rationalize their industry. Firms increased use of the more efficient argon-oxygen-decarbonization (AOD) process in production. Between 1975 and 1978, use of the AOD process increased from 60 percent to 95 percent of output. Improved efficiency enabled domestic firms to compete against some imports from abroad and to increase exports of certain specialty steel products. (USITC 968, 15–16)

The recession of the early 1980s adversely affected the domestic industry. In 1982, domestic prices fell and the US producer share of the US market declined; imports of stainless and alloy tool steel subject to the USITC investigation reached their highest recorded levels since 1978; while domestic consumption fell to its lowest level during the same period. As a result, there was significant idling of productive facilities; employment and hours worked declined substantially, and many firms were unable to earn profits. (USITC 1377, 78)

In 1983, some 29 US firms were producing stainless steel and/or alloy tool steel products. In 1984, US industry officials announced that planned investment in capital improvements and research and development had increased more than 66 percent for 1982–87 as compared with the 1974–79 period, and totaled nearly $1 billion. While acknowledging that import quotas had induced a "modest" recovery in stainless steel bar and rod and alloy tool steel production, industry officials claimed that subsidized imports of stainless steel sheet and strip continued to prevent progress in those segments of the domestic industry. (*International Trade Reporter*, 25 July 1984, 94)

Key Statistics

Imports from all sources

Year	Volume (thousand tons)	Value (million dollars)	Source
Before restraints			
1974	151	176	USITC 1377, A21; USITC 968, A79, A88
1975	154	195	USITC 1377, A21; USITC 968, A79, A88
During restraints			
1976	167	213	USITC 1377, A21; USITC 968, A79, A88
1977	141	211	USITC 1377, A21; USITC 968, A79, A88
1978	163	259	USITC 1377, A21; A96
1979	151	273	USITC 1377, A21; A96
Interim period			
1980	130	283	USITC 1377, A21; A96
1981	176	353	USITC 1377, A21; A96
1982	203	373	USITC 1377, A21; A96
During restraints			
1983	189	313	BC, IM 146
1984	231	404	BC, IM 146

Apparent consumption

Year	Volume (thousand tons)	Value[a] (million dollars)	Source
Before restraints			
1974	1,325	2,031	USITC 968, A3; authors' estimate
1975	850	1,465	USITC 968, A3; authors' estimate
During restraints			
1976	1,101	1,852	USITC 968, A3; authors' estimate
1977	1,143	2,035	USITC 968, A3; authors' estimate
1978	1,264	2,410	USITC 1377, A88; authors' estimate
1979	1,387	3,062	USITC 1377, A88; authors' estimate
Interim period			
1980	1,101	2,737	USITC 1377, A88; authors' estimate
1981	1,219	3,001	USITC 1377, A88; authors' estimate
1982	1,018	2,955	USITC 1377, A88; authors' estimate
During restraints			
1983	1,174[b]	3,003	authors' estimate
1984	1,377[b]	3,639	authors' estimate

a. These figures are based on the value of imports from all sources plus producers' shipments, excluding exports.

b. This estimate is based on the volume of imports from all sources plus US shipments.

Market share of imports (percentage of apparent consumption, by volume)

Year	Share	Source
Before restraints		
1974	11.4	USITC 968, A90
1975	18.1	USITC 968, A90
During restraints		
1976	15.2	USITC 968, A90
1977	12.3	USITC 968, A90
1978	12.9	USITC 1377, A88
1979	10.8	USITC 1377, A88
Interim period		
1980	11.8	USITC 1377, A88
1981	14.4	USITC 1377, A88
1982	19.9	USITC 1377, A88
During restraints		
1983	16.1	authors' estimate
1984	16.8	authors' estimate

Output of domestic industry[a]

Year	Volume (thousand tons)	Value (million dollars)	Source
Before restraints			
1974	1,264	1,997	USITC 968, A3; A92
1975	744	1,357	USITC 968, A3; A92
During restraints			
1976	994	1,744	USITC 968, A3; A92
1977	1,057	1,924	USITC 968, A3; A92
1978	1,152	2,251	USITC 1377, A88; USITC 968, A92
1979	1,311	2,958	USITC 1377, A88; USITC 1193, A116
Interim period			
1980	1,083	2,737	USITC 1377, A88; USITC 1193, A116
1981	1,108	2,813	USITC 1377, A88; USITC 1193, A116
1982	854	2,706	USITC 1377, A88; USITC 1508, 6
During restraints			
1983	985	3,048	USITC 1690, 5; USITC 1508, 6
1984	1,146	3,235	USITC 1690, 5; USITC 1666, 6

a. Producers' shipments.

Employment in domestic industry

Year	Production workers (average number)	Source
Before restraints		
1974	23,824	USITC 968, A3
1975	16,102	USITC 968, A3
During restraints		
1976	18,624	USITC 968, A3
1977	18,473	USITC 968, A3
1978	17,437	USITC 1377, A110
1979	18,347	USITC 1377, A110
Interim period		
1980	16,744	USITC 1377, A110
1981	16,137	USITC 1377, A110
1982	13,323	USITC 1377, A110
During restraints		
1983	11,737	USITC 1690, 7
1984	14,196	USITC 1690, 7

Wages and benefits[a]

Year	Dollars per hour	Source
Before restraints		
1974	6.41	BLS 1979, 139
1975	7.12	BLS 1979, 139
During restraints		
1976	7.79	BLS 1979, 139
1977	8.59	BLS 1983, 44
1978	13.55	USITC 1377, A114–15
1979	15.02	USITC 1377, A114–15
Interim period		
1980	17.11	USITC 1377, A114–15
1981	19.38	USITC 1377, A114–15
1982	22.29	USITC 1377, A114–15
During restraints		
1983	23.00	authors' estimate
1984	23.50	authors' estimate

a. The figures for 1974–77 reflect wages for workers in blast furnaces and steel mills generally. The figures for 1978–84 reflect average total hourly compensation paid to production and related workers producing stainless and alloy tool steel.

Industry profits[a] (million dollars)

Year	Profits (loss)[b]	Source
Before restraints		
1974	259	USITC 968, A128
1975	81	USITC 968, A128
During restraints		
1976	87	USITC 968, A128
1977	204	USITC 968, A128
1978	214	USITC 1377, A116
1979	308	USITC 1377, A116
Interim period		
1980	174	USITC 1377, A116
1981	108	USITC 1377, A116
1982	(94)	USITC 1377, A116
During restraints		
1983	103	USITC 1666, 6
1984	265	USITC 1666, 6

a. These figures represent US firms accounting for approximately 90 percent of US producers' shipments.
b. Net profits (loss) before taxes.

Industry capacity utilization[a]

Year	Percentage	Source
Before restraints		
1974	81.4	USITC 968, A99
1975	46.6	USITC 968, A99
During restraints		
1976	54.4	USITC 968, A99
1977	56.0	USITC 968, A99
1978	65.5	USITC 1377, A24
1979	70.0	USITC 1377, A24
Interim period		
1980	58.2	USITC 1377, A24
1981	56.9	USITC 1377, A24
1982	42.0	USITC 1377, A24
During restraints		
1983	56.0	authors' estimate
1984	70.0	authors' estimate

a. These figures represent the total average percentage for stainless steel (sheets and strip, plate, bars, wire rods) and alloy tool steel.

Quantitative Profile

Item	Amount	Source
Number of years restraints in force (1976–80, 1982–86)	8 years	
Induced increase in price of imported specialty steel	6 percent (1976–80) 25 percent (1983–85)	Morici, 22[a] authors' estimate[b]
Induced increase in price of domestic specialty steel (1983–85)	15 percent	authors' estimate
Coefficient of price response	0.6	authors' estimate
Quantity and value of imports (1984)	231,000 tons $404 million	BC, IM 146 BC, IM 146
Induced decrease in imports due to restraints	24,201 tons (1976–79) 44,000 tons (1983–85) $77 million (1983–85)	USITC 968, A144[c] authors' estimate[d] authors' estimate[d]
Quantity and value of domestic production (1984)	1,146,000 tons $3,235 million	USITC 1690, 5 USITC 1666, 6
Induced increase in domestic production due to restraints	21,000 tons (1976–77) 40,000 tons (1983–85)	USITC 968, A142[e] authors' estimate[d]
Coefficient of quantity response	0.9	authors' estimate
Elasticity of demand for imported specialty steel	1.5	authors' estimate
Elasticity of supply of domestic specialty steel	1.0	authors' estimate
Elasticity of demand for domestic specialty steel	0.8	USITC 968, A149[f]
Cross-elasticity of demand for domestic specialty steel relative to price of imported specialty steel	0.77 0.9	USITC 968, A141[f] authors' estimate
Cross-elasticity of output of domestic specialty steel relative to price of imported specialty steel	0.5	authors' estimate
Cross-elasticity of quantity of imported specialty steel relative to price of domestic specialty steel	6.0	authors' estimate
Cost of restraints to US consumers (1984)	$520 million	authors' estimate
Gain from restraints to US producers (1984)	$420 million	authors' estimate
Tariff revenue and implied average tariff rate (1983)	$32.5 million 10.2 percent	BC, IM 146 authors' estimate
Gain from restraints to foreigners (1984)	$50 million	authors' estimate
Efficiency loss of larger domestic production to the United States (1984)	$30 million	authors' estimate

Quantitative Profile (continued)

Item	Amount	Source
Welfare cost of restraints to the United States (1984)	$80 million	authors' estimate
Employment in protected US industry	16,102 (1975)	USITC 968, A3
	16,744 (1980)	USITC 1377, A110
	14,196 (1984)	USITC 1690, 7
Induced increase in employment (1984)	500	authors' estimate
Cost of restraints to US consumers per job saved (1984)	$1 million	authors' estimate
Gain from restraints to US producers per job (1984)	$60,000	authors' estimate

a. This figure reflects an estimate of the quota-induced increase in the price of imported stainless steel sheet and strip (these items accounted for two-thirds of domestic specialty steel production during this period). The figure does not include the tariff.

b. This figure includes a tariff of 10 percent and a quota premium of 15 percent.

c. This figure reflects USITC estimates of reduced stainless steel sheet and strip imports during the quota years 1976–79. According to USITC figures, those imports were reduced 21,313 tons (1976–77), 25,030 tons (1977–78), and 26,260 tons (1978–79) due to quotas, representing an annual average of 24,201 tons.

d. These figures assume that tariffs and VRAs caused imports to decline by 3.5 percent of domestic consumption, and domestic production to substitute for 90 percent of the import loss.

e. This figure is a USITC estimate of increased US shipments of stainless steel sheet and strip due to quotas during the first quota year (1976–77).

f. The coefficient refers only to demand for stainless steel sheet and strip products.

Hypothetical Adjustment Program

	1984	1985	1986	1987	1988	1989	1990
US consumption of specialty steel (thousand short tons)							
Assumed annual consumption growth of 0 percent	1,400	1,400	1,400	1,400	1,400	1,400	1,400
Imports from all sources							
Assumed annual consumption growth of 0 percent and no change in import restraints (thousand short tons)	230	230	230	230	230	230	230
Assumed annual consumption growth of 0 percent and quota expansion of 20 thousand tons per year (thousand short tons)	230	250	270	290	310	330	330

Hypothetical Adjustment Program (continued)

	1984	1985	1986	1987	1988	1989	1990
Import share of consumption with increasing quotas (percentage)	16.4	17.9	19.3	20.7	22.1	23.6	23.6
Hypothetical quota auction and tariff							
Quota auction							
Rate (percent)	—	11	7	3	—	—	—
Revenue (million 1984 dollars)	—	45	30	15	—	—	—
Tariff							
Rate (percent)	10	10	10	10	9	5	5
Revenue (million 1984 dollars)	40	45	50	50	50	30	30
Total							
Rate (percent)	10	21	17	13	9	5	5
Revenue (million 1984 dollars)	40	90	80	65	50	30	30
US production for the domestic market (thousand short tons)							
Assumed annual consumption growth of 0 percent and constant import share	1,170	1,170	1,170	1,170	1,170	1,170	1,170
Assumed annual consumption growth of 0 percent and rising import share	1,170	1,150	1,130	1,110	1,090	1,070	1,070
US employment in specialty steel (workers)							
Assumed 5 percent annual productivity growth and constant import share	4,200	13,520	12,880	12,270	11,680	11,130	10,600
Assumed 5 percent annual productivity growth and rising import share	4,200	13,290	12,400	11,640	10,880	10,180	9,690
Year-to-year employment changes (workers)							
Changes induced by consumption and productivity growth with constant import share	—	−680	−640	−610	−590	−550	−530

Hypothetical Adjustment Program (continued)

	1984	1985	1986	1987	1988	1989	1990
Changes induced by rising import share	—	−230	−250	−150	−170	−150	40
Total employment changes	—	−910	−890	−760	−760	−700	−490
Benefit and budget calculations (1984 prices)							
Annual wage cost per worker assuming constant $23 per hour and 1,500 hours (dollars)	35,000	35,000	35,000	35,000	35,000	35,000	35,000
Benefits calculated at two times annual wage cost per worker (million dollars)	—	64	62	53	53	49	28
Projected program surplus or deficit: tariff and quota revenue less benefits (million dollars)	—	26	18	12	−3	−19	2

— Not applicable.

BIBLIOGRAPHY

Chira, Susan. 1984. "The Fight Over Steel Quotas." *New York Times*, 22 August, D1.

Crandall, Robert W. 1978. "Federal Government Initiatives to Reduce the Price Level." *Brookings Papers on Economic Activity* 2.

Ericson, Helen. 1984. "Specialty Steel Presses for Quotas." *Journal of Commerce*, 6 September, 1A.

GATT Secretariat. 1978. "Modalities of Application of Article XIX." Report L/4679. Geneva, 5 July.

Morici, Peter, and Laura L. Megna. 1983. *US Economic Policies Affecting Industrial Trade: A Quantitative Assessment*. Report no. 200. Washington: National Planning Association.

Reagan, Ronald. 1983. "Specialty Steel Import Relief Determination." Memorandum for the US Trade Representative. Washington, 5 July.

"Trade Talks Intensify Over Specialty Steel." 1983. *Journal of Commerce*, 6 September, 1A.

US Department of Commerce. Bureau of the Census. 1983. *Imports for Consumption*. IM 146. Washington, December.

US Department of Labor. Bureau of Labor Statistics. 1979. *Employment and Earnings, United States, 1909–78*. Washington, July.

———. 1983. *Supplement to Employment and Earnings*. Washington, July.

US International Trade Commission. 1976. *Stainless Steel and Alloy Tool Steel: Report to the President on Investigation No. TA–210–5*. USITC Publication no. 756. Washington, January.

———. 1977a. *Certain Alloy Tool Steel: Report to the President on Investigation No. TA–203–2*. USITC Publication no. 805. Washington, February.

———. 1977b. *Stainless Steel and Alloy Tool Steel: Report to the President on Investigation No. TA–203–3*. USITC Publication no. 838. Washington, October.

———. 1979a. *Stainless Steel and Alloy Tool Steel*. USITC Publication no. 968. Washington, April.

———. 1979b. *Stainless Steel and Alloy Tool Steel: US Production, Shipments, Employment, Man-Hours, and Prices, First Calendar Quarter 1979*. USITC Publication no. 973. Washington, May.

———. 1983. *Stainless Steel and Alloy Tool Steel*. USITC Publication no. 1377. Washington, May.

———. 1984a. *Annual Survey on Certain Stainless Steel and Alloy Tool Steel*. USITC Publication no. 1508. Washington, March.

———. 1984b. *Quarterly Survey on Certain Stainless Steel and Alloy Tool Steel*. USITC Publication no. 1560. Washington, August.

———. 1984c. *1983 Annual Report*. USITC Publication no. 1580. Washington.

———. 1985a. *Quarterly Survey on Certain Stainless Steel and Alloy Tool Steel*. USITC Publication no. 1643. Washington, February.

———. 1985b. *Annual Survey on Certain Stainless Steel and Alloy Tool Steel*. USITC Publication no. 1666. Washington, March.

———. 1985c. *Quarterly Survey on Certain Stainless Steel and Alloy Tool Steel*. USITC Publication no. 1690. Washington, May.

CASE M–17

Nonrubber Footwear

PERIOD OF RELIEF

28 June 1977 to 30 June 1981

SUPPLIERS AFFECTED

Korea and Taiwan

RELIEF ACTION

The nonrubber footwear[1] industry has frequently sought relief under the trade laws, but its efforts have seldom been rewarded. Between 1963 and April 1975, acting under the authority of the Trade Expansion Act of 1962, the US Tariff Commission (USTC, later the US International Trade Commission [USITC]) conducted 155 nonrubber footwear investigations for firm and worker adjustment assistance. The Commission made affirmative findings in only 23 out of the 128 worker petitions filed, and in only 7 out of the 27 firm petitions filed. Since 1970, the Commission has conducted eight import relief investigations involving the nonrubber footwear industry. (USITC 799, A5; USITC 1545, A1, A96; USITC 1717, A1)

Between 1970 and 1985, the domestic industry filed five escape clause petitions and three other trade relief actions. On 15 July 1970, at the request of President Richard M. Nixon, the Commission instituted an escape clause investigation under the Trade Expansion Act of 1962. On 15 January 1971, the USTC was equally divided as to the existence of injury, or the threat of injury, and President Nixon decided against granting trade relief. (USITC 799, A5; USITC 1256, 21)

In 1974, the Treasury Department entered final countervailing duty orders against imports of nonrubber footwear from Brazil and Spain. In 1979, the Department entered a final countervailing duty order against imports of nonrubber footwear from

---

1. Nonrubber footwear is primarily vinyl and leather footwear provided for in Tariff Schedules of the United States (TSUS) items 700.05 through 700.45, inclusive; 700.56; 700.72 through 700.83, inclusive; and 700.95. (USITC 1545, A1)

India. On 24 May 1983, the USITC found that the US industry would not be materially injured if countervailing duty orders against imports from Brazil, Spain, and India were revoked. (USITC 1388, A8–13; USITC 1545, 1–5)

On 17 September 1975, in response to a petition filed by the American Footwear Industries Association, the Boot and Shoe Workers' Union, and the United Shoe Workers of America, the USITC initiated a second escape clause investigation under Section 201 of the Trade Act of 1974. The Commission found unanimously that increased imports were a substantial cause of serious injury to the domestic industry and, on 20 February 1976, recommended tariff increases, tariff-rate quotas, and adjustment assistance. On 16 April 1976, President Gerald R. Ford determined that adjustment assistance was the most effective remedy for the injury to the industry, and directed the Secretaries of the Departments of Commerce and Labor to expedite consideration of any petitions for assistance. (USITC 1256, 21; USITC 1545, 4, A2)

On 5 October 1976, in response to a resolution from the Senate Committee on Finance, the USITC initiated a third Section 201 investigation. On 3 February 1977, the Commission again unanimously found serious injury from increased imports and recommended tariff-rate quotas. On 1 April 1977, President Jimmy Carter took three actions: he rejected the tariff-rate quota, initiated a major trade adjustment assistance program, and directed the Special Trade Representative (STR) to negotiate orderly marketing agreements (OMAs) with Taiwan and Korea. (USITC 1545, A2)

The OMAs went into effect on 28 June 1977, and provided limits on nonrubber footwear exports from Taiwan and Korea (which together accounted for more than 50 percent of total US imports) for four years. President Carter also delegated authority to the STR to control import surges from other countries, although no agreements were negotiated. (USITC 1545, A2)

In December 1980, the USITC instituted a review investigation under Section 203 of the Trade Act of 1974 for the purpose of advising the President as to the probable economic effect of the extension, reduction, or termination of the OMAs. On 22 April 1981, the USITC unanimously advised that termination of the OMA with Taiwan would have a significant adverse effect on the domestic industry, and recommended a two-year extension of the OMA. In regard to Korea, it advised that termination of the OMA would not have a significant adverse effect. President Ronald Reagan later decided against extending import relief and the OMAs were allowed to expire on 30 June 1981. (USITC 1256, 22; USITC 1545, A2)

On 23 January 1984, the US nonrubber footwear industry again sought escape clause relief under Section 201 of the Trade Act of 1974. Petitioners requested global quotas limiting nonrubber footwear imports to 50 percent of the US market for five years. The USITC instituted an investigation on 8 February 1984, and on 6 July 1984 unanimously determined that imports were not a substantial cause of serious injury to the domestic industry, even though footwear imports were increasing. (USITC 1545, 1–3, A1–4)

After the USITC's "no injury" determination, the domestic industry turned to Congress for trade relief, achieving relaxation of the criteria by which the USITC made its finding in 1984. The Trade and Tariff Act of 1984, enacted 5 October 1984, modified Section 201 of the Trade Act of 1974 in a manner calculated to signal the USITC that the Senate was not satisfied with the 1984 footwear decision. In particular, Section 249 of the 1984 trade act made clear that prior plant closings and downward employment trends should be given weight, even if the surviving firms were profitable. Moreover, profits from the distribution of captive imports in the US market were not to be considered in determining the domestic industry's profitability. (US Congress, 49–50, 139–43; *Inside US Trade,* 12 September 1984, 7)

On 22 January 1985, following receipt of a resolution by the Senate Committee on Finance, the USITC instituted another escape clause investigation. On 22 May 1985, the Commission ruled by a 5 to 0 vote that imports of nonrubber footwear were causing or threatening serious economic damage to US shoe manufacturers. This decision came only 11 months after the Commission had found, also unanimously, that domestic shoemakers were not being injured. Although the decision was in part due to the broadened standards under the 1984 trade act, the Commission asserted that worsening economic developments had prompted the Commission's decision. Commission Chairwoman Paula Stern stated that "accelerating imports, the heightened pace of plant closures, increasing unemployment and diminishing profits" had convinced the Commission that imports were a serious threat to the domestic industry. (*Wall Street Journal,* 13 June 1985, 37; 23 May 1985, 35; *New York Times,* 23 May 1985, D1; *Journal of Commerce,* 23 May 1985, 1A)

On 12 June 1985, four of the five USITC commissioners recommended a five-year quota restricting imports of nonrubber footwear valued at over $2.50 a pair to 55 percent of the US market, the level that prevailed in 1981–82. The quota would have applied to leather shoes and boots, but would not have affected protective (rubber) footwear or canvas shoes.[2] (*Wall Street Journal,* 13 June 1985, 37; 23 May 1985, 35; *New York Times,* 13 June 1985, A1; *Journal of Commerce,* 23 May 1985, 1A)

The USITC vote marked the first time that a majority of the Commission called for a quota auction, an approach that was authorized by the Trade Agreements Act of 1979. Under the proposal, shoe importers, whether retailers, wholesalers, or subsidiaries of foreign companies based in the United States, would be allowed to bid at an auction held by the government for a license to import a certain amount of shoes from anywhere in the world. The highest bidder for a particular number or kind of shoes being auctioned would acquire the right to import those shoes. (*Washington Post,* 14 June 1985, F2; 13 June 1985, E1; *New York Times,* 13 June 1985, A1)

USITC Chairwoman Stern said the auction was proposed so that "costs to the US economy" of protecting the domestic industry "are minimized." According to government and private economists, the quota would save between 26,000 and 30,000 jobs, and would cost US consumers between $50,000 and $80,000 per job saved in an industry in which the average annual wage is about $14,000. The total cost to consumers is estimated to be between $1.3 billion and $2.5 billion a year. In response to a request from US Trade Representative (previously the Special Trade Representative) Clayton Yeutter for public comments, the Federal Trade Commission issued its report recommending adjustment assistance rather than import restrictions. The FTC estimated that direct assistance would cost only $77 million over five years while

---

2. See Case M–4, Rubber Footwear.

import restraints might cost as much as $940 million. (*New York Times*, 13 June 1985, A1; *Washington Post*, 14 June 1985, F2)

On August 28, following threats of retaliation from the European Community and other trading partners, and citing the costs to consumers of protectionism, President Ronald Reagan refused to impose quotas or other trade restraints on imports of nonrubber footwear. Instead, he authorized Secretary of Labor William E. Brock to develop an adjustment and retraining program for workers in the shoe manufacturing industry. In response to the President's decision, several key senators threatened to pass legislation limiting shoe imports. (*Washington Post*, 29 August 1985, A1)

The most-favored-nation (MFN) tariff rates on nonrubber footwear range from zero to 20 percent ad valorem. Since the late 1970s the average tariff has been 8.8 percent. The MFN tariff rates on rubber footwear are substantially higher, 35 percent to 40 percent. Nonrubber footwear was excluded from tariff cuts in the Tokyo Round of multilateral trade negotiations, is not eligible for duty-free treatment under the Generalized System of Preferences (GSP), and was excluded from duty-free treatment under the Caribbean Basin Economic Recovery Act of 1983. (USITC 1545, A8–9; Cline 1984, 13; *New York Times*, 23 May 1985, D1)

CHANGES IN THE INDUSTRY

In the past three decades, US imports have grown from less than 5 percent of US footwear consumption to approximately 60 percent by volume. Between 1966 and 1976, the share of the domestic nonrubber footwear market captured by imports jumped from 13 percent to 47 percent. Although the OMAs limited the volume of US imports from Taiwan and Korea, these countries countered the restraints by upgrading the quality of shoes exported, and by shipping shoes without soles that were not subject to the OMAs. Further, the quantitative restrictions were largely offset by sharp increases in nonrubber footwear imports from nonrestrained countries, primarily the Philippines (1,250 percent increase), Hong Kong (250 percent increase), Italy, and Thailand. (Cline 1984, 8; USITC 1256, 25; Morkre and Tarr, 104–21; Mutti and Bale, 5–6)

Although the US industry includes approximately 50 publicly owned corporations (four of which ranked among the 500 largest US companies in sales for 1982), the industry also includes a number of small privately owned firms. While approximately 70 percent of US producers make less than one million pairs annually, these small producers account for less than one-fifth of total US production.

The number of footwear factories has declined steadily in the past 15 years. In 1970, there were 1,100 plants nationwide. In 1981, 594 factories were manufacturing nonrubber footwear. During 1982, 10 factories started or resumed operations, while 33 closed down, lowering the total to 571 in December 1982. In 1984, 105 of the remaining plants closed down. Data show that 248 US firms (as opposed to factories) with 10 or more employees produced nonrubber footwear in 1982, as compared to 307 firms in 1979. The peak employment year for the industry was 1967, when employment reached 231,600. Employment has since dropped by almost 50 percent from that level. (*New York Times*, 28 May 1985, D1; USITC 799, C38; USITC 1545, A13–15)

Key Statistics

Imports affected from Taiwan and Korea

Year	Volume (million pairs)	Value (million dollars)	Source
Before restraints			
1975	119.3	210	Cline 1984, 9; 10
1976	199.6	444	Cline 1984, 9; 10
During restraints			
1977	225.2	576	Cline 1984, 9; 10
1978	147.8	558	Cline 1984, 9; 10
1979	149.3	630	Cline 1984, 9; 10
1980	181.0	883	Cline 1984, 9; 10
1981	162.5	934	Cline 1984, 9; 10
After restraints			
1982	273.8	1,398	Cline 1984, 9; 10
1983	362.3	1,780	USITC 1706, 9; 10
1984	425.4	2,131	USITC 1706, 9; 10

Imports from all sources

Year	Volume (million pairs)	Value (million dollars)	Source
Before restraints			
1975	287.7	1,131	Cline 1984, 9; 10
1976	370.0	1,448	Cline 1984, 9; 10
During restraints			
1977	368.1	1,598	Cline 1984, 9; 10
1978	373.5	2,057	Cline 1984, 9; 10
1979	404.6	2,429	Cline 1984, 9; 10
1980	365.7	2,298	USITC 1717, A15
1981	375.6	2,480	USITC 1717, A15
After restraints			
1982	479.7	3,083	USITC 1717, A15
1983	581.9	3,662	USITC 1717, A15
1984	725.9	4,651	USITC 1717, A15

Apparent consumption

Year	Volume (million pairs)	Value (million dollars)	Source
Before restraints			
1975	696.2	4,247	Cline 1984, 9; 10
1976	786.5	4,931	Cline 1984, 9; 10
During restraints			
1977	793.6	5,026	Cline 1984, 9; 10
1978	779.5	5,811	Cline 1984, 9; 10
1979	797.9	6,627	Cline 1984, 9; 10
1980	737.7	6,806	USITC 1717, A15; Cline 1984, 10
1981	739.2	7,123	USITC 1717, A15; Cline 1984, 10
After restraints			
1982	828.3	7,165	USITC 1717, A15; Cline 1984, 10
1983	915.8	8,330	USITC 1717, A15; USITC 1706, 4
1984	1,026.3	8,606	USITC 1717, A15; USITC 1706, 4

Market share of imports (percentage of apparent consumption, by volume)

Year	Affected imports	Total imports	Source
Before restraints			
1975	17.1	41.3	authors' estimate
1976	25.4	47.0	authors' estimate
During restraints			
1977	28.4	46.4	authors' estimate
1978	19.0	47.9	authors' estimate
1979	18.7	50.7	authors' estimate
1980	24.4	49.4	authors' estimate
1981	22.0	51.0	authors' estimate
After restraints			
1982	33.7	59.0	authors' estimate
1983	39.4	63.3	authors' estimate
1984	41.9	71.5	authors' estimate

Output of domestic industry

Year	Volume (million pairs)	Value (million dollars)	Source
Before restraints			
1975	413.1	3,145	Cline 1984, 9; 10
1976	422.5	3,520	Cline 1984, 9; 10

Output of domestic industry (continued)

Year	Volume (million pairs)	Value (million dollars)	Source
During restraints			
1977	430.9	3,464	Cline 1984, 9; 10
1978	412.9	3,799	Cline 1984, 9; 10
1979	402.6	4,269	Cline 1984, 9; 10
1980	387.9	4,620	Cline 1984, 9; 10
1981	372.0	4,834	Cline 1984, 9; 10
After restraints			
1982	342.4	4,186	Cline 1984, 9; 10
1983	344.3	4,758[a]	USITC 1706, 4
1984	298.5[b]	4,053[a]	USITC 1706, 4

a. The figures for 1983–84 are based on the value of US shipments.
b. Preliminary estimate.

Employment in domestic industry

Year	Production workers (average number)	Source
Before restraints		
1975	136,000	USITC 1139, G27
1976	144,000	USITC 1139, G27
During restraints		
1977	137,000	USITC 1139, G27
1978	138,000	USITC 1139, G27
1979	130,000	USITC 1139, G27
1980	124,600	USITC 1717, A44
1981	127,700	USITC 1717, A44
After restraints		
1982	121,800	USITC 1717, A44
1983	117,300	USITC 1717, A44
1984	108,200	USITC 1717, A44

Wages

Year	Dollars per hour	Source
Before restraints		
1975	3.75	USITC 1139, G29
1976	4.02	USITC 1139, G29

Wages (continued)

Year	Dollars per hour	Source
During restraints		
1977	4.32	USITC 1139, G29
1978	4.69	USITC 1139, G29
1979	5.22	USITC 1545, A58
1980	5.67	USITC 1545, A58
1981	6.22	USITC 1545, A58
After restraints		
1982	6.60	USITC 1545, A58
1983	6.80	USITC 1545, A58
1984	7.10	authors' estimate

Industry profits (million dollars)

Year	Profits[a]	Source
Prior to restraints		
1975	181	USITC 799, C56
1976[b]	235	USITC 799, C56
During restraints		
1977[b]	123	USITC 1139, G46
1978[b]	150	USITC 1139, G46
1979	198	USITC 1545, A37
1980	323	USITC 1545, A37
1981	423	USITC 1545, A37
After restraints		
1982	390	USITC 1545, A37
1983	499	USITC 1545, A37
1984	310	USITC 1717, A51

a. Net profits before taxes.

b. The 1976 figure is an annualized estimate based on net operating profit during the period January to June of $117.6 million. The figures for 1977–78 reflect the net income of firms accounting for approximately 42 percent of total domestic production.

Industry capacity utilization

Year	Percentage	Source
Before restraints		
1975	69.1	USITC 1139, G19
1976	75.9	USITC 1139, G19

Industry capacity utilization (continued)

Year	Percentage	Source
During restraints		
1977	76.0	USITC 1139, G19
1978	75.2	USITC 1139, G19
1979	75.5	USITC 1545, A26
1980	80.0	USITC 1545, A26
1981	80.5	USITC 1545, A26
After restraints		
1982	73.9	USITC 1545, A26
1983	72.1	USITC 1545, A26
1984	63.0	authors' estimate

Quantitative Profile

Item	Amount	Source
Number of years restraints in force (1977–81)	4 years	
Induced increase in price of imported footwear (1981)	18.5 percent	authors' estimate[a]
Induced increase in price of domestic footwear (1981)	2.74 percent	Cline 1984, 45[b]
	3.88 percent	USITC 1256, 25[b]
	5.55 percent	authors' estimate[c]
Coefficient of price response	0.3	authors' estimate
Quantity and value of imports (1981)	376 million pairs	Cline 1984, 9
	$2.5 billion	Cline 1984, 10
Induced decrease in imports due to restraints (1977–79 average)	29 million pairs	USITC 1256, 25[d]
	$176 million	USITC 1256, 25[d]
	41 million pairs	authors' estimate[e]
	$248 million	authors' estimate[e]
Quantity and value of domestic production (1981)	372 million pairs	Cline 1984, 9
	$4.8 billion	Cline 1984, 10
Induced increase in domestic production due to restraints (1977–79 average)	26 million pairs	USTIC 1256, 26[f]
	$272 million	USITC 1256, 26[f]
	37 million pairs	authors' estimate[e]
	$387 million	authors' estimate[e]
Coefficient of quantity response	0.9	authors' estimate
Elasticity of demand for imported footwear	1.5	Szenberg, 66–71
Elasticity of supply of domestic footwear	1.92	Cline 1984, 61
	1.67	Council, 17
	1.9	authors' estimate
Elasticity of demand for domestic footwear	0.12	USITC 1256, 89
	1.0	Council, 17
	0.5	authors' estimate

Quantitative Profile (continued)

Item	Amount	Source
Cross-elasticity of demand for domestic footwear relative to price of imported footwear	0.7	authors' estimate
Cross-elasticity of output of domestic footwear relative to price of imported footwear	0.6	authors' estimate
Cross-elasticity of quantity of imported footwear relative to price of domestic footwear	4.07 2.4	USITC 1259, 90 authors' estimate
Cost of restraints to US consumers	$1.04 billion (1980) $500 million (1977–79 average) $700 million (1981)	Munger, 9[g] Cline 1984, 42[g] authors' estimate
Gain from restraints to US producers (1981)	$250 million	authors' estimate
Tariff revenue and implied average tariff rate (1981)	8.8 percent $262 million	Cline 1984, 13 authors' estimate
Gain from restraints to foreigners (1981)	$220 million	authors' estimate
Efficiency loss from larger domestic production to the United States (1981)	$16 million	authors' estimate
Welfare cost of restraints to the United States (1981)	$236 million	authors' estimate
Employment in protected US industry	144,000 (1976) 127,700 (1981)	USITC 1139, G27 USITC 1545, A32
Induced increase in employment	15,100 (1977–79 average) 3,132 (1980) 12,700 (1981)	USITC 1256, 25[h] Pearson, 51 authors' estimate[i]
Cost of restraints to US consumers per job saved	$21,967 (1980) $55,000 (1981)	Pearson, 51 authors' estimate
Gain from restraints to US producers per job (1981)	$2,000	authors' estimate

a. This estimate reflects the effect of an 8.8 percent average ad valorem tariff (1979) plus Pearson's estimate that the OMA on imports of plastic and vinyl footwear from Taiwan (accounting for 66 percent of restricted imports in 1977–80) raised imports prices by 9.7 percent. (Pearson, 51)

b. These estimates reflect only the effect of the quantitative restraints.

c. This estimate reflects the effect of both the OMA and the normal tariff on domestic prices.

d. The USITC estimates that in the absence of the OMAs, the total level of imports in the three-year period (1977–79) would have been 87.9 million pairs higher than the actual level of imports, valued at $527 million (based on the unit value of US imports of nonrubber footwear in 1979). (USITC 1256, 25)

e. Our estimates include the effect of the normal tariff as well as that of the OMA. The increase in domestic production is based on the differential between our estimate and the USITC's estimates of domestic price effects due to the restraints. The estimated decrease in imports was derived using the coefficient of quantity response. *(continued overleaf)*

f. The USITC estimates that for the three-year period (1977–79) the OMAs increased domestic production by 76.9 million pairs, valued at $815 million (1979 dollars). (USITC 1256, 26)

g. The Munger estimate reflects the cost to consumers of the tariffs on nonrubber footwear, while the Cline estimate is based on a USITC study that calculated the costs of the OMAs.

h. This figure reflects the average increase in employment over the three-year period 1977–79, including induced changes in employment in related industries (e.g., leather tanning, plastics, textiles).

i. This figure reflects direct employment only, assuming increased domestic production of 37 million pairs.

BIBLIOGRAPHY

Brimmer and Company. 1977. *Cost to Consumers of Absolute Quotas on Imports of Footwear from Taiwan and Korea.* Washington.

Cline, William R. 1985. *Footwear Imports and the Consumer.* Washington: Volume Footwear Retailers of America.

———. 1985. "The Impact of Proposed Footwear Industry Protection on Consumers, Employment, and Industry Modernization." Washington: Volume Footwear Retailers of America.

Council on Wage and Price Stability. 1975. "Comments of the Council on Wage and Price Stability." Statement before the US International Trade Commission on Docket no. TA–201–7. Washington, 8 December.

Crandall, Robert W. 1977. "Comments of the Council on Wage and Price Stability on Footwear." Study prepared for the US International Trade Commission. Publication no. CWPS–217. Washington, 27 December.

Farnsworth, Clyde H. 1985. "Panel Asks Curb on Shoe Imports to Bolster Ailing Industry in US." *New York Times,* 13 June, A1.

Footwear Industries of America. 1983. *Footwear Manual 1983.* Arlington, Va.

Morici, Peter, and Laura L. Megna. 1983. *US Economic Policies Affecting Industrial Trade: A Quantitative Assessment.* Report no. 200. Washington: National Planning Association.

Morkre, Morris E., and David G. Tarr. 1980. *Effects of Restrictions on United States Imports: Five Case Studies and Theory.* US Federal Trade Commission, Bureau of Economics. Washington, June.

Munger, Michael C. 1983. *The Costs of Protectionism: Estimates of the Hidden Tax of Trade Restraint.* Working Paper no. 80. Washington University, Center for the Study of American Business, July.

Mutti, John H., and Malcom D. Bale. 1980. *Output and Employment Changes in a "Trade Sensitive" Sector: Adjustment in the US Footwear Industry.* World Bank Working Paper no. 430. Washington: World Bank, October.

Pearson, Charles. 1983. *Emergency Protection in the Footwear Industry.* Thames Essay no. 36. London: Trade Policy Research Centre.

Pine, Art. 1985. "Panel Rules Imports Hurt US Shoe Firms." *Wall Street Journal,* 23 May, 35.

———. 1985. "Import Quotas on Shoes Urged by Trade Panel." *Wall Street Journal,* 13 June, 37.

Seaberry, Jane. 1985. "Shoe Quota Cost Seen as Steep." *Washington Post,* 14 June, F2.

Suh, Joon H. 1981. *"Voluntary" Export Restraints and Their Effects on Exporters and Consumers: The Case of Footwear Quotas.* Washington University, Center for the Study of American Business, October.

Szenberg, M., J. W. Lombard, and E. V. Lee. 1977. *Welfare Effects of Trade Restrictions: A Case Study of the US Footwear Industry.* New York: Academic Press.

US Congress. House. 1984. *Trade and Tariff Act of 1984.* Conference Report no. 98–1156. 98 Cong., 2 sess., 5 October.

US International Trade Commission. 1976. *Footwear: Report to the President on Investigation No. TA–201–7.* USITC Publication no. 758. Washington, February.

———. 1977. *Footwear: Report to the President on Investigation No. TA–201–18.* USITC Publication no. 799. Washington, February.

———. 1981. *Footwear: Report to the President on Investigation No. TA–203–7.* USITC Publication no. 1139. Washington, April.

———. 1982. *Economic Effects of Export Restraints.* USITC Publication no. 1256. Washington, June.

———. 1983. *Certain Nonrubber Footwear from Brazil, India, and Spain.* USITC Publication no. 1388. Washington, May.

———. 1984. *Nonrubber Footwear.* USITC Publication no. 1545. Washington, July.

———. 1985a. *Nonrubber Footwear Quarterly Statistical Report.* USITC Publication no. 1706. Washington, June.

———. 1985b. *Nonrubber Footwear: Report to the President on Investigation No. TA–201–55.* USITC Publication no. 1717. Washington, July.

US Tariff Commission. 1969. *Nonrubber Footwear: Report to the President on Investigation No. 332–56.* USTC Publication no. 276. Washington.

———. 1971. *Nonrubber Footwear: Report to the President on Investigation No. TEA–I–18.* USTC Publication no. 359. Washington, January.

CASE M-18

Color Television Receivers

PERIOD OF RELIEF

1 July 1977 to 30 June 1982

SUPPLIERS AFFECTED

Japan, Korea, and Taiwan

RELIEF ACTION

On 22 September 1976, the Committee to Preserve American Color Television (COMPACT), an unincorporated association of 11 labor organizations and small firms in the electronics industry, filed a petition for escape clause relief under Section 201 of the Trade Act of 1974.[1] On 21 October 1976, the US International Trade Commission (USITC) instituted an escape clause investigation. (USITC 808, 1; Morici and Megna, 18)

On 22 March 1977, the USITC found that imports of color television receivers[2] were a substantial cause of serious injury to the domestic industry and recommended an average tariff increase of 16 percent for five years. The commissioners were divided as to the existence of injury from imports of monochrome (black and white) television receivers, which the Commission included in the investigation because the same establishments produce both color and monochrome televisions, and from imports of subassemblies of color television receivers. (USITC 1068, C3; USITC 808, 4)

Following the USITC determination, President Jimmy Carter instructed the US Special Trade Representative (STR) to seek an orderly marketing agreement (OMA) with

---

1. Since 1970, the US Tariff (later the International Trade) Commission has conducted 22 investigations concerning television receiving apparatus. The investigations involved countervailing and antidumping duty and escape clause investigations. (USITC 1514, A3)

2. This product category includes color television receiving sets, whether assembled or not assembled, and whether finished or not finished, provided for in item 685.20 of the Tariff Schedules of the United States (TSUS).

Japan rather than increase the tariff. On 20 May 1977, Japan agreed to an OMA on exports of complete and incomplete color television receivers (and subassemblies thereof) effective 1 July 1977 through 30 June 1980. The OMA limited Japanese exports to 1.75 million units annually (1.56 million units of complete color television receivers and 0.19 million units of incomplete color television receivers), about 70 percent of the 1976 Japanese import level. (Morici and Megna, 18; USITC 1068, C5)

In 1977–78, as a result of constraints on Japanese producers, imports of color television receivers from Taiwan and Korea increased fourfold. Consequently, in December 1978, Taiwan and Korea negotiated OMAs with the Carter administration that limited their exports of complete and incomplete color television receivers (and subassemblies thereof) for the period 1 February 1979 through 30 June 1980. During the period covered by the OMAs, Taiwan was allowed to export to the United States 500,000 complete color television receivers and 918,000 subassemblies of the kind covered by the agreement. Korea was allowed to export 289,000 units of the articles covered by the OMA, with no restrictions on the product mix. (Morici and Megna, 18; USITC 1514, A4; USITC 1256, 14; USITC 1068, C17)

The OMA with Japan expired 30 June 1980. The OMAs with Korea and Taiwan were extended for two years and then terminated on 30 June 1982.

CHANGES IN THE INDUSTRY

The number of firms producing color television receivers in the United States declined from 27 in 1960 to 12 in 1977, then increased to 17 in 1982. Labor requirements per unit of output in the US color television receiver industry have decreased steadily over the past decade, owing mainly to technological improvements such as increased utilization of printed circuit boards, reduced number of parts, and intensified use of automatic assembly equipment. (USITC 808, A8; USITC 841, 3)

During the three years Japanese imports were constrained, four major Japanese producers established plants in the United States, joining three other Japanese-owned companies. In 1982, a major Japanese-owned firm producing color television receivers in the United States was granted free-zone status by the Foreign Trade Zone Board; in 1983 and 1984, two other such Japanese-owned firms were also granted free-zone status. Since the OMAs, Sony and Matsushita have expanded their US facilities; Toshiba built a color television plant in Tennessee; and Sharp and Hitachi are also building US plants. Meanwhile, US companies have turned to importing incomplete color televisions. RCA Corporation, General Telephone and Electronics, General Electric, and Zenith have established subassembly operations in Mexico and Taiwan. (USITC 1256, 19; USITC 1396, A10; Morici and Megna, 18; Morkre and Tarr, 81)

Key Statistics

Imports affected from Japan, Taiwan, Korea[a,b]

Year	Volume (million units)	Value (million dollars)	Source
Before restraints			
1976	2.97	723	USITC 1396, A83–84, A86–88
During restraints			
1978	2.56	821	USITC 1396, A83–84, A86–88
1980	1.05	643	USITC 1514, A34–36
1982	1.92	854	USITC 1514, A34–36
After restraints			
1983	4.22	1,217	Summary, 18; authors' estimate

a. By 1979, Japanese imports of complete color television sets were only one-quarter of the 1976 level. However, from 1976 to 1979, imports of incomplete sets from all sources increased over 300 percent; imports of subassemblies not covered by the OMAs doubled. Thus, although the OMAs achieved part of their intended purpose in terms of trade with Japan, their overall impact was limited, first because of shifts in the source of imports, and second because of changes in the composition of imports. (Morici and Megna, 19)

b. Complete and incomplete sets.

Imports from all sources[a]

Year	Volume (million units)	Value[b] (million dollars)	Source
Before restraints			
1976	3.30	927	USITC 1396, A83–84, A86–88
During restraints			
1978	2.84	1,145	USITC 1396, A83–84, A86–88
1980	1.31	1,449	USITC 1514, A34–36
1982	2.35	1,543	USITC 1514, A34–36
After restraints			
1983	5.21	2,006	USITC 1514, A34–35; Summary, 18

a. Complete and incomplete sets.

b. These figures include imports of subassemblies.

Apparent consumption[a]

Year	Volume (million units)	Value (million dollars)	Source
Before restraints			
1976	8.57	2,591	USITC 1153, H2
During restraints			
1978	10.49	3,246	USITC 1153, H2
1980	11.02	3,654	USITC 1514, A37–38
1982	11.67	3,869	USITC 1514, A37–38
After restraints			
1983	15.25	4,525	USITC 1514, A37–38

a. Complete sets.

Market share of imports (percentage of apparent consumption, by volume)

Year	Affected imports	Total imports	Source
Before restraints			
1976	34.7	38.5	authors' estimate
During restraints			
1978	24.4	27.1	authors' estimate
1980	9.5	11.9	authors' estimate
1982	16.5	20.1	authors' estimate
After restraints			
1983	27.7	34.2	authors' estimate

Output of domestic industry[a]

Year	Volume (million units)	Value (million dollars)	Source
Before restraints			
1976	5.87	2,071	USITC 1153, A32
During restraints			
1978	8.28	2,668	USITC 1153, A32
1980	10.73	3,343	USITC 1514, A18
1982	9.71	3,336	USITC 1514, A18
After restraints			
1983	11.64	3,929	USITC 841, 15

a. Complete sets.

Employment in domestic industry[a]

Year	Production workers (average number)	Source
Before restraints		
1976	26,957	USITC 1153, H36
During restraints		
1978	23,854	USITC 1153, H36
1980	21,679	USITC 1153, H36
1982	21,350	USITC 1514, A21
After restraints		
1983	21,121	USITC 1514, A21

a. Part of the employment decline may reflect productivity increases, but the dominant explanation of higher production with fewer man-hours appears to be increased imports of incomplete color televisions and subassemblies. (Morkre and Tarr, 81)

Wages

Year	Dollars per hour	Source
Before restraints		
1977	5.66	USITC 1153, A49–50
During restraints		
1978	6.35	USITC 1153, A49–50
1980	8.20	USITC 1514, A21–23
1982	9.50	USITC 1514, A21–23
After restraints		
1983	10.33	USITC 1514, A21–23

Industry profits (million dollars)

Year	Profits (loss)[a]	Source
Before restraints		
1976	36.8	USITC 1396, A82
During restraints		
1978	(1.6)	USITC 1396, A82
1980	14.1	USITC 1514, A24
1982	(133.0)	USITC 1514, A24
After restraints		
1983	6.0	USITC 1514, A24

a. Net income (loss) before taxes.

Industry capacity utilization

Year	Percentage	Source
Before restraints		
1976	60.2	USITC 1396, A77
During restraints		
1978	79.6	USITC 1396, A77
1980	90.7	USITC 1514, A16
1982	76.5	USITC 1514, A16
After restraints		
1983	90.5[a]	USITC 1396, A19

a. This figure reflects industry capacity utilization for the period January to March 1983.

Quantitative Profile

Item	Amount	Source
Number of years restraints in force (1977–82)	5 years	
Induced increase in price of imported color televisions (1979)	6.7 to 13.4 percent 15 percent	Morici, 20 authors' estimate[a]
Induced increase in price of domestic color televisions (1979)	0.37 to 4.07 percent 6 percent	USITC 1256, 17[b] authors' estimate
Coefficient of price response	0.4	authors' estimate
Quantity and value of imports (1982)	2.35 million units $1,543 million	USITC 1514, A34–35 USITC 1514, A34–36
Induced decrease in imports due to restraints (average 1977–79)	0.37 million units $89 million 0.52 $125 million	USITC 1256, 15 USITC 1256, 15 authors' estimate authors' estimate
Quantity and value of domestic production (1982)	9.71 million units $3,336 million	USITC 1514, A18 USITC 1514, A18
Induced increase in domestic production due to restraints (average 1977–79)	0.32 million units 0.47 million units $166 million	USITC 1256, 18 authors' estimate authors' estimate
Coefficient of quantity response	0.9	authors' estimate
Elasticity of demand for imported color televisions	2.8 1.5	Morici, 15 authors' estimate
Elasticity of supply of domestic color televisions	2.0	authors' estimate
Elasticity of demand for domestic color televisions	0.31 1.4 0.5	USITC 1256, 18 USITC 808, 24[c] authors' estimate
Cross-elasticity of demand for domestic color televisions relative to price of imported color televisions	1.0	authors' estimate

Quantitative Profile (continued)

Item	Amount	Source
Cross-elasticity of output of domestic color televisions relative to price of imported color televisions	0.8	authors' estimate
Cross-elasticity of quantity of imported color televisions relative to price of domestic color televisions	9.0	authors' estimate
Cost of restraints to US consumers	none	Morkre, 197[d]
	none	Canto, 44[d]
	$500 million (1977)	Crandall 1978, 431[e]
	$600 million (1977)	Crandall 1977[f]
	$251 million (1980)	Munger, 14[f]
	$420 million (1982)	authors' estimate
Gain from restraints to US producers (1982)	$190 million	authors' estimate
Tariff revenue and implied average tariff rate (1982)	$77 million	authors' estimate
	5 percent	USITC 1068, A5
Gain from restraints to foreigners (1982)	$140 million	authors' estimate
Efficiency loss from larger domestic production to the United States (1982)	$7 million	authors' estimate
Welfare cost of restraints to the United States	$116 million (1977)	Crandall 1978, 431[e]
	$147 million (1982)	authors' estimate
Employment in protected US industry	26,957 (1976)	USITC 1153, H36
	21,350 (1982)	USITC 1514, A21
Induced increase in employment	4,755 (average 1977–80)	USITC 1256, 19[g]
	1,000 (1982)	authors' estimate
Cost of restraints to US consumers per job saved	$55,000 (1977)	Crandall 1978, 431[e]
	$420,000 (1982)	authors' estimate
Gain from restraints to US producers per job (1982)	$9,000	authors' estimate

a. This estimate includes the effect on prices of the normal ad valorem tariff of 5 percent plus a 10 percent price increase attributable to the OMAs.

b. This figure reflects the effect of OMAs during the three-year restraint period July 1977 to June 1980. The restraints on Korea and Taiwan after this period appear to have supported the effect of the initial three-year restraint period. Estimated increases in the annual average producer price of color television sets ranged from $1.29 per unit in the first OMA year (July 1977 to June 1978), to $11.05 in the second year (July 1978 to June 1979), to $14.30 in the third year (July 1979 to June 1980). (USITC 1256, 17)

c. This elasticity is for all television receivers.

d. These authors concluded that the OMA with Japan had negligible costs because Korea and Taiwan stepped in to replace the restricted imports. (Munger, 16)

e. This figure is based on the initial USITC recommendation with respect to imports from Japan, which were not fully implemented. It presumably represents the upper limits of the ultimate costs of the OMA with Japan. (Crandall 1978, 431)

f. These figures reflect USITC estimates that treat the OMA with Japan as if it covered all television imports. (Munger, 16)

g. During the three-year period July 1977 to June 1980, the estimated annual effects of the OMAs on employment ranged from an increase of 992 man-years in the third OMA year to an increase of 8,035 man-years in the second OMA year, or an annual average of 4,755 jobs. This estimate includes ripple effects on employment in related industries. (USITC 1256, 19)

BIBLIOGRAPHY

Canto, Victor A., and Arthur B. Laffer. 1983. "The Effectiveness of Orderly Marketing Agreements: The Color TV Case." *Business Economics* 18, no. 1 (January): 38–45.

Crandall, Robert W. 1977. "Comments of the Council on Wage and Price Stability on Investigation TA–201–19, Televisions." Study prepared for the US International Trade Commission. Washington, 18 January.

———. 1978. "Federal Government Initiatives to Reduce the Price Level." *Brookings Papers on Economic Activity* 2.

Cunningham, W. A., and C. Y. Lin. 1980. *The Effects of the Orderly Marketing Agreement Between Japan and the United States Regarding Color TV Sets*. Fayetteville, Ark.: University of Arkansas, December.

Morici, Peter, and Laura L. Megna. 1983. *US Economic Policies Affecting Industrial Trade: A Quantitative Assessment*. Report no. 200. Washington: National Planning Association.

Morkre, Morris E., and David G. Tarr. 1980. *Effects of Restrictions on United States Imports: Five Case Studies and Theory*. US Federal Trade Commission, Bureau of Economics, June.

Munger, Michael C. 1983. *The Costs of Protectionism: Estimates of the Hidden Tax of Trade Restraint*. Working Paper no. 80. Washington University, Center for the Study of American Business, July.

"Summary-Index of Week's News." 1984. *Weekly Television Digest with Consumer Electronics* 24, no. 12 (19 March): 11–20.

US International Trade Commission. 1977. *Television Receivers, Color and Monochrome, Assembled or Not Assembled, Finished or Not Finished, and Subassemblies Thereof*. USITC Publication no. 808. Washington, March.

———. 1980. *Color Televisions and Assemblies Thereof*. USITC Publication no. 1068. Washington, May.

———. 1981. *Television Receiving Sets from Japan*. USITC Publication no. 1153. Washington, June.

———. 1982. *Economic Effects of Export Restraints*. USITC Publication no. 1256. Washington, June.

———. 1983. *Color Television Receivers from the Republic of Korea and Taiwan*. USITC Publication no. 1396. Washington, June.

———. 1984a. *Color Television Receivers from the Republic of Korea and Taiwan*. USITC Publication no. 1514. Washington, April.

———. 1984b. *Summary of Trade and Tariff Information, Television Apparatus Except Cameras*. USITC Publication no. 841, control no. 6–5–33 (Supp.). Washington, September.

CASE M-19

Citizens Band (CB) Radio Transceivers

PERIOD OF RELIEF

11 April 1978 to 10 April 1981

SUPPLIERS AFFECTED

Global (primarily Hong Kong, Japan, Korea, and Taiwan)

RELIEF ACTION

On 10 August 1977, acting on a petition by the E. F. Johnson Company (then the largest US producer of CB radios), the US International Trade Commission (USITC) initiated an escape clause investigation pursuant to Section 201 of the Trade Act of 1974. In January 1978, the USITC rendered a split decision: two commissioners found imports of CB radios (TSUS 685.25) to be a substantial cause of serious injury that "threaten[ed] the domestic industry with extinction. . . ." Three commissioners found imports to be a threat of serious injury; one commissioner dissented. (Morkre and Tarr, 59; USITC 852, 1, 9)

The Commission was also divided as to recommended relief. Three commissioners recommended increased tariffs for five years (an increase of 30 percent in the first year with 5 percent annual reductions in each of the four successive years). The other three commissioners recommended trade adjustment assistance. (Morkre and Tarr, 59; USITC 852, 3)

On 11 April 1978, President Jimmy Carter decided to impose temporary tariff increases on CB radio transceivers (except hand-held). The tariff rose by 15 additional percentage points, to 21 percent in the first year, and then decreased 3 percentage points in each of the following two years before returning to 6 percent after escape clause relief expired on 10 April 1981. In addition, CB radios were denied duty-free entry under the Generalized System of Preferences (GSP) during the relief period. Thus, for Korea and Taiwan, the tariff increase was 21 percent in the first year for goods that formerly entered the United States under the GSP. (Morkre and Tarr, 59)

CHANGES IN THE INDUSTRY

Prior to 1970, there were fewer than one million users of CB radios; by 1980, there were estimated to be over 20 million users. In 1972, apparent US consumption of CB radios was valued at $47 million. Thereafter, demand for CB radios soared, reaching a peak in 1976 of $940 million, a twentyfold increase over 1972. The quantity of imports increased every year in the period 1972–76. After 1976, however, demand for CB radios dropped significantly. Between 1977 and 1978, apparent consumption fell by approximately 50 percent. (USITC 852, 5; Morkre and Tarr, 59–61)

In the peak year of 1976, five firms produced most of the CB radios. During 1977, however, plants representing approximately 25 percent of domestic capacity closed down. By 1980, the dominant firm in the industry (E. F. Johnson) was producing only negligible quantities of CB radios; two firms (Hy-Gain Electronics and Pearce-Simpson) had discontinued CB operations and filed for bankruptcy; and another firm (Motorola) had cut back its operations to supplying equipment for automobiles. According to the USITC, "the domestic industry may have lost more money in 1977 than it accumulated in profits [since] 1972. . . ." Despite trade relief, which is generally agreed to have come too late, the domestic industry has been nearly eliminated, mainly because demand for CB radios has collapsed. (USITC 852, 12, 119; Morkre and Tarr, 61–63, 75)

Key Statistics

Imports from all sources

Year	Volume (million units)	Value (million dollars)	Source
Before restraints			
1976	17.01	839	Morkre, 60
1977	11.05[a]	534	Morkre, 60
During restraints			
1978	4.85	194	Morkre, 60
1980	.92	37	BC, FT 246
1981	1.38	54	BC, FT 246
After restraints			
1982	1.39	52	BC, FT 246
1983	.91	34	BC, FT 246

a. This figure is based on a straight-line projection of import data during the period January to September 1977.

Apparent consumption[a]

Year	Volume (million units)	Value (million dollars)	Source
Before restraints			
1976	18.20	938	authors' estimate
1977	11.70	605	authors' estimate
During restraints			
1978	5.95	278	authors' estimate
1980	1.21	54	authors' estimate
1981	1.66	69	authors' estimate
After restraints			
1982	1.48	55	authors' estimate
1983	.94	35	authors' estimate

a. These figures reflect imports plus domestic production. Since US exports account for a small percentage of total shipments (CB radios are difficult to market abroad without substantial manufacturing alterations), and since the US accounts for about 90 percent of the world market in CB radios, US exports are not considered here. (USITC 852, A23; Morkre and Tarr, 60)

Market share of imports (percentage of apparent consumption, by volume)

Year	Share	Source
Before restraints		
1976	93.5	authors' estimate
1977	94.4	authors' estimate
During restraints		
1978	81.5	authors' estimate
1980	76.0	authors' estimate
1981	83.1	authors' estimate
After restraints		
1982	93.9	authors' estimate
1983	96.8	authors' estimate

Output of domestic industry[a]

Year	Volume[b] (million units)	Value (million dollars)	Source
Before restraints			
1976	1.22	102	Morkre, 60
1977	.76	64	Morkre, 60
During restraints			
1978	1.10	83	authors' estimate; BC, MA36N
1980	.29	18	authors' estimate; BC, MA36N
1981	.28	15	authors' estimate; BC, MA36N

Output of domestic industry[a] (continued)

Year	Volume[b] (million units)	Value (million dollars)	Source
After restraints			
1982	.09	4	authors' estimate; BC, MA36N
1983	.03	1	authors' estimate; BC, MA36N

a. Producers' shipments.

b. The figures for 1978–83 are based on the value estimates and reflect an estimated 10 percent price decrease in CB radio transceivers from the year 1977. The USITC indicates that domestic prices have fallen since 1977; an estimated 10 percent price decline appears to be conservative. (USITC 852, A24, A52)

Employment in domestic industry[a]

Year	Production workers (average number)	Source
Before restraints		
1976	3,312	USITC 852, A17
1977	2,061	USITC 852, A17
During restraints		
1978	2,175	authors' estimate
1980	805	authors' estimate
1981	775	authors' estimate
After restraints		
1982	325	authors' estimate
1983	300	authors' estimate

a. Since employment data for the CB radio industry are not available for years after 1977, the figures for 1978–83 are based on an approximate figure of 360 units per worker. (USITC 852, A16–18)

Wages[a]

Year	Dollars per hour	Source
Before restraints		
1976	5.69	BLS 1979, 330
1977	6.14	BLS 1983, 105
During restraints		
1978	6.62	BLS 1983, 105
1980	7.70	BLS 1983, 105
1981	8.52	BLS 1983, 105

Wages[a] (continued)

Year	Dollars per hour	Source
After restraints		
1982	9.48	BLS 1983, 105
1983	10.00	authors' estimate

a. The figures reflect production-worker average hourly earnings for employees producing radio and television communication equipment in general.

Industry profits (million dollars)

Year	Profits (loss)[a]	Source
Before restraints		
1976	44.3	USITC 852, A50
1977	(24.4)	USITC 852, A50
During restraints		
1978	n.a.	
1980	n.a.	
1981	n.a.	
After restraints		
1982	n.a.	
1983	n.a.	

n.a. Not available.

a. Net profits (loss) before taxes.

Industry capacity utilization[a]

Year	Percentage	Source
Before restraints		
1976	67	USITC 852, A16
1977	29	USITC 852, A16
During restraints		
1978	57	authors' estimate
1980	31	authors' estimate
1981	29	authors' estimate
After restraints		
1982	15	authors' estimate
1983	13	authors' estimate

a. The estimates for 1978–83 are based on USITC estimates of capacity decline, inventory buildup, and decreased production. The figure for 1977 reflects industry capacity utilization during the period January to June 1977, as compared to 83 percent during the period January to June 1976. The USITC found that substantial idling of productive facilities continued during July–December 1977. (USITC 852, 12, A16; USITC, 20 December 1977, unpublished studies)

Quantitative Profile[a]

Item	Amount	Source
Number of years restraints in force (1978–81)	3 years	
Induced increase in price of imported CB radios	$8 per unit (1980–81)	Morkre, 68
	15 percent (1980–81)	Morkre, 68
	21 percent (1978)	authors' estimate[b]
Induced increase in price of domestic CB radios	$8 per unit (1980–81)	Morkre, 68
	15 percent (1980–81)	Morkre, 68
	21 percent (1978)	authors' estimate
Coefficient of price response	1.0	authors' estimate
Quantity and value of imports (1978)	4.85 million units	Morkre, 60
	$194 million	Morkre, 60
Induced decrease in imports due to restraints (1978)	3.3 million units	Morkre, 67–68[c]
	$132 million	authors' estimate
Quantity and value of domestic production (1978)	1.10 million units	Morkre, 60
	$83 million	Morkre, 60
Induced increase in domestic production due to restraints (1978)	0.3 million units	authors' estimate[d]
Coefficient of quantity response	0.1	authors' estimate
Elasticity of demand for imported CB radios	2.0	Morkre, 67
Elasticity of supply of domestic CB radios	4.0	Morkre, 68
Elasticity of demand for domestic CB radios	2.0	Morkre, 67
Cross-elasticity of demand for domestic CB radios relative to price of imported CB radios	6.0	authors' estimate
Cross-elasticity of output of domestic CB radios relative to price of imported CB radios	4.0	authors' estimate
Cross-elasticity of quantity of imported CB radios relative to price of domestic CB radios	1.5	authors' estimate
Cost of restraints to US consumers	$40 million (1978–81 average)	Morkre, 71[e]
	$57 million (1980)	Munger, 10
	$55 million (1978)	authors' estimate
Gain from restraints to US producers	$2.3 million (1978–81 average)	Morkre, 71[f]
	$14 million (1978)	authors' estimate

Quantitative Profile[a] (continued)

Item	Amount	Source
Tariff revenue and implied average tariff rate (1977)	$32 million 6 percent	authors' estimate Morkre, 59[g]
Gain from restraints to foreigners	negligible	authors' estimate
Efficiency loss from larger domestic production to the United Sates (1978)	$5 million	authors' estimate
Welfare cost of restraints to the United States	$9 million (1978–81 average) $5 million (1978)	Morkre, 74 authors' estimate
Employment in protected US industry	2,175 (1978) 775 (1981)	authors' estimate authors' estimate
Induced increase in employment	472 (1978–81 average) 600 (1978)	Morkre, 74[h] authors' estimate
Cost of restraints to US consumers per job saved	$85,842 (1978–81 average) $93,000 (1978)	Morkre, 74[i] authors' estimate
Gain from restraints to US producers per job (1978)	$6,400	authors' estimate

a. Because of the "fad" nature of demand for CB radios in the late 1970s, data for the first year of restrictions, rather than the last year, have been used in these calculations.

b. Our estimate reflects the normal tariff of 6 percent plus the first year additional relief rate of 15 percent.

c. This figure reflects a price elasticity of demand of 2 and a 15 percent increase in the domestic price of CB radios.

d. Because of the high market penetration of imports and the declining demand pattern after 1978, the additional tariffs are credited with the entire increase in domestic production from 1977 to 1978.

e. Morkre and Tarr estimate the total cost of the tariff to US consumers to be $121.1 million during the three-year period 1978–81 ($48.8 million, $40.5 million, and $31.8 million in the three years, respectively), representing an average annual cost of $40 million. (Morkre and Tarr, 71)

f. Morkre and Tarr estimate the gain to US producers resulting from the three-year tariff increase to be $6.8 million during the period 1978–81 ($3.0 million, $2.2 million and $1.6 million in the three years, respectively), representing an average annual gain of $2.3 million. (Morkre and Tarr, 71)

g. Prior to 11 April 1978, the tariff rate was 6 percent. The total tariff in the three successive years was 21, 18, and 15 percent, respectively. Morkre and Tarr estimate that the increase in tariff revenues over the three-year restraint period was $34 million (1978–79), $29 million (1979–80), and $24 million (1980–81). (Morkre and Tarr, 59, 71)

h. Morkre and Tarr estimate that the number of jobs created over the three-year restraint period as a result of increased tariffs was 1,415 (587 in 1979, 461 in 1980, and 367 in 1981), representing an average annual increase of 472 jobs. (Morkre and Tarr, 63, 73)

i. Morkre and Tarr estimate that the total cost to US consumers per job created over the three-year restraint period was $257,526 ($83,073 in 1979, $87,764 in 1980, and $86,689 in 1981), representing an average annual cost of $85,842 per job created. (Morkre and Tarr, 74)

BIBLIOGRAPHY

Morkre, Morris E., and David G. Tarr. 1980. *Effects of Restrictions on United States Imports: Five Case Studies and Theory.* US Federal Trade Commission, Bureau of Economics. Washington, June.

Munger, Michael C. 1983. *The Costs of Protectionism: Estimates of the Hidden Tax of Trade Restraints.* Working Paper no. 80. Washington University, Center for the Study of American Business, July.

US Department of Commerce. Bureau of the Census. 1979–83. *Current Industrial Reports: Selected Electronic and Associated Products.* Publication no. MA–36N. Washington.

———. 1980–83. *US Imports for Consumption.* FT 246. Washington.

US Department of Labor. Bureau of Labor Statistics. 1979. *Employment and Earnings, United States, 1909–78.* Washington.

———. 1983. *Supplement to Employment and Earnings.* Washington, July.

US International Trade Commission. 1978. *Citizens Band Radio Transceivers.* USITC Publication no. 852. Washington, February.

———. Office of Economic Research. 1977a. "A Discussion of Impact on Consumers of Alternative Remedies for the Citizens Band Transceiver Industry (TA–201–29)." Washington, 20 December.

———. 1977b. "A Discussion of Remedy Alternatives for Citizens Band Transceivers (TA–201–29)." Washington, 20 December.

CASE M–20

Bolts, Nuts, and Large Screws of Iron or Steel

PERIOD OF RELIEF

4 January 1979 to 5 January 1982

SUPPLIERS AFFECTED

Global (primarily Japan)

RELIEF ACTION

In June 1977, the US Fastener Manufacturing Group, the United Steel Workers of America, and the International Association of Machinists and Aerospace Workers petitioned the US International Trade Commission (USITC), under Section 201 of the Trade Act of 1974, for escape clause relief from imports of bolts, nuts, and large screws of iron or steel. On 22 June 1977, the USITC instituted an investigation and eventually recommended five years of special protection through increased tariffs. In February 1978, however, President Jimmy Carter decided that the recommendation was not in the US economic interest. A congressional attempt to override his decision failed. (USITC 847, 1–2; USITC 924, A1)

On 3 August 1978, the Commission initiated another Section 201 investigation following receipt of a petition from the House Committee on Ways and Means, which had found good cause for reinvestigation within one year. In November the Commission again ruled affirmatively. Two commissioners found a threat of injury to the domestic industrial fastener industry, while one concluded that injury already existed. One commissioner dissented and two others did not participate. (USITC 924, 1–4)

This time, President Carter accepted the USITC decision and increased the duties to 15 percent ad valorem for all items included in the investigation while retaining the specific duties of 0.2 cent per pound on bolts and 0.1 cent per pound on nuts. Prior ad valorem duties were 9.5 percent on cap screws and other screws more than 0.24 inches in diameter and 12.5 percent on lag screws, with no ad valorem duties on bolts and nuts. Duty-free treatment for nuts and bolts under the Generalized System of Preferences was also suspended. The increased duties were on top of countervailing duties levied on screws from Italy, bolts and nuts from Japan, and certain industrial fasteners from India. (USITC 1193, A4, A6)

In June 1981, industry representatives filed a Section 203 petition with the USITC requesting a review investigation and extension of the relief period. Three commissioners noted that the condition of the industry had not improved significantly in the nearly three years of special protection but they blamed the industry's woes on cyclical factors affecting the overall demand for industrial fasteners, factors that would not be ameliorated by extended relief from imports. They also criticized domestic producers for not making sufficient efforts to adjust to imports. These commissioners recommended the immediate termination of special relief. Two commissioners dissented, arguing that industry efforts to adjust had been impeded by factors beyond its control, primarily the recession. They recommended that protection be continued for the full three years originally authorized. The relief period expired 6 January 1982 as scheduled. (USITC 1193, 1–15; USTR 197)

Ad valorem duties on screws were not reduced in the Tokyo Round of multilateral trade negotiations; specific duties on nuts and bolts were converted to ad valorem duties of 0.2 percent and 0.7 percent, respectively.

In 1982, the Department of Defense filed a petition with the Department of Commerce under Section 232 of the Trade Expansion Act of 1962, asserting that the domestic industry had deteriorated to a point that it would not be able to fulfill national defense requirements in an emergency. The Department of Commerce rejected the petition in March 1983, however, and market penetration by foreign competitors continues to rise. (BIE, 24–2)

CHANGES IN THE INDUSTRY

The health of the domestic fastener industry is largely dependent upon cyclical fluctuations in demand for industrial fasteners. Demand is derived from the demand for durable goods (particularly consumer durables), which is closely tied to the condition of the economy generally. In 1977 and 1978, the automotive and capital equipment markets strengthened, which led to large increases in output and consumption in 1979, the beginning of the relief period, and to increased employment, profitability, and capacity utilization in the industry. In 1980, however, declining demand in the automotive market, the capital equipment market, and the construction industry initiated a period of recession in the fastener industry that lasted for the remainder of the relief period. (IRA, 8)

Changing market conditions forced manufacturers to either alter their product mix or consolidate with other companies. Some firms simply eliminated their fastener operations and concentrated on the production of nonfastener products. Some of the large manufacturers shifted production from low-cost, high-volume standard fasteners to high-cost, low-volume special fasteners, thereby providing better immunity from import competition.[1] Some 85 percent to 90 percent of US imports are standards, while only about 20 percent (in terms of pieces) of US consumption of standards is domestically produced. The ratio of standards to specials in domestic consumption is about 2 to 1. (IRA, 8, 10; USITC 841)

---

1. "Standard fasteners are multipurpose products which are normally mass produced in long production runs. Special fasteners are designed and produced to fit a particular purchaser's requirements, and are usually not inventoried except at the request of an end-user." (IRA, v)

Key Statistics

Imports from all sources

Year	Volume (million pounds)	Value (million dollars)	Source
Before restraints			
1978	849	354	USITC 1193, A76
During restraints			
1979	793	375	USITC 1193, A76
1980	679	330	USITC 1193, A76
1981	677	336	BC, FT 246
After restraints			
1982	621	311	BC, FT 246

Apparent consumption

Year	Volume (million pounds)	Value (million dollars)	Source
Before restraints			
1978	2,074	1,413	IRA, K2, K3
During restraints			
1979	2,142	1,746	IRA, K2, K3
1980	1,624	1,504	IRA, K2, K3
1981	1,495	1,329	IRA, K2, K3
After restraints			
1982	1,245	979	IRA, K2, K3

Market share of imports (percentage of apparent consumption, by volume)

Year	Share	Source
Before restraints		
1978	40.9	authors' estimate
During restraints		
1979	37.0	authors' estimate
1980	41.8	authors' estimate
1981	45.3	authors' estimate
After restraints		
1982	49.9	authors' estimate

Output of domestic industry[a]

Year	Volume (million pounds)	Value (million dollars)	Source
Before restraints			
1978	1,442	1,142	IRA, K2, K3
During restraints			
1979	1,548	1,415	IRA, K2, K3
1980	1,066	1,238	IRA, K2, K3
1981	965	1,069	IRA, K2, K3
After restraints			
1982	814	806	IRA, K2, K3

a. Includes producers' shipments of US-made nuts, bolts, and large screws that are shipped to domestic customers, exported, or are transformed within the company for use in the manufacture of other products.

Employment in the domestic industry

Year	Production workers (average number)	Source
Before restraints		
1978	13,300	IRA, 43
During restraints		
1979	13,700	IRA, 43
1980	11,300	IRA, 43
1981	11,000	IRA, 43
After restraints		
1982	10,500	IRA, 43

Wages[a]

Year	Dollars per hour	Source
Before restraints		
1978	6.75	BC, MC82, 3
During restraints		
1979	7.22	BC, MC82, 3
1980	7.68	BC, MC82, 3
1981	8.43	BC, MC82, 3
After restraints		
1982	9.34	BC, MC82, 3

a. Average hourly earnings of workers producing bolts, nuts, rivets, screws, and washers (SIC 3452).

Industry profits (million dollars)

Year	Profits[a]	Source
Before restraints		
1978	75.3	USITC 1193, A103
During restraints		
1979	98.3	USITC 1193, A103
1980	59.1	USITC 1193, A103
1981	57.5	IRA, 27–28
After restraints		
1982	41.9	IRA, 27–28

a. Net profits before taxes.

Industry capacity utilization

Year	Percentage	Source
Before restraints		
1978	52.5	USITC 1193, A91
During restraints		
1979	58.4	USITC 1193, A91
1980	41.2	USITC 1193, A91
1981	43.0	IRA, 33
After restraints		
1982	36.0	IRA, 33

Quantitative Profile

Item	Amount	Source
Number of years restraints in force (1979–82)	3 years	
Induced increase in price of imported industrial fasteners (1981)	15 percent	authors' estimate
Induced increase in price of domestic industrial fasteners (1981)	6 percent	authors' estimate
Coefficient of price response	0.4	authors' estimate
Quantity and value of imports (1981)	677 million pounds	BC, FT 246
	$336 million	BC, FT 246
Induced decrease in imports due to restraints	20 million pounds	authors' estimate
	$10 million	authors' estimate
Quantity and value of domestic production (1981)	965 million pounds	IRA, K2
	$1,069 million	IRA, K3

Quantitative Profile (continued)

Item	Amount	Source
Induced increase in domestic production due to restraints	20 million pounds	authors' estimate
Coefficient of quantity response	1.0	authors' estimate
Elasticity of demand for imported fasteners	0.2	IRA, I2
Elasticity of supply of domestic fasteners	3.0	IRA, I2
Elasticity of demand for domestic fasteners	0.2	IRA, I2[a]
Cross-elasticity of demand for domestic fasteners relative to price of imported fasteners	1.3	authors' estimate
Cross-elasticity of output of domestic fasteners relative to price of imported fasteners	1.2	authors' estimate
Cross-elasticity of quantity of imported fasteners relative to price of domestic fasteners	4.0	authors' estimate
Cost of restraints to US consumers (1981)	$110 million	authors' estimate
Gain from restraints to US producers (1981)	$60 million	authors' estimate
Tariff revenue and implied average tariff rate (1978)	$16 million 4.5 percent	authors' estimate authors' estimate
Gain from restraints to foreigners	negligible	authors' estimate
Efficiency loss from larger domestic production to the United States (1981)	$1 million	authors' estimate
Welfare cost of restraints to the United States (1981)	$1 million	authors' estimate
Employment in protected US industry	13,700 (1979) 11,000 (1981)	IRA, 43 IRA, 43
Induced increase in employment (1981)	200	authors' estimate
Cost of restraints to US consumers per job saved (1981)	$550,000	authors' estimate
Gain from restraints to US producers per job (1981)	$5,500	authors' estimate

a. The elasticity figure represents the elasticity of demand for industrial fasteners in the United States regardless of whether they are imported or domestically produced.

BIBLIOGRAPHY

US Department of Commerce. Bureau of the Census. 1981. *US Imports for Consumption*. IM 146. Washington, December.

———. 1984. *1982 Census of Manufactures*. Publication no. MC82-I-34D-2(P). Washington.

———. Various years. *US Imports for Consumption and General Imports*. FT 246. Washington.

———. Bureau of Industrial Economics. 1984. *US Industrial Outlook*. Washington.

———. Industrial Resource Administration. 1983. *The Effect of Nuts, Bolts and Large Screws on the National Security*. Washington, February.

US International Trade Commission. 1977. *Bolts, Nuts, and Large Screws of Iron or Steel*. USITC Publication no. 847. Washington, December.

———. 1978. *Bolts, Nuts, and Large Screws of Iron or Steel*. USITC Publication no. 924. Washington, November.

———. 1981. *Bolts, Nuts, and Large Screws of Iron or Steel*. USITC Publication no. 1193. Washington, November.

———. October 1984. *Summary of Trade and Tariff Information: Bolts, Nuts and Large Screws of Iron or Steel*. USITC Publication no. 841, control no. 6-3-29 (Supp.). Washington, October.

US Trade Representative. 1982. *Annual Report of the President of the United States on the Trade Agreement Program, 1981-82*. Washington, November.

CASE M–21

Prepared Mushrooms

PERIOD OF RELIEF

1 November 1980 to 31 October 1983

SUPPLIERS AFFECTED

Global (primarily China, Hong Kong, Korea, Spain, and Taiwan)

RELIEF ACTION

On 14 March 1980, the American Mushroom Institute, a trade association representing domestic mushroom canners, filed a petition for escape clause relief under Section 201 of the Trade Act of 1974. On 24 March 1980, the US International Trade Commission (USITC) instituted an escape clause investigation, and on 18 August 1980, determined by a 4 to 0 vote that mushrooms provided for in item 144.20 of the Tariff Schedules of the United States (TSUS)[1] were being imported into the United States in such increased quantities as to be a substantial cause or threat of serious injury to the domestic industry producing like or directly competitive articles. (USITC 1089, 1–2)

The majority of commissioners recommended that, in order to prevent or remedy serious injury, quantitative restrictions be imposed on US imports of mushrooms for a three-year period commencing 1 July 1980. The quota was to be established at 86 million pounds (drained weight) for the first year, increasing by 9.7 percent in each subsequent year. The actual quantities on a drained weight basis were to be 94 million pounds in the second year and 103 million pounds in the third year. (USITC 1089, 1–2)

On 17 October 1980, President Jimmy Carter decided against imposing quotas and instead increased tariffs for three years effective 1 November 1980. Duties on prepared

---

1. The subject imports in this case are "mushrooms, otherwise prepared or preserved." While this item includes mushrooms in jars and frozen mushrooms, 97 percent of these imports are in cans. Furthermore, the vast majority of domestic production in these categories is canned, not jarred or frozen. (USITC 1089, 5)

and preserved mushrooms were increased by 20 percent ad valorem in the first year (1 November 1980 to 31 October 1981), and were reduced by 5 percentage points in each of the next two years.[2] (USITC 1293, A44–45; USTR 1983, 144)

On 14 May 1981, at the request of the US Trade Representative (USTR), the USITC instituted a review investigation under Section 203 of the Trade Act of 1974. On 11 September 1981, the USITC recommended termination of import relief for certain oriental and wild mushrooms. Accordingly, on 27 February 1982, President Ronald Reagan exempted these imports (less than 3 percent of total US imports of prepared and preserved mushrooms) from the increased tariff rates. (USTR 1982, 135; USITC 1239, 44)

On 29 December 1981, again at the request of the USTR, the USITC instituted another Section 203 review investigation. On 15 April 1982, the USITC recommended continued relief for certain buttered mushroom products, and further determined that the domestic mushroom industry continued to suffer serious harm from import competition. Thus, the increased tariff rates remained in effect until their scheduled expiration on 31 October 1983. (USTR 1982, 135; USITC 1293, 5)

On 9 July 1982, at the request of the American Mushroom Institute, the USITC initiated an investigation under Section 406 of the Trade Act of 1974 to determine whether imports of canned mushrooms from the People's Republic of China were causing market disruption. In its report of 30 September 1982, the USITC was evenly divided on the issue. In November 1982, President Reagan determined that imports from China were not disrupting the US market, and therefore did not impose trade restrictions. (USTR 1983, 145)

CHANGES IN THE INDUSTRY

The number of US firms producing canned mushrooms declined from 35 in 1972, to only 22 a decade later. Approximately 16 US firms produced frozen mushrooms in 1981 and 1982 (three of these also produced canned mushrooms). (USITC 1089, 15; USITC 1293, A11; USITC, TA–203–14)

Between 1 April 1976 and 28 February 1982, 18 firms petitioned the US Department of Commerce for adjustment assistance; the department certified 14 of these firms for $851,500. During the same period, the Department of Labor received petitions for adjustment assistance from three groups of workers. Two of these petitions were certified, resulting in 327 workers receiving a total of $643,249 in trade adjustment assistance. (USITC 1239, A55)

In 1981, the US industry completed a two-year technical assistance project funded by the Department of Commerce at a cost of $250,000. The project included research

---

2. The increased tariffs resulting from the escape clause investigation were in addition to the regular 10 percent ad valorem tariff plus a 3.2 cents per pound specific duty that has been in effect since 1963. With an average ad valorem equivalent of 13 percent to 14 percent, this is a borderline high tariff case under our methodology. However, we have treated mushrooms as an escape clause case only, with a November 1980 starting date and an October 1983 termination date.

on marketing, research and development, and diversification. US producers have recently developed a new processing method that reduces shrinkage by approximately 60 percent and enhances quality. Domestic investment in advanced equipment and improved growing and harvesting techniques has boosted yields over 17 percent. (USITC 1239, 6–8, A28)

Key Statistics

Imports from all sources

Year	Volume (million pounds)	Value[a] (million dollars)	Source
Before restraints			
1979	98.6	98.2	USITC 1239, A59
During restraints			
1980	117.3	121.9	USITC 1239, A59
1981	88.6	84.1	USITC 1239, A59
1982	101.6	92.4	USITC 1351; USITC, TA–203–14
1983	113.0[b]	109.6	USITC 1498, 1537; authors' estimate
After restraints			
1984	196.7[b]	190.8	authors' estimate

a. The estimates for 1983–84 reflect the average unit value 97 cents per pound for prepared or preserved mushroom imports during the period 1980–82. (USITC 1239, A59; USITC TA–203–14)

b. This figure is an annualized estimate based on imports of 147.49 million pounds during the period January to September 1984. Imports jumped 262 percent between the fourth quarter of 1983 (17.83 million pounds) and the first quarter of 1984 (46.69 million pounds). (USITC 1498, 1537, 1573, 1619)

Apparent consumption

Year	Volume (million pounds)	Value[a] (million dollars)	Source
Before restraints			
1979	190.4	206.5	USITC 1239, A63–64; authors' estimate
During restraints			
1980	234.7	267.4	USITC 1239, A63–64; authors' estimate
1981	196.1	218.5	USITC 1239, A63–64; authors' estimate
1982	217.0	226.2	USITC 1351; authors' estimate
1983	229.7	252.0	USITC 1498, 1537; authors' estimate

Apparent consumption (continued)

Year	Volume (million pounds)	Value[a] (million dollars)	Source
After restraints			
1984	315.2[b]	334.8	authors' estimate

a. The figures are derived from the value of imports and domestic output, with minor adjustments reflecting the value of exports.

b. This figure is an annualized estimate based on apparent consumption of 236.4 million pounds during the period January to September 1984. (USITC 1537, 1573, 1619)

Market share of imports (percentage of apparent consumption, by volume)

Year	Share	Source
Before restraints		
1979	51.8	authors' estimate
During restraints		
1980	50.0	authors' estimate
1981	45.2	authors' estimate
1982	46.8	authors' estimate
1983	49.2	authors' estimate
After restraints		
1984	62.4	authors' estimate

Output of domestic industry[a]

Year	Volume (million pounds)	Value[b] (million dollars)	Source
Before restraints			
1979	98.0	115.6	USITC 1239, A63–64; authors' estimate
During restraints			
1980	122.2	151.5	USITC 1239, A63–64; authors' estimate
1981	112.4	140.5	USITC 1239, A63–64; authors' estimate
1982	115.9	134.4	USITC 1351; authors' estimate
1983	117.2	143.0	USITC 1498, 1537; authors' estimate
After restraints			
1984	119.6[c]	145.9	authors' estimate

a. Producers' shipments.

b. These figures reflect the average US wholesale price per case (six cans) of 68-ounce cans of mushroom stems and pieces. The 1983 and 1984 value figures reflect the average US wholesale price during 1980–82 of $1.22 per pound. Since the price of mushroom stems and pieces in 68-ounce cans is lower than other varieties (e.g., slices and buttons) and packaging sizes (e.g., 4-ounce cans), these figures may be undervalued. (USITC 1293, A69–72)

c. This figure is an annualized estimate based on domestic output of 89.7 million pounds during the period January to September 1984. (USITC 1537, 1573, 1619)

Employment in domestic industry (average number of production workers)

Year	All operations	Canning and freezing	Source
Before restraints			
1979	3,022	1,218	USITC 1239, A17–19
During restraints			
1980	2,974	1,207	USITC 1239, A17–19
1981	3,063	1,187	USITC 1239, A17–19
1982	3,019	1,215	USITC 1239, 1293
1983	3,000	1,200	authors' estimate
After restraints			
1984	3,020	1,210	authors' estimate

Wages[a]

Year	Dollars per hour	Source
Before restraints		
1979	4.35	USITC 1239, A18
During restraints		
1980	4.66	USITC 1239, A18
1981	5.18	USITC 1239, A18
1982	5.66	authors' estimate
1983	6.00	authors' estimate
After restraints		
1984	6.50	authors' estimate

a. These figures reflect the average hourly wage rate for production and related workers in mushroom canning operations. The estimates for 1982–84 are based on the trend of increasing total wages and decreasing total hours in mushroom canning operations since 1979.

Industry profits (million dollars)

Year	Profits[a]	Source
Before restraints		
1979	3.16	USITC 1293, A61
During restraints		
1980	1.17	USITC 1293, A61
1981	0.32	USITC 1293, A61
1982	0.78	authors' estimate
1983	n.a.	

Industry profits (million dollars) (continued)

Year	Profits[a]	Source
After restraints		
1984	n.a.	

n.a. Not available.

a. These figures reflect the net operating profit before taxes for 18 out of approximately 24 firms (95 percent of total US sales volume in 1981). The figure for 1982 reflects the period January to June (as compared with a $1.49 million loss for the same period in 1981). (USITC 1293, A61)

Industry capacity utilization

Year	Percentage	Source
Before restraints		
1979	46	USITC 1293, A16
During restraints		
1980	58	USITC 1293, A16
1981	53	USITC 1293, A16
1982	47[a]	authors' estimate
1983	50	authors' estimate
After restraints		
1984	52	authors' estimate

a. This figure represents data for January to June 1982. (USITC 1293, A16)

Quantitative Profile

Item	Amount	Source
Number of years restraints in force (1980–83)	3 years	
Induced increase in price of imported mushrooms (1980–83)	20 percent	authors' estimate[a]
Induced increase in price of domestic mushrooms (1980–83)	10 percent	authors' estimate[a]
Coefficient of price response	0.5	authors' estimate
Quantity and value of imports (1983)	113 million pounds $110 million	USITC 1498, 1537 authors' estimate
Induced decrease in imports due to restraints	16 million pounds $16 million	authors' estimate authors' estimate
Quantity and value of domestic production (1983)	117 million pounds $143 million	USITC 1498, 1537 authors' estimate
Induced increase in domestic production due to restraints	11 million pounds $13 million	authors' estimate authors' estimate
Coefficient of quantity response	0.7	authors' estimate

Quantitative Profile (continued)

Item	Amount	Source
Elasticity of demand for imported mushrooms	0.21 to 1.13 0.3	Stern, 9[b] authors' estimate
Elasticity of supply of domestic mushrooms	1.0	authors' estimate
Elasticity of demand for domestic mushrooms	0.3	authors' estimate
Cross-elasticity of demand for domestic mushrooms relative to price of imported mushrooms	0.65	authors' estimate
Cross-elasticity of output of domestic mushrooms relative to price of imported mushrooms	0.5	authors' estimate
Cross-elasticity of quantity of imported mushrooms relative to price of domestic mushrooms	1.4	authors' estimate
Cost of restraints to US consumers (1983)	$35 million	authors' estimate
Gain from restraints to US producers (1983)	$13 million	authors' estimate
Tariff revenue and implied average tariff rate (1984)	$25 million 13.3 percent	authors' estimate authors' estimate[c]
Gain from restraints to foreigners (1983)	negligible	authors' estimate[d]
Efficiency loss from larger domestic production to the United States (1983)	$800,000	authors' estimate
Welfare cost of restraints to the United States (1983)	$800,000	authors' estimate
Employment in protected US industry	3,022 (1979) 3,000 (1983)	USITC 1239, A17–19 authors' estimate
Induced increase in employment (1983)	300	authors' estimate
Cost of restraints to US consumers per job saved (1983)	$117,000	authors' estimate
Gain from restraints to US producers per job (1983)	$4,300	authors' estimate

a. The import price increase is based on the USITC's estimate of an average price effect of about 7 percent over the three years plus the normal 13 percent tariff. The induced increase in domestic prices is derived from the USITC's estimate of the relative increases in import and domestic prices from the third quarter of 1980 to the first quarter of 1981. (USITC 1239, A24, A73)

b. This elasticity is for food products in general.

c. Since 1 July 1963, the average rate of duty has been 3.2 cents per pound plus 10 percent ad valorem. The ad valorem rate was temporarily increased, by the following amounts, as a result of the escape clause action: effective 1 November 1980, 20 percent ad valorem; effective 1 November 1981, 15 percent ad valorem; effective 1 November 1982, 10 percent ad valorem. (USITC 1239, A5)

d. Escape clause protection was implemented through higher tariffs. Accordingly, no quota rents accrued to foreign suppliers.

BIBLIOGRAPHY

Balassa, Carol. 1984. "Levels of Protection on Manufactured Goods: The US, EC, Canada, Japan." Office of the US Trade Representative. Washington.

Stern, Robert M. 1984. "Comments on Data, Elasticities, and Other Key Parameters." Seminar Discussion Paper no. 134. Paper read at conference, General Equilibrium Trade Policy Modelling, Columbia University, 5–6 April.

US Department of Agriculture. 1982. *The US Mushroom Industry: The Import Challenge.* Marketing Research Report no. 1131. Washington, July.

US International Trade Commission. 1980. *Mushrooms.* USITC Publication no. 1089. Washington, August.

———. 1981. *Processed Mushrooms: US Producers' Production, Sales, and Inventories, and US Imports, Exports, and Apparent Consumption. Fourteenth Quarterly Report: Second Calendar Quarter 1981.* USITC Publication no. 1179. Washington.

———. 1982a. *Certain Mushrooms.* USITC Publication no. 1239. Washington, April.

———. 1982b. *Canned Mushrooms from the People's Republic of China.* USITC Publication no. 1293. Washington, September.

———. 1983a. *Processed Mushrooms: US Producers' Production, Sales, and Inventories, and US Imports, Exports, and Apparent Consumption. Sixteenth Quarterly Report: Fourth Calendar Quarter 1982.* USITC Publication no. 1351. Washington, February.

———. 1983b. *USITC Factual Highlights, Certain Mushrooms.* Publication no. TA–203–14. Washington, May.

———. 1984a. *Processed Mushrooms: US Producers' Production, Sales, and Inventories, and US Imports, Exports, and Apparent Consumption. Eighteenth Quarterly Report: Fourth Calendar Quarter 1983.* USITC Publication no. 1498. Washington, February.

———. 1984b. *Processed Mushrooms: US Producers' Production, Sales, and Inventories, and US Imports, Exports, and Apparent Consumption. Nineteenth Quarterly Report: First Calendar Quarter 1984.* USITC Publication no. 1537. Washington, May.

———. 1984c. *Processed Mushrooms: US Producers' Production, Sales, and Inventories, and US Imports, Exports, and Apparent Consumption. Twentieth Quarterly Report: Second Calendar Quarter 1984.* USITC Publication no. 1573. Washington, August.

———. 1984d. *Processed Mushrooms: US Producers' Production, Sales, and Inventories, and US Imports, Exports and Apparent Consumption. Twenty-First Quarterly Report: Third Calendar Quarter 1984.* USITC Publication no. 1619. Washington, November.

US Trade Representative. 1982. *Twenty-Sixth Annual Report of the President of the United States on the Trade Agreements Program 1981–82.* Washington, November.

———. 1984. *Annual Report of the President of the United States on the Trade Agreements Program 1983.* Washington, April.

CASE M–22

Automobiles

PERIOD OF RELIEF

1 April 1981 to 31 March 1985, with continuing Japanese export restraints to present

SUPPLIERS AFFECTED

Japan

RELIEF ACTION

On 12 June 1980, the United Auto Workers (UAW) filed a petition with the US International Trade Commission (USITC) under Section 201 of the Trade Act of 1974. The petition claimed that the domestic industry producing on-the-highway passenger automobiles, automobile trucks, and bodies (including cabs) and chassis for automobile trucks (provided for in items 692.02, 692.03, 692.10, 692.11, 692.20, and 692.21 of the Tariff Schedules of the United States) was being seriously injured by foreign imports.[1] On 30 June 1980, the USITC instituted an escape clause investigation, and on 4 August 1980, the Ford Motor Company joined the investigation as a co-petitioner for import relief. (USITC 1110, A78, A85; USITC 1084)

On 10 July 1980, the USITC received a letter from President Jimmy Carter requesting that the Commission accelerate its investigation in view of the large number of businesses, workers, and consumers for whom an investigation taking the full six months "could cause major uncertainties." Similar requests were filed by several senators and congressmen, by the UAW, and by others. After considering these requests, and statements filed by opponents, the Commission decided to accelerate its investigation by approximately three weeks. (USITC 1110, A1)

---

1. The petitioners sought to have Canadian imports, which are accorded duty-free treatment under a 1965 agreement between the United States and Canada, excluded from the investigation. They argued that such imports are produced almost exclusively by subsidiaries of US companies and that the manufacturing operations of the two countries form a single industry. They further maintained that this fact is recognized by the Automotive Products Trade Act, which implemented the 1965 agreement. (USITC 1110, 12, A12)

On 10 November 1980, the USITC determined by a 3 to 2 vote that on-the-highway passenger automobiles and light trucks were not being imported into the United States in such increased quantities as to be a substantial cause of serious injury, or threat of serious injury, to the domestic industry. The majority of commissioners found the decline in demand for new automobiles and light trucks resulting from general recessionary conditions in the US economy to be a greater cause of injury to the domestic industry than increased imports. They also found that the structural shift in the automotive market, which increased the proportion of small, fuel-efficient vehicles demanded in relation to total vehicles demanded, was an important cause of injury, but not in and of itself a greater cause than the relative import increase. (USITC 1110, 34–35; USITC 1648, 1)

Following the USITC decision, the auto industry appealed to the Carter administration for trade restrictions against auto imports. The administration resisted the pressure and instead authorized massive Trade Adjustment Assistance (TAA) benefits. By early 1981, legislation to restrict Japanese auto imports was gaining broad support in Congress. On 5 February 1981, Senators John C. Danforth (R-Mo.) and Lloyd Bentsen (D-Tex.) introduced legislation (S 396) to limit automobile exports from Japan to 1.6 million units per year for 1981, 1982, and 1983. (Nanto, 14)

In April 1981, following meetings with US trade officials, the Japanese Ministry of International Trade and Industry (MITI) presented a proposal for voluntarily restraining auto exports to the United States to allow the US industry time to become more competitive with imports. Japan proposed to limit its auto exports to 1.6 million to 1.7 million units annually, to be enforced by MITI through administrative guidance. Japanese automakers were critical of the plan, stating that high demand for small cars and high US wages were responsible for the US auto industry slump. To complicate matters, the European Community (EC) contended that any restraint agreement with the United States should also limit Japanese shipments to the EC. (USITC 1648, 1–2; Feenstra, 37)

On 2 May 1981, MITI announced it had reached a voluntary restraint agreement (VRA) with the administration of President Ronald Reagan. The VRA reduced Japanese auto exports to the United States by 7.7 percent, from the 1980 level of 1.82 million units to 1.68 million units for the period 1 April 1981 through 31 March 1982. MITI indicated that a decision on a second year of restraints would be made after observing the 1981 market performance of the US industry. At a later date the Japanese announced that exports to the United States of four-wheel-drive station wagons and "jeep"-type vehicles would be limited to 82,500 units, and exports to Puerto Rico would not exceed 70,000 units. Thus, total Japanese exports of autos and "utility" vehicles to the United States for 1981 were set at 1,832,500 units. (USITC 1648, 2; Tarr and Morkre, 54)

In early February 1982, UAW-backed "domestic content" legislation was introduced in Congress (HR 5133), which would have required that a very high percentage of the value of motor vehicles sold in the United States—at least 90 percent in the case of firms selling more than 500,000 cars in the United States—consist of domestic parts and materials. On 29 March 1982, partly as a response to protectionist pressures on Capitol Hill, Japan renewed the VRA for the period April 1982 to March 1983 at the 1.68-million-unit ceiling, plus allowances for "utility" vehicles and exports to Puerto Rico. Despite a second year of voluntary restraints, HR 5133 passed the House on 15 December 1982 by a vote of 215 to 188; however, Congress adjourned before the Senate version of the bill (S 2300) could come to the floor. (Feenstra, 37; Nanto, 1; Cohen, 531)

On 3 February 1983, Congressman Richard L. Ottinger (D-NY) again introduced domestic content legislation, essentially identical to HR 5133, entitled the Fair Practices in Automotive Products Act (HR 1234). On 12 February 1983, again in response to congressional pressure, Japan renewed the VRA for a third year (April 1983 through March 1984) at the existing ceiling levels. On 3 November 1983, by a vote of 219 to 199, the House passed HR 1234. The Senate bill (S 707) was referred to the Senate Committee on Commerce but no action was taken prior to adjournment.

On 1 November 1983, the Japanese government announced that it would increase its voluntary export limit from 1.68 million to 1.85 million automobiles during the period 1 April 1984 to 31 March 1985. In addition, it announced that the four-wheel-drive and "jeep"-type vehicle limit would be increased to 90,848 units and exports to Puerto Rico would rise to 77,083 units. The total number of Japanese automobiles (excluding automobile trucks) exported to the United States during 1984 was to increase from 1,832,500 to 2,017,931 units, a 10.1 percent increase over the previous three-year level. (USITC 1648, 2; Nanto, 1)

In October 1984, Ford, Chrysler, American Motors, and the UAW urged the Reagan administration to extend the Japanese voluntary export restraints for a fifth year, from 1 April 1985 to 31 March 1986. At the same time, General Motors (GM) and the American International Automobile Dealers Association opposed continuation of the restraints. (*Washington Post,* 23 October 1984, D1)

On 30 January 1985, high-level officials of MITI disclosed that Japan's voluntary ceiling on automobile exports, scheduled to expire on 31 March 1985, would not be renewed. MITI indicated that the decision not to renew the restraints was based on the record 1984 earnings posted by the big US automakers plus the sharp reduction in unemployment in the US auto industry. Ministry officials stressed, however, that elimination of the four-year-old quota system would be accompanied by some new form of restriction such as traditional administrative guidance procedures, in order to prevent a sudden climb in auto shipments to the American market. (*Journal of Commerce,* 31 January 1985, 1A)

On 19 February 1985, the Cabinet Council on Commerce and Trade recommended to President Reagan that he not seek to change Japan's decision to discontinue its voluntary quotas on automobile exports for a fifth year. This recommendation came as key congressmen, organized labor, and three of the four US automakers pressed the White House to continue the restraints in light of the record US trade deficit with Japan. (*New York Times,* 20 February 1985, D1; *Washington Post,* 20 February 1985, A1)

In March 1985, President Reagan decided not to ask Japan to continue its voluntary auto restraints after the limit expired on 1 April 1985. Following this decision, and in part due to the introduction of a number of resolutions in Congress calling for continued automobile restraints, Japan announced that it would hold auto exports to the United States to 2.3 million units in 1985, up 24 percent from fiscal 1984. As a result, auto imports from Japan jumped to 19.2 percent of the US market in May and 21.2 percent in June, up from an average 16.9 percent in the first four months of the year. A Department of Commerce report estimated that lifting of its self-imposed restraints would allow Japan to export 3.1 million cars to the United States in 1987. (*Journal of Commerce*, 14 May 1985, 5A; *New York Times*, 20 February 1985, D1; *Wall Street Journal*, 11 July 1985, 1)

CHANGES IN THE INDUSTRY

Since 1979, offshore automakers have committed $1.9 billion for new US manufacturing ventures and investments in domestic auto companies. Honda constructed an auto assembly plant at Marysville, Ohio. Toyota agreed to a joint venture with GM to produce Toyota-designed cars in Fremont, California. Ford is planning a $500 million investment project in Mexico, where it will assemble a Toyo Kogyo subcompact. In June 1984, GM and the Dao Motor Company signed a $426 million agreement to produce 167,000 cars a year in South Korea by 1987. (Simison, 1; Temple, 8; Reich; *New York Times*, 9 July 1984, D1)

The domestic industry has modernized production facilities, adopting robotics on a large scale, and become more competitive in the small-car market.[2] US automakers have closed 10 assembly plants, reorganized major divisions to increase efficiency, increased component outsourcing, lowered inventory carrying costs, and made significant gains in quality control. By increasing productivity while cutting both the salaried and hourly work force and renegotiating wages and work rules, the auto industry managed to reduce labor costs in the early 1980s. However, in September 1984, GM and the UAW signed a new three-year contract that raised wages and fringe benefits from about $22.80 an hour to about $27.80 an hour and widened further the production cost disadvantage vis-à-vis Japan—from about $1,500 to about $2,000 per car. Furthermore, the productivity increases and labor cost gains achieved have been largely offset by the overvalued dollar, which gives the Japanese an additional and significant price advantage. (Wharton, 4–5; USITC 1648, vi; Samuelson, 49)

Employment by the six domestic auto producers dropped each year from 1979 to 1982. In 1982, 289,000 auto workers were placed on temporary or indefinite layoff. Although employment rebounded by almost 100,000 by mid-1984 as a result of the 1984 sales recovery, the UAW was still 170,000 automotive jobs short of the 1978 level, a decline of 23 percent, with over 90,000 auto workers on indefinite layoff. Some experts estimate that by 1982, productivity increases had resulted in a permanent reduction of over 150,000 jobs (compared to the 1978–79 peak of almost one million workers). (USITC 1648, vi; Temple, i; *Wall Street Journal*, 31 May 1984, 14; Wharton, 17)

Despite some $50 billion in investment, the domestic industry is relying increasingly on Japan for subcompact technology. Auto production for the US market is now

---

2. In January 1985, General Motors announced plans for a totally new small car to be built by a separate, wholly-owned subsidiary called the Saturn Corporation. According to company representatives, this new car is aimed at making GM "cost competitive with the lowest-priced imports." (*Journal of Commerce*, 9 January 1985, 1A; *New York Times*, 9 January 1985; D1)

viewed as a "mature" industry with long-term growth limited to the rate of growth of real income.[3] Nevertheless, in 1984, the US auto industry had its best profit year since 1977. In *Forbes* listing of the largest 500 US companies according to profit, GM ranked third, Ford Motor Company ranked fourth, and Chrysler ranked ninth. These rankings jumped from their 1983 levels of fourth, sixth, and forty-fourth, respectively. (Wharton, 4–5; Samuelson; Fisher, 20; Altshuler, 110; *Forbes*, 174)

---

3. Average annual car mileage has declined 12 percent since 1978 to 8,037 miles, and new-car buyers are keeping their cars an average of 5.1 years, more than one year longer than in 1978. In addition, higher gasoline prices have crimped US demand for automobile services. After the rapid increase in the price of gasoline during 1979–80, consumers changed their purchases of mostly large autos to that of smaller, more fuel-efficient models. As the price of gasoline leveled and the general economy improved in late 1982, many consumers switched from smaller domestic models to larger models. (USITC 1648, v; *Wall Street Journal*, 3 May 1984, 1)

Key Statistics

Imports affected from Japan

Year	Volume (million units)	Value (billion dollars)	Source
Before VRA			
1979	1.62	6.47	USITC 1419, 4
1980	1.99	8.23	USITC 1419, 4
During VRA			
1981	1.91	9.49	USITC 1419, 4
1982	1.80	9.61	USITC 1419, 4
1983	1.87	10.76	USITC 1648, 42
1984	1.97	12.50	USITC 1648, 42

Imports from all sources[a]

Year	Volume (million units)	Value (billion dollars)	Source
Before VRA			
1979	3.01	14.85	USITC 1419, 4
1980	3.11	16.68	USITC 1419, 4

Imports from all sources[a] (continued)

Year	Volume (million units)	Value (billion dollars)	Source
During VRA			
1981	2.86	17.69	USITC 1419, 4
1982	2.93	20.18	USITC 1419, 4
1983	3.69	24.17	USITC 1650, 2
1984	3.56	29.26	USITC 1650, 2

a. US imports fluctuated little from 1979 to early 1983 due in large part to the VRA, which held Japanese imports constant during the latter part of this period. However, in 1983–84, US imports rose to 3.6 million units owing to increased demand for automobiles produced by US subsidiaries in Canada and for West German automobiles, and an increase in the level of the Japanese VRA from 1.68 million units to 1.85 million units. (USITC 1648, vii)

Apparent consumption

Year	Volume (million units)	Value[a] (billion dollars)	Source
Before VRA			
1979	10.64	59.85	USITC 1419, 2; authors' estimate
1980	8.97	53.57	USITC 1648, 36; authors' estimate
During VRA			
1981	8.53	58.74	USITC 1648, 36; authors' estimate
1982	7.98	55.74	USITC 1648, 36; authors' estimate
1983	9.18	65.54	USITC 1648, 36; authors' estimate
1984	10.40	86.05	USITC 1648, 36; authors' estimate

a. These figures are derived from the value of imports from all sources and domestic output, minus the value of exports.

Market share of imports (percentage of apparent consumption, by volume)

Year	Affected imports	Total imports	Source
Before VRA			
1979	15.2	28.3	authors' estimate
1980	22.2	34.7	authors' estimate
During VRA			
1981	22.4	33.5	authors' estimate
1982	22.6	36.7	authors' estimate
1983	20.4	40.2	authors' estimate
1984	18.9	34.2	authors' estimate

Output of domestic industry[a]

Year	Volume (million units)	Value[b] (billion dollars)	Source
Before VRA			
1979	8.41	49.60	USITC 1648, 18; USITC 1110, A49
1980	6.38	40.79	USITC 1648, 18; authors' estimate
During VRA			
1981	6.26	44.95	USITC 1648, 18; authors' estimate
1982	5.07	38.46	USITC 1648, 18; authors' estimate
1983	5.98	45.57	USITC 1648, 18; authors' estimate
1984[c]	7.77	61.69	USITC 1648, 18; authors' estimate

a. Producers' shipments.

b. The 1979 figure is the value of producers' shipments. The 1980–84 figures were derived using the export unit values for those years. (USITC 1585, 3; USITC 1650, 4)

c. Preliminary estimates.

Employment in domestic industry

Year	Production workers (average number)	Source
Before VRA		
1979	779,121	USITC 1648, 9
1980	609,315	USITC 1648, 9
During VRA		
1981	602,264	USITC 1648, 9
1982	509,195	USITC 1648, 9
1983	543,849	USITC 1648, 9
1984	605,065[a]	USITC 1648, 9

a. This figure reflects employment during January to June.

Wages and benefits[a]

Year	Dollars per hour	Source
Before VRA		
1979	13.68	Crandall, 11
1980	16.29	Crandall, 11
During VRA		
1981	17.28	Crandall, 11
1982	18.66	Crandall, 11
1983	19.02	Crandall, 11
1984	22.80	Samuelson

a. The UAW "gave back" about $2 billion in wages and benefits in the contract expiring fall 1984, compared with the prior contract. Japanese firms are estimated to have an $8-to-$10-an-hour advantage in labor costs. (Fisher, 21; *Wall Street Journal*, 14 May 1984, 1)

Industry profits[a] (billion dollars)

Year	Profits (loss)[b]	Source
Before VRA		
1979	(0.4)	USITC 1648, 13
1980	(4.7)	USITC 1648, 13
During VRA		
1981	(2.3)	USITC 1648, 13
1982	(0.6)	USITC 1648, 13
1983	5.3	USITC 1648, 13
1984[c]	10.4	USITC 1648, 13

a. During the period of the VRA, the four domestic auto companies (General Motors, Ford, Chrysler, and American Motors) registered total net profits of almost $13.0 billion on their US operations. (USITC 1648, vii)

b. Net profits (loss) before taxes.

c. This figure reflects an annualized estimate of profits reported by the six US producers of automobiles during January to June 1984.

Industry capacity utilization[a]

Year	Percentage	Source
Before VRA		
1979	82.9	USITC 1648, 18
1980	65.0	USITC 1648, 18
During VRA		
1981	67.8	USITC 1648, 18
1982	54.6	USITC 1648, 18
1983	69.6	USITC 1648, 18
1984	86.8	USITC 1648, 18

a. Capacity for the US production of autos decreased from 10.1 million units in 1979 to 8.6 million in 1983 before rising to 9.0 million in 1984. (USITC 1648, v)

Quantitative Profile

Item	Amount	Source
Number of years restraints in force (imposed by US, 1981–85)	4 years, with continuing Japanese restraints thereafter	
Induced increase in price of imported autos	7.9 percent (1981–84 average)	USITC 1648, 36[a]
	2.4 percent	Feenstra, 38[b]
	9.6 percent (1981)	Tarr, 65[c]
	10 percent (1981–84 average)	Hickok, 8
	15.3 percent ($1,000 per auto)	Crandall, 16
	11 percent (1981–84 average)	authors' estimate[d]

Quantitative Profile (continued)

Item	Amount	Source
Induced increase in price of domestic autos	5.0 percent (1981–83) or $400 per auto	Crandall, 16
	4.0 percent (1984)	Hickok, 8
	4.4 percent (1981–84 average)	authors' estimate[e]
Coefficient of price response	0.4	authors' estimate
Quantity and value of imports (1984)	3.56 million units	USITC 1650, 2
	$29.3 billion	USITC 1650, 2
Induced decrease in imports due to restraints	7 percent	Harbridge, 1
	0.5 million units	USITC 1648, 42
	0.7 million units	authors' estimate
	$5.8 billion	authors' estimate
Quantity and value of domestic production (1984)	7.77 million units	USITC 1648, 18
	$61.7 billion	authors' estimate
Induced increase in domestic production due to restraints	0.6 million units	USITC 1648, ix
	8 percent	USITC 1648, ix
	0.7 million units	authors' estimate
Coefficient of quantity response	1.0	authors' estimate
Elasticity of demand for imported autos (Japan basic car)	3.5	Council, A2
	2 to 3	Feenstra, 54
	2.53	Hickok, 9
Elasticity of supply of domestic autos	0.3	authors' estimate
Elasticity of demand for domestic autos	1.0 to 1.5	Wharton, 26
	2 to 3 (small cars)	Wharton, 26
	1.0	USITC 1110, A59
	1.5	authors' estimate
Cross-elasticity of demand for US basic car relative to price of Japan basic car	0.78	Council, A2
	0.72	authors' estimate
Cross-elasticity of output of domestic autos relative to price of imported autos	0.12	authors' estimate
Cross-elasticity of quantity of imported autos relative to price of domestic autos	0.67	authors' estimate
Cost of restraints to US consumers	$3.9 billion (1981–84 average)	USITC 1648, ix[f]
	$4.3 billion (1983)	Crandall, 16
	$4.5 billion (1984)	Hickok, 8
	$5.8 billion (1984)	authors' estimate
Gain from restraints to US producers	$115 million (1983)	Tarr, 56
	$2.6 billion (1984)	authors' estimate

Quantitative Profile (continued)

Item	Amount	Source
Tariff revenue and implied average tariff rate (1984)	$790 million 2.7 percent	authors' estimate Tarr, 66
Gain from restraints to foreigners	$824 million (1983) $2.2 billion (1984)	Tarr, 56 authors' estimate
Efficiency loss from larger domestic production to the United States (1984)	$200 million	authors' estimate
Welfare cost of restraints to the United States	$2 billion (1981–83 average) $994 million (1983) $2.4 billion (1984)	Crandall, 13 Tarr, 56 authors' estimate
Employment in protected US industry	779,121 (1979) 605,065 (1984)	USITC 1648, 9 USITC 1648, 9[g]
Induced increase in employment	4,600 5,600 to 11,100 26,200 44,100 55,000	Tarr, 70 Feenstra, 54[h] Crandall, 16 USITC 1648, 4 authors' estimate[i]
Cost of restraints to US consumers per job saved	$241,235 (1983) $160,000 (1983) $105,000 (1984)	Tarr, 58 Crandall, 16 authors' estimate
Gain from restraints to US producers per job (1984)	$4,300	authors' estimate

a. According to USITC estimates, transaction prices of Japanese automobiles sold in the United States in 1984 averaged $1,300 more per auto as a result of the VRA than they would otherwise have been. The estimated VRA-induced price increase of Japanese autos in the US rose from $185 per auto in 1981 to $359 in 1982, and to $831 more per auto by 1983. This reflects an average VRA-induced price increase of $670 per Japanese auto during the period 1981–84. (USITC 1648, viii)

b. In addition to the scarcity rent import price increase of 2.4 percent, Feenstra calculates a price increase due to quality upgrading of 6.0 percent. (Feenstra, 52)

c. According to Tarr and Morkre, the unit value of Japanese automobiles rose 20 percent in 1981. Of this increase, 1.7 percent resulted from an increase in the cost of inputs; 2.7 percent resulted from exchange rate changes; 6 percent resulted from additional costs required to produce higher quality vehicles; and 9.6 percent resulted from the VRA. (Tarr and Morkre, 65–66)

d. This estimate includes the effect of the regular ad valorem tariff of 2.7 percent, plus an average 8 percent increase due to the VRA.

e. According to Wharton Econometrics, the average new car selling price has increased nearly $2,600 (35 percent) since April 1981. In common with other observers, we attribute only a small part of this increase to the VRA. (Wharton, 8)

f. According to USITC staff estimates, the VRA cost US consumers an additional $835 million in 1981, $1.65 billion in 1982, $4.68 billion in 1983, and $8.52 billion in 1984, for a combined total of $15.7 billion during 1981–84. (USITC 1648, ix)

g. This figure reflects employment in the US industry during the period January to June 1984.

h. This figure reflects an import demand elasticity of 2 to 3.

i. Our estimate is based on the ratio between the induced increase in domestic production (0.7 million units) and the 1984 level of domestic production (7.96 million units), times the 1984 level of employment (605,065).

Hypothetical Adjustment Program[a]

	1984	1985	1986	1987	1988	1989	1990
US purchases of automobiles (million units)							
Assumed annual consumption growth of 2 percent	10.40	10.61	10.82	11.04	11.26	11.48	11.71
Imports from all sources							
Assumed annual consumption growth of 2 percent and no change in import restraints (million units)	3.50	3.57	3.64	3.71	3.79	3.86	3.94
Assumed annual consumption growth of 2 percent and degressive tariff (price elasticity of 3.5) (million units)	3.50	3.69	3.89	4.12	4.37	4.62	4.91
Import share of consumption with degressive tariff (percentage)	33.7	34.8	35.9	37.3	38.8	40.2	41.9
Hypothetical quota auction and existing tariffs							
Tariff equivalent of existing tariff and quota auction (degressive at 1 percentage point per year) (percent)	11	10	9	8	7	6	5
Quota auction and existing tariff revenue (billion 1984 dollars)	—	3.1	3.0	2.9	2.7	2.5	2.2
US production for domestic market[b] (million units)							
Assumed annual consumption growth of 2 percent and constant import share	6.90	7.04	7.18	7.33	7.47	7.62	7.77
Assumed annual consumption growth of 2 percent and rising import share	6.90	6.92	6.93	6.92	6.89	6.86	6.80
US employment in automobile industry (thousand workers)							
Assumed 5 percent annual productivity growth and constant import share	605	587	570	554	538	522	497

Hypothetical Adjustment Program[a] (continued)

	1984	1985	1986	1987	1988	1989	1990
Assumed 5 percent annual productivity growth and rising import share	605	587	559	532	507	483	460
Year-to-year employment changes (thousand workers)							
Changes induced by consumption and productivity growth with constant import share	—	−18	−17	−16	−16	−16	−15
Changes induced by rising import share	—	—	−11	−11	−9	−8	−8
Total employment changes	—	−18	−28	−27	−25	−24	−23
Benefit and budget calculations (1984 prices)							
Annual wage cost per worker assuming constant $22 per hour and 1,600 hours (dollars)	—	35,000	35,000	35,000	35,000	35,000	35,000
Benefits calculated at two times annual wage cost per worker (billion dollars)	—	1.3	2.0	1.9	1.8	1.7	1.6
Projected program surplus or deficit: tariff and quota revenue less benefits (billion dollars)	—	1.8	1.0	1.0	0.9	0.8	0.6

— Not applicable.

a. This program assumes that Japanese export restraints are replaced by a quota auction administered by the United States.

b. The figures are calculated as US purchases less imports.

BIBLIOGRAPHY

Altshuler, Alan, Martin Anderson, Daniel Jones, Daniel Roos, and James Womack. 1984. *The Future of the Automobile: The Report of MIT's International Automobile Program.* Cambridge, Mass.: MIT Press.

Auerbach, Stuart, and David Hoffman. 1985. "Car Quotas to be Left Up to Japan." *Washington Post,* 20 February, A1.

Balassa, Carol. 1984. "Levels of Protection on Manufactured Goods: The US, EC, Canada, Japan." Office of the US Trade Representative. Washington.

Boyd, Gerald M. 1985. "US Aides Ask for End to Car Quotas." *New York Times,* 20 February, D1.

Cohen, Robert B. 1983. "The Prospects for Trade and Protectionism in the Auto Industry." In *Trade Policy in the 1980s*. Edited by William R. Cline. Washington: Institute for International Economics.

Council of Economic Advisers. 1982. "Domestic Content Requirements for US Auto Sales: An Economic Assessment." Executive Office of the President. Washington, 24 May.

Crandall, Robert W. 1984. "Import Quotas and the Automobile Industry: The Costs of Protectionism." *Brookings Review* 2, no. 4 (Summer): 8–16.

Cullison, A. E. 1985. "Japan Won't Renew US Car Export Ceiling." *Journal of Commerce*, 31 January, 1A.

Feenstra, Robert C. 1984. "Voluntary Export Restraint in US Autos, 1980–81: Quality, Employment, and Welfare Effects." In *The Structure and Evolution of Recent US Trade Policy*. Edited by Robert Baldwin and Anne O. Krueger. National Bureau of Economic Research Conference Report. Chicago: University of Chicago Press.

Fisher, Anne B. 1984. "Can Detroit Live Without Quotas?" *Fortune* 109, no. 13 (June): 20–25.

"The Forbes Profits 500." 1985. *Forbes*, 29 April.

Harbridge House. 1982. *Domestic Content Legislation, A Tax on the American Auto Consumer*. Study prepared for the American International Automobile Dealers Association. Washington, July.

Hickok, Susan. 1985. "The Consumer Cost of US Trade Restraints." *Federal Reserve Bank of New York: Quarterly Review* 10, no. 2 (Summer): 1–12.

Holusha, John. 1984. "A Race for Greater Auto Profits." *New York Times*, 30 September, III, 1.

Morici, Peter, and Laura L. Megna. 1983. *US Economic Policies Affecting Industrial Trade: A Quantitative Assessment*. Report no. 200. Washington: National Planning Association.

Nanto, Dick K. 1983. *Automobiles Imported from Japan*. Issue Brief no. IB80030. US Congressional Research Service. Washington, 7 December.

Reich, Robert B. 1984. "Quotas Allow Auto Makers Not to Invest in Future." *Los Angeles Times*, 13 May, IV, 3.

Samuelson, Robert J. 1984. "Pampering the Auto Industry." *Newsweek*, 8 October.

Simison, Robert L. 1984. "Despite Strong Sales, Auto Makers Believe Real Booms Are Over." *Wall Street Journal*, 3 May, 1.

Tarr, David G., and Morris E. Morkre. 1984. *Aggregate Costs to the United States of Tariffs and Quotas on Imports: General Tariff Cuts and Removal of Quotas on Automobiles, Steel, Sugar, and Textiles*. US Federal Trade Commission, Bureau of Economics Staff Report. Washington, December.

Temple, Barker & Sloane. 1984. *The Imported Automobile Industry in America*. Study prepared for the American International Automobile Dealers Association, January.

US International Trade Commission. 1980a. *Certain Motor Vehicles and Certain Chassis and Bodies Therefor*. USITC Publication no. 1110. Washington, December.

———. 1980b. *Annual Report 1980*. USITC Publication no. 1084. Washington.

———. 1981. *Automotive Trade Statistics 1964–1980*. USITC Publication no. 1171. Washington, August.

———. 1983. *The US Auto Industry: US Factory Sales, Retail Sales, Imports, Exports, Apparent Consumption, Suggested Retail Prices, and Trade Balances with Selected Countries for Motor Vehicles, 1964–82*. USITC Publication no. 1419. Washington, August.

———. 1984a. *The US Automobile Industry: Monthly Report on Selected Economic Indicators*. USITC Publication no. 1527. Washington, May.

———. 1984b. *The US Automobile Industry: Monthly Report on Selected Economic Indicators*. USITC Publication no. 1541. Washington, June.

———. 1984c. *The US Automobile Industry: Monthly Report on Selected Economic Indicators.* USITC Publication no. 1551. Washington, July.

———. 1984d. *The US Automobile Industry: Monthly Report on Selected Economic Indicators.* USITC Publication no. 1564. Washington, August.

———. 1984e. *The US Auto Industry: US Factory Sales, Retail Sales, Imports, Exports, Apparent Consumption, Suggested Retail Prices, and Trade Balances with Selected Countries for Motor Vehicles, 1964–83.* USITC Publication no. 1585. Washington, September.

———. 1985a. *A Review of Recent Developments in the US Automobile Industry Including an Assessment of the Japanese Voluntary Restraint Agreements.* USITC Publication no. 1648. Washington, February.

———. 1985b. *The US Automobile Industry: Monthly Report on Selected Economic Indicators.* USITC Publication no. 1650. Washington, February.

———. 1985c. *The US Automobile Industry: Monthly Report on Selected Economic Indicators.* USITC Publication no. 1715. Washington, June.

US Trade Representative. 1981. *Twenty-fifth Annual Report of the President of the United States on the Trade Agreements Program 1980–81.* Washington.

———. 1982. *Twenty-sixth Annual Report of the President of the United States on the Trade Agreements Program 1981–82.* Washington, November.

———. 1984. *Annual Report of the President of the United States on the Trade Agreements Program 1983.* Washington, April.

Wayne, Leslie. 1984. "The Irony and Impact of Auto Quotas." *New York Times*, 8 April, F1.

Wharton Econometric Forecasting Associates. 1983. *Impact of Local Content Legislation on US and World Economies, "The Fair Practices in Automotive Products Act,"* HR 1234 (abridged and unabridged). Study prepared for the Japan Automobile Manufacturers Association. Philadelphia and Washington, July.

CASE M-23

Heavyweight Motorcycles (over 700 cc)

PERIOD OF RELIEF

16 April 1983 to 15 April 1988

SUPPLIERS AFFECTED

Global (primarily Japan)

RELIEF ACTION

On 1 September 1982, Harley-Davidson Motor Company and Harley-Davidson York, Inc. filed a petition, under Section 201 of the Trade Act of 1974, for escape clause relief from imports of heavyweight motorcycles.[1] The US International Trade Commission (USITC) initiated an investigation on 16 September 1982 and on 1 February 1983 reported to President Ronald Reagan that imports of heavyweight motorcycles were a substantial cause of serious injury to the domestic industry. The USITC did not find imported engines and power train subassemblies and parts to be a threat of injury. The USITC recommended an increase in duties for a five-year period (to 45 percent ad valorem in the first year of protection, falling to 10 percent in the fifth year). (Hatch 334; USITC 1342, 1–2, A1)

President Reagan accepted the USITC recommendation in part and, on 1 April 1983, announced the implementation of increased duties and imposition of tariff-rate quotas (TRQ). Thus, only imports above the quota level are subject to the higher tariffs. This action was intended to assure continued access to the US market for relatively low volume exporters. The TRQ for West Germany, which accounted for only 0.4 percent of US motorcycle imports in 1981, started at 5,000 units in 1983 and will increase to

---

1. Harley-Davidson succeeded in having the affected domestic industry defined as including those firms manufacturing motorcycles with a total piston displacement of over 700 cc, despite the fact that most of its own sales are of motorcycles over 1,000 cc. The firm failed, however, to convince the USITC that Japanese-owned firms manufacturing such vehicles should be excluded because they use mostly imported parts. (Hatch 335–36)

10,000 units by 1988. For all other exporters, except Japan, the TRQ began at 4,000 units and will increase by 1,000 units each year for the next four years. (Hatch 326, N6; USTR 1984, 144)

Japan, which in 1981 accounted for 93 percent of all motorcycle imports, was granted an initial quota of 6,000 units, with increases of 1,000 units per year through 1988, when special relief is to terminate. Japan regarded the TRQ as unfairly favorable to its European competitors and threatened to file a complaint of discriminatory treatment under Article XIII of the General Agreement on Tariffs and Trade (GATT). No formal action was taken, however. (Hatch 327; *Journal of Commerce,* 25 May 1984, 1A)

CHANGES IN THE INDUSTRY

"Since the first motorcycle was manufactured commercially in 1901, there have been approximately 150 producers of motorcycles in the United States. As of 1978, however, only one US-owned firm, Harley-Davidson, remained in operation in the United States, along with two Japanese-owned producers, Kawasaki and Honda America. Harley-Davidson and Honda America both produce only heavyweight motorcycles, while Kawasaki produces both heavy- and medium-weight vehicles." Until 1984, when the increased tariffs forced it to shift more of its heavyweight motorcycle production from Japan to its US facilities, Kawasaki accounted for less than 10 percent of domestic production. (Hatch 332; McElroy)

Harley-Davidson plans to modernize its facilities and introduce "a more competitive, smaller line of motorcycles in the 800 cc–1,000 cc range." One reason the USITC recommended the level and period of relief that it did was to give the firm sufficient time to carry out those plans. (Hatch 339)

The Japanese producers, Kawasaki and Honda, have responded to the tariffs by increasing production of heavyweight motorcycles in their US plants, and by reducing the engine displacement of what otherwise would have been 750 cc bikes to between 690 cc and 700 cc. Imports of motorcycle parts other than engines increased 82 percent in 1983 and more than 200 percent in the first half of 1984. The USITC estimated that 50 percent to 70 percent of the value of completed motorcycles from the two Japanese-owned plants is imported as parts. (BIE, 50–6)

Harley-Davidson has used the relief period to modify its management style, cut costs, and improve quality. The company has adopted some of the management methods of its Japanese competitors, lowered its inventory, and improved management-labor relations by maintaining an open door policy and allowing more employee input into decision-making. Harley has increased its share of the domestic market but its sales are still declining because the market continues shrinking. Company management is hoping for a resurgence in the market and cites demographic evidence of growing numbers of 25-to-45 year olds, the age group most likely to buy motorcycles. Other analysts are more skeptical, however, and contend that "motorcycles are out of vogue in a yuppie age." (*New York Times,* 3 October 1985, D1)

Key Statistics

Import from all sources

Year	Volume (million units)	Value (million dollars)	Source
Before restraints			
1980	196	393	USITC 1342, A18
1981	202	440	USITC 1342, A18
1982	224	474	USITC 1342, A18; 1420
During restraints			
1983	94	229	USITC 1420, 1456, 1493
1984	38	124	USITC 1533, 1570, 1614, 1652

Apparent consumption[a]

Year	Volume (million units)	Value (million dollars)	Source
Before restraints			
1980	326	850	authors' estimate
1981	327	855	authors' estimate
1982	324	812	authors' estimate
During restraints			
1983	194	643	authors' estimate
1984	159	635	authors' estimate

a. These estimates were derived by adding imports and domestic output; exports are small. The estimates do not take into account the large inventories built up in 1982 just before restraints went into effect.

Market share of imports (percentage of apparent consumption, by volume)

Year	Share	Source
Before restraints		
1980	60	authors' estimate
1981	62	authors' estimate
1982	69	authors' estimate
After restraints		
1983	48	authors' estimate
1984	31	authors' estimate

Output of domestic industry

Year	Volume[a] (million units)	Value[b] (million dollars)	Source
Before restraints			
1980	130	457	Motorcycle 1983, 12; authors' estimate
1981	125	415	Motorcycle 1983, 12; authors' estimate
1982	100	347	Motorcycle 1983, 12; authors' estimate
During restraints			
1983	100	414	Motorcycle 1984, 12; authors' estimate
1984	121	511	USITC 1533, 1570, 1614, 1652; authors' estimate

a. Production figures were estimated by the Motorcycle Industry Council, Inc., based on new registrations and information provided by US manufacturers.

b. The value of output was estimated using the average unit value of US-produced heavyweight motorcycles. The figures for 1980–82 are based on the unweighted average of prices for motorcycles in the 851 cc to 1025 cc range and for those over 1025 cc.

Employment in domestic industry

Year	Production workers (average number)	Source
Before restraints		
1980	2,702	McElroy
1981	2,924	McElroy
1982	2,230	McElroy
During restraints		
1983	3,199	USITC 1420, 1455, 1493
1984	3,357	USITC 1533, 1570, 1614, 1652

Wages[a]

Year	Dollars per hour	Source
Before restraints		
1980	6.89	BIE, 50–15
1981	7.82	BIE, 50–15
1982	8.96	BIE, 50–15
During restraints		
1983	9.41	BIE, 50–2
1984	9.87	BIE, 50–2

a. These figures are for workers in the motorcycle and bicycle production industries. The 1983 and 1984 figures are estimates by the Bureau of Industrial Economics.

Industry profits

Figures on profits are not available in the public record.

Industry capacity utilization

Figures on capacity utilization are not available in the public record.

Quantitative Profile

Item	Amount	Source
Number of years restraints in force (1983–88)	5 years	
Induced increase in price of imported motorcycles	25 percent (1983) 30 percent (1984)	USITC 1342, 19 authors' estimate[a]
Induced increase in price of domestic motorcycles (1984)	15 percent	authors' estimate
Coefficient of price response	0.5	authors' estimate
Quantity and value of imports (1984)	38,000 units $124 million	USITC 1533, 1570, 1614, 1652
Induced decrease in imports due to restraints (1984)	50,000 units $163 million	authors' estimate authors' estimate
Quantity and value of domestic production (1984)	121,000 units $511 million	USITC 1533, 1570, 1614, 1652
Induced increase in domestic production due to restraints (1984)	25,000 units	authors' estimate
Coefficient of quantity response	0.5	authors' estimate
Elasticity of demand for imported motorcycles	2.3 2.0	Stern, 9[b] authors' estimate
Elasticity of supply of domestic motorcycles	0.5	authors' estimate
Elasticity of demand for domestic motorcycles	2.0	authors' estimate
Cross-elasticity of demand for domestic motorcycles relative to price of imported motorcycles	6.4 1.3	Stern, 9[b] authors' estimate
Cross-elasticity of output of domestic motorcycles relative to price of imported motorcycles	0.3	authors' estimate
Cross-elasticity of quantity of imported motorcycles relative to price of domestic motorcycles	0.5	authors' estimate

Quantitative Profile (continued)

Item	Amount	Source
Cost of restraints to US consumers	$47 million (1983)	Consumers[c]
	$400 to $600 per unit	Consumers
	$100 million (1983)	BIE, 50–6
	$104 million (1984)	authors' estimate
Gain from restraints to US producers (1984)	$67 million	authors' estimate
Tariff revenue and implied average tariff rate (1982)	$21 million 4.4 percent	authors' estimate USITC 1342, A6
Gain from restraints to foreigners (1984)	negligible	authors' estimate
Efficiency loss from larger domestic production to the United States (1984)	$17 million	authors' estimate
Welfare cost of restraints to the United States (1984)	$17 million	authors' estimate
Employment in protected US industry	2,230 (1982) 3,357 (1984)	McElroy McElroy
Induced increase in employment (1984)	700	authors' estimate
Cost of restraints to US consumers per job saved (1984)	$150,000	authors' estimate
Gain from restraints to US producers per job (1984)	$20,000	authors' estimate

a. This estimate reflects the normal tariff of about 5 percent and an increase in price due to escape clause relief of about 25 percent.

b. The Stern elasticity estimates apply to transportation equipment in general.

c. This figure is based on an average $500 per unit cost on 94,000 units.

BIBLIOGRAPHY

Balassa, Carol. 1984. "Levels of Protection on Manufactured Goods: The US, EC, Canada, Japan." Office of the US Trade Representative. Washington.

Consumers for World Trade. 1984. "How Much Do Consumers Pay for US Trade Barriers?" CWT Information Paper. Washington, Winter.

Hatch, Josiah, III. 1984. "Recent Decision: The Harley-Davidson Case, Escaping the Escape Clause." *Law and Policy in International Business* 16, pp. 325–49.

McElroy, James (US International Trade Commission). 1985. By communication, 4 June.

Motorcycle Industry Council. 1983, 1984. *Motorcycle Statistical Annual*. Arlington, Va.

Stern, Robert M. 1984. "Comments on Data, Elasticities, and Other Key Parameters." Seminar Discussion Paper no. 134. Paper read at conference, General Equilibrium Trade Policy Modelling, Columbia University, 5–6 April.

US Department of Commerce. Bureau of Industrial Economics. 1985. *US Industrial Outlook*. Washington.

US International Trade Commission. 1983a. *Heavyweight Motorcycles and Engines and Power Train Subassemblies Therefor.* USITC Publication no. 1342. Washington, February.

———. 1983b. *Heavyweight Motorcycles: First Quarterly Report (Covering Fourth Quarter of 1982 and First and Second Quarters of 1983) on Selected Economic Indicators.* USITC Publication no. 1420. Washington, August.

———. 1983c. *Heavyweight Motorcycles: Second Quarterly Report (Covering Third Quarter of 1983) on Selected Economic Indicators.* USITC Publication no. 1455. Washington, November.

———. 1984a. *Heavyweight Motorcycles: Quarterly Report (Covering Fourth Quarter of 1983) on Selected Economic Indicators.* USITC Publication no. 1493. Washington, February.

———. 1984b. *Heavyweight Motorcycles: Selected Economic Indicators, First Quarter 1984.* USITC Publication no. 1533. Washington, May.

———. 1984c. *Heavyweight Motorcycles: Selected Economic Indicators, Second Quarter 1984.* USITC Publication no. 1570. Washington, August.

———. 1984d. *Heavyweight Motorcycles: Selected Economic Indicators, Third Quarter 1984.* USITC Publication no. 1614. Washington, November.

———. 1985. *Heavyweight Motorcycles: Selected Economic Indicators, Fourth Quarter 1984.* USITC Publication no. 1652. Washington, February.

US Trade Representative. 1984. *Annual Report of the President of the United States on the Trade Agreements Program 1983.* Washington, April.

CASE S-1

Maritime Industries

PERIOD OF RELIEF

1789 to present

SUPPLIERS AFFECTED

Global

RELIEF ACTION

Since the beginning of the Republic, the maritime industries[1] have benefited from a wide variety of on-budget and off-budget aids. In recent years, the administration of President Ronald Reagan has sought to reduce direct subsidies; however, most of the protective apparatus remains.

Early Programs

The second act passed by the first Congress was the Tariff Act of 1789, which established different tonnage tax rates for foreign and American ships. Foreign-owned and foreign-built ships were taxed at a rate of 50 cents per ton each time they entered a US port. American-owned and American-built ships were taxed only 6 cents per ton and paid the tax just once a year. The act also provided a 10 percent reduction in customs duties to importers using American vessels. (Jantscher, 46; Heine, 4)

International law recognizes the right of nations to reserve coastal trade to their national fleets. The first US cabotage law was passed in 1817 and, after being suspended for a time during World War I, was reinstated by the Jones Act of 1920 (46 USC 883). The law reserves trade between US ports to US-owned and US-built ships, manned by US crews.[2] As new territories were added, the scope of the law

---

1. The maritime industries are the shipbuilding, repair, and ship operation industries.

2. Originally, the law reserved domestic trade to US-flag ships which, by definition, were American-built, American-owned, and manned by American citizens. Since 1912, foreign-built ships have been admitted to US registry; requirements regarding citizenship of the owners and crew have been maintained. (Jantscher, 11)

was broadened so that today it includes intercoastal trade and trade between the mainland United States and its noncontiguous areas, Alaska, Hawaii, Puerto Rico, and the US territories and possessions. (Janstcher, 45–48; Heine, 4)

Another major form of off-budget aid is cargo preference. The Military Transportation Act of 1904 (10 USC 2631) requires that all supplies intended for US armed forces abroad that travel by sea must do so in US-flag vessels unless the rate charged is "excessive or otherwise unreasonable." In 1934, Public Resolution 17 expressed the intent of Congress that whenever a loan is made by a government agency (e.g., the US Export-Import Bank) to foster exports, those goods should be carried in US bottoms. The resolution is not legally binding and, in practice, about half of such shipments are transported in US-flag ships. Finally, the Cargo Preference Act of 1954 (46 USC 1241[b]), also known as the 50-50 law, amended the Merchant Marine Act of 1936 to require that 50 percent of certain government-impelled cargoes should be shipped in US-flag vessels, if they are available at "fair and reasonable" rates. Military cargoes make up the majority of government-impelled cargoes. These requirements may be waived in case of emergency. (Jantscher, 69–80)

In late 1983, Representative Lindy Boggs (D-La.) and Senator Paul Trible (R-Va.) introduced companion bills (HR 6222 and S 1624) seeking "to promote increased ocean transportation of bulk commodities by US-flag ships in the foreign commerce of the United States." The bills would require all US importers and exporters to transport 5 percent of their bulk cargo on US-flag carriers one year after enactment of the legislation. The percentage would rise one percentage point each year to a maximum of 20 percent at the end of 15 years. However, at the end of the first five years, US shipbuilders and operators are required to show that they have reduced their costs (in real terms) by 15 percent under HR 6222, and 20 percent under S 1624, in order for the share of impelled cargo to increase. The legislation was never acted upon, but Boggs has indicated that she will reintroduce it in the 1985–86 session. (USITC 1676, 62)

Cargo preference has come under increasing criticism from exporters, particularly agricultural interests, whose sales abroad have already been reduced by the strong dollar. Secretary of Agriculture John R. Block announced in June 1985 that cargo preference would not apply to the Department of Agriculture's new bonus incentive commodity export program. (*Washington Post*, 31 May 1985, A3; *Journal of Commerce*, 6 June 1985, 22B)

The Merchant Marine Acts of 1936 and 1970

The US government provided indirect subsidies, through the extension of mail contracts, to the privately owned US merchant marine beginning in 1891. Mismanagement and corruption plagued this program and contributed little to promotion of the US-flag commercial fleet. Following an investigation of the program by a special Senate committee chaired by Senator Hugo Black, President Franklin D. Roosevelt, in 1935, proposed the substitution of direct subsidies for mail contracts. Congress passed the Merchant Marine Act establishing the operation differential subsidy (ODS) and construction differential subsidy (CDS) programs in 1936. Both programs were retained in modified form by the Merchant Marine Act of 1970. The act, under Article XI, also provides government guarantees for the financing of ship construction, a program that has become increasingly important in recent years with the limitation of direct subsidies. (Heine, 4–9, 13–14; Jantscher, 17; Poole, 1226)

Under the 1936 Act, ODS was provided only to liner operators on trade routes considered essential.[3] To be eligible, the vessel must be American-built and registered, and all crew and officers must be American citizens. Further, the company that owns the ships is not permitted to own any foreign-built ships. The operating subsidy is intended to offset the lower operating costs of foreign competitors. The bulk of the differential serves as an offset to higher manpower costs—due both to higher wages and overmanning of ships. In 1969, manpower costs accounted for 67 percent of subsidies paid out. By 1981, the figure had increased to 87 percent. ODS also applies to any differential in uninsured repair costs charged by US yards as compared to foreign yards. US-flag operators are encouraged to repair their vessels domestically by a 50 percent ad valorem duty on repairs done or replacement equipment purchased abroad, unless it can be shown that foreign repairs were necessary for the safety of the ship. (Jantscher, 20–35; GAO, 5)

The Merchant Marine Act of 1970 modified the ODS program. First, it broadened the eligibility for subsidies to include bulk carriers, which had become increasingly important in world trade.[4] This action required changing the "essential route" criterion to an "essential services" criterion. Nonetheless, liners continued to receive most of the benefits and comprised 80 percent of the subsidized fleet in 1981. Next, the 1970 act changed the manner in which the wage subsidy was calculated. Previously, the subsidy had been based on the difference between a "fair and reasonable" US wage cost and that of foreign competitors. The 1970 act established an index to be used to determine a "subsidized wage cost." This was intended to force ship operators to become tougher negotiators with the unions. (Jantscher, 23–25; GAO, 2)

The CDS program was designed to cover the difference in construction costs between US and foreign shipyards. The subsidy limit was originally 33.3 percent of the ship's cost. Between 1960 and 1970, the limit was raised to 55 percent. The 1970 act set the legal limit at 50 percent and established guidelines for reducing that limit to 35 percent by 1976. That goal was abandoned as unrealistic and the Negotiated Shipbuilding Contracting Act of 1976 confirmed the 50 percent level. Recent studies revealed that even a 50 percent subsidy was often insufficient to cover the higher cost of US construction. (Jantscher, 36–43; Heine, 17; GAO, 7–9)

The Reagan Administration Maritime Program

President Reagan has sought to reduce the level of government intervention in the maritime industry. A primary target has been direct subsidies. In order to increase the competitiveness of US shipping firms, the administration and Congress have tried to loosen the restrictions on buying foreign-built ships. These efforts are opposed by

---

3. Liners usually carry mixed cargos for different shippers and sail along fixed routes on a regular schedule. (Jantscher, 19)

4. Bulk carriers generally "are chartered for one or more voyages to carry a single cargo occupying much of their capacity." These vessels do not operate on fixed schedules or routes. (Jantscher, 24)

the shipbuilding industry, which fears the loss of business to lower cost Asian producers.

President Reagan requested no new funds for CDS for fiscal year 1982 but, instead, allowed $49.5 million to be carried over from 1981. The administration also announced that, while existing ODS contracts would be honored, no new contracts would be signed. Congressional opponents were unable to reverse this policy and took steps to release subsidized operators from their "Buy America" obligations. The new rules allowed subsidized operators to buy foreign vessels in 1982 if there were no CDS funds available, yet remain eligible for ODS. Eleven foreign-built ships were delivered in 1984 and 1985 as a result of this waiver. (OTA, 203; *Congressional Quarterly Weekly Report*, 15 August 1981, 1988; Washington)

In late 1982, disagreement between Congress and the President led to continued suspension of CDS and resurrection of the rule that ship operators could not buy foreign vessels unless they sacrificed their operating subsidies. (*Congressional Quarterly Weekly Report*, 2 October 1982, 2443; 25 December 1982, 3091)

In the spring of 1983, Senator Ted Stevens (R-Ala.) introduced a bill (S 1038) containing the administration's proposals for the maritime industry. The legislation focused on ship operators rather than shipyards.[5] S 1038 would have revived the provision allowing operators to buy ships abroad while retaining their ODS eligibility. It also would have permitted money from tax-deferred capital construction funds, previously reserved for US shipyards, to be used to buy foreign-built ships. Finally, S 1038 sought to encourage foreign investment in the US merchant marine by allowing the share of foreign ownership of a US-flag vessel to increase from the current 49 percent to 75 percent. None of these controversial proposals was included in the final Senate bill.

However, the Senate-approved legislation included an administration proposal to allow ships built with CDS funds to repay the subsidies with interest and enter the coastal trade. The House version would have permitted such paybacks only on a case-by-case basis. Supporters of the House version feared that the proposed rule "would allow vessels that benefited from cheaper construction costs to compete unfairly in an already crowded domestic shipping trade." The proposed rule would be of interest primarily to tanker operators wishing to enter the Alaskan oil trade. House and Senate disagreement resulted in a stalemate. (*Congressional Quarterly Weekly Report*, 16 April 1983, 763; 7 May 1983, 894; 5 November 1983, 2341; 12 November 1983, 2375; 26 November 1983, 2483)

The fiscal year 1985 maritime authorization included none of the controversial provisions that had blocked passage in 1982 and 1983. All parties agreed to maintain the status quo. As a result, at the beginning of 1985, there were no construction subsidies; operating subsidies were limited to past commitments; and firms that received operating subsidies could not purchase foreign vessels. (*Congressional Quarterly Weekly Report*, 12 May 1984, 1137; 8 September 1984, 2223; 13 October 1984, 2683)

---

5. In fact, virtually the only initiative by the administration to assist shipbuilders has been the Navy's shipbuilding program. (*Congressional Quarterly Weekly Report*, 16 April 1983, 763; OTA, 203)

Recent Department of Transportation rulings have revived many of the controversial provisions. On 4 May 1985, Secretary Elizabeth Hanford Dole issued a rule allowing seven supertankers to pay back construction subsidies over a one-year period and enter the Alaskan oil trade. On the following day, it was revealed that a Houston ship operator had received approval from the US Maritime Administration (MARAD) to sell the rights to his operating subsidies on three ships. Once sold, the subsidies can be used for foreign-built ships. The owner of the company purchasing the subsidy rights said they would be used on East-Asian-built ships because one "can't afford to build a ship in the US today." Critics charged that the sale of ODS rights perverted congressional intent. The department's decision on CDS payback was also attacked by operators in the Alaskan trade who fear they will be displaced. The department estimated that the CDS ruling could save $800 million to $3 billion in shipping costs. Critics, however, contend that as many as 8,000 seamen could lose their jobs and that it could cost the government $477 million. (*Washington Post,* 4 May 1985, C1; 5 May 1985, F1; *Journal of Commerce,* 24 May 1985, 1A; 6 June 1985, 1B)

Secretary Dole has asked Congress to grant the Department of Transportation permanent authority to permit ODS recipients to build abroad. She expressed the administration's support for the cargo preference laws while indicating opposition to "either the expansion or contraction of those laws." Dole has also proposed that US-flag operators that acquire new ships abroad be immediately eligible to use them for carriage of preference cargoes. (*Journal of Commerce,* 20 May 1985, 1C)

CHANGES IN THE INDUSTRY

The active fleet of ocean-going, US-owned and operated ships has plunged from 1,170 in 1950 to 413 in 1984 and carries only about 6 percent of US waterborne commerce moving to and from foreign destinations. US shipyards are in even worse shape as no new orders for commercial ships have been placed since August 1982.

The Reagan administration argues that the Navy's shipbuilding program will sustain an adequate shipbuilding base. Industry spokesmen contend that the Navy program provides work for only a few yards and that "the nation's shipbuilding base soon will be too small to support the Navy's needs in time of war. . . ." The industry's national security argument has been undermined by several recent developments. First, many defense analysts believe that the next major war will allow no time for ship construction, conversion, or repair. Second, even most industry proponents agree that past subsidy programs have not been adequate to maintain the US-flag merchant marine. Finally, a joint Department of Defense-MARAD study completed in 1984 concluded that the Navy program could sustain a sufficient base to meet foreseeable emergencies. Former MARAD Administrator, Admiral Harold Shear, when advocating that subsidized US operators be allowed to build abroad, said, "It's not that we're unpatriotic, we'd like to build American . . . but I see no way we can build a competitive commercial ship in the US." (*Journal of Commerce,* 20 May 1985, 13C; 23 May 1985, 1B; *Christian Science Monitor,* 4 September 1984)

Key Statistics: Maritime Services

Imports from all sources[a]

Year (during restraints)	Volume (million short tons)	Value (billion dollars)	Source
1970	502	3	Heine, 253; authors' estimate
1975	654	7	Heine, 253; authors' estimate
1977	829	10	Heine, 253; authors' estimate
1979	788	15	USITC 1676, 54; authors' estimate
1980	744	18	USITC 1676, 54; authors' estimate
1981	726	19	USITC 1676, 54; authors' estimate
1982	645	17	USITC 1676, 54; authors' estimate
1983	593	15	USITC 1676, 54; authors' estimate

a. These figures reflect US waterborne foreign trade transported in foreign flag ships to or from foreign destinations. Import values are based on the assumption that the cost to shippers is 7 percent of the value of goods transported.

Apparent consumption[a]

Year (during restraints)	Volume (million short tons)	Value (billion dollars)	Source
1970	770	7	authors' estimate
1975	923	12	authors' estimate
1977	1,117	16	authors' estimate
1979	1,128	22	authors' estimate
1980	1,102	26	authors' estimate
1981	1,082	27	authors' estimate
1982	987	24	authors' estimate
1983	943	23	authors' estimate

a. These figures are based on the sum of imported (i.e., foreign-supplied) shipping services and shipping services provided by domestic carriers, both in the Jones Act and foreign trades. Jones Act commerce includes coastal, intercoastal, and trade with noncontiguous US territories. Foreign waterborne US commerce refers to goods transported between US and foreign ports (henceforth referred to as foreign commerce).

Market share of imports[a] (percentage of apparent consumption, by volume)

Year (during restraints)	Share	Source
1970	65.2	authors' estimate
1975	70.9	authors' estimate
1977	74.2	authors' estimate
1979	69.9	authors' estimate

Market share of imports[a] (percentage of apparent consumption, by volume) (continued)

Year (during restraints)	Share	Source
1980	67.5	authors' estimate
1981	67.1	authors' estimate
1982	65.3	authors' estimate
1983	62.3	authors' estimate

a. US-flag ships carry only about 6 percent of commerce transported between US and foreign ports. Most of US-flag tonnage is in Jones Act trade.

Volume of domestic output[a] (million short tons)

Year (during restraints)	Foreign commerce	Jones Act commerce	Source
1970	28	240	Heine 102–03, 253
1975	35	234	Heine 102–03, 253
1977	39	249	Heine 102–03, 253
1979	35	305	USITC 1676, 54; BC, 641
1980	28	330	USITC 1676, 54; BC, 641
1981	34	322	USITC 1676, 54; BC, 641
1982	31	311	USITC 1676, 54; BC, 641
1983	37	313	USITC 1676, 54; Wilve

a. These figures reflect the volume of US waterborne commerce transported in US ships.

Value of domestic output (billion dollars)

Year (during restraints)	Foreign commerce[a]	Jones Act commerce[b]	Source
1970	1.1	2.5	Heine 255; authors' estimate
1975	2.4	2.5	Heine 255; authors' estimate
1977	3.7	2.6	Heine 255; authors' estimate
1979	4.0	3.2	USITC 1676, 54; authors' estimate
1980	4.6	3.5	USITC 1676, 54; authors' estimate
1981	4.9	3.4	USITC 1676, 54; authors' estimate
1982	4.5	3.3	USITC 1676, 54; authors' estimate
1983	4.8	3.3	USITC 1676, 54; authors' estimate

a. These figures are based on the assumption that the cost to domestic shippers of transporting cargoes between US and foreign ports is 11 percent of the total value of that commerce.

b. Estimates of the value of Jones Act trade are based on the assumption that 50 percent of shipping costs are proportional to the relative numbers of ships in the foreign and Jones Act trades while the other 50 percent of costs are proportional to the relative numbers of seamen in the two trades. The figure for 1983 is based on data for the first quarter only.

Employment in domestic industry

Year (during restraints)	Shipboard jobs (average number)	Source
1970	37,249	MARAD
1975	21,100	MARAD
1977	20,888	MARAD
1979	19,993	MARAD
1980	19,638	MARAD
1981	18,513	MARAD
1982	16,986	MARAD
1983	15,162	MARAD
1984	13,767	MARAD

Wages[a]

Year (during restraints)	Dollars per hour	Source
1970	3.54	BC, 626
1975	4.72	BC, 626
1977	5.65	BC, 626
1979	6.72	BC, 626
1980	7.44	BC, 626
1981	8.30	BC, 626
1982	9.03	BC, 626
1983	9.94	BC, 626

a. These figures reflect the average of East Coast and West Coast basic monthly wage rates for an able-bodied seaman, exclusive of subsistence, overtime, and other fringe benefits.

Industry profits (million dollars)

Year (during restraints)	Profits (loss)[a]	Source
1977	64	OTA, 65
1979	33	OTA, 65
1980	160	OTA, 65
1981	99	OTA, 65
1982	187	OTA, 65
1983	(22)	OTA, 65

a. Net profits (loss) after taxes.

Maritime subsidies[a] (million dollars)

Fiscal year (during restraints)	CDS	ODS	Source
1975	240	243	OTA, 154
1977	219	344	OTA, 154
1979	201	301	OTA, 154
1980	265	341	OTA, 154
1981	208	335	CBO, 102
1982	184	401	CBO, 102
1983	—	454	Congressional Quarterly
1984	—	401	Congressional Quarterly
1985	—	378	Congressional Quarterly

— Not applicable.

CDS Construction differential subsidies.

ODS Operating differential subsidies.

a. The figures for 1983–85 reflect congressional authorizations rather than actual outlays for construction and operating differential subsidies. (*Congressional Quarterly Weekly Report*, 25 December 1982, 309; 7 May 1983, 894; 5 November 1983, 2341; 13 October 1984, 2683)

Key Statistics: Shipbuilding and Repair

Imports from all sources[a]

Year (during restraints)	Ships (number delivered)	DWT (thousand tons)	Source
1979	12	456	Washington
1980	11	493	Washington
1981	24	956	Washington
1982	14	1,039	Washington
1983	8	455	Washington
1984	1	94	Washington

DWT Deadweight tonnage.

a. These figures reflect the number of ships, and their deadweight tonnage, delivered by foreign shipyards to US owners for registration under foreign flags. It was impossible to estimate the value of such purchases because of the variety of countries and different types of ships involved. In 1984, seven ships were built abroad for US owners under the exemption allowing them to retain operating subsidies.

Apparent consumption

Year (during restraints)	Ship purchases[a]	DWT (thousand tons)	Source
1979	27	2,450	authors' estimate
1980	21	961	authors' estimate
1981	36	1,386	authors' estimate
1982	26	1,500	authors' estimate
1983	20	934	authors' estimate
1984	6	663	authors' estimate

DWT Deadweight tonnage.
a. Purchases of ships by US owners, registered in the United States or abroad.

Market share of imports (percentage of apparent consumption)

Year (during restraints)	Ships	DWT	Source
1979	44	19	authors' estimate
1980	52	51	authors' estimate
1981	67	69	authors' estimate
1982	54	69	authors' estimate
1983	40	49	authors' estimate
1984	17	14	authors' estimate

DWT Deadweight tonnage.

Volume of domestic output[a]

Year (during restraints)	Ships delivered	DWT (thousand tons)	Source
1979	15	1,994	Washington
1980	10	468	Washington
1981	12	430	Washington
1982	12	461	Washington
1983	12	479	Washington
1984	5	569	Washington

DWT Deadweight tonnage.
a. The number of merchant ships ordered from US shipyards dropped from 41 in 1973 to 11 in 1975, increased to 30 in 1978 before slumping to 7 in 1980 and 0 in 1983. (CBO, 43)

Value of domestic output (million dollars)

Year (during restraints)	Ship construction		Repair and reconversion		Source
	Commercial	Military	Commercial	Military	
1979	1,890	2,152	1,052	969	USITC 1676, 11, 14
1980	1,810	2,838	1,397	1,095	USITC 1676, 11, 14
1981	1,542	3,351	1,601	1,251	USITC 1676, 11, 14
1982	1,240	3,518	1,588	1,386	USITC 1676, 11, 14
1983	873	3,893	1,596	1,819	USITC 1676, 11, 14
1984	600	3,847	915	1,909	USITC 1676, 11, 14

Employment in domestic industry[a]

Year (during restraints)	Production jobs (average number)	Source
1979	33,600	USITC 1676, 18
1980	19,317	USITC 1676, 18
1981	20,282	USITC 1676, 18
1982	21,233	USITC 1676, 18
1983	10,853	USITC 1676, 18
1984	7,926	USITC 1676, 18

a. Commercial shipbuilding and repair.

Wages[a]

Year (during restraints)	Dollars per hour	Source
1979	7.64	USITC 1676, 22
1980	8.54	USITC 1676, 22
1981	9.40	USITC 1676, 22
1982	10.23	USITC 1676, 22
1983	10.70	USITC 1676, 22
1984	10.99	USITC 1676, 22

a. Commercial shipbuilding and repair.

Industry profits[a] (million dollars)

Year (during restraints)	Profits (loss)[b]	Source
1979	109	USITC 1676, 23
1980	(3)	USITC 1676, 23
1981	(3)	USITC 1676, 23

Industry profits[a] (million dollars) (continued)

Year (during restraints)	Profits (loss)[b]	Source
1982	40	USITC 1676, 23
1983	67	USITC 1676, 23
1984	40	USITC 1676, 23

a. Commercial shipbuilding and repair.
b. Net profits (loss) before taxes.

Industry capacity utilization (percentage)

Year (during restraints)	Shipbuilders	Ship repairs	Source
1979	95.7	85.2	USITC 1676, 16–17
1980	58.1	72.1	USITC 1676, 16–17
1981	25.6	82.3	USITC 1676, 16–17
1982	25.8	60.7	USITC 1676, 16–17
1983	20.2	63.4	USITC 1676, 16–17
1984	8.9	62.0	USITC 1676, 16–17

US-flag active fleet

Year (during restraints)	Ships[a]	Source
1975	507	Heine, 346
1977	547	Heine, 346
1979	536	Heine, 346
1980	537	MARAD
1981	521	MARAD
1982	493	MARAD
1983	448	MARAD
1984	413	MARAD

a. Annual average number, privately owned ships.

Quantitative Profile[a]

Item	Amount	Source
Number of years restraints in force (since 1789)	196	
Induced increase in price of imported shipping services (1984)	negligible	authors' estimate[b]

Quantitative Profile[a] (continued)

Item	Amount	Source
Induced increase in price of domestic shipping services (1984)	60 percent	authors' estimate
Coefficient of price response	n.a.	authors' estimate[b]
Quantity and value of imported shipping services (1983)	593 million short tons $15 billion	USITC 1676, 54 authors' estimate
Induced decrease in imports due to restraints (1983)	250 million short tons $7 billion	authors' estimate[c] authors' estimate[c]
Quantity and value of domestic shipping services (1983)	350 million short tons $8.1 billion	USITC 1676, 12 authors' estimate
Induced increase in domestic production due to restraints (1983)	250 million short tons	authors' estimate[c]
Coefficient of quantity response	1.0	authors' estimate
Elasticity of demand for imported shipping services	0.1	authors' estimate
Elasticity of supply of domestic shipping services	1.0	authors' estimate
Elasticity of demand for domestic shipping services	0.1	authors' estimate
Cross-elasticity of demand for domestic shipping services relative to price of imported shipping services	1.1	authors' estimate
Cross-elasticity of output of domestic shipping services relative to price of imported shipping services	1.0	authors' estimate
Cross-elasticity of quantity of imported shipping services relative to price of domestic shipping services	0.1	authors' estimate
Cost of restraints to US consumers and taxpayers (1983)	$1.3 billion $3.0 billion	CBO, 64[d] authors' estimate[e]
Gain from restraints to US producers (1983)	$2.0 billion	authors' estimate
Tariff revenue and implied average tariff rate (annual average)	$10 million 0 percent	CBO, 63[f] authors' estimate[g]
Gain from restraints to foreigners (1983)	negligible	authors' estimate
Efficiency loss of larger domestic production to the United States (1983)	$1 billion	authors' estimate
Welfare cost of restraints to the United States (1983)	$1 billion	authors' estimate
Employment in protected US industry (shipping services only)	19,993 (1979) 13,767 (1984)	MARAD MARAD

Quantitative Profile[a] (continued)

Item	Amount	Source
Induced increase in employment (1983)	11,000	authors' estimate
Cost of restraints to US consumers per job saved (1983)	$270,000	authors' estimate
Gain from restraints to US producers per job (1983)	$130,000	authors' estimate

n.a. Not applicable.

a. For this section it is assumed that higher US shipbuilding costs are reflected in higher operating costs. Hence, only the shipping services industry is considered here.

b. In recent years, little or no increase in the price of imported shipping services has occurred because protection was implemented through subsidization and cargo preference.

c. This figure assumes that all foreign origin and destination waterborne commerce carried in US-flag vessels would be carried in foreign flag vessels and that about two-thirds of Jones Act commerce would be carried in foreign flag vessels.

d. This estimate reflects the cost to consumers of cabotage only.

e. This estimate includes the cost of ODS subsidies ($0.4 billion), plus the Congressional Budget Office estimate of the cost of cabotage ($1.3 billion), and an estimate that the cost of cargo preference on foreign commerce is $1.3 billion.

f. This figure reflects a CBO estimate for ship repairs abroad only. (CBO, 63)

g. In relation to total imports of shipping services, the tariff on ship repairs is negligible. There is no tariff on ships themselves because they are not considered an article of international commerce.

Hypothetical Adjustment Program

	1984	1985	1986	1987	1988	1989	1990
US purchases of maritime services (million short tons)							
Assumed annual consumption growth of 3 percent	1,000	1,030	1,061	1,093	1,126	1,159	1,194
Imports from all sources							
Assumed annual consumption growth of 3 percent and no change in import restraints[a] (million short tons)	650	670	690	710	732	753	776
Assumed annual consumption growth of 3 percent and import share rising at 2 percent (million short tons)	650	690	732	776	822	869	919

Hypothetical Adjustment Program (continued)

	1984	1985	1986	1987	1988	1989	1990
Import share of consumption with liberalized protection (percentage)	65	67	69	71	73	75	77
Hypothetical quota auction rate[b]							
Quota auction rate degressive at 5 percentage points[c] (percent)	60	55	50	45	40	35	30
Quota auction revenue (million 1984 dollars)	—	2,710	2,380	2,065	1,760	1,470	1,190
US production for the domestic market (million short tons)							
Assumed annual consumption growth of 3 percent and constant import share	350	360	371	383	394	406	418
Assumed annual consumption growth of 3 percent and rising import share	350	340	329	317	304	290	275
US employment in domestic shipping operations							
Assumed 6 percent annual productivity growth and constant import share	13,770	13,360	12,990	12,650	12,280	11,940	11,590
Assumed 6 percent annual productivity growth and rising import share	13,770	12,620	11,520	10,470	9,470	8,530	7,620
Year-to-year employment changes (workers)							
Changes induced by consumption and productivity growth with constant import share	—	−410	−370	−340	−370	−340	−350
Changes induced by rising import share	—	−740	−730	−710	−630	−600	−560
Total employment changes	—	−1,150	−1,100	−1,050	−1,000	−940	−910
Benefit and budget calculations (1984 prices)							
Annual wage cost per worker assuming	36,000	36,000	36,000	36,000	36,000	36,000	36,000

Hypothetical Adjustment Program (continued)

	1984	1985	1986	1987	1988	1989	1990
constant $18 per hour and 2,000 hours (dollars) Benefits calculated at two times annual wage cost per worker (million dollars)	—	83	79	76	72	68	66
Projected program surplus or deficit: tariff revenue less benefits (million dollars)	—	2,627	2,301	1,989	1,688	1,402	1,124

— Not applicable.

a. Imports remain at 65 percent of consumption.

b. The quota auction applies only to Jones Act and cargo preference shipments.

c. These estimates assume a domestic supply elasticity of about 1.0.

BIBLIOGRAPHY

Hanson, David P. 1980. "Regulation of the Shipping Industry: An Economic Analysis of the Need for Reform." *Law and Policy in International Business* 12, pp. 973–99.

Hawkins, Harry C. 1951. *Commercial Treaties and Agreements: Principles and Practice.* New York: Rinehart and Co.

Heine, Irwin M. 1980. *The US Maritime Industry: In the National Interest.* Washington: National Maritime Council.

Jantscher, Gerald R. 1975. *Bread upon the Waters: Federal Aids to the Maritime Industries.* Washington: Brookings Institution.

Poole, Gordon L., Barbara B. Powell, and David T. Gray. 1982. "Financing of United States Flag Vessels." *Tulane Law Review* 56 (June): 1172–1284.

US Congress. Office of Technology Assessment. 1983. *An Assessment of Maritime Trade and Technology.* Washington.

US Congressional Budget Office. 1984. *US Shipping and Shipbuilding: Trends and Policy Choices.* Washington, August.

US Department of Commerce. Bureau of the Census. 1985. *Statistical Abstract of the United States.* Washington.

US General Accounting Office. 1981. "Maritime Subsidy Requirements Hinder US-Flag Operators' Competitive Position." Washington.

US International Trade Commission. 1985. *Analysis of the International Competitiveness of the US Commercial Shipbuilding and Repair Industries.* USITC Publication no. 1676. Washington.

US Maritime Administration. Office of Maritime Labor and Training. 1984. "Seafaring Employment, Oceangoing Commercial Ships, 1,000 Gross Tons and Over." Washington. Processed.

Washington, Dorothy (Office of Trade Studies and Statistics, US Maritime Administration). 1985. By communication, June.

Wilve, Gloria (US Army Corps of Engineers, Statistics Branch, New Orleans). 1985. By communication, 29 May.

CASE A-1

Sugar

PERIOD OF RELIEF

Jones-Costigan quotas: 1934–41
Sugar Act of 1948: 1948–74
Target price era: 1976 to present

SUPPLIERS AFFECTED

Global

RELIEF ACTION

Rising Tariffs (1914–34)

The US tariff on sugar from sources other than Hawaii, Puerto Rico, and the Philippines was increased from 1.0 cent a pound during the 1914–21 period, to 1.76 cents a pound in the Fordney-McCumber Tariff of 1922, and to 2.0 cents a pound in the Tariff Act of 1930 (the Smoot-Hawley tariff). Rising tariffs previewed more serious efforts to separate the US sugar market from the world sugar market. (House Committee on Agriculture, 13)

The Jones-Costigan Era (1934–41)

In 1934, the Jones-Costigan Act established a quota framework for regulating domestic production and imports of sugar. The Secretary of Agriculture was authorized to determine the sugar consumption requirements of the United States so that prices would maintain the domestic industry yet be "fair and reasonable" to consumers. The Secretary allocated consumption requirements to domestic and foreign producing areas on the basis of market shares in the years 1931–34 (a period of reduced imports because of the high Smoot-Hawley tariff). The Jones-Costigan Act also imposed a processing tax of 0.5 cents a pound on both domestic and imported sugar, with proceeds used to pay domestic producers to limit their output. The basic architecture of the Jones-Costigan Act remains in place to this day. (House Committee on Agriculture, 14; DOA 1984a, 33)

Following a January 1936 decision in which the Supreme Court struck down the processing tax provisions of the Jones-Costigan Act, Congress passed the Sugar Act of 1937. An excise tax replaced the processing tax, with proceeds paid into general Treasury receipts. The statute itself allocated percentage-of-market quotas to domestic producers and foreign countries; the allocations followed the historical base-year approach used by the Secretary of Agriculture under the Jones-Costigan Act. (House Committee on Agriculture, 14–15; DOA 1984a, 33)

In 1941, with the onset of World War II, quotas were suspended, and the United States purchased virtually all sugar produced in Cuba. (House Committee on Agriculture, 15)

The Sugar Act of 1948 (1948–74)

In 1948, Congress passed the Sugar Act of 1948, which assigned fixed tonnage quotas to domestic producing areas and the Philippines, and assigned 98.64 percent of residual consumption requirements (as determined by the Secretary of Agriculture) to Cuba and 1.36 percent to other countries. The excise tax and domestic payment plans were essentially unchanged from the Sugar Act of 1937. (House Committee on Agriculture, 15)

In 1951, Congress amended the Sugar Act of 1948 to increase the tonnage assigned to Puerto Rico and the Virgin Islands and to increase the quota for foreign countries other than Cuba and the Philippines, from 1.36 percent to 4 percent of residual consumption. (House Committee on Agriculture, 17)

In 1956, Congress again amended the 1948 act to assign domestic producing areas 55 percent of the increase in consumption requirements over 8.35 million tons (the 1955 consumption level) and to assign the remaining 45 percent of the increase to Cuba (29.59 percent) and to other countries (15.41 percent). In 1962 and again in 1965, the 1948 act was further amended. In 1971, Congress amended the 1948 act once more to assign 65 percent of the change in required consumption to domestic producers and to assign 35 percent to foreign producers. (House Committee on Agriculture, 17; AID, 7; DOA 1984a, 33–34)

On 1 January 1974, President Gerald R. Ford imposed a global annual import quota of 7 million short tons, instead of increasing the tariff, as a means of increasing domestic sugar prices. Ford later allowed the Sugar Act of 1948 to expire (on 31 December 1974), during a period of booming sugar prices. (Morkre and Tarr, 89; Senate Committee on Agriculture, 103; DOA 1984a, 34)

The Target Price Era (1976 to Present)

On 21 September 1976, the Ford administration raised the tariff on sugar to 1.875 cents a pound (from 0.625 cents a pound) using the authority of headnote 2 of the Tariff Schedules of the United States (TSUS). This action followed a Senate Committee on Finance resolution directing the US International Trade Commission (USITC) to conduct an escape clause investigation under Section 201 of the Trade Act of 1974. During this episode, support began to grow among domestic sugar producers to use the apparatus of quotas, tariffs, fees, and price support programs to ensure domestic target prices that would afford an adequate return to domestic growers. (Morkre and Tarr, 89)

In May 1977, President Jimmy Carter rejected the USITC's recommendation, which included relief in the form of annual quotas (approximately 4.275 million short tons). Instead, Carter instituted by regulation (under authority of the Agricultural Act of 1949) a direct income-support payment program to pay any difference between market prices and a domestic price objective of 13.5 cents a pound. Under the payment program, processors received $237.5 million. (Senate Committee on Agriculture, 103; Morkre and Tarr, 89; Crafts)

In September 1977, unable to override President Carter's rejection of the USITC recommendation, Congress enacted the Food and Agricultural Act of 1977, which provided price supports via loan and purchase programs for sugar beets and sugar cane. The support price for 1977 was set at 13.5 cents a pound. In November 1977, the new loan program superseded the direct payments. (Senate Committee on Agriculture, 103; Crafts)

In November 1977, with sugar prices plunging, President Carter increased the 1976 headnote 2 tariff and imposed a sugar import fee under the authority of Section 22 of the Agriculture Adjustment Act of 1933. (Section 22 authorizes the President to impose a fee, up to 50 percent ad valorem, or to impose quotas limiting imports to 50 percent of levels in a previous representative period, but not both simultaneously.[1]) This raised the total headnote 2 tariff and Section 22 fee from 1.975 cents a pound to 5.513 cents a pound, effective 1 January 1978. Because the November proclamation did not adequately distinguish between fees on raw and on refined sugar, it was replaced in January 1978. The new fees were 2.7 cents a pound for raw sugar and 3.22 cents a pound for refined sugar. The raw sugar duty remained at 2.8125 cents a pound. The support price for the 1978 crop was increased to 14.73 cents a pound. To protect the support program, a target price of 15 cents was established and maintained through duties and fees. (Morkre and Tarr, 90; Crafts)

The International Sugar Agreement (ISA), which resulted from a 72-nation sugar conference held in October 1977, was ratified by the Senate at the end of 1979. The ISA called for export quotas for the major sugar producers, a buffer stock arrangement, and a price range objective for raw sugar ranging from 11 cents to 21 cents a pound. (Morkre and Tarr, 89–90)

The 1979–81 crops were not designated to receive price support in the Food and Agricultural Act of 1977, though the 15 cents-a-pound price target continued. Consequently, price support authority reverted to Section 301 of the Agricultural Act of 1949. A loan rate of 13 cents a pound was adopted for 1979. No price support was in effect for 1980 or 1981. Effective 1 January 1979, the previously fixed Section 22 fee became variable, based on the difference between the 15-cent target price and the landed price of sugar. With the rise in world prices, the fee fell to zero in the fall of 1979 and President Carter reduced the duty to the 0.625-cent-a-pound minimum in February 1980. (DOA 1984a, 34–35; Crafts)

In 1981, with White House acquiescence, Congress passed the Agriculture and Food Act of 1981, which directed the executive to use price support programs and to

---

1. See Case A–2, Dairy Products, for a fuller discussion of Section 22 procedures.

control both domestic production and imports so that specified price targets would be met for sugar at the farm gate. The support price target was 16.75 cents a pound for the 1982 crop, escalating to 18 cents a pound for the 1985 crop. The Senate Committee on Agriculture urged the administration to meet these price objectives without federal budget expenditures on crop loans or other price support programs. The administration adopted a no-budget-cost policy. (DOA 1984a, 35)

On 22 December 1981, President Ronald Reagan raised the headnote 2 tariff on sugar to the statutory maximum of 2.8125 cents a pound. Section 22 fees were also imposed, which escalated from 2.1418 cents a pound on 24 December 1981, to 3.0703 cents a pound on 1 April 1982, to 4.0703 cents a pound on 21 April 1982. (DOA 1984a; Crafts)

On 5 May 1982, after five months of attempted protection through the use of the headnote 2 tariff and Section 22 fees, the Section 22 fee was abandoned. Instead, the Reagan administration resorted to Section 22 quotas. The headnote 2 tariff duty remained at its maximum rate of 2.8125 cents a pound. To ensure that the government acquired no sugar as a result of the price support program, the Department of Agriculture established import quotas designed to ensure prices on landed raw sugar about 3.5 cents a pound higher than the farm gate price targets. In fiscal year 1984, the so-called domestic market stabilization price (MSP) for raw sugar was 21.17 cents a pound. In 1984, this entailed a quota of 3 million tons. For fiscal year 1985 the MSP was 21.57 cents a pound; the consequent quota was 2.55 million tons initially. The sharp reduction in the import quota was occasioned by continued inroads on sugar usage made by corn sweeteners. (Presidential proclamation 4941, 5 May 1982; DOA, 1984a, 35–136; Crafts)

On 1 January 1985, the Department of Agriculture reimposed a fee on sugar imports. Four days after announcing an increase in the fee from 0.28 cents to 2.71 cents a pound, the department rescinded the fee, claiming it was unnecessary with the quotas already in place. On 28 January 1985, President Reagan issued an emergency proclamation placing additional quotas on imports of sweetened cocoa, pancake and flour mixes, and TSUS category 183.05, "edible preparations," a catchall category that includes everything not covered elsewhere. The action was taken because the "government thinks people are sneaking in food products made with sugar and then extracting and selling the sugar" in order to take advantage of the large gap between US and world prices. The quotas created enormous problems for importers of products in the edible preparations category that contain only minimal amounts of sugar, which could not possibly be extracted, but that nonetheless were excluded until October 1985 because the quota was filled as of early March. (*Wall Street Journal*, 23 April 1985, 1; *Journal of Commerce*, 23 May 1985, 16A)

CHANGES IN THE INDUSTRY

The US sugar industry has been challenged in recent years by changes in consumer tastes and by the increasing use of sugar substitutes such as high-fructose corn syrup. In fact, high-fructose corn syrup is a major beneficiary of sugar quotas and high domestic sugar prices: consumption of corn syrup rose 61 percent between 1981 and 1984, to reach 4.3 million short tons. Meanwhile, health and fitness concerns have reduced the overall level of demand for sugar while increasing that for noncaloric sweeteners. Corn syrup use and health concerns partially account for the declining number of farms and processing plants involved in sugar production. Sugar beet production has ceased entirely in Arizona, Washington, New Mexico, and Utah because of the closure of processing facilities in those areas. (DOA 1984a, 5, 36–40; *Wall Street Journal*, 6 February 1985, 41)

In February 1985, the US Cane Sugar Refiners Association (CSRA) sought a special exemption to import about 1.5 million short tons of raw sugar for conversion into syrup that would compete with high-fructose corn syrup in the soft drink market. The CSRA pointed out that five domestic refinery plants have closed since 1982, and 3,000 to 4,000 people have lost jobs. It claimed that the exemption would serve to increase world sugar prices by 3 cents to 4 cents a pound. The exemption was vigorously opposed by the Corn Refiners Association. (*Wall Street Journal*, 6 February 1985, 41; *Journal of Commerce*, 23 May 1985, 16A)

In a House Committee on Agriculture field hearing held on 18 May 1985, representatives of sugar refiners claimed that they were bearing a "disproportionate share of industry losses in comparison with domestic beet and cane growers" due to import quotas and support prices. Ken Robinson of Revere Sugar called for a reduction in the MSP from 21.5 cents to 14 cents a pound and an end to import quotas. He recommended institution of a "fees-and-tariff" system instead. (*Journal of Commerce*, 21 May 1985, 15A)

Key Statistics

Imports from all sources

Year	Volume (million tons)	Value (million dollars)	Source
Interim period			
1974	5.8	1,217	USITC 977, A50; DOA 1979, 568
1975	3.9	1,865	USITC 977, A50; BC 1984, 840
1976	4.7	1,154	USITC 977, A50; BC 1984, 840
During restraints			
1977	6.1	1,076	USITC 977, A50; BC 1984, 840
1978	4.7	723	USITC 977, A50; BC 1984, 840
1979	5.0	974	USITC 1462, A10; BC 1984, 840
1980	4.5	1,988	USITC 1462, A10; BC 1984, 840
1981	5.0	2,142	USITC 1462, A10; BC 1984, 840
1982	3.0	863	USITC 1462, A10; BC 1984, 840
1983	3.2	1,047	USITC 1462, A10
1984	3.4	1,258	BC, FT 990
1985	2.6[a]	n.a.	Bureau, 308

n.a. Not available.

a. This figure is based on the 1985 quota for sugar imports.

Apparent consumption

Year	Volume (million tons)	Value[a] (million dollars)	Source
Interim period			
1974	11.5	3,421	USITC 977, A50; authors' estimate
1975	10.2	2,891	USITC 977, A50; authors' estimate
1976	11.1	2,228	USITC 977, A50; authors' estimate
During restraints			
1977	11.4	2,170	USITC 977, A50; authors' estimate
1978	11.0	1,895	USITC 977, A50; authors' estimate
1979	11.0	2,416	USITC 1462, A10; authors' estimate
1980	10.4	4,149	USITC 1462, A10; authors' estimate
1981	10.0	3,583	USITC 1462, A10; authors' estimate
1982	9.4	2,357	USITC 1462, A10; authors' estimate
1983	9.0	2,580	USITC 1462, A10; authors' estimate
1984	9.1	2,791	Bureau 308; authors' estimate

a. These figures are derived from the value of imports and domestic production. Exports are negligible. The estimates should be taken as rough estimates since the production values are for crop years while import values are on a calendar year basis.

Market share of imports (percentage of apparent consumption, by volume)

Year	Share	Source
Interim period		
1974	50.3	USITC 977, A50
1975	38.2	USITC 977, A50
1976	42.0	USITC 977, A50
During restraints		
1977	53.8	USITC 977, A50
1978	42.4	USITC 977, A50
1979	45.4	authors' estimate
1980	43.3	authors' estimate
1981	50.0	authors' estimate
1982	31.9	authors' estimate
1983	35.5	authors' estimate
1984	34.5	authors' estimate

Output of domestic industry

Year	Volume (million tons)	Value (million dollars, crop year[a])	Source
Interim period			
1974	6.0	n.a.	USITC 977, A50
1975	6.6	2,204	USITC 977, A50; DOA 1984a, 46
1976	7.1	1,026	USITC 977, A50; DOA 1984a, 46
During restraints			
1977	6.4	1,074	USITC 977, A50; USITC 1253, A13
1978	5.8	1,094	USITC 977, A50; USITC 1253, A13
1979	6.0	1,172	USITC 1462, A10; USITC 1253, A13
1980	5.9	1,442	USITC 1462, A10; USITC 1253, A13
1981	6.2	2,161	USITC 1462, A10; USITC 1253, A13
1982	5.9	1,441	USITC 1462, A10; DOA 1984a, 46
1983	5.8	1,495	USITC 1462, A10; DOA 1984a, 46
1984	5.7	1,533	Bureau, 308; Barry

n.a. Not available.

a. A crop year runs from 1 October through 30 September.

Employment in domestic industry[a]

Year	Production workers (average number)	Source
1973	28,500	BLS 1979, 483
Interim period		
1974	27,600	BLS 1979, 483
1976	29,000	BLS 1979, 483
During restraints		
1978	24,000	BLS 1983, 148
1980	21,100	BLS 1983, 148
1982	21,700	BLS 1983, 148
1983	20,400	BLS 1984, 168

a. Refinery operations only.

Wages[a]

Year	Dollars per hour	Source
Interim period		
1974	4.57	BLS 1979, 484
1976	5.51	BLS 1979, 484

Wages[a] (continued)

Year	Dollars per hour	Source
During restraints		
1978	6.63	BLS 1984, 168
1980	7.90	BLS 1984, 168
1982	8.70	BLS 1984, 168
1983	9.31	BLS 1984, 168

a. Refinery operations only.

Acreage (million acres in production)

Crop year[a]	Beet sugar	Cane sugar	Source
Interim period			
1975	1.2	0.69	DOA 1984a, 45
1976	1.5	0.73	DOA 1984a, 45
During restraints			
1977	1.5	0.83	USITC 1253, A13
1978	1.2	0.84	USITC 1253, A13
1979	1.3	0.80	USITC 1253, A13
1980	1.1	0.78	USITC 1253, A13
1981	1.2	0.77	USITC 1253, A13
1982	1.2	0.79	USITC 1253, A13
1983	1.0	0.72	DOA 1984a, 45
1984	1.1	0.73	DOA 1984a, 45

a. A crop year runs from 1 October through 30 September.

Sugar processing facilities[a]

Year	Mills[b]	Factories[c]	Source
Interim period			
1974	75	55	DOA 1984a, 10, 13
1975	73	56	DOA 1984a, 10, 13
1976	71	56	DOA 1984a, 10, 13
During restraints			
1977	68	51	DOA 1984a, 10, 13
1978	58	49	DOA 1984a, 10, 13
1979	54	43	DOA 1984a, 10, 13
1980	52	43	DOA 1984a, 10, 13
1981	50	43	DOA 1984a, 10, 13

Sugar processing facilities[a] (continued)

Year	Mills[b]	Factories[c]	Source
1982	48	38	DOA 1984a, 10, 13
1983	48	41	DOA 1984a, 10, 13

a. Producers' estimates reveal a relatively constant level of capacity to process sugar beets and a 5 percent increase in sugar cane refining capacity from 1978 to 1981. Capacity utilization in that period is estimated to have increased from 86 percent to 96 percent for beet processors and from 89 percent to 92 percent for cane refiners. (USITC 1253, A25)

b. Number of mills producing sugar from cane.

c. Number of factories processing sugar beets.

Raw sugar prices (cents per pound, average)

Year	World	United States	Source
Interim period			
1974	31.63	29.50	USITC 977, A54
1975	20.49	22.47	DOA 1984b, 33
1976	11.58	13.31	DOA 1984b, 33
During restraints			
1977	8.11	11.00	DOA 1984b, 33
1978	7.82	13.93	DOA 1984b, 33
1979	9.66	15.56	DOA 1984b, 33
1980	29.04	30.11	DOA 1984b, 33
1981	16.93	19.73	DOA 1984b, 33
1982	8.42	19.92	DOA 1984b, 33
1983	8.49	22.04	DOA 1984b, 33
1984	5.20	21.74	IMF, 76

Quantitative Profile

Item	Amount	Source
Number of years restraints in force (since 1934, with interruptions during World War II and 1975–76)	43 years	
Induced increase in price of imported sugar (average 1977–84)	4.6 cents/pound 30 percent	authors' estimate[a] authors' estimate
Induced increase in price of domestic sugar (average 1977–84)	4.6 cents/pound 30 percent	authors' estimate[a] authors' estimate
Coefficient of price response	1.0	authors' estimate

Quantitative Profile (continued)

Item	Amount	Source
Quantity and value of imports (average 1977–84)	4.4 million tons $1,259 million	authors' estimate authors' estimate
Induced decrease in imports due to restraints (average 1977–84)	4.5 million tons $1,288 million	authors' estimate[b] authors' estimate
Quantity and value of domestic production (average 1977–84)	6.0 million tons $1,426 million	authors' estimate authors' estimate
Induced increase in domestic production due to restraints (average 1977–84)	4.5 million tons	authors' estimate[b]
Coefficient of quantity response	1.0	authors' estimate
Elasticity of demand for imported sugar	2.3	authors' estimate
Elasticity of supply of domestic sugar	1.66	Morkre, 94
Elasticity of demand for domestic sugar	0.2	Morkre, 94
Cross-elasticity of demand for domestic sugar relative to price of imported sugar	1.9	authors' estimate[c]
Cross-elasticity of output of domestic sugar relative to price of imported sugar	1.7	authors' estimate[c]
Cross-elasticity of quantity of imported sugar relative to price of domestic sugar	2.3	authors' estimate[c]
Cost of restraints to US consumers	$660 million (1978)	Crandall
	$1,000 million/quotas (1981)	Consumers
	$1,742 million/tariffs (1980)	Munger 10, 14; Consumers
	$2,400 million (FY 1983)	DOA 1984a, 38
	$1,880 million (FY 1983)	Dardis, 127
	735 million (1983)	Tarr, 76[d]
	$1,000 million (1984)	Hickok, 7
	$3,000 million (1984)	Mirsky[e]
	$930 million (average 1977–84)	authors' estimate[f]
Gain from restraints to US growers and processors	$1,500 million (1982–83) of which: $900 million to growers $600 million to processors	DOA 1984a, 37
	$782 million (FY 1983)	Dardis, 127
	$550 million (average 1977–84)	authors' estimate[g]
Tariff revenue and implied average tariff rate (1983)	$5.4 million 0.5 percent	BC, IM 146[h] authors' estimate

Quantitative Profile (continued)

Item	Amount	Source
Gain from restraints to foreigners	$495 million (FY 1983)	Dardis, 127
	$238 million (1983)	Tarr, 76
	$410 million (average 1977–84)	authors' estimate[i]
Efficiency loss from larger domestic production to the United States	$384 million (FY 1983)	Dardis, 127
	$130 million (average, 1977–84)	authors' estimate
Welfare cost of restraints to the United States	$57 million (1977)	Crandall, 431
	$975 million (FY 1983)	Dardis, 127
	$960 million (1983)	Tarr, 76
	$540 million (average 1977–84)	authors' estimate
Employment in protected US refinery industry	29,000 (1976)	BLS 1979, 483
	20,400 (1983)	BLS 1984, 168
Induced increase in refinery employment (1983)	15,300	authors' estimate
Cost of restraints to US consumers per job saved in refinery operations (average 1977–84)	$60,000	authors' estimate
Gain from restraints to US refineries per job (average 1977–84)	$27,000	authors' estimate[j]
Agricultural land in US sugar-growing operations	2.3 million acres (1976)	USITC 1253, A13
	1.8 million acres (1984)	USITC 1253, A13
Induced increase in acreage due to import restraints (1983)	1.35 million acres	authors' estimate
Cost of restraints to US consumers per acre saved in sugar growing (average 1977–84)	$690	authors' estimate
Gain from restraints to US growers per acre in sugar growing (average 1977–84)	$180	authors' estimate[j]
Gain from restraints to US producers per farm		
Beet	$43,400	DOA 1984a, 37
Cane	$98,000	DOA 1984a, 37

a. These figures assume that in the absence of protection, US sugar prices would equal world prices, and that world prices would rise by 3.0 cents/pound. For the period 1977 to 1984, the average world price was 11.7 cents/pound, while the average US price was 19.3 cents/pound, a difference of 7.6 cents/pound. Subtracting 3.0 cents/pound gives an indicated price impact of 4.6 cents/pound.

b. This figure assumes that, in the absence of US protection, imported sugar would replace 75 percent of domestic production (essentially all beet sugar and some cane sugar).

c. The cross-elasticity estimates are based on the assumption that imports are not restrained by quotas.

d. This is a conservative estimate because it is based on a long-run analysis in which the world price of sugar is assumed to be 15 cents/pound. The actual world price in 1983 was 9.4 cents/pound. (Tarr and Morkre, 76)

e. This is an estimate of the cost of import quotas and price supports to the consumer; cited by Paul Mirsky, president of Refined Sugars, Inc. (*Journal of Commerce,* 21 May 1985, 15A)

f. This figure assumes that import restrictions induce a 4.6 cents/pound increase in price on US consumption of 10.1 million short tons (20.2 billion pounds).

g. This figure assumes that import restrictions induce a 4.6 cents/pound increase in price on US production of 6.0 million short tons (12 billion pounds).

h. This estimate is based on the collected duty as calculated by the Census Bureau. The specific duty in the tariff schedule is 2.8125 cents/pound which, based on average world prices for 1982–84, would have an average ad valorem equivalent of 33 percent. The actual tariff revenue is much smaller, however, because the majority of US suppliers do not have to pay the duty because of their GSP eligibility.

i. This figure is based on a 4.7 cents/pound quota rent on average imports of 4.4 million short tons (8.8 billion pounds).

j. This figure assumes that 60 percent of the benefits to processors and growers combined are received by growers and 40 percent of the benefits are received by processors. (DOA 1984a, 37)

Hypothetical Adjustment Program

	1984	1985	1986	1987	1988	1989	1990
US purchases of sugar (million short tons)							
Assumed annual consumption growth of 0 percent	9.1	9.1	9.1	9.1	9.1	9.1	9.1
Imports from all sources							
Assumed annual consumption growth of 0 percent and no change in import restraints[a] (million short tons)	3.4	2.6	2.6	2.6	2.6	2.6	2.6
Assumed annual consumption growth of 0 percent and quota expansion of 0.3 million tons per year (million short tons)	3.4	3.7	4.0	4.3	4.6	4.9	5.2
Import share of consumption with quota expansion (percentage)	37.4	40.7	44.0	47.3	50.5	53.8	57.1
Hypothetical quota auction and existing tariffs							
Assumed world sugar price (cents/pound)[b]	12	12	12	12	12	12	12

APPENDIX 297

Hypothetical Adjustment Program (continued)

	1984	1985	1986	1987	1988	1989	1990
Tariff equivalent of headnote 2 duty plus hypothetical quota (percent)	30	27	24	21	18	15	12
Tariff and quota auction revenue (million 1984 dollars)	—	240	230	217	199	166	150
US production for the domestic market (million short tons)							
Assumed annual consumption growth of 0 percent and constant import share	5.7	6.5	6.5	6.5	6.5	6.5	6.5
Assumed annual consumption growth of 0 percent and rising import share	5.7	5.4	5.1	4.8	4.5	4.2	3.9
US employment in sugar refining (thousand workers)							
Assumed annual productivity growth of 2 percent and constant import share	20.0	22.4	22.0	21.5	21.1	20.7	20.3
Assumed annual productivity growth of 2 percent and rising import share	20.0	18.6	17.3	15.9	14.6	13.4	12.2
Year-to-year employment changes (thousand workers, refinery operations only)							
Changes induced by consumption and productivity growth with constant import share	—	2.4	−0.4	−0.5	−0.5	−0.4	−0.4
Changes induced by rising import share	—	−3.8	−0.9	−0.9	−0.8	−0.8	−0.8
Total employment changes	—	−1.4	−1.3	−1.4	−1.3	−1.2	−1.2

Hypothetical Adjustment Program (continued)

	1984	1985	1986	1987	1988	1989	1990
US acreage in sugar (million acres)							
Assumed annual productivity growth of 2 percent and constant import share							
Beet	1.10	1.23	1.21	1.18	1.16	1.14	1.11
Cane	0.73	0.82	0.80	0.78	0.77	0.75	0.74
Assumed annual productivity growth of 2 percent and rising import share[c]							
Beet	1.10	0.88	0.78	0.67	0.57	0.47	0.37
Cane	0.73	0.82	0.80	0.78	0.77	0.75	0.74
Year-to-year acreage changes (million acres)							
Land retirement induced by consumption and productivity growth, with constant import share							
Beet	—	0.13	−0.02	−0.02	−0.02	−0.02	−0.03
Cane	—	0.09	−0.02	−0.02	−0.01	−0.02	−0.01
Land retirement induced by rising import share							
Beet	—	−0.35	−0.08	−0.09	−0.08	−0.08	−0.07
Cane	—	—	—	—	—	—	—
Total land retirement							
Beet	—	−0.22	−0.10	−0.11	−0.10	−0.10	−0.10
Cane	—	0.09	−0.02	−0.02	−0.01	−0.02	−0.01
Benefit and budget calculations (1984 prices)							
Annual wage cost per worker assuming constant $10 per hour and 1,500 hours (dollars)	15,000	15,000	15,000	15,000	15,000	15,000	15,000
Benefits calculated at two times annual wage cost per worker (million dollars)	—	42	39	42	39	36	36
Agricultural land retirement calculated at $1,000 per acre (million dollars)	—	220	120	130	110	120	110

Hypothetical Adjustment Program (continued)

	1984	1985	1986	1987	1988	1989	1990
Projected program surplus or deficit: tariff and quota auction revenue less benefits (million dollars)	—	−22	71	45	50	10	4

— Not applicable.

a. The no change estimate assumes that lower sugar prices would arrest the inroads made by corn sweeteners. The estimates reflect the actual quota for FY 1984 and the preliminary quota for FY 1985. Thereafter, the quota is held at 30 percent of the domestic market. In fact, many observers believe that the present policy of domestic price escalation will require a decline in imported sugar to 1.0 to 2.0 million tons by 1990. (Crafts)

b. This figure is based on the average annual price, 1977 to 1984. Past experience indicates that the world price of sugar fluctuates violently from year to year. The figures here represent a hypothetical average over a longer period of time.

c. These figures assume that all land retirements resulting from import expansion occur in beet sugar production.

BIBLIOGRAPHY

Addison, Paul. 1982. "Hawaii is Rebuilding on Shaken Foundations." *Far Eastern Economic Review*, 5 November, pp. 74–76.

Balassa, Carol. 1984. "Levels of Protection on Manufactured Goods: The US, EC, Canada, Japan." Office of the US Trade Representative. Washington.

Barry, Robert (US Department of Agriculture, Economic Research Service). 1985. By communication, 19 April.

Bureau of National Affairs. 1984. *International Trade Reporter.* 19 September, p. 308.

Consumers for World Trade. 1984. "How Much Do Consumers Pay for US Trade Barriers?" CWT Information Paper. Washington, Winter.

Crafts, Donald (US Treasury Department). 1984. By communication, November.

Crandall, Robert W. 1978. "Federal Government Initiatives to Reduce the Price Level." *Brookings Papers on Economic Activity* 2.

Dardis, Rachel, and Carol Young. 1985. "The Welfare Loss from the New Sugar Program." *Journal of Consumer Affairs* 19, pp. 119–29.

Gemmill, Gordon. 1977. "An Equilibrium Analysis of US Sugar Policy." *American Journal of Agricultural Economics* 19 (November): 609–18.

Hickok, Susan. 1985. "The Consumer Cost of US Trade Restraints." *Federal Reserve Bank of New York: Quarterly Review* 10, no. 2 (Summer): 1–12.

International Monetary Fund. 1985. *International Financial Statistics, Monthly Bulletin.* Washington, April.

Jay, Keith. 1971. *The Nature and Impact of the International Market for Sugar.* AID Discussion Paper no. 24. Washington, November.

Morkre, Morris E., and David G. Tarr. 1980. *The Effects of Restrictions on United States Imports: Five Case Studies and Theory.* US Federal Trade Commission, Bureau of Economics. Washington, June.

Munger, Michael C. 1983. *The Costs of Protectionism: Estimates of the Hidden Tax of Trade Restraint.* Working Paper no. 80. Washington University, Center for the Study of American Business, July.

Tarr, David G., and Morris E. Morkre. 1984. *Aggregate Costs to the United States of Tariffs and Quotas on Imports: General Tariff Cuts and Removal of Quotas on Automobiles, Steel, Sugar, and Textiles.* US Federal Trade Commission, Bureau of Economics. Washington, December.

US Congress. House. Committee on Agriculture. 1961. *Special Study on Sugar.* 87 Cong., 1 sess., 14 February.

US Congress. Senate. Committee on Agriculture, Nutrition and Forestry. 1981. *Agriculture and Food Act of 1981.* Report no. 97–126. 97 Cong., 1 sess., 27 May.

US Department of Agriculture. 1979, 1982. *Agricultural Statistics.* Washington.

———. 1984a. *Sugar: Background for 1985 Legislation.* Agriculture Information Bulletin 478. Washington.

———. Foreign Agricultural Service. 1984b. *Foreign Agriculture Circular: Sugar, Molasses, and Honey.* Washington, May.

US Department of Commerce. Bureau of the Census. Various issues. *Highlights of US Export and Import Trade.* FT 990. Washington.

———. Various years. *US Imports for Consumption.* IM 146. Washington, December.

———. 1984. *Statistical Abstract of the United States, 1983–1984.* Washington.

US Department of Labor. Bureau of Labor Statistics. 1979. *Employment and Earnings, 1909–78.* Washington, July.

———. 1983, 1984. *Supplement to Employment and Earnings.* Washington, July.

US International Trade Commission. 1979. *Sugar from Canada.* USITC Publication no. 977. Washington, May.

———. 1982. *Sugar: Report to the President on Investigation no. 22–45 Under Section 22 of the Agricultural Adjustment Act.* USITC Publication no. 1253. Washington, June.

———. 1983. *Certain Articles Containing Sugar.* USITC Publication no. 1462. Washington, December.

US Trade Representative. 1984. *Annual Report of the President of the United States on the Trade Agreements Program 1983.* Washington, April.

CASE A–2

Dairy Products

PERIOD OF RELIEF

1953 to present

SUPPLIERS AFFECTED

Global

RELIEF ACTION

Imports of most dairy[1] and certain other agricultural products are regulated under Section 22 of the Agricultural Adjustment Act of 1933 (1935 amendments).[2] Section 22 authorizes the President to restrict imports of agricultural products by imposing fees, not to exceed 50 percent ad valorem, or quotas (but not both together) if such imports threaten to undermine domestic price support or other agricultural programs. "It should be emphasized that Sections 22 and 32 [relating to export subsidies] were not originally intended to provide extra protection to the United States farmer against foreign competition. . . . On the contrary, their purpose was to keep the effects of governmental aid to agricultural products from spilling over into the international market to such an extent as to transfer markets in the opposite direction, i.e., from the domestic to the foreign farmer." The language of the amendment did not make the intent clear, however, and it was used increasingly for protectionist purposes after World War II. (Leddy, 175–226; DOA 1981)

Imports of butter and several other commodities were controlled under the Second War Powers Act of 1942. These controls, continued after the war in order to facilitate

---

1. Primarily cheese, butter, and powdered milk.

2. At various times, Section 22 controls have been imposed on imports of wheat, almonds, flaxseed, linseed oil, filberts, rye and its products, and barley and its products. In addition, agreements in lieu of Section 22 controls with Canada at various times limited its oat and potato exports; agreements with Argentina and Paraguay restricted exports of tung nuts and oil to the United States. In addition to dairy products, Section 22 controls currently limit imports of sugar, peanuts, and cotton. See also Cases A–1, Sugar, and A–3, Peanuts. The impact of Section 22 controls on cotton imports is very slight.

surplus disposal, were scheduled to lapse in June 1951. The Secretary of Agriculture requested that they be allowed to lapse and anticipated a period of decontrol with the later imposition of less restrictive Section 22 fees or quotas if necessary. (Leddy, 211–12)

Congress replaced the obsolete war controls with Section 104, an amendment to the Defense Production Act of 1950, which was passed in response to the hostilities in Korea. Section 104, also known as the cheese amendment, extended the previous controls to all dairy products and made the criteria for controls more restrictive. Although nine countries that were entitled to concessions on dairy products because of prior trade agreements formally protested US actions under the General Agreement on Tariffs and Trade (GATT), only the Netherlands exercised its right to compensation and imposed controls on imports of American wheat flour. (Leddy, 212–15)

In April 1953, the administration of President Dwight D. Eisenhower imposed Section 22 controls on butter, dried milk products, and cheese (as well as the other commodities covered under Section 104). In response to the President's increased willingness to use Section 22 procedures, Congress allowed Section 104 to expire later that year. (Leddy, 217)

In 1951, Congress asserted the primacy of Section 22 over GATT obligations undertaken by the United States by affirming its role "irrespective of any U.S. international obligation." In 1953, the United States petitioned GATT to allow exceptional quota treatment, if the quotas were used to reinforce domestic supply controls. In 1955, the GATT Contracting Parties bowed to political necessity and granted the United States a waiver for its use of fees and quotas under Section 22. (Leddy, 204–21)

During the Tokyo Round, the United States agreed to restructure and enlarge its Section 22 restrictions on cheese imports, effective 1 January 1980. This concession was used to expand US access to foreign agricultural markets and to balance other foreign concessions. The United States cheese quota was enlarged from about 210 million pounds to approximately 246 million pounds. At the same time, the United States applied quota restrictions to some cheeses not previously covered. As a result of the changes, about 85 percent of all cheese imports enter the United States under quota, including almost all cow's milk cheeses (except for soft-ripened and specialty cheeses). (Houck, 286; DOA 1981, 4–5)

CHANGES IN THE INDUSTRY

Congress restructured the domestic dairy program three times between 1981 and 1984. Expenditures for the purchase of surplus milk, butter, and cheese were $1.9 billion in 1981, $2.6 billion in 1983, and $1.6 billion in 1984. The 1984 program established a price support level of $12.60 per hundred weight (112 pounds) of milk, and established a "diversion" plan that offered farmers $10.00 per hundred pounds of milk not produced. The diversion plan was financed by an assessment on all dairies of 50 cents per hundred pounds of milk produced. The Department of Agriculture hoped that production would be reduced by 10 percent, but in fact 1984 production was cut by only 3 percent because of the diversion program. In the first nine months of 1984, the assessment raised $711 million and diversion outlays totaled only $536 million. In 1985, the Reagan administration's proposal to phase out the diversion program and end mandatory federal purchases of surplus dairy products was strongly opposed by dairy interests. (*Washington Post,* 22 March 1985, A4)

On 17 December 1984, the United States notified GATT of its intention to withdraw from the International Dairy Agreement (IDA), effective in 60 days. Department of Agriculture Secretary John R. Block explained that the United States had reduced its supplies of exportable dairy products and had "no intention of breaking the world market with dairy products." Block stated that "withdrawing from the IDA is consistent with USDA's goal of removing restrictions on agricultural trade." The IDA, established in the Tokyo Round in 1979, sets minimum export prices for dairy products shipped by its 20-plus signatories and encourages the exchange of information. The United States justified its withdrawal by arguing that members had not abided by price provisions of the agreement. (*Journal of Commerce,* 19 December 1984, 9A)

Key Statistics

Imports from all sources

Year (during restraints)	Volume (million pounds)			Value[a] (million dollars)	Source
	Cheese	Butter	Nonfat dry milk		
1978	244.9	0.7	2.5	324	DOA 1982, 356, 531
1979	248.5	0.8	2.2	388	DOA 1982, 356, 531
1980	231.5	0.6	4.9	462	DOA 1982, 356, 531
1981	247.9	1.8	2.8	524	DOA 1982, 356, 531
1982	269.2	2.2	2.2	610	DOA 1984a, 11, 16, 21; BIE 1985, 40–11
1983[b]	286.8	1.9	2.2	588	DOA 1984a, 11, 16, 21; BIE 1985, 40–11

a. All manufactured dairy products.
b. Preliminary estimates.

Apparent consumption

Year (during restraints)	Volume (million pounds)			Value[a] (million dollars)	Source
	Cheese	Butter	Nonfat dry milk		
1978	3,736	966	745	11,289	DOA 1982, 352; authors' estimate
1979	3,837	1,005	807	12,485	DOA 1982, 352; authors' estimate
1980	3,974	1,013	751	14,511	DOA 1982, 352; authors' estimate
1981	4,154	982	651	19,097	DOA 1982, 352; authors' estimate
1982	4,633	1,072	695	17,145	DOA 1984a, 13, 18, 23; authors' estimate
1983[b]	4,870	1,194	801	17,818	DOA 1984a, 13, 18, 23; authors' estimate

a. These figures are derived from the value of imports of all manufactured dairy products plus the value of domestic production of cheese, butter, and nonfat dry milk with an adjustment for exports.

b. Preliminary estimates.

Market share of imports[a] (percentage of apparent consumption, by volume)

Year (during restraints)	Share	Source
1978	4.5	authors' estimate
1979	5.1	authors' estimate
1980	4.1	authors' estimate
1981	4.4	authors' estimate
1982	4.3	authors' estimate
1983	4.2	authors' estimate

a. The market share of dairy imports in US consumption of all dairy products is estimated to be limited to about 1.5 percent to 2.0 percent by Section 22 quotas. These figures are for cheese, butter, and dried milk only. (*Inside US Trade*, 21 September 1984, 4; DOA 1984a, 27)

Output of domestic industry

Year (during restraints)	Volume (million pounds)			Value (million dollars)	Source
	Cheese	Butter	Nonfat dry milk		
1978	3,530	995	927	11,171	DOA 1982, 355–6; BIE 1981, 394
1979	3,751	986	915	12,291	DOA 1982, 355–6; BIE 1983, 37–2
1980	3,972	1,145	1,161	14,311	DOA 1982, 355–6; BIE 1983, 37–2
1981	4,192	1,238	1,314	18,956	DOA 1982, 355–6; BIE 1984, 38–11
1982	4,633	1,258	1,401	16,944	DOA 1984a, 10, 15, 20; BIE 1985, 40–11
1983[a]	4,854	1,291	1,500	17,665	DOA 1984a, 10, 15, 20; BIE 1985, 40–11

a. Preliminary estimates.

Employment in domestic industry[a]

Year (during restraints)	Production workers (average number)	Source
1978	96,800	BLS, 159
1979	96,700	BLS, 159
1980	96,100	BLS, 159
1981	93,800	BLS, 159
1982	93,100	BLS, 159
1983	94,300	BLS, 159

a. Dairy products processing.

Wages[a]

Year (during restraints)	Dollars per hour	Source
1978	5.79	BLS, 159
1979	6.32	BLS, 159
1980	6.86	BLS, 159
1981	7.53	BLS, 159
1982	8.10	BLS, 159
1983	8.52	BLS, 159

a. Dairy products processing.

Farm inventory

Year (during restraints)	Milk cows[a] (millions)	Source
1965	15.4	DOA 1982, 326
1970	12.1	DOA 1982, 326
1975	11.2	DOA 1982, 326
1978	10.9	DOA 1982, 326
1979	10.8	DOA 1982, 326
1980	10.8	DOA 1982, 326
1981	10.9	DOA 1982, 326
1982	11.0	DOA 1982, 326
1983	11.1	DOA 1984a, 33
1984	11.1	DOA 1984a, 33

a. Including heifers that have calved.

Dairy and slaughter cow prices[a] (dollars per head)

Year (during restraints)	Dairy cows	Slaughter cows	Difference	Source
1970	332	256	76	DOA 1984a, 7
1975	412	253	159	DOA 1984a, 7
1978	674	441	233	DOA 1984a, 7
1979	1,044	601	443	DOA 1984a, 7
1980	1,195	549	646	DOA 1984a, 7
1981	1,201	503	698	DOA 1984a, 7
1982	1,100	480	620	DOA 1984a, 7
1983	1,020	472	548	DOA 1984a, 7

a. Received by farmers.

Cheddar cheese prices[a] (cents per pound)

Year (during restraints)	World	United States	Source
1978	n.a.	130.1	Commodity
1979	53.3	141.4	Paddock; Commodity
1980	70.3	156.2	Paddock; Commodity
1981	86.1	167.2	Paddock; Commodity
1982	79.3	168.5	Paddock; Commodity
1983	65.2	168.2	Paddock; Commodity

n.a. Not available.

a. The world cheese price is for cheddar cheese and for 1979–82 it represents the average price in the fall of each year. The price for 1983 is the average price for the whole year. The US price is the wholesale price of American-type cheeses, which are for the most part cheddar.

Industry income (million dollars)

Year (during restraints)	Receipts[a]	Source
1965	5,213	DOA 1982, 340
1970	6,663	DOA 1982, 340
1975	10,063	DOA 1982, 340
1978	12,798	DOA 1982, 340
1979	14,776	DOA 1982, 340
1980	16,708	DOA 1982, 340
1981	18,128	Carman
1982	18,273	Carman
1983	18,808	Carman

a. Gross receipts of dairy farms.

Quantitative Profile

Item	Amount	Source
Number of years restraints in force (1953 to present)	32 years	
Induced increase in price of imported dairy products (1980–83)	80 percent	authors' estimate[a]
Induced increase in price of domestic dairy products (1980–83)	40 percent	authors' estimate
Coefficient of price response	0.5	authors' estimate
Quantity and value of imports (1983)	291 million pounds	DOA 1984a, 11, 16, 21
	$588 million	BIE 1985, 40–11
Induced decrease in imports due to restraints	2,000 million pounds	authors' estimate
	$2,300 million	authors' estimate
Quantity and value of domestic production (1983)	7,645 million pounds	DOA 1984a, 10, 15, 20
	$17,665 million	BIE 1985, 40–11
Induced increase in domestic production due to restraints	2,000 million pounds	authors' estimate
Coefficient of quantity response	1.0	authors' estimate
Elasticity of demand for imported dairy products	3.0	authors' estimate
Elasticity of supply of domestic dairy products	0.2 to 0.25	Novakovic 1984
	0.5 over four years	DOA 1984a, 5
	0.5	authors' estimate
Elasticity of demand for domestic dairy products	0.4	Novakovic 1984
	0.7 to 0.8	DOA 1984a, 10
	0.7	authors' estimate

Quantitative Profile (continued)

Item	Amount	Source
Cross-elasticity of demand for domestic dairy products relative to price of imported dairy products	0.6	authors' estimate
Cross-elasticity of output of domestic dairy products relative to price of imported dairy products	0.4	authors' estimate
Cross-elasticity of quantity of imported dairy products relative to price of domestic dairy products	18	authors' estimate
Cost of restraints to US consumers	$500 million (1973)	Bergsten, 4
	$1.5 to $4.9 billion (1984)	Consumers
	$5.5 billion (1983)	authors' estimate
Gain from restraints to US dairy producers (1983)	$5.0 billion	authors' estimate
Tariff revenue and implied average tariff rate (1983)	$33.7 million	BC, IM 146
	8.4 percent	authors' estimate
Gain from restraints to foreigners (1983)	$250 million	authors' estimate
Efficiency loss from larger domestic production to the United States (1983)	$1,370 million	authors' estimate
Welfare cost of restraints to the United States (1983)	$1,600 million	authors' estimate
Employment in protected US industry (processing plants)	96,800 (1978)	BLS, 159
	94,300 (1983)	BLS, 159
Induced increase in employment (1983)	25,000	authors' estimate
Cost of restraints to US consumers per job saved in processing plants (1983)	$220,000	authors' estimate
Gain from restraints to US producers per job (1983)	$53,000	authors' estimate
Milk cows in protected industry	10.9 million (1978)	DOA 1982, 326
	11.1 million (1983)	DOA 1984a, 33
Induced increase in milk cows (1983)	3.0 million	authors' estimate
Costs of restraints to US consumers per milk cow saved (1983)	$1,800	authors' estimate
Gain from restraints to US producers per milk cow (1983)	$450	authors' estimate

a. This figure includes the existing tariff of about 8 percent and a quota premium of about 72 percent.

Hypothetical Adjustment Program

	1984	1985	1986	1987	1988	1989	1990
US purchases of dairy products (million pounds of cheese, butter, and nonfat dry milk)							
Assumed annual consumption increase of 4 percent	7,000	7,280	7,570	7,870	8,190	8,520	8,860
Imports from all sources							
Assumed annual consumption increase of 4 percent and no change in import restraints[a] (million pounds of cheese)	300	313	326	338	352	366	381
Assumed annual quota expansion of 100 million pounds per year (million pounds of cheese)	300	400	500	600	700	800	900
Import share of consumption with quota expansion (percentage)	4.3	5.5	6.6	7.6	8.5	9.4	10.2
Hypothetical quota auction and existing tariffs							
Assumed world price of cheeses imported by United States (1984 dollars per pound)	1.25	1.25	1.25	1.25	1.25	1.25	1.25
Tariff equivalent of existing tariff and hypothetical quota (percent)	80	72	65	60	56	52	49
Revenue from existing tariff and quota auction (million 1984 dollars)	—	360	406	450	490	520	551
US production for the domestic market (million pounds)							
Assumed annual consumption increase of 4 percent and constant import share	6,700	6,967	7,244	7,532	7,838	8,154	8,479
Assumed annual consumption increase of 4 percent and rising import quota	6,700	6,880	7,070	7,270	7,490	7,720	7,960

Hypothetical Adjustment Program (continued)

	1984	1985	1986	1987	1988	1989	1990
US employment in dairy processing plants (thousand workers)							
Assumed annual productivity growth of 8 percent and constant import share	94	90	87	84	80	77	74
Assumed annual productivity growth of 8 percent and rising import share	94	89	85	81	76	73	69
Year-to-year employment changes (thousand workers, processing operations only)							
Changes induced by consumption and productivity growth with constant import share	—	−4.0	−3.0	−3.0	−4.0	−3.0	−3.0
Changes induced by rising import share	—	−1.0	−1.0	−1.0	−1.0	−1.0	−1.0
Total employment changes	—	−5.0	−4.0	−4.0	−5.0	−4.0	−4.0
US dairy herd (million milk cows)							
Assumed annual productivity growth of 2 percent and constant import share	11.1	10.8	10.5	10.2	9.9	9.6	9.3
Assumed annual productivity growth of 2 percent and rising import share	11.1	10.7	10.2	9.9	9.5	9.1	8.7
Year-to-year dairy herd changes (million milk cows)							
Livestock retirement induced by consumption and productivity growth, with constant import share	—	−0.3	−0.3	−0.3	−0.3	−0.3	−0.3
Livestock retirement induced by rising import share	—	−0.1	−0.1	−0.1	−0.1	−0.1	−0.1
Total livestock retirement	—	−0.4	−0.4	−0.4	−0.4	−0.4	−0.4

Hypothetical Adjustment Program (continued)

	1984	1985	1986	1987	1988	1989	1990
Benefit and budget calculations (1984 prices)							
Annual wage cost per worker assuming constant $10 per hour and 1,500 hours (dollars)	15,000	15,000	15,000	15,000	15,000	15,000	15,000
Benefits calculated at two times annual wage cost per worker (million dollars)	—	150	120	120	150	120	120
Dairy herd retirement calculated at $600 per milk cow (million dollars)	—	240	240	240	240	240	240
Projected program surplus or deficit: tariff revenue less benefits (million dollars)[b]	—	−30	46	90	100	160	191

— Not applicable.

a. These estimates reflect a quota equal to 4.3 percent of the US market.

b. These figures do not reflect costs or savings from reform of the domestic dairy program.

BIBLIOGRAPHY

Bergsten, C. Fred. 1973. *The Cost of Import Restrictions to American Consumers.* New York: American Importers Association.

Carman, Cliff (US Department of Agriculture, Animal Products Branch). 1984. By communication, 14 November.

Commodity Research Bureau. 1984. *1984 Commodity Year Book.* Jersey City, NJ

Consumers for World Trade. 1984. "How Much Do Consumers Pay for US Trade Barriers?" CWT Information Paper. Washington, Winter.

Hammond, Jerome, and Karen Brooks. 1985. *Federal Price Programs for the American Dairy Industry: Issues and Alternatives.* Washington: National Planning Association.

Houck, James P. 1980. "US Agricultural Trade and the Tokyo Round." *Law and Policy in International Business* 12, pp. 265–95.

Leddy, John M. 1963. "United States Commercial Policy and the Domestic Farm Program." In *Studies in United States Commercial Policy.* Edited by William B. Kelly, Jr. Chapel Hill: University of North Carolina Press.

Novakovic, Andrew M., and Robert L. Thompson. 1977. "The Impact of Imports of Manufactured Milk Products on the US Dairy Industry." *American Journal of Agricultural Economics* 59 (August): 507–19.

Novakovic, Andrew M. (Cornell University, Agricultural Economics Department). 1984. By communication, 19 October.

Paddock, William (US Department of Agriculture, Foreign Agricultural Service). 1984. By communication, 14 November.

US Department of Agriculture. 1981. "Import Controls under Section 22 of the Agricultural Adjustment Act, as Amended." Washington, February.

———. 1982. *Agricultural Statistics*. Washington.

———. 1984. *Dairy: Background for 1985 Farm Legislation*. Washington.

———. Foreign Agricultural Service. 1984. *Foreign Agricultural Circular: World Dairy Situation and Outlook*. Washington, May.

US Department of Commerce. Bureau of the Census. Various years. *US General Imports*. FT 155. Washington.

———. Various years. *US Imports for Consumption*. IM 146. Washington, December.

———. 1984. *Statistical Abstract of the United States, 1983–1984*. Washington.

———. Bureau of Industrial Economics. Various years. *US Industrial Outlook*. Washington.

US Department of Labor. Bureau of Labor Statistics. 1984. *Supplement to Employment and Earnings*. Washington, July.

CASE A-3

Peanuts

PERIOD OF RELIEF

1953 to present

SUPPLIERS AFFECTED

Global

RELIEF ACTION

Peanuts came under the production control and diversion provisions of the Agricultural Adjustment Act of 1933 (AAA) after being designated a "basic crop" in April 1934. The AAA provided benefit payments to farmers for taking part of their land out of production. The payments were financed out of a processing tax on the commodities involved. In 1936, the Supreme Court invalidated the processing tax provisions of the act; as a consequence, Congress passed the Soil Conservation and Domestic Allotment Act later that year. Under this legislation, farmers could receive payments for shifting acreage from soil-depleting crops (including peanuts) to soil-conserving crops. (DOA, 10).

The Agricultural Adjustment Act of 1938, as amended in 1941, established market quotas and a price support system based on "parity" for peanuts. This program was modified by the Food and Agriculture Act of 1977, which was designed to lower its cost. The 1977 legislation retained acreage allotments and price supports but introduced a two-tier quota program with much lower prices for over-quota "additional" peanuts. The act also provided for annual decreases in the minimum poundage quota. The 1981 legislation further reduced poundage quotas and suspended acreage allotments. Thus, anyone is now eligible to grow peanuts but "additionals" receive the lower support price and are still subject to marketing controls. The 1984 price support for quota peanuts was $440 per ton while that for additionals was $185 per ton. The minimum Commodity Credit Corporation (CCC) export resale price for 1984 for additionals was $425 per ton. (DOA, 11–14)

In order to prevent imports from undermining the price support program, a strict import quota has been established as provided under Section 22 of the Agricultural

Adjustment Act of 1933 (1935 amendments).[1] Since 1953, the annual import quota has remained at 1.71 million pounds (shelled basis), except in 1954 and 1981 when larger quantities were imported under emergency quotas to compensate for domestic production shortfalls. (DOA, 11)

CHANGES IN THE INDUSTRY

"The 1977 and 1981 peanut programs were designed to reduce Government costs, bring domestic supply of quota supported peanuts more in line with demand, and recognize the possibility of expanding exports. These programs helped move producers toward increased market orientation and, at the same time, eased the transition for peanut allotment holders and the communities which had become dependent on the old program." (DOA, 17–18)

---

1. See Case A–2, Dairy Products, for a fuller description of Section 22 procedures.

Key Statistics

Unless otherwise specified, data are on a crop year basis. A crop year runs from 1 September to 31 August. For example, the 1974 crop year would be 1 September 1974 to 31 August 1975.

Imports from all sources

Year (during restraints)	Volume (million pounds in-shell) Crop year	Calendar year	Value (million dollars, calendar year)	Source
1974	1	0.7	0.3	BC, FT 246; Commodity, 252; BC, FT 246
1976	1	0.7	0.4	BC, FT 246; Commodity, 252; BC, FT 246
1978	1	0.7	0.7	BC, FT 246; Commodity, 252; BC, FT 246
1980	40[1]	1.0	0.5	BC, FT 246; Commodity, 252; BC, FT 246
1981	2	408.9	289.0	BC, FT 246; Commodity, 252; BC, FT 246
1982	2	2.9	2.0	BC, FT 246; Commodity, 252; BC, FT 246
1983	2	3.3	1.5	BC, FT 210; Commodity, 252; BC, FT 210

Apparent consumption

Year (during restraints)	Volume (million pounds in-shell)	Value[a] (million dollars)	Source
1974	2,929	524	DOA, 20, 21; authors' estimate
1976	2,957	591	DOA, 20, 21; authors' estimate
1978	2,818	594	DOA, 20, 21; authors' estimate
1980	2,201	741	DOA, 20, 21; authors' estimate
1981	3,406	916	DOA, 20, 21; authors' estimate
1982	2,762	693	DOA, 20, 21; authors' estimate
1983	2,524	608	DOA, 20, 21; authors' estimate

a. These figures are derived from the value of domestic output, with an adjustment for exports. Because of the relatively small figures involved, the value of imports has been included only in the 1980 figure. It was not used in the 1981 value figure because of the difference between crop and calendar years.

Market share of imports

The proportion of imports in US consumption is generally insignificant. In 1981, owing to a domestic crop failure, the ratio of imports to consumption reached 12.0 percent by volume.

Output of domestic industry

Year (during restraints)	Volume (million pounds in-shell)	Value (million dollars)	Source
1974	3,668	658	DOA, 20; 24
1976	3,739	747	DOA, 20; 24
1978	3,952	834	DOA, 20; 24
1980	2,303	578	DOA, 20; 24
1981	3,982	1,070	DOA, 20; 24
1982	3,440	862	DOA, 20; 24
1983	3,296	786	DOA, 20; 24

Acreage (million acres)

Year (during restraints)	Planted	Harvested	Source
1974	1.52	1.47	DOA, 20
1976	1.55	1.52	DOA, 20
1978	1.54	1.51	DOA, 20
1980	1.52	1.40	DOA, 20
1981	1.51	1.49	DOA, 20
1982	1.31	1.28	DOA, 20
1983	1.41	1.37	DOA, 20

Yield

Year (during restraints)	Pounds per acre	Source
1974	2,491	DOA, 20
1976	2,464	DOA, 20
1978	2,619	DOA, 20
1980	1,645	DOA, 20
1981	2,675	DOA, 20
1982	2,696	DOA, 20
1983	2,399	DOA, 20

Employment in domestic industry

Year (during restraints)	Workers in peanut-growing[a]	Source
1974	6,080	authors' estimate
1976	6,200	authors' estimate
1978	6,160	authors' estimate
1980	6,080	authors' estimate
1981	6,040	authors' estimate
1982	5,240	authors' estimate
1983	5,640	authors' estimate

a. Estimates based on the assumption that one man-year is required per 250 acres of harvested peanuts.

Returns to farmers (million dollars)

Year (during restraints)	Income[a]	Source
1976	396	DOA, 9
1978	379	DOA, 9
1980	57	DOA, 9
1981	351	DOA, 9
1982	269	DOA, 9
1983	205	DOA, 9

a. Value of production less cash expenses, by crop year.

Peanut prices (cents per pound)

Crop year (during restraints)	Prices received by US farmers	World prices	Source
1974	17.9	33.5	DOA, 22; IMF 1983
1976	20.0	19.2	DOA, 22; IMF 1983
1978	21.1	28.6	DOA, 22; IMF 1983
1980	25.1	22.0	DOA, 22; IMF 1984
1981	26.9	28.2	DOA, 22; IMF 1984
1982	25.1	17.4	DOA, 22; IMF 1984
1983	24.1	15.8	DOA, 22; IMF 1984
1984[a]	25.8	15.8	Hacklander; IMF 1984

a. These prices are for the period January–June 1984.

Net budget outlay (million dollars)

Fiscal year (during restraints)	Program payments (receipts)[a]	Source
1974	4	DOA, 23
1976	250	DOA, 23
1978	(39)	DOA, 23
1980	28	DOA, 23
1981	12	DOA, 23
1982	6	DOA, 23
1983	n.a.	
1984	n.a.	

n.a. Not available.

a. These figures reflect loans and purchases, storage and handling expenses, and other outlays less sales proceeds, loan repayments, and other receipts, excluding PL 480 cost.

Quantitative Profile

Item	Amount	Source
Number of years restraints in force (since 1953)	32 years	
Induced increase in price of imported peanuts (1980–84)	28 percent 5.6 cents/pound	authors' estimate[a] authors' estimate
Induced increase in price of domestic peanuts (1980–84)	28 percent 5.6 cents/pound	authors' estimate authors' estimate
Coefficient of price response	1.0	authors' estimate
Quantity and value of imports (1983)	3.3 million pounds $1.5 million	Commodity BC, FT 210
Induced decrease in imports due to restraints	440 million pounds $200 million	authors' estimate authors' estimate

Quantitative Profile (continued)

Item	Amount	Source
Quantity and value of domestic production (1983)	3,296 million pounds $786 million	DOA, 20 DOA, 24
Induced increase in domestic production due to restraints	440 million pounds	authors' estimate
Coefficient of quantity response	1.0	authors' estimate
Elasticity of demand for imported peanuts	1.0	authors' estimate
Elasticity of supply of domestic peanuts	0.43	Langley[b,c]
Elasticity of demand for domestic peanuts (for food use)	0.11	Langley[c]
Cross-elasticity of demand for domestic peanuts relative to price of imported peanuts	0.5	authors' estimate
Cross-elasticity of output of domestic peanuts relative to price of imported peanuts	0.4	authors' estimate
Cross-elasticity of quantity of imported peanuts relative to price of domestic peanuts	8	authors' estimate
Costs of restraints to US consumers (1983)	$200 million $170 million	Consumers authors' estimate
Gain from restraints to US producers (1983)	$170 million	authors' estimate
Tariff revenue and implied average tariff rate (1981)	$9.2 million 3 percent	BC, IM 146 authors' estimate[d]
Gain from restraints to foreigners	negligible	authors' estimate
Efficiency loss from larger domestic production to the United States (1983)	$14 million	authors' estimate
Welfare cost of restraints to the United States (1983)	$14 million	authors' estimate
Agricultural land in US peanut growing operations	1.5 million acres (1974) 1.4 million acres (1983)	DOA, 20 DOA, 20
Induced increase in acreage due to import restraints (1983)	0.17 million acres	authors' estimate
Cost of restraints to US consumer per acre saved in peanut growing (1983)	$1,000	authors' estimate
Gain from restraints to US growers per acre in peanut growing (1983)	$120	authors' estimate

a. The figure includes the existing tariff of about 3 percent, and a quota premium of about 25 percent.

b. The supply coefficient is the elasticity of acreage planted with respect to the support price.

c. Preliminary estimates.

d. The year 1981 (crop year 1980) was an unusual year in which a large quantity of imports was allowed to make up for a domestic shortfall in production.

Hypothetical Adjustment Program

	1984	1985	1986	1987	1988	1989	1990
US purchases of peanuts (million pounds in shell)							
Assumed annual consumption increase of 0 percent	2,900	2,900	2,900	2,900	2,900	2,900	2,900
Imports from all sources							
Assumed annual consumption increase of 0 percent and no change in import restraints (million pounds, in shell)	neg.	neg.	neg.	neg.	neg.	neg.	neg.
Assumed annual quota expansion of 30 million pounds per year (million pounds, in shell)	neg.	30	60	90	120	150	180
Import share of consumption with quota expansion (percentage)	neg.	1.0	2.1	3.1	4.1	5.2	6.2
Hypothetical quota auction and existing tariffs							
Assumed world peanut price[a] (cents/pound)	20	20	20	20	20	20	20
Tariff equivalent of existing tariff and hypothetical quota auction (percent)	28	26	24	22	20	18	16
Revenue from existing tariff and hypothetical quota auction revenue (million 1984 dollars)	—	1.6	2.9	4.0	4.8	5.4	5.8
US production for the domestic market (million pounds in shell)							
Assumed annual consumption increase of 0 percent and constant import share	2,900	2,900	2,900	2,900	2,900	2,900	2,900

Hypothetical Adjustment Program (continued)

	1984	1985	1986	1987	1988	1989	1990
Assumed annual consumption increase of 0 percent and rising import share	2,900	2,870	2,840	2,810	2,780	2,750	2,720
US acreage in peanuts (million acres)							
Assumed annual productivity growth of 0 percent and constant import share	1.400	1.400	1.400	1.400	1.400	1.400	1.400
Assumed annual productivity growth of 0 percent and rising import share	1.400	1.385	1.370	1.355	1.340	1.325	1.310
Year-to-year acreage change (million acres)							
Land retirement induced by consumption and productivity growth, with constant import share	neg.	neg.	neg.	neg.	neg.	neg.	neg.
Land retirement induced by rising import share	—	−0.015	−0.015	−0.015	−0.015	−0.015	−0.015
Total land retirement	—	−0.015	−0.015	−0.015	−0.015	−0.015	−0.015
Benefit and budget calculations (1984 prices)							
Agricultural land retirement calculated at $1,500 per acre (million dollars)	—	22.5	22.5	22.5	22.5	22.5	22.5
Program surplus or deficit: tariff and quota revenue less benefits (million dollars)	—	−20.9	−19.6	−18.5	−17.7	−17.1	−16.7

— Not applicable.

neg. Negligible.

a. This figure is based on the average annual price, 1980–84.

BIBLIOGRAPHY

Commodity Research Bureau. 1984. *1984 Commodity Year Book.* Jersey City, NJ

Consumers for World Trade. 1984. "How Much Do Consumers Pay for US Trade Barriers?" CWT Information Paper. Washington, Winter.

Hacklander, Duane (US Department of Agriculture, Crops Branch). 1984. By communication, 5 November.

International Monetary Fund. 1983. *International Financial Statistics Yearbook.* Washington.

———. 1984. *International Financial Statistics, Monthly Bulletin.* Washington, October.

Langley, Suchada V. (Consultant to US Department of Agriculture). 1984. Letter dated 8 November.

US Department of Agriculture. 1984. *Peanuts: Background for 1985 Farm Legislation.* Washington.

US Department of Commerce. Bureau of the Census. 1983. *US Imports.* FT 210. Washington.

———. Various years. *US Imports for Consumption.* IM 146. Washington, December.

———. Various years. *US Imports for Consumption and General Imports.* FT 246. Washington.

US International Trade Commission. 1982. *Summary of Trade and Tariff Information: Peanuts and Coconuts for Edible Purposes.* USITC Publication no. 841, control no. 1–9–18. Washington, February.

CASE A-4

Meat

PERIOD OF RELIEF

January 1965 to present

SUPPLIERS AFFECTED

Global (primarily Australia, Canada, several Central American countries, Mexico, and New Zealand)

RELIEF ACTION

In November 1963, the Senate Committee on Finance directed the US Tariff Commission to investigate imports of meat,[1] pursuant to Section 332 of the Tariff Act of 1930. In mid-1964, based on the Commission's investigation, the Committee concluded that "imported meat has played an important part in creating the distressed market conditions" in the domestic industry. On 22 August 1964, Congress enacted the Meat Import Act of 1964, effective 1 January 1965, which limited imports of fresh, chilled, or frozen beef and veal, and mutton and goats (except lambs) (an insignificant item). (USITC 834, A6, A15; USITC 842, 96; USTC 128)

The limit is stated in terms of "adjusted base quantity." The base quantity is 725.4 million pounds, and the adjustment factor is the ratio of average annual domestic commercial production in the current and two preceding calendar years to average annual production for the years 1959–63. If meat imports are expected to exceed the adjusted base quantity by 10 percent or more (the "trigger level"), the President is required to proclaim a quota. However, under Section 2(d) of the Meat Act, the quota may be suspended for "overriding economic or national security interests of the United States." To avoid the imposition of quotas, administrations have regularly negotiated "voluntary" restraints with principal, and sometimes smaller, suppliers pursuant to Section 204 of the Agricultural Act of 1956 (7 USC 1854). (USITC 842, 96–102)

---

1. "Meat" includes fresh, chilled, and frozen beef and veal provided for in Tariff Schedules of the United States (TSUS) items 106.10, 106.80, and 106.85; 107.20 and 107.25; 107.40 through 107.60, inclusive; and 107.75. (USITC 834, 4)

On 17 March 1977, a coalition of US meat associations filed a petition for escape clause relief under Section 201 of the Trade Act of 1974. The US International Trade Commission (USITC) initiated an investigation on 26 March 1977, and on 17 September 1977 found that imports were not a substantial cause of serious injury, or threat of serious injury, to the domestic industry. On 31 May 1977, in response to congressional urging, the USITC instituted a Section 332 investigation to explore avenues of relief not available under Section 201. The report was published in November 1977, but led to no new import restraints. (USITC 834, 1–3; USITC 842)

During the 1979 Tokyo Round of multilateral trade negotiations (MTN), 23 participating countries signed an Arrangement Regarding Bovine Meat which took effect 1 January 1980. The objectives of the arrangement are to promote the expansion, greater liberalization, and stability of the international meat and livestock market. It provides for a comprehensive information and cooperation mechanism applicable to live bovine animals and the bovine meat sector. The arrangement also established an International Meat Council, which evaluates and prepares annual reports on the world market. (USTR, 101)

The most-favored-nation (MFN) tariff on meat (TSUS 106.10) has remained at 3 cents a pound since 1948. The ad valorem equivalent of this rate was approximately 5 percent in 1976 and approximately 3 percent in 1983. (USITC 842, 93)

CHANGES IN THE INDUSTRY

In 1967, 2.2 million US farms and ranches handled cattle; by 1976, this figure dropped to 1.8 million. In 1969, there were 190,000 cattle feedlots in the United States; by 1976, this number had declined to 134,000. By 1983, the number of US farms and ranches handling cattle had dropped to 1.6 million, and the number of US cattle feedlots had declined to 64,000. (USITC 842, 16–19; American Meat Institute, 4–5)

In the 1970s, the beef industry was strongly influenced by grain prices and by US economic policies. In late 1971, meat prices rose in response to increased consumer demand for beef and reduced beef supplies resulting from the 1970 corn blight. In 1973, packers and retailers curtailed beef operations because of retail price ceilings, reduced marketings, and rising live cattle prices. (USITC 842, 54–58)

Since 1973, rising costs of operations have placed the cattle industry under financial stress. Beef production has followed a long-term upward trend because of increased numbers slaughtered and the increased average weight of cattle. Higher production has attracted larger imports since, under the Meat Act, imports can rise when domestic production increases, even if part of the production increase is due to herd liquidation. (USITC 842, E30–31)

Key Statistics

Imports from all sources[a]

Year	Volume (million pounds)	Value (million dollars)	Source
Before restraints			
1964	706	229	USITC 834, A36
During restraints			
1965	584	196	USITC 834, A36
1970	1,131	568	USITC 834, A36
1975	1,208	580	USITC 834, A36
1980	1,549	1,780	DOA, 139; 137
1982	1,460	1,364	DOA, 139; 137
1983	1,455	1,363	American Meat, 35; 34

a. The figures for 1964–75 reflect imports of beef and veal covered by the Meat Import Act of 1964. The figures for 1980–83 reflect total imports of beef and veal. All figures reflect product weight.

Apparent consumption[a]

Year	Volume (million pounds)	Value (million dollars)	Source
Before restraints			
1964	19,889	7,238	USITC 842, B4; authors' estimate
During restraints			
1965	20,052	7,700	USITC 842, B4; authors' estimate
1970	23,507	11,243	USITC 842, B4; authors' estimate
1975	26,274	19,217	USITC 842, B4; authors' estimate
1980	23,368	23,705	authors' estimate
1982	24,134	25,038	authors' estimate
1983	24,833	26,006	authors' estimate

a. The figures for 1964–75 reflect carcass-weight-equivalent basis. The figures for 1980–83 reflect slaughtered-weight-equivalent basis. The estimates for 1980–83 reflect the volume of domestic output, plus total imports, minus total US exports of beef and veal. The value estimates were derived in the same manner. (American Meat, 8, 135; DOA, 522, 138–39)

Market share of imports[a] (percentage of apparent consumption, by volume)

Year	Share	Source
Before restraints		
1964	3.6	authors' estimate
During restraints		
1965	2.9	authors' estimate
1970	4.9	authors' estimate
1975	4.6	authors' estimate
1980	6.6	authors' estimate
1982	6.1	authors' estimate
1983	5.9	authors' estimate

a. The figures for 1964–75 reflect the market share of imports covered by the Meat Import Act of 1964. The figures for 1980–83 reflect the market share of total imports.

Output of domestic industry[a]

Year	Volume (million pounds)	Value (million dollars)	Source
Before restraints			
1964	19,469	7,009	American Meat, 8; authors' estimate
During restraints			
1965	19,747	7,504	American Meat, 8; authors' estimate
1970	22,240	10,675	American Meat, 8; DOA, 134
1975	24,849	18,637	American Meat, 8; DOA, 134
1980	22,044	22,925	American Meat, 8; DOA, 134
1982	22,984	23,674	American Meat, 8; DOA, 134
1983	23,695	24,643	American Meat, 8; DOA, 134

a. Producers' shipments.

Employment in domestic industry[a]

Year	Production workers (average number)	Source
Before restraints		
1963	189,200	USITC 834, A55
During restraints		
1967	184,600	USITC 834, A55
1972	187,500	USITC 834, A55
1975	183,000	American Meat, 31
1980	182,800	American Meat, 31
1982	173,300	American Meat, 31
1983	167,900	American Meat, 31

a. Meat packing and processing.

Farm inventory

Year	Cattle (thousands of head)	Source
Before restraints		
1964	107,903	American Meat, 2
During restraints		
1965	109,000	American Meat, 2
1970	112,369	American Meat, 2
1975	132,028	American Meat, 2
1980	111,192	American Meat, 2
1982	115,604	American Meat, 2
1984	114,040	American Meat, 2

Wages

Year	Dollars per hour	Source
Before restraints		
1963	2.72	USITC 834, A55
During restraints		
1967	3.14	USITC 834, A55
1972	4.37	USITC 834, A55
1975	5.52	American Meat, 31
1980	8.28	American Meat, 31
1982	9.04	American Meat, 31
1983	8.82	American Meat, 31

Industry profits (million dollars)

Year	Profits[a]	Source
Before restraints		
1964	182	USITC 834, A127
During restraints		
1965	142	USITC 834, A127
1970	244	USITC 834, A127
1974	380	USITC 834, A127
1980	480	American Meat, 32
1982	404	American Meat, 32
1983	n.a.	

n.a. Not available.
a. Net profits after taxes, meat-packing industry.

Meat prices[a] (dollars per pound)

Year (during restraints)	Import	Domestic	Source
1972	0.67	0.72	USITC 834, A59
1973	0.92	0.92	USITC 834, A59
1974	0.72	0.77	USITC 834, A59
1975	0.61	0.63	USITC 834, A59
1976	0.71	0.74	USITC 834, A59
1977	0.72	0.74	USITC 834, A59
1980	1.15	1.26	American Meat, 26; authors' estimate
1982	0.93	1.11	American Meat, 26; authors' estimate
1983	n.a.	n.a.	

n.a. Not available.

a. These figures reflect the US price of imported 85 percent chemical lean beef, Chicago port of entry, and the domestic price of 85 percent chemical lean beef, sold to domestic users. Freight is included in the Chicago price of imports. (USITC 834, A58)

Quantitative Profile

Item	Amount	Source
Number of years restraints in force (since 1965)	20 years	
Induced increase in price of imported meat	3.5 percent (1970)	Magee, 673
	10 percent (1970)	Mintz, 75
	14 percent (1980–82)	authors' estimate[a]
Induced increase in price of domestic meat	2 to 4 percent (1977)	Crandall 1978, 431
	3.5 percent (1978)	Magee, 673
	7 percent (1980–82)	authors' estimate
Coefficient of price response	0.5	authors' estimate[b]
Quantity and value of imports (1983)	1,455 million pounds	American Meat, 35
	$1,363 million	American Meat, 34
Induced decrease in imports due to restraints	307 million pounds (1976)	USITC 842, 88
	1,600 million pounds (1983)	authors' estimate
	$1,500 million (1983)	authors' estimate
Quantity and value of domestic production (1983)	23,695 million pounds	American Meat, 8
	$24,643 million	DOA, 522, 134
Induced increase in domestic production due to restraints (1983)	1,600 million pounds	authors' estimate
Coefficient of quantity response	1.0	authors' estimate
Elasticity of demand for imported meat	10.0	Magee, 673
Elasticity of supply of domestic meat	1.0	authors' estimate

Quantitative Profile (continued)

Item	Amount	Source
Elasticity of demand for domestic meat (fed and processed beef)	1.4 to 2.0 1.6	USITC 842, E14 authors' estimate
Cross-elasticity of demand for domestic meat relative to price of imported meat	0.63 to 1.37 1.3	USITC 842, E14 authors' estimate
Cross-elasticity of output of domestic meat relative to price of imported meat	0.5	authors' estimate
Cross-elasticity of quantity of imported meat relative to price of domestic meat	1.5	authors' estimate
Cost of restraints to US consumers	$600 million (1970)	Mintz, 75
	$400 to $800 million (1977)	Crandall 1978, 431
	$1,362 million (1980)	Munger, 14
	$1,800 million (1983)	authors' estimate
Gain from restraints to US producers (1983)	$1,600 million	authors' estimate
Tariff revenue and implied average tariff rate	$42 million (1977)	USITC 842, D8
	5 percent	USITC 842, 93
	$44 million (1983)	authors' estimate
	3 percent	authors' estimate
Gain from restraints to foreigners	$53 million (1970)	Mintz, 76
	$9.3 million (1971)	Magee, 673
	$135 million (1983)	authors' estimate
Efficiency loss from larger domestic production to the United States (1983)	$145 million	authors' estimate
Welfare cost of restraints to the United States	$12.5 million (1971)	Magee, 673
	$5 to $19 million (1977)	Crandall 1978, 431
	$280 million (1983)	authors' estimate
Employment in protected US industry	189,200 (1963)	USITC 834, A55
	167,900 (1983)	American Meat, 31
Induced increase in employment (1983)	11,000	authors' estimate
Cost of restraints to US consumers per job saved (1983)	$160,000	authors' estimate
Gain from restraints to US producers per job (1983)	$9,500	authors' estimate
Livestock in protected US industry	108 million head (1964)	American Meat, 2
	114 million head (1984)	American Meat, 2
Induced increase in livestock (1983)	8 million head	authors' estimate

Quantitative Profile (continued)

Item	Amount	Source
Cost of restraints to US consumers per head of livestock saved (1983)	$225	authors' estimate
Gain from restraints to US producers per head of livestock (1983)	$20	authors' estimate

a. This figure is based on the average premium of wholesale domestic over import prices for boneless beef, for the two years 1980 and 1982. The figure includes the effect of the normal 3 percent tariff plus the effect of the quantitative restraints estimated at 11 percent. (American Meat, 26)

b. A coefficient of price response of 0.5 is assumed because imported beef (largely hamburger meat) does not directly compete with the more extensive range of domestically produced beef, including high-quality beef.

Hypothetical Adjustment Program

	1984	1985	1986	1987	1988	1989	1990
US purchases of meat (beef and veal) (billion pounds)							
Assumed annual consumption growth of 1 percent	25.00	25.25	25.50	25.75	26.02	26.28	26.54
Imports from all sources							
Assumed annual consumption growth of 1 percent and no change in import restraints (billion pounds)	1.50	1.52	1.53	1.55	1.56	1.58	1.59
Assumed annual consumption growth of 1 percent and quota increasing at 1 percentage point per year (billion pounds)	1.50	1.77	2.04	2.32	2.60	2.89	3.18
Import share of consumption with increasing quotas (percentage)	6.0	7.0	8.0	9.0	10.0	11.0	12.0
Hypothetical quota auction and existing tariffs							
Quota increasing at 1 percentage point per year[a] (percent)	14	12	10	8	6	4	2
Quota and tariff revenue (million 1984 dollars)	—	198	190	173	145	108	59

Hypothetical Adjustment Program (continued)

	1984	1985	1986	1987	1988	1989	1990
US production for the domestic market (billion pounds)							
Assumed annual consumption growth of 1 percent and constant import share	23.50	23.73	23.97	24.21	24.46	24.70	24.95
Assumed annual consumption growth of 1 percent and rising import share	23.50	23.48	23.46	23.44	23.42	23.39	23.36
US employment in the packing and processing industry (thousand workers)							
Assumed 3 percent annual productivity growth and constant import share	168.0	164.7	161.5	158.3	155.2	152.2	149.2
Assumed 3 percent annual productivity growth and rising import share	168.0	163.0	158.1	153.3	148.6	144.1	139.7
Year-to-year employment changes (thousand workers)							
Changes induced by consumption and productivity growth with constant import share	—	−3.3	−3.2	−3.2	−3.1	−3.0	−3.0
Changes induced by rising import share	—	−1.7	−1.7	−1.6	−1.6	−1.5	−1.4
Total changes	—	−5.0	−4.9	−4.8	−4.7	−4.5	−4.4
US livestock herd (million head)							
Assumed annual productivity growth of 0 percent and constant import share	114	115	116	117	118	119	120
Assumed annual productivity growth of 0 percent and rising import share	114	114	114	114	114	114	114

Hypothetical Adjustment Program (continued)

	1984	1985	1986	1987	1988	1989	1990
Year-to-year livestock changes (million head)							
Livestock growth induced by consumption	—	1.0	1.0	1.0	1.0	1.0	1.0
Livestock shrinkage induced by rising import share	—	−1.0	−1.0	−1.0	−1.0	−1.0	−1.0
Total livestock change	—	0.0	0.0	0.0	0.0	0.0	0.0
Benefit and budget calculations (1984 prices)							
Annual wage cost per worker assuming constant $10 per hour and 2,000 hours (dollars)	20,000	20,000	20,000	20,000	20,000	20,000	20,000
Benefits calculated at two times annual wage cost per worker (million dollars)	—	200	196	192	188	180	176
Livestock reduction calculated at $500/head	—	—	—	—	—	—	—
Projected program surplus or deficit: quota auction revenue less benefits (million dollars)	—	−2	−6	−19	−43	−72	−117

— Not applicable.

a. These figures assume that a quota increase equal to 1 percent of the domestic market increases the quantity of inputs by about 16 percent and depresses the quota auction rate by about 2 percent.

BIBLIOGRAPHY

American Meat Institute. 1984. *Meatfacts 1984 Edition.* Arlington, Va., July.

Balassa, Carol. 1984. "Levels of Protection on Manufactured Goods: The US, EC, Canada, Japan." Office of the US Trade Representative. Washington.

Bergsten, C. Fred. 1972. *The Cost of Import Restrictions to American Consumers.* New York: American Importers Association.

Crandall, Robert W. 1977. "Comments of the Council on Wage and Price Stability on Investigations TA–201–25 and TA–332–85, Meat." Study prepared for the US International Trade Commission. Washington, 12 August.

———. 1978. "Federal Government Initiatives to Reduce the Price Level." *Brookings Papers on Economic Activity* 2.

Freebairn, J. W., and G. C. Ransser. 1975. "Effects of Changes in the Level of US Beef Imports." *American Journal of Agricultural Economics* 57 (November): 676–88.

Houck, James P. 1974. "The Short-Run Impact of Beef Imports on US Prices." *Australian Journal of Agricultural Economics* 18, pp. 60–72.

Magee, Stephen P. 1972. "The Welfare Effects of Restrictions on US Trade." *Brookings Papers on Economic Activity* 3.

Mintz, Ilse. 1973. *US Import Quotas: Costs and Consequences.* Domestic Affairs Study 10. Washington: American Enterprise Institute for Public Policy Research, February.

Morkre, Morris E., and David G. Tarr. 1980. *Effects of Restrictions on United States Imports: Five Case Studies and Theory.* US Federal Trade Commission, Bureau of Economics. Washington, June.

Munger, Michael C. 1983. *The Costs of Protectionism: Estimates of the Hidden Tax of Trade Restraint.* Working Paper no. 80. Washington University, Center for the Study of American Business, July.

US Department of Agriculture. Economic Research Service. 1983. *Livestock and Meat Statistics: Supplement for 1982,* Statistical Bulletin no. 522. Washington, October.

US Department of Labor. Employment and Training Administration. 1981. *Employment and Training Report of the President.* Washington.

US International Trade Commission. 1977a. *Live Cattle and Certain Edible Meat Products of Cattle.* USITC Publication no. 834. Washington, September.

———. 1977b. *Conditions of Competition in US Markets Between Domestic and Foreign Live Cattle and Cattle Meat Fit for Human Consumption.* USITC Publication no. 842. Washington, November.

US Tariff Commission. 1964. *Report on Investigation No. 332–44 (Beef and Beef Products) Under Section 332 of the Tariff Act of 1930 Pursuant to a Resolution of the Committee on Finance of the United States Senate Adopted November 20, 1963.* USTC Publication no. 128. Washington, June.

US Trade Representative. 1982. *A Preface to Trade.* Washington, September.

CASE A-5

Fish in the Conservation Zone

PERIOD OF RELIEF

1977 to present

SUPPLIERS AFFECTED

Global

RELIEF ACTION

The US fishing industry was an early, though indirect, recipient of protection from imports as far back as the presidency of George Washington. Since 1812, coastal trade, including fishing, has been reserved to US-built and US-owned vessels manned by US citizens. Additional protection was provided by the Nicholson Act (46 USC Sec. 24 (1)(a)), passed in 1950. This act, while intended to promote the shipping industry, also aided fishermen by prohibiting the unloading, in US ports, of fish caught by foreign vessels in US waters. Fish landed under such circumstances must leave US waters and be processed in some form before they can be imported. This provision was given greater geographic scope by the 200-mile conservation zone. (Freese; Jantscher, 45-48)

Since the early 1950s, the US fishing industry has regularly petitioned the US Tariff Commission and the US International Trade Commission (USITC) for relief under the escape clause and the countervailing duty statutes.

In 1951-52, the US Tariff Commission investigated an escape clause petition under Section 7 of the Trade Agreements Extension Act of 1951 and found no injury. (USITC 1066, A13)

In 1954 and again in 1956, the Tariff Commission found injury under the escape clause, but in both cases President Dwight D. Eisenhower refused to grant the recommended trade relief. (USITC 1066, A13-14)

In 1964, pursuant to Section 225(b) of the Trade Expansion Act of 1962, the Tariff Commission found that the domestic industry was still injured by imports. This finding precluded tariff reductions in the Kennedy Round of multilateral trade negotiations. (USITC 1066, A14)

In 1977, 1978, and 1980, the Treasury Department waived the imposition of countervailing duties on groundfish (a group of species accounting for 30 percent of US fish consumption in 1978). In 1978, and again in 1979 and 1980, the USITC investigated whether imports of these subsidized duty-free fish (principally cod from Canada) were a cause of material injury to the domestic industry. No injury was found in any of these cases. In 1980, the USITC investigated an escape clause petition under Section 201 of the Trade Act of 1974 and again found no injury. (USITC 1066, A3, A14; USITC 1028; USITC 919, 2; *Federal Register,* 13 April 1977, 19327; 5 January 1979, 1372; 8 January 1979, 1728)

The US Congress responded to the grievances of the fishing industry in 1976 with the passage of the Magnuson Fishery Conservation and Management Act (16 USC 1801), which established a 200-nautical-mile limit for US jurisdiction over fisheries, the so-called fishery conservation zone (FCZ). The act allocates fishing rights to foreign countries with the principal objective of ensuring that US fishermen have first call on fishing within the FCZ (Sections 201(d)(2) and 303(a)(4)). In August 1978, Congress amended the act to extend its benefits to domestic processors. Foreign fish processors had been setting up waterborne plants just outside US territorial waters (three miles), and their activities adversely affected US processing firms. The amendments directed the Secretary of Commerce to issue permits to foreign processors to operate in the FCZ "only if U.S. processors could not or would not process such fish." The Magnuson Act thus combined territorial acquisition, conservation, and protection; moreover, the act replaced the tariff and the quota as the principal tools for advancing the fortunes of the US fishing industry. (Dopico, 1333)

CHANGES IN THE INDUSTRY

Establishment of the FCZ, though primarily designed to promote the US fishing fleet, has, in some cases, constrained it through its conservation regulations. The USITC found that, while production and capacity utilization of the Atlantic groundfish fleet increased significantly in 1977–78, just after the zone was established, the fleet was prevented from operating at full capacity by conservation regulations. (USITC 919, A18)

In 1984, the New England fishing industry petitioned the USITC to initiate a Section 332 fact-finding investigation. The fishermen alleged that Canada subsidizes its fishing industry, thus enabling its fleet to sell their catch at prices that could eventually force New England fishermen out of business. (*Washington Post,* 9 September 1984, F1; Cory)

Key Statistics

Imports from all sources[a]

Year	Volume (million pounds, round weight[b])	Value (million dollars)	Source
Before 200-mile limit			
1970	3,767	812	NMFS 1976, 44; 29
1972	4,454	1,233	NMFS 1976, 44; 29
1974	4,142	1,495	NMFS 1976, 44; 29
1976	4,629	1,914	NMFS 1983, 46[b]
During 200-mile limit			
1978	4,958	2,256	NMFS 1983, 46
1980	4,352	2,687	NMFS 1983, 46
1982	4,683	3,202	NMFS 1983, 46
1983	5,175	3,627	NMFS 1983, 46

a. Edible fishery products.
b. Fish measured on a round weight basis include heads, tails, etc.
c. See NMFS 1983, 46; but cf. 62.

Apparent consumption[a]

Year	Volume (million pounds, round weight[b])	Value[c] (million dollars)	Source
Before 200-mile limit			
1970	6,213	1,357	NMFS 1976, 44; authors' estimate
1972	6,889	1,935	NMFS 1976, 44; authors' estimate
1974	6,559	2,308	NMFS 1976, 44; authors' estimate
1976	7,404	3,171	NMFS 1983, 62; authors' estimate
During 200-mile limit			
1978	8,135	3,989	NMFS 1983, 62; authors' estimate
1980	8,006	4,779	NMFS 1983, 62; authors' estimate
1982	7,968	5,249	NMFS 1983, 62; authors' estimate
1983	8,412	5,830	NMFS 1983, 62; authors' estimate

a. Edible fishery products.
b. Fish measured on a round weight basis include heads, tails, etc.
c. These figures are derived from the value of imports and domestic output.

Market share of imports (percentage of apparent consumption, by volume)

Year	Share	Source
Before 200-mile limit		
1970	59.2	NMFS 1976, 44
1972	64.7	NMFS 1976, 44
1974	63.2	NMFS 1976, 44
1976	62.5	NMFS 1983, 62
During 200-mile limit		
1978	60.9	NMFS 1983, 62
1980	54.4	NMFS 1983, 62
1982	58.7	NMFS 1983, 62
1983	61.5	NMFS 1983, 62

Landings of domestic industry[a]

Year	Volume (million pounds, round weight[b])	Value (million dollars)	Source
Before 200-mile limit			
1970	2,537	565	NMFS 1976, 6
1972	2,435	702	NMFS 1976, 6
1974	2,417	813	NMFS 1976, 6
1976	2,775	1,257	NMFS 1976, 6
During 200-mile limit			
1978	3,177	1,733	NMFS 1983, 6
1980	3,654	2,092	NMFS 1983, 6
1982	3,285	2,047	NMFS 1983, 6
1983	3,238	2,203	NMFS 1983, 6

a. Edible fishery products.
b. Fish measured on a round weight basis include heads, tails, etc.

Ex vessel prices[a]

Year	Index (1967 = 100)	Source
Before 200-mile limit		
1974	238.7	NMFS 1979, 65
1976	299.1	NMFS 1979, 65
During 200-mile limit		
1978	391.4	NMFS 1979, 65
1980	399.9	NMFS 1983, 74
1982	484.3	NMFS 1983, 74
1983	478.5	NMFS 1983, 74

a. All fish.

Employment in domestic industry

Year	Fishermen (average number)	Source
Before 200-mile limit		
1965	128,565	NMFS 1976, 74
1970	140,538	NMFS 1976, 74
1972	139,000	NMFS 1983, 86
1974	161,361	NMFS 1977, 82
1976	172,900	NMFS 1979, 82
During 200-mile limit		
1977	182,000	NMFS 1983, 86
1979	184,000	NMFS 1980, 94
1981	197,000	NMFS 1982, 80
1982	216,000	NMFS 1983, 86

Fish catch in the Fishery Conservation Zone

Year	Domestic harvest (million pounds)	Foreign allocation (million pounds)	Foreign harvest (million pounds)	Source
Before 200-mile limit				
1969	n.a.	—	5,516	NMFS, DMSD, 52
1970	n.a.	—	6,840	NMFS, DMSD, 61
1972	n.a.	—	7,281	NMFS, DMSD, 82
1974	n.a.	—	6,840	NMFS, DMSD, 104
1976	1,603	—	5,516	NMFS 1977, iv; NMFS, DMSD, 125
During 200-mile limit				
1978	1,323	4,633	3,972	NMFS 1978, iv; xxi; iv
1980	2,064	4,854	3,527	NMFS 1980, iv; 103; iv
1982	2,427	4,190	3,089	NMFS 1983, iv; 93; 21
1983	2,648	4,190	2,868	NMFS 1983, iv; 93; 24

n.a. Not available.

— Not applicable.

Quantitative Profile

Item	Amount	Source
Number of years restraints in force (since Magnuson Act)	8 years	
Induced increase in price of imported fish (1983)	10 percent	authors' estimate[a]

Quantitative Profile (continued)

Item	Amount	Source
Induced increase in price of domestic fish (1983)	10 percent	authors' estimate
Coefficient of price response	1.0	authors' estimate
Quantity and value of imports (1983)	5,175 million pounds $3,627 million	NMFS 1983, 46 NMFS 1983, 46
Induced decrease in imports due to restraints (1983)	400 million pounds $280 million	authors' estimate authors' estimate
Quantity and value of domestic production (1983)	3,238 million pounds $2,203 million	NMFS 1983, 6 NMFS 1983, 6
Induced increase in domestic production due to restraints (1983)	400 million pounds	authors' estimate
Coefficient of quantity response	1.0	authors' estimate
Elasticity of demand for imported fish	0.2	authors' estimate
Elasticity of supply of domestic fish	0.32	FTC, appendix A, 15[b]
Elasticity of demand for domestic fish	0.2 to 0.3	USITC 1066, A5: N.1[c]
Cross-elasticity of demand for domestic fish relative to price of imported fish	0.5	authors' estimate
Cross-elasticity of output of domestic fish relative to price of imported fish	0.3	authors' estimate
Cross-elasticity of quantity of imported fish relative to price of domestic fish	0.2	authors' estimate
Cost of restraints to US consumers (1983)	$560 million	authors' estimate
Gain from restraints to US producers (1983)	$200 million	authors' estimate
Tariff revenue and implied average tariff rate (1983)	$177 million 4.9 percent	NMFS 1983, 46 authors' estimate
Gain from restraints to foreigners (1983)	$170 million	authors' estimate
Efficiency loss from larger domestic production to the United States (1983)	$15 million	authors' estimate
Welfare cost of restraints to the United States (1983)	$185 million	authors' estimate
Employment (fishermen) in protected US industry	172,900 (1976) 216,000 (1982)	NMFS 1979, 82 NMFS 1983, 86
Induced increase in employment (1983)	27,000	authors' estimate
Cost of restraints to consumers per job saved (1983)	$21,000	authors' estimate

Quantitative Profile (continued)

Item	Amount	Source
Gain from restraints realized by producers per job (1983)	$900	authors' estimate

a. Between 1976 and 1983, fish prices increased by 60 percent. By comparison, imported beef rose 54 percent during this period. We think a conservative estimate of the induced increase in fish prices on account of the Magnuson Act is 5 percent. In addition, the existing tariff rate is about 5 percent.

b. The staff of the Federal Trade Commission (FTC) regards this elasticity estimate as the best available coefficient; however, it refers to all fish and forestry products.

c. This coefficient is taken from a 1968 study by Frederick W. Bell that estimates the elasticity of demand for several classes of groundfish, including cod, haddock, and yellowtail flounder. The USITC did not have sufficient information to update the coefficient.

Hypothetical Adjustment Program

	1984	1985	1986	1987	1988	1989	1990
US purchases of fish (million pounds, round weight)							
Assumed annual consumption increase of 2.5 percent	8,600	8,820	9,040	9,260	9,490	9,730	9,970
Imports from all sources							
Assumed annual consumption increase of 2.5 percent and no change in import restraints[a] (million pounds, round weight)	5,160	5,290	5,420	5,560	5,690	5,840	5,980
Assumed annual consumption increase of 2.5 percent and quota expansion of 0.5 percent per year, about 45 million pounds (million pounds, round weight)	5,160	5,340	5,510	5,690	5,880	6,080	6,230
Import share of consumption with quota expansion (percentage)	60.0	60.5	61.0	61.5	62.0	62.5	62.5
Hypothetical quota auction and existing tariffs							
Assumed world fish price (cents/pound, round weight)	70	70	70	70	70	70	70

Hypothetical Adjustment Program (continued)

	1984	1985	1986	1987	1988	1989	1990
Tariff equivalent of existing tariffs plus hypothetical quota auction (percent)	10	8	6	4	2	—	—
Revenue from existing tariffs and quota auction (million 1984 dollars)	360	300	230	160	80	—	—
US fish catch for the domestic market (million pounds, round weight)							
Assumed annual consumption increase of 2.5 percent and constant import share	3,440	3,530	3,620	3,700	3,800	3,890	3,990
Assumed annual consumption increase of 2.5 percent and rising import share	3,440	3,480	3,530	3,570	3,610	3,650	3,740
US employment in fishing (thousand fishermen)							
Assumed annual productivity growth of 0 percent and constant import share	200	205	210	215	220	225	230
Asssumed annual productivity growth of 0 percent and rising import share	200	202	205	207	209	211	216
Year-to-year employment changes (thousand fishermen)							
Changes induced by consumption growth with constant import share	—	5.0	5.0	5.0	5.0	5.0	5.0
Changes induced by rising import share	—	−3.0	−2.0	−3.0	−3.0	−3.0	0.0
Total employment changes	—	2.0	3.0	2.0	2.0	2.0	5.0
Benefit and budget calculations (1984 prices)							
Annual wage cost per worker assuming constant $10 per hour and 1,500 hours (dollars)	15,000	15,000	15,000	15,000	15,000	15,000	15,000

Hypothetical Adjustment Program (continued)

	1984	1985	1986	1987	1988	1989	1990
Projected program surplus: tariff and quota revenue less benefits (million dollars)	360	300	230	160	80	—	—

— Not applicable.

a. Imports remain at 60 percent of US consumption.

BIBLIOGRAPHY

Bell, Frederick W. 1968. *Food from the Sea: The Economics and Politics of Ocean Fisheries.* Boulder, Colo.: Westview Press.

Cory, Roger (US International Trade Commission). 1985. By communication, 20 May.

Dopico, Jorge. 1978. "Amendments to the Fishery Conservation and Management Act of 1976: The Path to Expanded Protection for American Fish Processors." *Law and Policy in International Business* 10, pp. 1325–37.

Freese, Steve (National Marine Fisheries Service). 1984. By communication, September.

Jantscher, Gerald R. 1975. *Bread upon the Waters: Federal Aids to the Maritime Industries.* Washington: Brookings Institution.

US Congress. House. Committee on Merchant Marine and Fisheries. 1985. *Fishery Conservation and Management Improvement.* Report 99–165, accompanying HR 1533. 99 Cong., 1 sess., 10 June.

US Department of Commerce. National Marine Fisheries Service. Various years. *Fisheries of the United States.* Washington.

———. 1983. *Magnuson Fishery Conservation and Management Act* (as amended through 12 January 1983). Washington, March.

———. Data Management and Statistics Division. 1984. Washington, 14 August. Processed.

US International Trade Commission. 1978. *Certain Fish from Canada.* USITC Publication no. 919. Washington, September.

US Federal Trade Commission. 1984. *Proceedings before the US International Trade Commission: Certain Canned Tuna Fish.* Prehearing brief. Washington, May.

———. 1980. *Fish, Fresh, Chilled, or Frozen, Whether or Not Whole, But Not Otherwise Prepared or Preserved, from Canada.* USITC Publication no. 1066. Washington, May.

———. 1984. *Conditions of Competition Affecting the Northeastern US Groundfish and Scallop Industries in Selected Markets.* USITC Publication no. 1662. Washington, December.

CASE E-1

Petroleum

PERIOD OF RELIEF

1959 to 1973

SUPPLIERS AFFECTED

Global (with special exemptions for Western Hemisphere suppliers)

RELIEF ACTION

Between 1959 and 1973, the US oil industry was protected from foreign competition by a variety of quantitative and tariff controls intended to keep the domestic price above the world price. The OPEC price shock of 1973–74 made further protection unnecessary. Until decontrol in 1981, debate focused on whether and how fast to allow domestic prices to increase to world levels. More recently, petroleum refiners have sought relief from imports of petroleum products. A crude oil import fee has also been considered as a means of raising revenue while world oil prices are declining. No action has been taken thus far.

Internal Revenue Act of 1932

The first duty was levied on imports of crude oil and products in 1932 under the Internal Revenue Act. At a time when the price of crude oil in the field was about $1.00 a barrel and gasoline was $0.10 a gallon, import fees of $0.21 a barrel on crude oil, residual fuel oil, and some products, $1.05 a barrel on gasoline, and $1.68 a barrel on lubricating oil were quite restrictive. These fees were lowered over the years by a series of agreements with Mexico and Venezuela. The Trade Expansion Act of 1962 preserved fees of $0.0525 a barrel on crude and residual fuel oils of less than 25 degrees gravity and $0.165 a barrel on those oils above 25 degrees gravity while halving the fees on other petroleum products from their 1932 level. These fees remained in effect throughout the period of the voluntary and mandatory oil import programs and were finally terminated in 1973 when both the fees and the quotas were replaced with a more complex (but economically less significant) license-fee system.[1] (Bohi, 231)

---

1. Imports of petroleum and products, and other imports controlled under national security provisions, were not subject to the 10 percent import surcharge imposed for balance of payments reasons from 15 August to 20 December 1971. (Bohi, 231, N. 93)

The Voluntary Program

State prorationing of crude oil production began in the 1930s when major new discoveries and slack demand resulted in lowered prices. In this period the United States was a net oil exporter and the US price was the world price. After World War II, however, increasing supplies from the Middle East contributed to a lower world price and a growing differential between US and world prices. States initially responded by cutting back domestic production but the imposition of import controls was inevitable if US price levels were to be maintained. (Bohi, 251–53)

By 1954, concern over rising oil imports triggered the appointment of a cabinet advisory committee to study the problem. The committee's report concluded that oil imports above the 1954 market penetration level (about 10 percent of domestic production) would be a potential threat to national security. Nevertheless, only voluntary measures were recommended and, for the moment, the only other action taken was to instruct the Office of Defense Mobilization (ODM) to monitor imports and report to the President if they reached levels that would threaten national security. This provision was embodied in the Trade Agreements Extension Act of 1955 and, as eventually incorporated in the Trade Expansion Act of 1962, authorized the President, following a recommendation from the director of ODM, "to take whatever action, for such time deemed necessary, to limit imports threatening national security. . . ." (Bohi, 27)

Pressure from the petroleum industry for mandatory import controls mounted throughout 1955 and the first part of 1956. In the fall of 1956, supply interruptions resulting from the Suez Canal crisis temporarily eased pressure. The pressure for controls resumed early in 1957 and, in April, the ODM director certified to the President that oil imports had reached a potentially threatening level. President Dwight D. Eisenhower appointed another special committee in June 1957; in July the voluntary oil import program was established. (Bohi, 40–42)

Eisenhower's special committee recommended that imports of crude oil be limited to 1,031,000 barrels a day (about the pre-Suez level) as compared to a planned 1,266,700 barrels a day. The recommended level was approximately 12 percent of domestic production. West Coast (District V) imports and exports of petroleum products were left uncontrolled. The 756,000 barrels a day to be allowed into Districts I, II, III, and IV were not much less than the 1957 import levels but were well below planned levels.[2] (Bohi, 44–46)

Quota allocations were established for 22 known importers; little account was taken of new entrants. There was no enforcement mechanism other than the threat of mandatory controls. Support for the program deteriorated steadily throughout 1957–58. The administration responded in March 1958 by ordering all government agencies to buy only domestic or "complying" imported crude oil. The order could not be

---

2. Petroleum imports into the West Coast area were not controlled because it was an oil deficit area. The districts were the five US regions created to control oil supply and distribution for defense purposes. District V included the West Coast states (California, Washington, and Oregon) plus Arizona, Nevada, Alaska, and Hawaii. The other four districts covered all the other states. (Bohi, 45)

fully implemented, however, because so few companies had been in compliance with recommended quota levels that government needs could not be met. (Bohi, 54–57)

By the winter of 1958–59, the lack of compliance, requests by new importers for allocations, and increasing imports of uncontrolled petroleum products all combined to fatally undermine the voluntary import control program. It was abolished by executive order and a new mandatory program established in its place on 10 March 1959. (Bohi, 58–61)

The Mandatory Oil Import Program

As with previous control efforts, the Mandatory Oil Import Program (MOIP) was based on a national security rationale. In 1959, the US price for crude oil was just under $3 a barrel while the world price was well under $2 a barrel. It was argued that unrestrained imports would force the US price down to world levels thereby making some high-cost wells unprofitable and inhibiting additions to reserves. The United States would become more dependent on imports and, hence, more vulnerable to supply disruption of economic or military origin. In order to reassure the public, the announcement of mandatory controls explicitly stated that controls would not be used to raise the domestic price of oil but only to stabilize it. The American public accepted the national security rationale until the costs of the program reached conspicuously high levels. (Cabinet, 19–20; Bohi, 2, 70, 211)

The director of the Office of Civil and Defense Mobilization (previously ODM) certified to the President in February 1959 that oil imports were a threat to national security; on 6 March 1959, the President's Special Committee to Investigate Crude Oil Imports recommended imposition of a mandatory program. Following the President's announcement of 10 March, the Department of the Interior, with the responsibility for administering MOIP, published the provisions of the program, effective 1 April 1959. (Bohi, 68)

The major elements of the program were the following:

- Three geographic areas were designated—Districts I–IV, District V, and Puerto Rico—each to be subject to a different set of regulations.
- Residual fuel oil (resid) was differentiated from crude and unfinished oils and finished products.[3]

---

3. Residual fuel oil is an extremely heavy oil used primarily as utility and industrial fuel. The principal US market for resid was along the East Coast, in District I. Until 1970, US producers were more interested in the higher priced lighter fuel oils and treated resid as a byproduct, minimizing its proportion in the refining process. Thus, resid imports were treated as supplementing rather than displacing domestic production. In fact, the inclusion of resid in MOIP reflected concerns of the coal industry, which is competitive with resid, not pressure from oil producers. After a number of adjustments, resid was effectively decontrolled in April 1966, although the formal mechanisms remained in place for potential reinstatement. (Bohi, 144–51)

- Allocations were made to refiners on the basis of refinery capacity, giving due attention to historical imports and quota allocations under the voluntary program so as to avoid drastic cutbacks for any particular importer.

- The maximum level of imports of petroleum and products, except resid, into Districts I–IV was established at 9 percent of total demand. Within that overall level, finished product imports could not exceed the relative level of such imports in 1957; unfinished oils were limited to 10 percent of permissible imports of crude oil and unfinished oils.

- The crude oil import level for District V, because it was an oil deficit area, was based on the difference between estimated domestic supply and estimated total demand. Product levels were the same as in the rest of the country.

- Resid imports were to be monitored and adjusted at the discretion of the Secretary of the Interior using the 1957 level as a base.

- Imports into Puerto Rico were restricted to the level of 1958.

- Provisions were made for importing fuel under bond for ship and airplane use.

- An Oil Import Appeal Board was established and authorized to grant relief on the basis of hardship, error, or any other "relevant" consideration. However, a grant of additional importing authority to one entity meant a reduction elsewhere since the overall import ceiling could not be breached. (Bohi, 68–69)

Just a month later in May 1959, the first exemption from controls was granted for overland oil imports, which could not logically be included under a national security rationale based on fear of military interdiction of ocean routes. Only Canada and Mexico were eligible and, in reality, only Canada could take advantage of the exception since Mexico did not have the transportation facilities to move significant quantities of oil overland.[4] At the time the exemption was granted, imports of Canadian oil were only 56,000 barrels a day. By 1963, however, they had grown to 119,200 barrels a day. (Bohi, 106)

On 5 December 1962, President John F. Kennedy addressed the problem of growing Canadian imports by bringing them under the overall import limit. Canadian oil could still be imported freely, but now only at the expense of third-party exporters. Petroleum from Canada continued to come in at increasing levels and mandatory controls eventually were imposed in March 1970. (Bohi, 107; Dam, 31)

Kennedy's announcement also included a change in the way in which the overall quota level was determined. The Bureau of Mines consistently had overestimated domestic demand so that imports were always greater than the desired 9 percent of demand. Henceforth, allowable imports were to be calculated as 12.2 percent of actual production. This level was also seldom maintained, however, because Canadian

---

4. Small quantities of Mexican oil did come into Texas as a result of a State-Department-negotiated loophole called the "Brownsville shuffle." This contrivance allowed Mexican oil to be shipped by tanker to Brownsville and unloaded in bond. It was then trucked across the border into Mexico, after which the trucks simply turned around and the oil was imported into the United States under the overland exemption. The loophole was finally abolished in 1971 and a straightforward country quota granted to Mexico. (Bohi, 132–34)

exports, which had just been brought under the overall ceiling, were usually underestimated. (Bohi, 107)

Other changes effectively allowing further increases in import levels were announced in June 1963. At that time, the base for calculating import quotas was shifted from actual to prospective domestic production, a significant change in a growing market, and a potential source for misestimation by the Bureau of Mines. From this point on, the 12.2 percent ceiling became the rallying point for domestic producers. Domestic consumers and overseas suppliers never launched a direct attack on the 12.2 figure. Rather, they whittled away at the ceiling by arguing for a variety of special programs and exemptions, justifying the need for lower priced imported oil by citing temporary shortages and excessive domestic prices. (Bohi, 107–9)

Of these special programs, the ones dealing with residual fuel oil and hemispheric preferences (which included various inducements to import Venezuelan oil) were the most important. Other special provisions were made for the "islands program," which established special allocations for refiners willing to establish plants, provide employment, and promote development in Puerto Rico, the Virgin Islands, and Guam. Consumer pressure in the Northeast resulted in the frequent use of hardship allocations to allow increased imports of No. 2 fuel oil, used primarily for home heating. Asphalt imports were decontrolled and special allowances made for importers of crude and unfinished oils used in low-sulfur resid (a result of air pollution concerns). (Bohi, 131–85)

Cabinet Task Force on Oil Import Control

By the late 1960s, special programs had contributed to the effective unraveling of MOIP. In March 1969, President Richard M. Nixon appointed a special cabinet task force chaired by Secretary of Labor George P. Shultz to study the oil import issue and its relationship to national security. (Bohi, 189–92)

The task force concluded that the existing system of import controls was not contributing to the national security because it was too rigid and often internally inconsistent. The group found that a gradual liberalization of controls would not impair national security but it did not recommend the complete abolition of controls. Instead, it recommended that tariffs be substituted for the quota system. It suggested that the tariffs be established so as to allow the US price for crude oil to decline from its $3.30 a barrel level to about $3.00 a barrel. Shultz personally recommended that prices eventually be allowed to go as far down as $2.50 a barrel. World prices at the time averaged $2.00 a barrel. (Cabinet, 90–91, 134–39)

The report came under heated attack from industry representatives and oil-state congressmen. Perhaps because of the strength of the response, President Nixon announced, when formally releasing the report in February 1970, that no action would be taken until after congressional hearings and discussion with affected foreign governments. No direct action was taken on oil imports for the next three years, but anti-inflationary policies exerted a dampening effect on imports even as rising world oil prices negated the original rationale for controls. (Bohi, 198–210)

CHANGES IN THE INDUSTRY

To combat accelerating inflation, President Nixon imposed wage and price controls in August 1971. Under the inflation-fighting scheme, higher imported oil prices could not be passed on to the consumer until phase four of the program, starting in December 1973. Faced with declining profit margins, the oil companies "voluntarily" limited their imports into the United States. (Bohi, 208)

By early 1973, world oil prices were rising to and exceeding the level of US prices. The combination of rising world prices and domestic price controls provided no incentives to increase either domestic production or imports, or to reduce consumption. On 18 April 1973, President Nixon announced that, effective immediately, he was lifting the quota controls and the old fee system, and substituting a license-fee system. (Bohi, 218)

In relation to rapidly rising world oil prices, the new fees were nearly insignificant and had little effect on imports. "The new system did provide a cost differential between crude and product fees to help encourage domestic refinery construction." From this point until 1981, however, the issue was whether to decontrol domestic prices and allow them to rise to world levels. (Bohi, 232–35)

Key Statistics

Imports from all sources

Year	Volume[a] (million barrels) Crude and products	Resid	Value[b] (million dollars)	Source
Before restraints				
1954	255	129	828	Bohi, 146; BEA, 148; American Petroleum
Voluntary restraints				
1957	402	173	1,548	Bohi, 146; BEA, 148; American Petroleum
Mandatory restraints				
1959	426	223	1,529	Bohi, 146; BEA, 148; American Petroleum
1965	556	345	2,149	Bohi, 146; BEA, 148; BM
1967	530	396	2,207	Bohi, 146; BEA, 148; BM
1969	655	462	2,691	Bohi, 146; BEA, 148; BM
1971	855	578	3,350	Bohi, 146; BEA, 148; BM
1973	1,607	676	7,858	Bohi, 146; BEA, 148; BM

Imports from all sources (continued)

Year	Volume[a] (million barrels) Crude and products	Resid	Value[b] (million dollars)	Source
After restraints				
1975	1,763	447	25,156	BEA, 148–150; BEA 148–150; BM

a. The figures for crude oil include imports of other unfinished oils and refined products other than residual fuel oil. Figures for residual fuel oil have been broken out separately because of its special status in the import control program and its effective decontrol by the mid-1960s.

b. These figures include the value of imports of petroleum and all petroleum products.

Apparent consumption

Year	Volume (million barrels) Crude and products	Resid	Value[a] (million dollars)	Source
Before restraints				
1954	2,565	521	7,253	BEA, 148; Bohi, 146; authors' estimate
Voluntary restraints				
1957	3,073	544	9,627	BEA, 148; Bohi, 146; authors' estimate
Mandatory restraints				
1959	3,349	554	9,002	BEA, 148; Bohi, 146; authors' estimate
1965	4,184	574	10,307	BEA, 148; Bohi, 146; authors' estimate
1967	4,474	640	11,585	BEA, 148; Bohi, 146; authors' estimate
1969	5,092	723	13,118	BEA, 148; Bohi, 146; authors' estimate
1971	5,570	838	15,043	BEA, 148; Bohi, 146; authors' estimate
1973	6,894	1,030	20,916	BEA, 148; Bohi, 146; authors' estimate
After restraints				
1975	6,822	898	48,272	BEA, 148; Bohi, 146; authors' estimate

a. These figures are derived from the value of domestic production of crude oil plus the value of all imports of petroleum and petroleum products.

Market share of imports (percentage of apparent consumption, by volume)

Year	Crude and products	Resid	Source
Before restraints			
1954	9.9	24.8	authors' estimate; Bohi, 146
Voluntary restraints			
1957	13.1	31.8	authors' estimate; Bohi, 146
Mandatory restraints			
1959	12.7	40.1	authors' estimate; Bohi, 146
1965	13.3	60.1	authors' estimate; Bohi, 146
1967	11.8	61.9	authors' estimate; Bohi, 146
1969	12.9	63.9	authors' estimate; Bohi, 146
1971	15.3	68.9	authors' estimate; Bohi, 146
1973	23.3	65.6	authors' estimate; Bohi, 146
After restraints			
1975	25.8	49.8	authors' estimate

Output of domestic industry[a]

Year	Volume (million barrels)	Value (million dollars)	Source
Before restraints			
1954	2,315	6,425	Bohi, 23; American Petroleum
Voluntary restraints			
1957	2,617	8,079	Bohi, 23; American Petroleum
Mandatory restraints			
1959	2,575	7,473	Bohi, 23; American Petroleum
1965	2,849	8,158	Bohi, 23; BM
1967	3,216	9,378	Bohi, 23; BM
1969	3,204	10,427	Bohi, 23; BM
1971	3,297	11,693	Bohi, 23; BM
1973	3,206	13,058	Bohi, 23; BM
After restraints			
1975	2,923	23,116	Bohi, 23; BM

a. Crude oil only.

Employment in domestic industry

Year	Production workers (average number)	Source
Before restraints		
1954	140,000	BLS, 24
Voluntary restraints		
1957	132,000	BLS, 24
Mandatory restraints		
1959	118,000	BLS, 24
1965	88,000	BLS, 24
1967	82,000	BLS, 24
1969	75,000	BLS, 24
1971	75,000	BLS, 24
1973	70,000	BLS, 24
After restraints		
1975	78,000	BLS, 24

Wages

Year	Dollars per hour	Source
Before restraints		
1954	2.15	BLS, 24
Voluntary restraints		
1957	2.47	BLS, 24
Mandatory restraints		
1959	2.65	BLS, 24
1965	3.03	BLS, 24
1967	3.25	BLS, 24
1969	3.59	BLS, 24
1971	4.15	BLS, 24
1973	4.79	BLS, 24
After restraints		
1975	6.01	BLS, 24

Crude oil prices (dollars per barrel)

Year	United States[a]	Venezuela	Saudi Arabia	Source
Before restraints				
1955	2.77	1.35	1.93	Bohi, 211; IMF, 80–81; IMF, 80–81
Mandatory restraints				
1960	2.88	1.48	1.50	Bohi, 211; IMF, 80–81; IMF, 80–81
1965	2.86	1.73	1.33	Bohi, 211; IMF, 80–81; IMF, 80–81
1970	3.18	1.73	1.30	Bohi, 211; IMF, 80–81; IMF, 80–81
1973	3.89	3.56	2.70	Bohi, 211; IMF, 80–81; IMF, 80–81
After restraints				
1975	7.56	10.89	10.72	Bohi, 211; IMF, 80–81; IMF, 80–81

a. These figures reflect the average wellhead price.

Quantitative Profile

Item	Amount	Source
Number of years restraints in force (1959–73)	14 years	
Induced increase in price of imported oil (average 1960–70)	$1.46/barrel 96 percent	authors' estimate[a] authors' estimate
Induced increase in price of domestic oil (average 1960–70)	$1.46/barrel 96 percent	authors' estimate authors' estimate
Coefficient of price response	1.0	authors' estimate
Quantity and value of imports (1971)	1,433 million barrels $3,350 million	Bohi, 146; BEA, 148 BM
Induced decrease in imports due to restraints (1971)	2,800 barrels $6,550 million	Bohi, 277 authors' estimate
Quantity and value of domestic production (1971)	3,297 million barrels $11,693 million	Bohi, 23 BM
Induced increase in domestic production due to restaints (1971)	1,900 million barrels	Bohi, 277
Coefficient of quantity response	0.68	authors' estimate
Elasticity of demand for imported oil	0.79 to 0.96	Stern, 9[b]
Elasticity of supply of domestic oil	0.93	Bohi, 273[c]
Elasticity of demand for domestic oil	0.5	Bohi, 275

Quantitative Profile (continued)

Item	Amount	Source
Cross-elasticity of demand for domestic oil relative to price of imported oil	0.34 to 2.36 1.4	Stern, 9[b] authors' estimate
Cross-elasticity of output of domestic oil relative to price of imported oil	0.9	authors' estimate
Cross-elasticity of quantity of imported oil relative to price of domestic oil	1.9	authors' estimate
Cost of restraints to US consumers	$4.4 billion (average 1960–70) $5.9 billion (1969) $4.9 billion (1969) $6.2 billion (1969) $0.8 billion (1969) $6.9 billion (1971)	Bohi, 285 Bohi, 285 Cabinet, 26 Bohi, 198[d] Oil companies, in Bohi, 198[e] authors' estimate
Gain from restraints to US producers[f]	$3.1 billion (1969) $4.8 billion (1971)	Bohi, 289 authors' estimate
Tariff revenue and implied average tariff rate (1969)	$70 million 2.6 percent	authors' estimate authors' estimate[g]
Gain from restraints to foreigners[h]	$819 million (1969) $600 million (1969) $2.0 billion (1971)	Bohi, 290 Cabinet, 89 authors' estimate
Efficiency loss from larger domestic production to the United States (1971)	$3.0 billion	authors' estimate
Welfare cost of restraints to the United States (1969)	$2.3 billion (1969) $5.0 billion (1971)	Bohi, 289[i] authors' estimate
Employment in protected US industry	140,000 (1954) 75,000 (1971)	BLS, 24 BLS, 24
Induced increase in employment (1971)	43,000	authors' estimate
Cost of restraints to consumers per job saved (1971)	$160,000	authors' estimate
Gain from restraints to producers per job (1971)	$61,500	authors' estimate

a. This figure includes the effect of the small tariff (under 3 percent) as well as the effect of quantitative restraints.

b. The coefficients refer to demand for refined petroleum products.

c. The supply coefficient reflects the estimated long-run price elasticity of new discoveries. (Bohi, 274)

d. This is an estimate by Charles River Associates cited by Bohi and Russell.

e. This figure is the average of estimates by Shell Oil, Standard of Indiana, and Standard of New Jersey. (Bohi, 198)

f. "Producers" includes both refiners and the owners of crude oil resources.

g. Derived from average duties imposed on imports of crude oil, distillates, and residual fuel oil. (Cabinet, 91)

h. Quota rents in this case accrued to domestic rather than foreign producers since quotas were allocated directly to the refineries.

i. This figure represents the resource cost due to "excess resources engaged in production and unnecessary idle capacity." (Bohi, 289)

BIBLIOGRAPHY

American Petroleum Institute. Various years. *Petroleum Facts and Figures.* Washington.

Bohi, Douglas R., and Milton Russell. 1978. *Limiting Oil Imports: An Economic History and Analysis.* Baltimore, Md.: Johns Hopkins University Press.

Burrows, James C., and Thomas A. Domencich. 1970. *An Analysis of the United States Oil Import Quota.* Prepared for Energy Policy Staff, Office of Science and Technology. Washington.

Cabinet Task Force on Oil Import Control. 1970. *The Oil Import Question: A Report on the Relationship of Oil Imports to the National Security.* Washington.

Charles River Associates. 1969. *An Analytical Framework for Evaluating the Oil Import Quota.* Lexington, Mass.: D. C. Heath and Co.

Cichetti, Charles J., and William J. Gillen. 1973. "The Mandatory Oil Import Quota Program: A Consideration of Economic Efficiency and Equity." *Natural Resources Journal* 13 (July): 399–430.

Dam, Kenneth. 1971. "Implementation of Import Quotas: The Case of Oil." *Journal of Law and Economics* (April): 1–60.

International Monetary Fund. 1982. *International Financial Statistics Yearbook.* Washington.

Stern, Robert M. 1984. "Comments on Data, Elasticities, and Other Key Parameters." Seminar Discussion Paper no. 134. Paper read at conference, General Equilibrium Trade Policy Modelling, Columbia University, 5–6 April.

US Department of Commerce. Bureau of Economic Analysis. 1980. *Business Statistics 1979.* Washington.

US Department of Interior. Bureau of Mines. Various years. *Minerals Yearbook.* Washington.

US Department of Labor. Bureau of Labor Statistics. 1979. *Employment and Earnings, United States, 1909–78.* Washington.

CASE E-2

Lead and Zinc

PERIOD OF RELIEF

October 1958 to October 1965

SUPPLIERS AFFECTED

Global

RELIEF ACTION

In 1939, the ad valorem equivalent (AVE) of the specific duty on lead was 45.8 percent, while the AVE for zinc was 65.3 percent. The specific duties on lead and zinc were reduced 50 percent and 60 percent, respectively, as a result of concessions in the initial negotiations of the General Agreement on Tariffs and Trade (GATT). Successive GATT negotiations reduced the ad valorem equivalent rates to 6.5 percent and 8.4 percent, respectively, by 1956. (USTC 1958, 12–14)

The combination of GATT concessions on tariffs and US government efforts to promote world production of lead and zinc during the Korean War contributed to excess supply and falling prices in the mid-to-late 1950s. In 1953, representatives of lead and zinc miners and refiners first petitioned for escape clause relief under Section 7 of the Trade Agreements Extension Act of 1951, as amended. In May 1954, the US Tariff Commission reported its unanimous finding of serious injury to the domestic industry due to imports and recommended increased tariffs. President Dwight D. Eisenhower, however, decided not to take the recommended steps; instead, he authorized increased purchases of the two metals for government stockpiles. This had the desired but temporary effect of increasing prices. (USTC 1958, 32–34; USTC 157, 4)

In September 1957, the Emergency Lead-Zinc Committee filed another escape clause petition with the Tariff Commission claiming injury from increased imports. The Commission instituted an investigation on 4 October 1957, and, following a series of public hearings in November, reported to the President its unanimous decision that unmanufactured lead and zinc were being imported in such increased quantities as to seriously injure domestic producers. The Commission split, however, on its recommendations for relief: three commissioners called for a combination of higher tariffs and quotas; the other three recommended higher tariffs alone. (USTC 1958, 3)

President Eisenhower accepted the Commission's findings but differed slightly on relief, establishing import quotas but taking no action on tariffs. Effective 1 October 1958, import quotas on lead and zinc were imposed at 80 percent of average annual imports in the period 1953–57. Quotas were established on a quarterly basis and were set at 33,650 tons for lead-bearing ores and materials; 55,030 tons for unwrought lead and lead waste and scrap; 94,960 tons for zinc-bearing ores and materials; and 35,280 tons for unwrought zinc and zinc waste and scrap. (USTC 157, 24, 10)

CHANGES IN THE INDUSTRY

The restrictions on imports significantly reduced the level of imports of lead and zinc into the United States and, by 1963–64, domestic demand and prices were on the rise. In March 1964, President Lyndon B. Johnson asked the US Tariff Commission to conduct an investigation into the probable economic effects on the domestic industries of lifting the import quotas. The Commission found that the industries had improved their competitive position through consolidation into larger and more efficient facilities and that those facilities—both at the mining and at the smelting and refining levels—had been mechanized and modernized. The commissioners found that termination of the quotas was unlikely to have a detrimental effect on domestic producers unless world demand declined substantially. The quotas were lifted on 23 October 1965, despite protests from the lead and zinc industries. (USTC 157, 6–10; *New York Times*, 23 October 1965, A36)

Key Statistics

Imports from all sources[a]

	Volume (thousand tons)		Value (million dollars)		
Year	Lead	Zinc	Lead	Zinc	Source
Before restraints					
1957	512	882	153	153	USTC 1958, tables 7, 8
During restraints					
1958	529	661	126	88	USTC 157, table 5; 39, 45
1960	354	502	75	73	USTC 157, table 5; 39, 45
1962	340	510	65	70	USTC 157, table 5; 39, 45
1964	342	488	69	72	USTC 157, table 5; 39, 45
After restraints					
1966	356	677	91	127	BM 1967

a. These figures are based on the lead and zinc content of metal-bearing ores and scrap.

Apparent consumption

	Volume (thousand tons)		Value[a] (million dollars)		
Year	Lead	Zinc	Lead	Zinc	Source
Before restraints					
1957	1,145	1,250	395	332	USTC 1958, tables 7, 8; authors' estimate
During restraints					
1958	986	1,142	289	227	USTC 157, table 5; authors' estimate
1960	1,021	1,159	244	262	USTC 157, table 5; authors' estimate
1962	1,110	1,333	196	256	USTC 157, table 5; authors' estimate
1964	1,200	1,470	289	318	USTC 157, table 5; authors' estimate
After restraints					
1966	1,324	1,424	361	382	BM 1970; authors' estimate

a. These figures are derived from the value of output plus the value of imports.

Market share of imports (percentage of apparent consumption, by volume)

Year	Lead	Zinc	Source
Before restraints			
1957	50.2	76.1	USTC 1958, tables 7, 8
During restraints			
1958	53.6	57.9	USTC 157, table 5
1960	34.7	43.3	USTC 157, table 5
1962	30.7	38.3	USTC 157, table 5
1964	28.0	33.0	USTC 157, table 5
After restraints			
1966	26.9	47.5	authors' estimate

Output of domestic industry[a]

	Volume (thousand tons)		Value (million dollars)		
Year	Lead	Zinc	Lead	Zinc	Source
Before restraints					
1957	822	783	242	179	USTC 1958, tables 7, 8; authors' estimate

Output of domestic industry[a] (continued)

Year	Volume (thousand tons)		Value (million dollars)		Source
	Lead	Zinc	Lead	Zinc	
During restraints					
1958	669	642	163	139	USTC 157, table 5; authors' estimate
1960	717	701	169	189	USTC 157, table 5; authors' estimate
1962	681	768	131	186	USTC 157, table 5; authors' estimate
1964	807	872	220	246	USTC 157, table 5; authors' estimate
After restraints					
1966	900	851	270	255	BM 1970; authors' estimate

a. Production figures include output of both primary and secondary (recovered from scrap) lead and zinc.

Employment in domestic industry (thousand production workers)

Year	Mining, milling	Smelting, refining	Source
Before restraints			
1957	14.3	14.1	USTC 157, tables 24, 29
During restraints			
1958	8.6	10.9	USTC 157, tables 24, 29
1960	7.8	10.7	USTC 157, tables 24, 29
1962	6.9	9.7	USTC 157, tables 24, 29
1964	8.2	10.4	BM 1968
After restraints			
1966	8.7	11.0	BM 1968

Wages[a] (dollars per hour)

Year	Mining, milling	Smelting, refining	Source
Before restraints			
1957	2.19	2.39	USTC 157, table 24
During restraints			
1958	2.38	2.46	USTC 157, table 24
1960	2.43	2.60	USTC 157, table 24
1962	2.63	2.69	USTC 157, table 24
1964	2.96	3.11	BLS, 9, 13
After restraints			
1966	3.17	3.28	BLS, 9, 13

a. The 1964–66 figures are for workers in metal mining and primary metal manufacturing generally.

Industry profits (million dollars)

Year	Profits[a]	Source
Before restraints		
1957	n.a.	
During restraints		
1958	n.a.	
1961	20.9	USTC 157, table 35
1962	24.1	USTC 157, table 35
1963	40.2	USTC 157, table 35
After restraints		
1966	n.a.	

n.a. Not available.
a. Net profits before taxes.

Lead prices (cents per pound)

Year	Domestic[a]	World[b]	Source
Before restraints			
1957	14.7	12.1	USTC 1958, table 14
During restraints			
1958	12.2	9.1	IMF, 78–79
1960	11.8	9.0	USTC 157, table 11
1962	9.6	7.0	USTC 157, table 11
1964	13.6	12.6	USTC 157, table 11
After restraints			
1966	15.0	11.9	IMF, 78–79

a. New York price of common lead.
b. London metal exchange price.

Zinc prices (cents per pound)

Year	Domestic[a]	World[b]	Source
Before restraints			
1957	11.4	10.2	USTC 1958, table 15
During restraints			
1958	10.8	8.3	IMF, 80–81
1960	13.5	11.2	USTC 157, table 12
1962	12.1	8.5	USTC 157, table 12
1964	14.1	14.7	USTC 157, table 12
After restraints			
1966	15.0	12.8	IMF, 80–81

a. New York price of prime western zinc.
b. London metal exchange price.

Quantitative Profile

Item	Amount	Source
Number of years restraints in force (1958–65)	7 years	
Induced increase in price of imported lead and zinc	9.5 percent	authors' estimate[a]
Induced increase in price of domestic lead and zinc	9.5 percent	authors' estimate
Coefficient of price response	1.0	authors' estimate
Quantity and value of imports (1966)		
Lead	356,000 tons	BM 1967
	$91 million	BM 1967
Zinc	677,000 tons	BM 1967
	$127 million	BM 1967
Induced decrease in imports due to restraints		
Lead	100,000 tons	authors' estimate
	$26 million	authors' estimate
Zinc	100,000 tons	authors' estimate
	$19 million	authors' estimate
Quantity and value of domestic production (1966)		
Lead	900,000 tons	BM 1968
	$270 million	authors' estimate
Zinc	851,000 tons	BM 1968
	$255 million	authors' estimate
Induced increase in domestic production due to restraints		
Lead	100,000 tons	authors' estimate
Zinc	100,000 tons	authors' estimate
Coefficient of quantity response	1.0	authors' estimate
Elasticity of demand for imported lead and zinc	0.67 to 1.38	Stern, 9[b]
	1.0	authors' estimate
Elasticity of supply of domestic lead and zinc	1.0	authors' estimate
Elasticity of demand for domestic lead and zinc	1.0	authors' estimate
Cross-elasticity of demand for domestic lead and zinc relative to price of imported lead and zinc	0.81 to 1.43	Stern, 9[b]
	1.1	authors' estimate
Cross-elasticity of output of domestic lead and zinc relative to price of imported lead and zinc	1.0	authors' estimate
Cross-elasticity of quantity of imported lead and zinc relative to price of domestic lead and zinc	1.7	authors' estimate
Cost of restraints to US consumers (1964)	$67 million	authors' estimate
Gain from restraints to US producers (1964)	$46 million	authors' estimate

Quantitative Profile (continued)

Item	Amount	Source
Tariff revenue and implied average tariff rate (1964)	$11 million 7.5 percent	authors' estimate authors' estimate
Gain from restraints to foreigners (1964)	$4 million	authors' estimate
Efficiency loss from larger domestic production to the United States (1964)	$5 million	authors' estimate
Welfare cost of restraints to the United States (1964)	$9 million	authors' estimate
Employment in protected US industry[c]	28,400 (1957) 19,700 (1966)	USTC 157 BM 1968
Induced increase in employment (1964)	2,200	authors' estimate
Cost of restraints to US consumers per job saved (1964)	$30,000	authors' estimate
Gain from restraints to producers per job (1964)	$2,300	authors' estimate

a. This figure includes a quota premium estimated at about 2 percent and the existing tariff estimated at about 7.5 percent.

b. These coefficients refer to demand for nonferrous-metal-based industries.

c. These figures include workers involved in mining, milling, smelting, and refining of lead and zinc.

BIBLIOGRAPHY

International Monetary Fund. 1982. *International Financial Statistics Yearbook*. Washington.

Stern, Robert M. 1984. "Comments on Data, Elasticities, and Other Key Parameters." Seminar Discussion Paper no. 134. Paper read at conference, General Equilibrium Trade Policy Modelling, Columbia University, 5–6 April.

US Department of Interior. Bureau of Mines. Various years. *Minerals Yearbook*. 3 vols. Washington.

US Department of Labor. Bureau of Labor Statistics. 1979. *Employment and Earnings, United States, 1909–78*. Washington, July.

US Tariff Commission. 1958. *Lead and Zinc, Report to the President on Escape Clause Investigation No. 65 Under the Provisions of Section 7 of the Trade Agreements Extension Act of 1951, as Amended*. Washington.

———. 1965. *Lead and Zinc*. USTC Publication no. 157. Washington.

Other Publications from the Institute

POLICY ANALYSES IN INTERNATIONAL ECONOMICS SERIES

1 **The Lending Policies of the International Monetary Fund**
  John Williamson/August 1982

2 **"Reciprocity": A New Approach to World Trade Policy?**
  William R. Cline/September 1982

3 **Trade Policy in the 1980s**
  C. Fred Bergsten and William R. Cline/November 1982

4 **International Debt and the Stability of the World Economy**
  William R. Cline/September 1983

5 **The Exchange Rate System,** Second Edition
  John Williamson/September 1983, rev. June 1985

6 **Economic Sanctions in Support of Foreign Policy Goals**
  Gary Clyde Hufbauer and Jeffrey J. Schott/October 1983

7 **A New SDR Allocation?**
  John Williamson/March 1984

8 **An International Standard for Monetary Stabilization**
  Ronald I. McKinnon/March 1984

9 **The Yen/Dollar Agreement: Liberalizing Japanese Capital Markets**
  Jeffrey A. Frankel/December 1984

10 **Bank Lending to Developing Countries: The Policy Alternatives**
   C. Fred Bergsten, William R. Cline, and John Williamson/April 1985

11 **Trading for Growth: The Next Round of Trade Negotiations**
   Gary Clyde Hufbauer and Jeffrey J. Schott/September 1985

12 **Financial Intermediation Beyond the Debt Crisis**
   Donald R. Lessard and John Williamson/September 1985

13 **The United States–Japan Economic Problem**
   C. Fred Bergsten and William R. Cline/October 1985

14 **Deficits and the Dollar: The World Economy at Risk**
   Stephen Marris/December 1985

15 **Trade Policy for Troubled Industries**
   Gary Clyde Hufbauer and Howard F. Rosen/March 1986

BOOKS

IMF Conditionality
John Williamson, editor/1983

Trade Policy in the 1980s
William R. Cline, editor/1983

Subsidies in International Trade
Gary Clyde Hufbauer and Joanna Shelton Erb/1984

International Debt: Systemic Risk and Policy Response
William R. Cline/1984

Economic Sanctions Reconsidered: History and Current Policy
Gary Clyde Hufbauer and Jeffrey J. Schott, assisted by Kimberly Ann Elliott/1985

SPECIAL REPORTS

1 **Promoting World Recovery: A Statement on Global Economic Strategy** by Twenty-six Economists from Fourteen Countries/December 1982

2 **Prospects for Adjustment in Argentina, Brazil, and Mexico: Responding to the Debt Crisis**
John Williamson, editor/June 1983

3 **Inflation and Indexation: Argentina, Brazil, and Israel**
John Williamson, editor/March 1985

4 **Global Economic Imbalances**
C. Fred Bergsten, editor/March 1986

FORTHCOMING

Domestic Adjustment and International Trade
Gary Clyde Hufbauer and Howard F. Rosen, editors

Toward A New Development Strategy for Latin America
Bela Balassa, Gerardo M. Bueno, Pedro-Pablo Kuczynski, and Mario Henrique Simonsen

Another Multi-Fiber Arrangement?
William R. Cline

The Politics of Anti-Protection
I. M. Destler and John S. Odell

Japan in the World Economy
Bela Balassa and Marcus Noland

International Trade in Automobiles: Liberalization or Further Restraint?
William R. Cline

The Multiple Reserve Currency System
C. Fred Bergsten and John Williamson

New International Arrangements for Foreign Direct Investment
C. Fred Bergsten and Jeffrey J. Schott

Toward Cartelization of World Steel Trade?
William R. Cline

Trade Controls in Three Industries: The Automobile, Steel, and Textiles Cases
William R. Cline